LANDSCAPES OF KOREAN AND KOREAN AMERICAN BIBLICAL INTERPRETATION

INTERNATIONAL VOICES IN BIBLICAL STUDIES

Jione Havea
Jin Young Choi
Musa W. Dube
David Joy
Nasili Vaka'uta
Gerald O. West

Number 10

LANDSCAPES OF KOREAN AND KOREAN AMERICAN BIBLICAL INTERPRETATION

Edited by
John Ahn

Atlanta

Copyright © 2019 by SBL Press

All rights reserved. No part of this work may be reproduced or transmitted in any form or by any means, electronic or mechanical, including photocopying and recording, or by means of any information storage or retrieval system, except as may be expressly permitted by the 1976 Copyright Act or in writing from the publisher. Requests for permission should be addressed in writing to the Rights and Permissions Office, SBL Press, 825 Houston Mill Road, Atlanta, GA 30329 USA.

Library of Congress Control Number: 2019938032

Printed on acid-free paper.

For our parents, grandparents, and mentors

Rev. Dr. Joshua Yoo K. Ahn, PhD and Ruth Soon Hee Ahn (John Ahn)

Sarah Lee and Memory of Du Soon Lee (Hannah S. An)

Chun Hee Cho and Soon Ja Cho (Paul K.-K. Cho)

SooHaeing Kim and Memory of DaeJak Ha (SungAe Ha)

Rev. Soon-Young Hong and Hae-Sun Park (Koog-Pyoung Hong)

Rev. Seok-Gu Kang and Tae-Soon Kim (Sun-Ah Kang)

Rev. Dong Bin Kim and Bong Joo Lee (Hyun Chul Paul Kim)

Namkyu Kim and Rev. Dr. Gilsoon Park, PhD (Sehee Kim)

Rev. Yong Soon Lim and Sang Nan Yoo (Eunyung Lim)

Rev. Dr. Chae-Woon Na, PhD, LittD and Young-Soon Choe (Kang-Yup Na)

Kyoung Hee Nam and Soon Young Kang (Roger S. Nam)

Kyung-Jin Kwon and Kathleen Greider (Hee-Kyu Heidi Park)

Ye Hun Park and Young Sook Shin (Kyungmi Park)

Ho Neung Shin and Young Bok Lee (SuJung Shin)

Contents

Preface ix
Abbreviations xi

Introduction: Toward a Methodology for Korean and Korean
American Biblical Interpretation 1
John Ahn

The Case of Suspected Adultery (Num 5:11–31)
in Light of the Hittite Instructions for the Priests and
Temple Officials (CTH 264) 19
Hannah S. An

Divine Jealousy, Human Zeal: Self-Psychology and the Kenotic
Spirituality of קנא in Numbers 25 37
Hee-Kyu Heidi Park

State, War, and Women 49
Kyungmi Park

A "Dialogic" Hero David from the Perspective of "Internally
Persuasive Words" in the Narrative of Samuel 59
SuJung Shin

Murder, Adultery, and Theft 73
John Ahn

Ethics of Remembering: Scapegoating Manasseh after the
Sewol Ferry Tragedy 99
Koog-Pyoung Hong

Half Speak Ashdodite and None Can Speak Judean:
Code-Switching in Ezra-Nehemiah as an Identity Marker for
Repatriate Judeans and Koreans 119
Roger S. Nam

Rereading "a Virtuous Woman (*'ēšet hayil*)" in Proverbs 31:10–31 133
Sun-Ah Kang

Job the Penitent: Whether and Why Job Repents (Job 42:6) 145
Paul K.-K. Cho

An Invitation for Postcolonial Reading of the Prophetic
Tradition Claiming Imperial Powers as God's Agents in the
Context of American Colonialism in Korea 175
SungAe Ha

Perils of Betraying a Deity: Parallels between Ezekiel 16
and The Sumerian Myth "Unfaithfulness" 187
Sehee Kim

Crossing Boundaries: Daniel's Three Friends Meet Rev.
Ki-chol Chu of Colonized Korea 195
Hyun Chul Paul Kim

Of Great Walls, DMZs, and Other Lines in the Sand:
Galatians Demythologized and Deconstructed 217
Kang-Yup Na

Eve and Norea Retold: The Power of Storytelling in
Nature of the Rulers 241
Eunyung Lim

Bibliography 251

List of Contributors 277

Index of Primary Sources 279

Index of Modern Authors 289

Preface

The present volume represents the work of Korean and Korean American biblical scholars from South Korea (Republic of Korea) and the United States. First and foremost, the contributors have made the volume possible. Much appreciation goes out to each contributor. Collectively, the volume has given voice and birth to a new consciousness. Culturally speaking, because Koreans and Korean Americans prefer to work and operate independently, this collective effort is a true milestone.

As the current president of the Korean Biblical Colloquium (KBC), I express my deepest gratitude to John Kutsko and the Society of Biblical Literature Council for having envisioned the 2016 International Meeting of the Society of Biblical Literature (IMSBL) in Seoul, South Korea with other leaders, including Yun Lak Chung (Anyang University), Koog- Pyoung Hong (Yonsei University), and especially Tai Il Wang (Methodist Theological University). The IMSBL in 2016 was a seminal venue for all Korean, diaspora Korean, and Korean American biblical scholars.

I also express my deepest gratitude to Jione Havea, Monica Melanchthon, Bob Buller, and the editorial board of the International Voices in Biblical Studies for accepting this work for publication. Finding the right home for a new volume is no easy task. I want to thank the anonymous peer reviewers who offered helpful insights and input and also for endorsing this volume for publication. Much appreciation also goes out to Nicole Tilford.

Lastly, but not least, the dedication and exceptional work of three graduate students, Isaiah Ahn, Joe Harris, and Jamila Bess-Johnson have been instrumental in bringing the present volume to completion.

John Ahn
Washington, DC

ABBREVIATIONS

AB	Anchor Bible
ABD	Freedman, D. N., ed. *Anchor Bible Dictionary*. 6 vols. New York: Doubleday, 1992.
ABG	Arbeiten zur Bibel und ihrer Geschichte
AfOB	Archiv für Orientforschung: Beiheft
AIL	Ancient Israel and Its Literature
ANET	Pritchard, J. B., ed. *Ancient Near Eastern Texts relating to the Old Testament*. 3rd ed. Princeton: Princeton University Press, 1969.
ASR	*American Sociological Review*
ASV	American Standard Version
ATAT	Arbeiten zu Text und Sprache im Alten Testament
BA	*Biblical Archaeologist*
BAR	*Biblical Archeology Review*
BASOR	*Bulletin of the American Schools of Oriental Research*
BBB	Bonner biblische Beiträge
BBR	*Bulletin for Biblical Research*
BDB	Brown F., S. R. Driver, and C. A. Briggs. *A Hebrew and English Lexicon of the Old Testament*. Oxford: Clarendon, 1907.
BE	Biblische Enzyklopädie
BibInt	*Biblical Interpretation*
BibOR	Biblica et orientalia
BHS	Elliger, K., and W. Rudolph, eds. *Biblia Hebraica Stuttgartensia*. Stuttgart: Deutsche Bibelgesellschaft, 1983.
BJS	Brown Judaic Studies
BKAT	Biblischer Kommentar, Altes Testament
BN	*Bilische Notizen*
BR	*Biblical Research*
BRS	Biblical Resource Series
BT	*Bible Translator*
BTB	*Biblical Theology Bulletin*
BWANT	Beiträge zur Wissenschaft vom Alten und Neuen Testament
BZ	*Biblische Zeitschrift*
BZAW	Beihefte zur Zeitschrift für die alttestamentliche Wissenschaft

CAD	Gelb, Ignace J., et al. *The Assyrian Dictionary of the Oriental Institute of the University of Chicago*. Chicago: The Oriental Institute of the University of Chicago, 1956–2010.
CANE	Sasson, J., ed. *Civilizations of the Ancient Near East*. 4 vols. New York: Scribner's Sons, 1995.
CBQ	*Catholic Biblical Quarterly*
CHD	Güterbock, Hans G., Harry A. Hoffner Jr., and Theo P. J. van den Hout, eds. *The Hittite Dictionary of the Oriental Institute of the University of Chicago*. Chicago: The Oriental Institute of Chicago, 1980–.
CTH	*Catalogue des texts hittites*; supplements in RHA 30 (1972) 94-133 and RHA 33 (1975) 68-71
CTJ	*Calvin Theological Journal*
DBAT	*Dielheimer Blätter zum Alten Testament und seiner Rezeption in der Aten Kirche*
DJD	Discoveries in the Judean Desert
DMOA	Documenta et monumenta Orientis antiqui
ESHM	European Seminar in Historical Methodology
Evth	*Evangelische Theologie*
FAT	Forschungen zum Alten Testament
FMR	*Forced Migration Review*
FOLT	Forms of the Old Testament Literature
FRLANT	Forschungen zur Religion und Literatur des Alten und Neuen Testaments
GBS	Guides to Biblical Studies
GK (GKC)	Kautzsch, E., ed. *Gesnius' Hebrew Grammar*. Translated by A. E. Cowley. 2nd ed. Oxford: Clarendon, 1910.
HALOT	Koehler, L., W. Baumgartner, and J. J. Stamm. *The Hebrew and Aramaic Lexicon of the Old Testament*. Translated and edited under the supervision of M. E. J. Richardsho. 4 vols. Leiden: Brill, 1994–1999
HAR	*Hebrew Annual Review*
HAT	Handbuch zum Alten Testament
HBM	Hebrew Bible Monographs
HBT	*Horizons in Biblical Theology*
HCOT	Historical Commentary on the Old Testament
HED	Puhvel, Jann. *Hittite Etymological Dictionary*. Berlin, 1984–.
HKAT	Handkommentar zum Alten Testament
HSM	Harvard Semitic Monographs
HSS	Harvard Semitic Studies
HTR	*Harvard Theological Review*
HUCA	*Hebrew Union College Annual*

IBC	Interpretation: A Bible Commentary for Teaching and Preaching
ICC	International Critical Commentary
IEJ	*Israel Exploration Journal*
IMR	*International Migration Review*
Int	*Interpretation*
ISBL	Indiana Studies in Biblical Literature
ITC	International Theological Commentary
JAAR	*Journal of American Academy of Religion*
JANES	*Journal of Ancient Near Eastern Studies*
JAOS	*Journal of the American Oriental Society*
JB	Jerusalem Bible
JBL	*Journal of Biblical Literature*
JBQ	*Jewish Biblical Quarterly*
JCS	*Journal of Cuneiform Studies*
JDS	Judean Desert Studies
JJS	*Journal of Jewish Studies*
JNES	*Journal of Near Eastern Studies*
JNWSL	*Journal of Northwest Semitic Languages*
JPS	Jewish Publication Society
JQR	*Jewish Quarterly Review*
JR	*Journal of Religion*
JRS	*Journal of Refugee Systems*
JSOT	*Journal for the Study of Old Testament*
JSOTSup	Journal for the Study of the Old Testament Supplemental Series
JSS	*Journal of Semitic Studies*
JTS	*Journal of Theological Studies*
KAT	Kommentar zum Alten Testament
KBL	Koehler, L., and W. Baumgartnew. *Lexicon in Veteris Testament libros*. 2nd ed. Leiden: Brill, 1958.
KHAT	Kurzer Hand-Kommentar zum Alten Testament
KJV	King James Version
KTU	Dietrich, M., O. Loretz, and J. Sanmartín, eds. *Die keilalphbetischen Texte aus Ugarit, Ras Ibn Hani und anderen Orten*. AOAT 24.1. Neukirchen-Vluyn, 1976. 2nd enlarged ed. of KTU: *The Cuneiform Alphabetic Texts from Ugarit, Ras Ibn Hani, and Other Places*. Edited by M. Dietrich, O. Loretz, and J. Sanmartín. Münster, 1995 (=*CTU*).
LHBOTS	Library of Hebrew Bible/Old Testament Studies
LNTS	The Library of New Testament Studies
MBPS	Mellen Biblical Press Series
NABC	New American Bible Commentary
NASB	New American Standard Bible

NAV	New American Version
NCBC	New Century Bible Commentary
NIB	Keck, Leander E., ed. *The New Interpreter's Bible*. 12 vols. Nashville: Abingdon, 1994–2004.
NICOT	New International Commentary on the Old Testament
NIV	New International Version
NJB	New Jerusalem Bible
NJPS	*Tanakh: The Holy Scriptures: The New JPS Translation according to the Traditional Hebrew Text*
NRSV	New Revised Standard Version
OBL	Orientalia et biblica lovaniensia
OBO	Orbis biblicus et orentalis
OBT	Overtures to Biblical Theology
OLA	Orientalia lovaniensia analecta
OLP	Orientalia loveniensia periodica
OR	*Orientalia*
OrAnt	*Oriens antiquus*
OTG	Old Testament Guides
OTL	Old Testament Library
OTS	Old Testament Studies
OtSt	*Oudtestamentische Studiën*
PEQ	*Palestine Exploration Quarterly*
PRSt	*Perspectives in religious Studies*
RA	*Revue d'assyriologie et d'archéologie orientale*
RB	*Revue Biblique*
RSV	Revised Standard Version
SBLDS	Society of Biblical Literature Dissertation Series
SBLMS	Society of Biblical Literature Monograph Series
SBLSP	Society of Biblical Literature Seminar Papers
SBT	Studies in Biblical Theology
SBTh	*Studia biblica et Theologica*
SJLA	Studies in Judaism in Late Antiquity
SJT	*Scottish Journal of Theology*
SO	Symbolae osloenses
SVT	Supplements to Vetus Testamentum
TDOT	Botterweck, G. J., and H. Ringgren, eds. *Theological Dictionary of the Old Testament*. Translated by J. T. Willis, G. W. Bromiley, and D. E. Green. 8 vols. Grand Rapids: Eerdmans, 1974–2006.
TLOT	Jenni, E., ed. with assistance from C. Westermann. *Theological Lexicon of the Old Testament*. Translated by M. E. Biddle. 3 vols. Peabody, MA: Hendrickson, 1997.

ThWAT	Botterweck, G. J. and H. Ringgren, eds. *Theologisches Wörterbuch zum Alten Testament*. Stuttgart: Kolhammer, 1970–.
TRS	Test-Reader Series
UF	*Ugarit-Forschungen*
VT	*Vetus testamentum*
VTSup	*Vetus Testamentum Supplements*
WAW	Writings from the Ancient World
WC	Westminster Commentaries
WBC	Word Biblical Commentary
WDWLS	W. D. Whitney Linguistic Series
WMANT	Wissenschaftliche Monographien zum Alten und Neun Testament
WUNT	Wissenschaftliche Untersuchungen zum Neun Testament
WW	*Word and World*
ZA	*Zeitschrift für Assyriologie*
ZAW	*Zeitschrift für die alttestamentliche Wissenschaft*
ZDMGsuppl	Zeitschrift der deutschen morgenländischen Gesellschaft Supplementbände

INTRODUCTION: TOWARD A METHODOLOGY FOR KOREAN AND KOREAN AMERICAN BIBLICAL INTERPRETATION

John Ahn

In 2016, the International Meeting of the Society of Biblical Literature was held in Seoul, South Korea—on the campus of Yonsei University. Five guilds—the Society of Biblical Literature (SBL), the Korean Society of Old Testament Studies (KSOTS), the New Testament Society of Korea (NTSK), the Society of Asian Biblical Studies (SABS), and the Korean Biblical Colloquium (KBC)—worked collaboratively to ensure a positive "outcome."[1] This volume pays tribute to the historical precedence of hosting the meeting in Seoul with an acclaimed body of international scholars. A large number of diaspora Korean biblical scholars living in Australia, the United Kingdom, Germany, Israel, Canada, the United States, and elsewhere—as Koreans or Australians, British citizens, Israelis, Canadians, and Americans—returned to their motherland to present papers.

The essays in this volume have been selected from keynote addresses and papers presented at the meeting. The essays offer landscapes of current biblical scholarship undertaken by Korean and Korean American biblical scholars. For quite some time, it has been the volition and goal of both Korean and Korean American biblical scholars to foster voice exchange through critical scholarship. This volume is a long-awaited endeavor.

The volume echoes Knut Holter and Louis C. Jonker's observation that, in their case, a southern (African and Latin American) point of view to complement the northern (Europe and North American) is very much needed.[2] In our case, the scope is East-West, Korean and Korean American. In addition, as Jean-Pierre Ruiz's observation of Fernando F. Segovia's attempt to map a place of cultural

---

[1] See Andrew Abbott, "The Idea of Outcome," in *Processual Sociology* (Chicago: University of Chicago Press, 2016), 166–97.

[2] See Knut Holter, "Geographical and Institutional Aspects of Global Old Testament Studies," in *Global Hermeneutics: Reflections and Consequences*, ed. Knut Holter and Louis C. Jonker (Atlanta: Society of Biblical Literature, 2010), 3–14, 83–85; Louis C. Jonker, "The Global Context and Its Consequences for Old Testament Interpretation," in *Global Hermeneutics*, 47–56; Jonker, "Living in Different Worlds Simultaneously: Pleas for Contextual Integrity," in *African and European Readers of the Bible in Dialogue: In Quest of a Shared Meaning*, ed. J. H. de Wit and G. O. West (Leiden: Brill, 2008), 107–19.

hermeneutics of Latino/a theology, which then gave rise to a more nuanced work on Latino/a (Latinx) biblical studies,[3] this volume bypasses the traditional undertaking by first producing a broad theological or interdisciplinary set of essays, then moving to more nuanced work. We have consciously, deliberately, and directly moved into biblical studies without a precursor.

Any time a new volume attempts to break new ground, there is celebration, guarded optimism, and calculated risk. The essays in the volume offer traditional historical critical, newer approaches, and an amalgam of approaches. Although there is a plethora of scholarship undertaken by Korean and Korean American biblical scholars,[4] this work marks the collective entry point for our field. There is much anticipation for this work in Korea, the United States, and elsewhere.

---

[3] Jean-Pierre Ruiz, "The Bible and Latino/a Theology," in *The Wiley Blackwell Companion to Latino/a Theology*, ed. Orlando O. Espin (West Sussex, UK: Wiley & Sons, 2015), 111–28; Efrain Agosto and Jacqueline M. Hidalgo, eds., *Latinxs, the Bible and Migration* (London: Palgrave Macmillan, 2018).

[4] John Ahn, "Rising from Generation to Generation: Lament, Hope, Consciousness, Home, and Dream," in *The Oxford Handbook of the Psalms*, ed. William P. Brown (New York: Oxford University Press, 2014), 459–74; Yoon Kyoung Lee, "Postexilic Jewish Experience and Korean Multiculturalism," in *Migration and Diaspora: Exegetical Voices from Northeast Asian Women*, ed. Hisako Kinukawa (Atlanta: Society of Biblical Literature, 2014), 3–18; Young-Sung Ahn, "For a Better Future in Korean Biblical Studies: Dialoguing within Myself in a Different Context," in *The Future of a Biblical Past: Envisioning Biblical Studies on a Global Key*, ed. Roland Boer and Fernando R. Segovia (Atlanta: Society of Biblical Literature, 2012), 67–79; Kyung-Sook Lee, "Neo-Confucian Ideology in the Interpretation of the Book of Ruth: Toward a Cross-Checking hermeneutics," in *Korean Feminists in Conversation with the Bible, Church and Society*, ed. Kyung Sook Lee and Kyung Mi Park (Sheffield: Sheffield Phoenix, 2011), 1–13; Seong Hee Kim, *Mark, Women and Empire: A Korean Postcolonial Perspective*. Bibles in the Modern World (Sheffield: Sheffield Phoenix, 2010); Tai Il Wang, "Performing the Scripture: Understanding the Bible from Korean Biblical Hermeneutics," in *Mapping and Engaging the Bible in Asian Cultures: Congress of the Society of Asian Biblical Studies 2008 Seoul Conference*, ed. Yeong Mee Lee and Yoon Jong Yoo (Seoul: Christian Literature Society of Korea, 2009), 37–52; Elaine Howard Ecklund, *Korean American Evangelicals: New Models for Civic Life* (New York: Oxford University Press, 2008); John Ahn, "A Light to the Nations: The Sociological Approach in Korean American Approach," in *Ways of Being, Ways of Reading*, ed. Mary F. Foskett and Jeffrey Kah-Jin Kuan (St. Louis: Chalice, 2006), 112–22; Se-Hoon Jang, *Particularism and Universalism in the Book of Isaiah: Isaiah's Implications for a Pluralistic World from a Korean Perspective* (Bern: Lang, 2005); Ho-Young Kwon and Kwang Chung Kim, *Korean Americans and Their Religions: Pilgrims from a Different Shore* (University Park: Penn State University Press, 2001); Wayne Patterson, *The Ilse: First-Generation Korean Immigrants in Hawaii 1903–1973* (Honolulu: University of Hawai'i Press, 2000); Kyeyoung Park, *The Korean American Dream: Immigrants and Small Business in New York City* (Ithaca, NY: Cornell University Press, 1997); Cyris Heesuk Moon, *A Korean Minjung Theology: An Old Testament Perspective* (Maryknoll,

A First Composite Volume

As the first Korean and Korean American biblical studies compendium, the primary inquiries are: What features effectuate a Korean or Korean American perspective? What modes of reading beyond cultural hermeneutics, if any, shape Korean and Korean American biblical interpretation? How is the interpretative task different from an Asian American one? Benny Liew has underscored a parallel set of inquiries in *What Is Asian American Biblical Hermeneutics? Reading the New Testament*.[5] For Liew, the pan Asian American task of locating meaning and interpreting occurs in a hybrid world of rapidly changing centers and peripheries. For Koreans and Korean Americans, we also begin with our social location. Ethnically, we are Koreans. But culturally and generationally, we are diverse. To redefine and refine our inquiries: What constitutes, demarcates, fosters, and makes Korean and Korean American biblical interpretation distinctive from Asian American or other cultural interpretations? If social location is seminal, what additional noticeable similarities or differences are found in interpretation framed by a South Korean point of view over against a North Korean, or for that matter, a Korean American one? If language, customs, and even food are indicators of distinctive cultural variance, a hallmark of Korean and Korean American biblical scholarship may be the Korean and Korean American church(es), which brings everything Korean under the umbrella of "cultural intelligence."[6] The others are education—a powerful form of assimilation—generational consciousness, and global issues.

For some Korean and Korean American biblical scholars, actualizing the center and periphery[7] are central. For others, the question of center and periphery are puzzling. Yet, for others, multiple centers and equal or unequal number of peripheries help them to reconsider Immanuel Wallerstein's "core, periphery, and semi-periphery."[8] The construct of a center and periphery or centers and peripheries,

---

NY: Orbis Books, 1995); Chan-Hie Kim, "Reading the Bible as Asian Americans," *NIB* 1:161–66.

[5] Tat-siong Benny Liew, *What Is Asian American Biblical Hermeneutics: Reading the New Testament* (Honolulu: University of Hawaii Press, 2008).

[6] Soon Ang and Linn Van Dyne, eds., *Handbook of Cultural Intelligence: Theory Measurement and Application* (New York: Routledge, 2008).

[7] Edward Albert Shils, *Center and Periphery: Essay in Macrosociology* (Chicago: University of Chicago, 1975).

[8] Immanuel Wallerstein, *Essential Wallerstein* (New York: The New Press, 2000); Wallerstein, *The Modern World System: Capitalist Agriculture and the Origins of the European World-Economy in the Sixteenth Century* (New York: Academic Press, 1974); Wallerstein, *The Modern World System II: Mercantilism and the Consolidation of the European World Economy 1600–1750* (New York: Academic Press, 1980); Wallerstein, *The Modern World System III: The Second Era of Great Expansion of the Capitalist World-Economy, 1730–1840* (New York: Academic Press, 1989).

however, continues to be relevant for Korean and Korean American biblical interpretation. The diachronic task of historical and textual criticism and the synchronic task of locating the *Mitte* are necessary for a better understanding of the text. These foundational German (protestant) approaches are embedded in the scholarships undertaken by Koreans and Korean Americans. There is a consensus that, in Korean and Korean American biblical interpretation, our task is not to replace existing modes of interpretations, but rather, as biblical scholars, work within biblical studies and with social sciences, ethnic studies, and global issues to create and foster something distinctive. If the outcome is a carefully constructed new creation, a new transnational mode of interpretation, which encompasses past and present methods, factoring in social constructions of realities, solving critical problems, bringing awareness to important modern and ancient issues, and offering new insights, a synthesized model has been achieved. If not, much work remains ahead of us.

In the foreground, biblical scholars in South Korea appear to have complete academic freedom like their Korean American counterparts. In the background, however, for some South Korean biblical scholars, limitations are set by the Korean church(es) and their respective institutions. Korean church leaders question advancements in progressive scholarship. They prefer scholarships that reflect their communities' values. Interpretations that fall outside certain faithful dispositions are questioned. These Korean biblical scholars appear to be caught between pre-Vatican II Catholic biblical scholarship[9] and (post) Vatican II (1994).[10] Others, parallel Korean American biblical scholars with freedom to pursue scholarship without any limits or restraints. Some are attempting to bridge the poles – by introducing Korean folklores, select Korean traditions, and various settings of ancient and modern history to constructively expand the "historical and contextul"—along the lines of cultural diffusion—through an amalgation of approaches.

The essays in this volume directly and indirectly address these and other inquiries framed in historical, literary, theological, sociological, feminist, postmodern, and postcolonial approaches. Several essays cross boundaries by innovatively taking risk—reframing "social location and Korean history"—to guide their interpretive task (Hyun Chul Paul Kim and Kang-Yup Na). From a broad perspective then, social location or "locative" (to locate or denote location, home,

---

[9] Jose Granados, Carlos Granados, and Luis Sanchez-Navarro, eds., *Opening Up the Scriptures: Joseph Ratzinger and the Foundations of Biblical Interpretations* (Grand Rapids: Eerdmans, 2008); Heinrich Denzinger-Peter Hunermann, *Enchiridion Symbolorum*: *A Compendium of Creeds, Definitions and Declarations of the Catholic Church* (San Francisco: Ignatius Press, 2012).

[10] See "The Interpretation of the Bible in the Church," http://catholic-resources.org/ChurchDocs/PBC_Interp-FullText.htm?fbclid=IwAR0Jo4pSIs6MX5KX0ei-91yLfMw6cwfEwWUCgIXahFHomHZdqJ4x4nlcLlo, accessed June 10, 2018.

domī at the center or periphery) and the "text" unify this volume. Every contributor in the volume agrees on the importance of the text—there is a text. The social location of the reader's academic training that substantively defines the scholar's methodological approach without compromising "the text" (*textus receptus*) is essential. This is what demarcates Korean and Korean American from an Asian and Asian American reading. I call this a "locative textual approach."

LOCATIVE TEXTUAL APPROACH

By "locative" or "sociolocative," I am acknowledging the traditions of sociology of knowledge and traditional grammar, but also include classic and contemporary approaches in biblical studies as noted above.[11] In our undertaking, scholars locate and denote the base or home of their academic training. Their current state of evolution in their academic career and comfortability with that social location either confirms, reaffirms, modifies, or rejects the base. The task of addressing critical problems or interpreting texts begins through those operative lenses.

By textual, it is an amalgamation of canonical criticism (James Sanders), canonical approach (Brevard Childs), and canonical consciousness (Michael Fishbane). This may or may not be further juxtaposed with the view of an earlier epic and the construct that "the text is just a text" (David Clines, Philip Davies, and Claudia Camp)—a redacted composite ancient literature set in various genres.

Interpreters acknowledge, seek clarity, or wrestle with the text. For many, the text is scripture. For others, the text is a mythopoetic construct with literary contours, capturing ancient imagination, which includes social, political, and religious concerns. In select communities, the text is binding, the source for religious construction of identity. For others, it is a Western text that has come to dominant and displace Asian religious (Buddhist) and nonreligious (Confucian) texts. For some, the Bible has replaced ancient Korean foundations and traditions. For others, the Bible has liberated Koreans and Korean Americans from Shamanism and other forms of idolatrous ideologies.

Viewing the text sociologically and canonically (Robert Wilson and Brevard Childs), which includes the historical and literary, advocating the locative textual approach in Korean and Korean American biblical interpretation is broad enough

---

[11] Robert Morgan, *Biblical Interpretation* (Oxford: Oxford University Press, 1988); John Barton, *The Nature of Biblical Criticism* (Louisville: Westminster John Knox, 2007); A. K. M. Adam, ed., *Handbook of Postmodern Biblical Interpretation* (St. Louis: Chalice, 2000); R. S. Sugirtharajah, *Exploring Postcolonial Biblical Criticism: History, Method, Practice* (Chichester, West Sussex: Wiley-Blackwell, 2011); Louise Schottroff and Marie-Theres Wacker, eds., *Feminist Biblical Interpretation: A Compendium of Critical Commentary on the Books of the Bible and Related Literature* (Grand Rapids: Eerdmans, 2012); Mark Boda et al., eds., *The Prophets Speak on Forced Migration* (Atlanta: SBL Press, 2015); Elizabeth Boase and Christopher G. Frechette, eds., *Bible through the Lenses of Trauma* (Atlanta: SBL Press, 2016).

to advance and engage biblical studies, Korean and Korean American interpretation, and other cultural interpretations without being limited to just cultural appropriation. The sociocanonical method driving Korean and Korean American biblical interpretation is centered on *communication and reproduction* (Niklas Luhmann). It embraces then goes beyond ethnic and cultural demarcations by including generational consciousness. Indeed, the methodology is comprehensive and pervasive enough to engage fully, local and global communities, especially those that have experienced any form of migration (voluntary or involuntary) across time and space. In other words, the locative (sociolocative) textual approach is generative, thick, and catholic to engage all social constructions of realities.

Social Presentation of the Group (First and 1.5 Generation)

In Peter Berger and Thomas Luckman's *The Social Construction of Reality* and Erving Goffman's *The Presentation of the Self in Everyday Life*, identity, belonging, and the construction of reality is framed by an individual's (or a group's) understanding of the self in relation to the other(s).[12] Perceptions, actions, and social interactions with others have forged and framed the self (group). There is deliberate and conscious passivity—a system of culturally conditioned Confucian hegemony—that has shaped Koreans and some first and 1.5 generation Korean Americans. In other words, what others say and do—especially those who are older and more seasoned—concerning an individual or group is more determinative than one's own projection of the self (group). The 1.5 generation (a designation credited to Karl Mannhiem[13]) Korean Americans[14] reflect on the phenomenology of liminality and marginality to constitute their sense of being.[15]

---

[12] Peter Berger and Thomas Luckmann, *The Social Construction of Reality* (New York: Anchor Books, 1966); Erving Goffman, *The Presentation of the Self in Everyday Life* (Garden City, NY: Doubleday, 1959).

[13] David M. McCourt, "The 'Problem of Generations' Revisited: Karl Mannheim and the Sociology of Knowledge in International Relations," in *The Theory and Application of the "Generation" in International Relations and Politics*, ed. Brent J. Steele and Jonathan M. Acuff (New York: Palgrave Macmillan, 2012), 47–70; See Karl Mannheim, "The Problem of Generations," in *Karl Mannheim: Essays*, ed. Paul Kecskemeti (New York: Routledge, 1972), 276–322.

[14] Mary Yu Danico, *The 1.5 Generation: Becoming Korean American in Hawai'i* (Honolulu: University of Hawai'i Press, 2004); Sucheng Chan, ed., *The Vietnamese American 1.5 Generation: Stories of War, Revolution, Flight and New Beginnings* (Philadelphia, PA: Temple University Press, 2006).

[15] Sang Hyun Lee, *From a Liminal Place: An Asian American Theology* (Minneapolis: Fortress, 2010); Jung Young Lee, *Marginality: The Key to Multicultural Theology* (Minneapolis: Fortress, 1995).

When issues become heated or difficult, the solution is to circumvent and circumspect. The perception from the outside looking in is a stereotype—passive, quiet or not involved, speaks only when spoken to. However, the reality is, there are keen observations made internally with opinions and thoughts that are reserved for the sake of the other. The mode is: "less is more," fostering an internal cultural place of "belonging."[16]

Second, Third, and Fourth Generations

For second generation Korean Americans, "less is less, and more is more." Their social construction of reality is forged through assimilation to the dominant culture. Their everyday interactions occur with multiple social groups. There are many centers and peripheries. They weave in and out of various groups that constitute community, belonging, and identity. However, because of what they have seen and experienced, that is, the put downs and dismissals of the previous and even current generations by the dominant groups that they have joined, many are vocal and outspoken. Some even attempt to reform the center and bridge the periphery. They speak out on behalf of the endured silence as *Fighting Words*.[17] And because of their outspokenness, ironically, new caricatures develop. They are there, but not there. They are heard, but not heard. They are seen, yet unseen.

The social constructions for the third and fourth generations are on the horizon. This is the most exciting aspect of the unknown future. In short, the third and fourth generations of formally trained Korean American biblical scholars will need to discover their own voices by accepting, emending, and even rejecting before transcending future communications set in this and ensuing volumes.[18]

---

[16] Bell Hooks, *Belonging: A Culture of Place* (New York: Routledge, 2009).
[17] Patricia Hill Collins, *Fighting Words: Black Women and the Search for Justice* (Minneapolis: University of Minnesota Press, 1998).
[18] For example, Exod 34:7 "down to the third and fourth generation," which gets reversed in Deut 24:16; the redacted section in 2 Kgs 14:5–6; Jer 31:29–30; Ezek 18:1–4; and other narratives that especially pertain to third and fourth generations like the Jacob cycle, Joseph novella, and the Letter to the Ephesians. See George Lawson, "Within and Beyond the 'Fourth Generation' of Revolutionary Theory," *Sociological Theory* 34.2 (2016): 106–27; John Foran, "Theories of Revolution Revisited: Toward a Fourth Generation?," *Sociological Theory* 11.1 (1993): 1–21; Paul Hyun Chul Kim, "Reading the Joseph Story (Gen 37–50) as a Diaspora Narrative," *CBQ* 75.2 (2013): 219–38; Dominik Markl, "The Sociology of the Babylonian Exile and Divine Retribution "to the third and fourth generation," in *The Dynamics of Early Judean Law: Studies in the Diversity of Ancient Social and Communal Legislation*, ed. Sandra Jacobs, BZAW (Berlin: de Gruyter, forthcoming).

Primary and Secondary Socializations

For Berger and Luckmann, performances and roles that communicate and shape the "here and now," the everyday social interactions that are centrally responsible for cultural and social identity formation, the objective and subjective reality that produce the self-other dichotomy all occur through the dialectic of the individual and various groups that enter into both primary and secondary socializations. Effective members of society *produce*. They further perpetuate and collect then pass down a body of stock knowledge—something that is tangible and worthwhile. All of this is produced by society, notes Berger and Luckmann. For Koreans and Korean Americans, primary socializations take place through language, code-switching (Nam's essay in this volume), cultural acculturations to the dominant American or Korean contexts, and other social groups that help bridge and foster individual and group constructions of reality. In part, as scholars, this primary society is our respective guilds: the Society of Biblical Literature, the Korean Society of Old Testament Studies, the New Testament Society of Korea, et cetera.

Actualization of Niklas Luhmann's Theory

Returning to the task of the "locative textual approach," the work of Niklas Luhmann is an important cornerstone. His critical theories have revolutionized every sector of today's society: politics, economics, education, social theories, religion, and biblical studies.[19] Luhmann suggests, as Geertz did for the American Anthropological Association (AAA), that sociologists stop citing past (dead) giants in their respective fields. For Luhmann, society is no longer about the "actors" or "actions" in society. Rather, it is fundamentally and purely *communication*.

> Accordingly, communication is understood as a mode of operation that reproduces itself from its own products. Stated another way, it is the operational mode of an "autopoietic" system, and it demands that a synthesis of information, utterance [*Mitteilung*], and understanding be achieved to such a degree that

---

[19] Niklas Luhmann, *Die Gesellschaft der Gesellschaft* (Frankfurt am Main: Suhrkamp, 1997); Luhmann, "Society, Meaning, Religion—Based on Self Reference," *Sociological Analysis* 46 (1985): 5–20; Luhmann, *The Differentiation of Society* (New York: Columbia University Press, 1982); Luhmann, *Die Funktion der Religion* (Frankfurt: Suhrkamp, 1977). The key difference between Jürgen Habermas (*kommunikatives Handeln*) and Niklas Luhmann is the form and function of communication. For Habermas, who has the most to lose, communication is an action in the classical sociological sense. However, for Luhmann, though action is a necessity, communication is a synthesis of utterance, information, and understanding. Action accounts for utterance and information, but it does not account for understanding. In a self-referential system, the basic unit is communication, not action (or outcome).

communication can be continued. In every communicative operation, constative (informative) and performative (utterative) components of communication have to be balanced and understood in relation to one another.[20]

Have we also arrived at such a juncture when we ought to stop citing past giants in biblical studies? Is this the fundamental chain of our discipline that holds us back from true advancements? Drawing on just one issue, namely, centers and margins, can we arrive at a place in communication when we process and ascertain information regardless of where that information is coming from? As this volume consciously seeks unity and diversity across locations and methodologies, if the language or communicating from the center or periphery must remain for the sake of structure or order, the essays in this volume do come from the epicenters of South Korea and the United States, respectively Seoul and Washington, DC. But having said this, many Korean and Korean American biblical scholars also choose to stand with those on the periphery.[21]

Another important contribution from Luhmann is the concept of *autopoiesis*. The term is generally associated with a system that is concerned with self-reproduction—in a biological sense. Think of the cardiovascular system or the respiratory system that reproduces its own cells (so cardiovascular cells do not become respiratory cells). Each set or system acts independently, but also communicates with others. The cells in one system communicate within its own system and further carries that information to another set. Also, think of a university, with various schools and departments. They are all independent of each other, operating independently, self-producing scholarship, with its own set of faculties, students, and et cetera. Yet, communication takes place. Autopoiesis is functionally a system's approach to communication and reproduction. Communication according to Luhmann must reproduce. Luhmann notes three central components in his system's approach: a stock of knowledge or the synthesis of the past and present set of information (studied knowledge), utterance which can be oral or written, and understanding from the body that is producing the communication. The sharp contrast of the Luhmannian view is that a social system of self-reproduction no longer begins with humanity or ends with mere positive outcomes. Rather, that which is being communicated is the goal. Communication for the sake of communication, exegesis for the sake of exegesis, or Korean and Korean American biblical interpretation for the sake of Korean and Korean American biblical interpretation. When Koreans and Korean Americans understand this communication as "word(s) reproduce word(s)," this communicative system makes sense as texts indeed reproduce texts.

---

[20] Niklas Luhmann, *A Systems Theory of Religion*, trans. David A. Brenner with Adrian Hermann (Stanford: Stanford University Press, 2013), 27.

[21] R. S. Sugirtharajah, ed., *Still at the Margins: Biblical Scholarship Fifteen Years after Voices from the Margin* (New York: T&T Clark, 2008).

To understand these things, it is critical that we also (indeed, that we absolutely) make reference to the observational operations of communication. One should not be misled in everyday communication by those who make "humanity"—and not communication—responsible for things that cannot be observed or by those who argue that weaknesses in seeing or expressing religious (e.g., mystically inclined) communication are [is] basic human conditions. These are only some of the semantic forms of concealing the deeper paradox of the communicatively produced unobservability of observation. And if I am correct here, *sociology*—and not psychology or anthropology—is the most *appropriate science of religion*. (my emphasis)[22]

In my view, this is the visible hallmark of Korean and Korean American biblical interpretation—not "communicative action" (Jürgen Habermas) but communication (sociological) and reproduction (canonical) of scholarship (mirroring texts reproducing texts)—a synthesis of information gathered from our mentors or *Doctorvater* and institution(s), reproducing and passing down a stock of knowledge.

If one was a student or trained under Marvin Sweeney, Fernando Segovia, or Brevard Childs and Robert Wilson, that social construction of reality will be communicated and reproduced in our scholarship. What is emended or added to this on-going communication is direct or indirect outlook or some broader consciousness to help Koreans, Korean Americans, and others—the global community—to collectively reflect on issues and concerns that are intrinsically and extrinsically canonical and communal. This is the mantle that is upon every Korean and Korean American biblical scholar—to produce for the guild and also for one's respective community. However, at the moment, even if Korean and Korean American biblical scholars contribute and advance their specialization, far too many established scholars, for whatever reason, still do not cite published works by Korean and Korean American biblical scholars.[23] This is what I mean by the center-periphery debate. Hopefully, scholars will take notice and fully advance scholarship.

Fresh scholarship should be consciously inclusive—women and men, established and emerging scholars, North and South America, Europe and Australia, and Asia and Africa—with traditional and/or new methods, if applicable. This volume celebrates and attempts to set a (bench)mark of diversity and inclusivity (see the index of modern scholars), especially between eastern and western biblical scholars. Pressing this issue in contemporary biblical scholarship, are we producing works that are provincial, national, or global? Is there diversity and

---

[22] Luhmann, *Systems Theory of Religion*, 29.
[23] Randall C. Bailey, Tat-siong Benny Liew, and Fernando F. Segovia, eds., *They Were All Together in One Place? Toward Minority Biblical Criticism* (Atlanta: Society of Biblical Literature, 2009).

plurality in the construction of scholarship, or is the work in consideration a product of monolithic isolation? Again, these are the layered questions surrounding the center-perphery debate.

Inasmuch as society externally shapes identity and constructs reality through the other, when it comes to cadres then, "the vast majority of social structures are not corporations or even formal organizations. They are things like neighborhoods, occupations, newspaper readerships, church congregations, social classes, ethnicities, technological communities, and consumption groups: often disorganized or unorganized but nonetheless consequential as social structures."[24] This is the secondary socialization that completes and complements the primary spheres of influence that shape Koreans and Korean Americans. Those who are from the same place or location often find comfort, encouragement, and strength by being around each other. Family, home, culture, faith, school, and community make up the other *Mitte* in the formation and collective outcomes of Korean and Korean American identity and belonging.

Collective Outcomes

Andrew Abbott, a leading American social theorist reflecting on social structures, advances two important cross-sections concerning professions and outcomes—grand or provisional—both in the historicity of individuals and collective. For Abbot, individuals process and produce exceptional outcomes. However, at the collective level, all outcomes are provisional.[25] In place of a definitive permanent outcome, all outcomes at the collective entity are on-going. It is this definition of "outcome" with which we emend Luhmann's narrow view of "action" or outcome in communication. In other words, the reason why Luhmann opposed "action or outcome" was due to the limited onetime event. However, in Abbott's words: "It just keeps on going."[26] Collective outcomes are fluid.[27] As previously noted, a new volume that attempts to break new ground is open ended, not definitive, hoping to give birth to ensuing volumes.

On the whole, the ongoing process of fostering a wider cultural and global reading is also fluid. In this volume, some contributors begin and end without ever departing from the traditional methods of historical, literary, or sociological. Others begin with Korean history or current events and then, move into a specific biblical text. For example, Korea's colonization by Japan (1910), the issue of

---

[24] Abbott, *Processual Sociology*, 8.
[25] Abbott, *Processual Sociology*, 166–97.
[26] Abbott, *Processual Sociology*, 4.
[27] Alpheus Masoga, et al., *Reading the Bible in the Global Village: Cape Town* (Leiden: Brill, 2002); Heikki Raisanen, et al., *Reading the Bible in the Global Village: Helsinki* (Atlanta: Society of Biblical Literature, 2000).

Comfort Women, the Korean War (1950–1953), which resulted in the demarcation on the thirty-eighth parallel, more commonly known as the demilitarized zone (DMZ), the failed Korean economy of the 1990s, and the Sewol Ferry incident (2014) are social-historical starting points, not an eisegetical reading.

Theologically speaking, for several decades, Korean theology has centered around Ahn Byung-Mu's Minjung theology. Today, Korean feminists[28] interpretations have emerged. With South Korea's new found place among global leaders in technology (memory, semiconductor), ship building, chemical, automobiles, heavy construction, advancements in plastic surgery, and even highly sought after school academies, a connection to the protestant ethic and the rise of capitalism attempts to explain the rapid growth and transformation.[29] More indigenously, however, are "self-sufficiency" and working with "speed," South Korea's two organic traits. Interestingly, North Korea has its own self sufficient endemic ideology called "Juche."[30]

On the religious side, the Nevius approach to mission in Korea was just that, an endemic local approach to the dissemination of Christianity in Korea by Koreans, whereas missionary efforts in China and Japan failed because of nonacculturation or assimilation to the dominant culture. The 1907 Great Awakening in Pyongyang (North Korea), parallel to America's Great Awakening, is considered by experts as the burgeoning of Korean Christianity.[31] Indeed, Christianity for all of Korea began in what is now called North Korea.

For Korean Americans, the memory and story begin in 1903—on the sugar plantations of Hawaii.[32] The first wave of 102 Koreans set sail on the USS Gaelic

---

[28] Kyung Sook Lee and Kyung Mi Park, eds., *Korean Feminists in Conversation with the Bible, Church, and Society* (Sheffield: Sheffield Phoenix, 2011).

[29] Max Weber, *Protestant Ethic and the Spirit of Capitalism*, trans. Talcott Parsons (London: Routledge, 2001).

[30] Juche is the dominant ideology of North Korea. The ten guiding principles reflect on self guidance and governance of the nation. The origins and development of the ten principles can be traced back to the "Decalogue," the Ten Commandments, with all religiosity and God-langugage removed, anticipating a three generational reign as their trinity. Kim Il Sung's mother was a devote Christian. Although Kim Il Sung's writings may suggest otherwise, in North Korea, there is a fascination for the history and literature of ancient Israel. Also, Juche was advanced in the Black Panther Party movement (Professor Hyun Sik Kim, former professor of Russian Literature, Pyongyang University [Kim Il Sung University], former visiting professor, Yale University, and former private tutor and educator to Kim Il Sung's children, personal communication, October 1, 2003).

[31] Eunsik Cho, "The Great Revival of 1907 in Korea: Its Cause and Effect," *Missiology* 26.3 (1998): 289–300; Sebastian C. H. Kim and Kirsteen Kim, *A History of Korean Christianity* (New York: Oxford University Press, 2015); Samuel Moffet, *History of Christianity in Asia*, vol. 2 (Maryknoll, NY: Orbis Books, 2005).

[32] David K. Yoo, *Contentious Spirits: Religion in Korean American History 1903–1945* (Stanford: Stanford University Press, 2010); Marn J. Cha, *Koreans in Central California (1903–1957): A Study of Settlement and Transnational Politics* (Lanham, MD: University

from Incheon and arrived in Honolulu. Revision history reveals much more hardships and compromises than previously recorded. To have set foot on the same sugar plantation in June of 2018 was a remarkable and moving experience. Many of the first settlers dreamed of making it in America. However, the reality was, they were abused and mistreated. The work was not what they were promised. It was unrelenting and arduous, physically and emotionally back-breaking. Recovery and restoration were not in sight. Many wanted to return home but could not afford to go back. For others, picture brides were brought in from Korea. These brides were also misled. Husband and wife worked side by side on those sugar plantations. Eventually, in due course with sacrifice and their immigrant work ethos and praxis, some made it out. They made their way to Los Angeles, New York, Chicago, and Washington DC to start anew.

With the Immigration Act of 1965,[33] which ended the Naturalization Act of 1790, granting Asians, Eastern European Catholics, and Jews privilege to enter the United States, a new wave of Koreans entered the United States. The Korean American scholars in this volume have been the beneficiaries of the 1965 immigration act. Our parents came in the mid-1960s and early 1970s. Some came alone as exchange students in the 1980s. Others arrived even later as graduate students. Most of us were infants or toddlers. Others were born here. Today, collectively, we are at home or metaphorically, at multiple homes, as cultural memory carriers of the Korean American heritage.[34]

AT HOME IN CULTURAL INTERPRETATION

The present volume finds a shared home in the company of African American, Asian American, Latinx American, feminist-womanist, and global readings.[35] In

---

Press of America, 2010); Young-Ho Ch'oe, ed., *From the Land of Hibiscus: Koreans in Hawai'i 1903–1950* (Honolulu: University of Hawai'i Press, 2006).

[33] Gabriel J. Chin and Rose Cuison Villazor, eds., *The Immigration and Nationality Act of 1965: Legislating a New America* (New York: Cambridge University Press, 2015).

[34] Astrid Eril and Ansgar Nünning, eds., *A Companion to Cultural Memory Studies* (Berlin: de Grutyer, 2010); Lewis A. Coser, ed., *Maurice Halbwachs On Collective Memory* (Chicago: University of Chicago Press, 1992); Jan Assmann, *Religion und kulturelles Gedächtnis* (München: Beck, 2000); Assmann, *Religion and Cultural Memory*, trans. Rodney Livingstone (Stanford, CA: Stanford University Press, 2006); see John Ahn, "Story and Memory," in *The Oxford Encyclopedia of the Bible and Theology*, ed. Samuel E. Balentine (New York: Oxford University Press, 2014), 332–43.

[35] Jione Havea and Peter H. W. Lau, eds., *Reading Ruth in Asia* (Atlanta: SBL Press, 2015); Jione Havea, Margaret Aymer, and Steed Vernyl Davidson, eds., *Island, Islanders, and the Bible* (Atlanta: SBL Press, 2015); Judith E. McKinlay, *Troubling Women and Land Reading Biblical Texts in Aotearoa New Zealand* (Sheffield: Sheffield Phoenix, 2014); Nasil Vaka'uta, *Reading Ezra 9–10 Tu'a-Wise: Rethinking Biblical Interpretation in Oceania* (Atlanta: Society of Biblical Literature, 2011).

1991, Cain Hope Felder's *Stony the Road We Trod: African American Biblical Interpretation*[36] profoundly changed the landscape of biblical interpretation. The Euro-American center was introduced to fresh biblical scholarship by African American biblical scholars. Much of the work in that volume wrestled with not only higher and lower criticism but added an important cultural dimension. A comment made by an older African American woman unabashedly captures the spirit of the volume: "I don't understand Paul, how can he say, 'Slaves obey your masters.'" Now, any explanation offered—denoting that in the socioeconomic context of the Roman Empire, even a freed person could become an indentured-economic slave because of the high tax rate, or for that matter, Paul's qualification that a *doulous* was bound to his lord, and some slaves, like those who belonged to Caesar or Christ (King) had tremendous power and prestige—misses the mark. Even the fact that perhaps, Paul never spoke those words, they are an interpolation, misses the problem that the reader raises.

In 2002, another volume entitled *Yet with a Steady Beat* followed. Edited by Randall C. Bailey, the work pressed for an Afrocentric reading. The volume pushed for a steady beat of counter-narratives that begins with the reader's experience as an African American. The reader's response and cultural interpretation was deemed more seminal than the historical. Additional works followed. This time, by ensuing generations of African American biblical scholars: *True to Our Native Land*, edited by Brian K. Blount,[37] *The Africana Bible*, edited by Hugh R. Page Jr.,[38] and more recently, Gay L. Byron and Vanessa Lovelace's *Womanist Interpretations of the Bible: Expanding the Discourse* (2016)[39] have all moved the discourse of communication with reproduction.

In 2002, Tat-siong Benny Liew's *The Bible in Asian America*[40] offered an interdisciplinary study of Asian American studies with biblical studies. As a first of its kind, eighteen contributors read the Bible from cultural, theological, historical, and biblical studies. Of the eighteen contributors, however, only four were biblical scholars. The volume nevertheless paved the way for *Ways of Being, Ways of Reading*,[41] edited by Mary F. Foskett and Jeffrey Kah-Jin Kuan. *Ways* is a landmark. It offers new inroads on biblical studies from Asian (India, China,

---

[36] Cain Hope Felder, ed., *Stony the Road We Trod: African American Biblical Interpretation* (Minneapolis: Fortress, 1991).

[37] Brian Blount, ed., *True to Our Native Land: An African American New Testament Commentary* (Minneapolis: Fortress, 2007).

[38] Hugh R. Page Jr., ed., *The Africana Bible: Reading Israel's Scriptures from Africa and the African Diaspora* (Minneapolis: Fortress, 2010).

[39] Gay Byron and Vanessa Lovelace, eds., *Womanist Interpretations of the Bible: Expanding the Discourse* (Atlanta: SBL Press, 2016).

[40] Tat-siong Benny Liew, ed., *The Bible in Asian America* (Atlanta: Society of Biblical Literature, 2002).

[41] Mary F. Foskett and Jeffrey Kah-Jin Kuan, eds., *Ways of Being, Ways of Reading* (St. Louis: Chalice, 2006).

Korea, and the Southeast) and Asian American perspectives. Twelve years later, *The Handbook on Asian American Hermeneutics* (T&T Clark), edited by Uriah Kim and Seung Yi Yang, is currently in circulation.

In 2014, Francisco Lozada and Fernando F. Segovia edited a volume entitled *Latino/a Biblical Hermeneutics: Problematics, Objectives, Strategies*. This work complements Fernando F. Segovia's previous work, *Decolonizing Biblical Studies*, *Interpreting Beyond Borders*, among others. Returning to the mid-1990s, Fernando F. Segovia and Mary Ann Tolbert in *Reading from This Place* (Volume 1: interpretation in the United States [1995] and Volume 2: global perspective [2000]) anticipated an innovative approach, which is conventional today, using social location as a hermeneutical key. That adumbration has been fully actualized.

As noted at the outset of this introduction, Knut Holter and Louis Jonker's edited volume on *Global Hermeneutics* (2010) has truly fostered creative scholarship, engaging the global stage. Other works have followed: Oceania (2011), South Africa (2012), Jewish Exegesis (2013), Women in Northeast Asian Countries (2014), Asia (2015), Samoan (2017), Filipino Resistance (2019), and now, Korean and Korean American (2019).[42]

We do not need to rehearse the rich gift of feminist interpretations from Phyllis Trible to Jacqueline Lapsley and womanists Wil Gafney to Mitzi Smith. Moreover, today, we also add acclaimed Black women social and cultural theorists: Bell Hooks, Patricia Hill Collins, Hortense Spillers, among others. Of the fourteen essays in this volume, eight are authored by Korean and Korean-American women. In fact, following this introduction, we open and close the volume with contributions from Korean and Korean American women Old and New Testament scholars. The Korean and Korean American reading strategy builds on these and other previous generations of social location readings without diminishing the historical critical approach.[43] I do not foresee the eclipse of our critical foundation, but rather, advancing creative dialogue and voice exchange with newer methods.

---

[42] Vaka'uta, *Reading Ezra 9–10 Tu'a-Wise: Rethinking Biblical Interpretation in Oceania*; Christo Lombaard, *The Old Testament and Christian Spirituality: Theoretical and Practical Essays from a South African Perspective* (Atlanta: Society of Biblical Literature, 2012); Michael Avioz, *Zer Rimonim: Studies in Biblical Literature and Jewish Exegesis* (Atlanta: Society of Biblical Literature, 2013); Hisako Kinukawa, *Migration and Diaspora: Exegetical Vocies of Women in Northeast Asian Countries* (Atlanta: SBL Press, 2014); Jione Havea and Peter H. W. Lau, eds., *Reading Ruth in Asia*; Vaitusi Nofoaiga, *A Samoan Reading of Discipleship in Matthew* (Atlanta: SBL Press, 2017); Lily Fetalsana-Apura, *A Filipino Resistance Reading of Joshua 1:1–9* (Atlanta: SBL Press, 2019).

[43] John J. Collins, *The Bible after Babel: Historical Criticism in a Postmodern Age* (Grand Rapids: Eerdmans, 2005).

Hebrew Bible/Old Testament and New Testament/Nag Hammadi

We open with Hannah S. An's "The Case of the Suspected Adultery (Num 5:11–31) in Light of the Hittite Instructions for the Priests and Temple Officials (CTH 264)." Both the Hittite Instructions for Priests and Temple Officials (CTH 264) and Num 5:11–31 are notable texts that reference a drinking ordeal to resolve a woman accused or suspected of adultery. An offers a comparative study of the legal assumptions underlying the Hittite and biblical texts' particular expression תשא את־עונה (Num 5:31). The literary unit belies rhetorical emphasis to preclude the potential loophole in the Israelite ritual system.

Hee-Kyu Heidi Park's "Divine Jealousy, Human Zeal: Self-Psychology and the Kenotic Spirituality of קנא in Numbers 25," engages self-psychology to interpret the spirituality of kenosis expressed in Phinehas (Num 25). The intense emotion of jealousy that dominates the text results from the anxious process of generation transition in the context of historical trauma. Self-psychologist Heinz Kohut's understanding of narcissistic transference of grandiosity finds good breeding ground in such context. Park argues that when a grandiose leader claims kenotic spirituality that channels the divine without filtering through his or her own personality, such a leader may foster gross religious violence.

In "State, War, and Women," Kyungmi Park traces the historical convergence of Koreans and Japanese coming to terms with the issue of "comfort women." Park reviews the historical sequences that resulted in the divided Koreas. She examines Judg 11 and 19, exploring the geopolitical context of violence and war. The stories of Jephthah's daughter and the Concubine and the Levite, who experienced kidnap and exploitation, are reflected through young Korean girls and women who were also kidnapped and exploited into forced sexual service for the Imperial Japanese Army from 1930 to the end of World War II.

SuJung Shin's "A 'Dialogic' Hero David from the Perspective of 'Internally Persuasive Words' in the Book of Samuel" highlights David's authority in both the surface structure of the text and in its deep structure. Shin offers a literary analysis of "internally persuasive" words, which are used to reinterpret and reexamine the text through a Bakhtinian reading.

In "Murder, Adultery, and Theft," John Ahn highlights adultery codes found in the ancient Near Eastern law collections with modern sociological case studies to situate the vetitive לא תנאף (do not commit adultery) in the context of the Decalogue's לא תרצח, לא תנאף, and לא תגנב. David's affair with Bathsheba in 2 Sam 11–12 is suggested as the backdrop to the codes. He concludes with an examination of self-identity and social reflexivity of David and Bathsheba through Anthony Giddens's work on social sequestration.

Koog-Pyoung Hong, "Ethics of Remembering: Scapegoating Manasseh after the Sewol Ferry Tragedy," begins by recalling the terrible Sewol Ferry accident which claimed 476 lives on April 16, 2014. Hong moves to read the DtrH's scapegoat theory on blaming Manasseh for the fall of Judah. He wrestles with the DrtH's theodicy—a God who remains silent when tragedy strikes—and implements current research on memory to compare the works of the DtrH and the Chronicler's account of Manasseh.

In "Half Speak Ashdodite and None Can Speak Judean: Code-Switching in Ezra-Nehemiah as an Identity Marker for Repatriate Judeans and Koreans," Roger S. Nam uses a sociolinguistics phenomenon of code switching to explain the bilingual features of Aramaic and Hebrew in Ezra-Nehemiah. He notes the importance of social intentions or situations that call for a specific (linguistic) register. Code switching offers a unique and distinctive set of cultural and political awareness to foster command of a particular situation, but moreover, it is a key marker for self-identity. Korean Americans' use of code switching offers additional insights to explain the function and purpose of bilingualism.

In "Rereading 'a Virtuous Woman (*'ēšet hayil*)' in Proverbs 31:10–31," Sun-Ah Kang interjects Michel Foucault's panopticon as a hermeneutical lens to help Korean women discipline Korean Confucianism's ideal wife. *Naehun*, to be supportive, obedient, and dutiful among other everyday images of the Korean wife and mother, are offered to reframe contemporary and ancient issues that signify a better understanding of the text and Korean social constructions of women's identities.

In Paul K.-K. Cho's "Job the Penitent: Whether and Why Job Repents (Job 42:6)," the theological theme of whether Job repents and for what reason(s) are taken up. First, using Roman Jakobson's translation process, which raises the issue of inadequacy in correct renderings, Cho situates Job 42:6 in a new literary context. Cho argues that Job repents of his hubris in Job 29–31 and 38:1–42:6. The compositional history of the book as well as Job the defiant and Job the pious are discussed in light of the Joban tale (Job 1; 42:11–17).

In "An Invitation for Postcolonial Reading of the Prophetic Tradition Claiming Imperial Powers as God's Agents in the Context of American Colonialism in Korea," SungAe Ha offers the legacy of missionary activity in Korea, which, on the one hand, is celebrated but, on the other, is cast as a form of western imperialism. She reads select passages in the books of Jeremiah (27:1–15) and Second Isaiah (44:28–45:13), examining references to the Babylonian and Persian empires as God's agents, a conduit for a theology of retribution. American imperialism and the Korean church are also read as such agents.

In "Perils of Betraying a Deity: Parallels between Ezekiel 16 and The Sumerian Myth 'Unfaithfulness,'" Sehee Kim reads Ezek 16 with Inanna's divine union with a human king. The infidelity of Dumuzi, which underscores Jerusalem's unfaithfulness to Yahweh, offers a contextual ancient Near East comparison.

Hyun Chul Paul Kim's "Crossing Boundaries: Daniel's Three Friends Meet Rev. Ki-chol Chu of Colonized Korea," the Korean American Hebrew Bible/Old

Testament keynote address from Seoul, examines cultural setbacks and renegotiations of faith and customs based on Shinto shrines established by the Japanese in the 1920s and 1930s in Korea for the promulgation of its imperial ideology. Daniel and his three friends receive a cultural reinterpretation in light of one of the most celebrated and remembered resistance fighters during Korea's colonized period, the Rev. Ki-chol Chu.

In "Of Great Walls, DMZs, and Other Lines in the Sand: Galatians Demythologized and Deconstructed," the Korean American New Testament keynote address also from Seoul, Kang-Yup Na traces the history of both Koreas and the sociopolitical context of the letter to the Galatians. He suggests that the author, the text, and the reader (encoder, code, and decoder) receive culturally conditioned markers to create meaning.

We conclude with Eunyung Lim's "Eve and Norea Retold: The Power of Storytelling in Nature of the Rulers." The Hypostatis of the Archons is read in light of Gen 1–6. Lim pushes the marker of canonicity by engaging the Eve of Gen 1–6 with Norea in the Nature (or Reality) of the Rulers, Nag Hammadi library (NHC II 4), with Michael Jackson's *The Politics of Storytelling*. Accordingly, when the female principle departs from her carnal form, and laughs at the ruler's foolishness, challenging the "social convention of male domination and female submission," Lim suggests power relations are re-ordered and re-distributed.

The fourteen essays in this volume offer diverse scholarship undertaken by Korean and Korean American biblical scholars. The essays address: women, adultery, and sex-sexuality-power (An, K. Park, Ahn, Kang, S. Kim, and Lim), Korean history, borders, and colonialism (Hong, H. Kim, and Na), sociolinguistics, language, and lexemes (Shin, Nam), and spirituality, mission, and theology (H. Park, Ha, and Cho).

In the broadest sense, *Landscapes of Korean and Korean American Biblical Interpretation* marks a locative textual approach, collectively offering and highlighting communication and reproduction. Three years have passed since the 2016 International Meeting of the Society of Biblical Literature in Seoul. *Landscapes* in 2019 breaks new ground. The volume marks the formal entrance of Korean and Korean American biblical interpretation into the field of biblical studies for the twenty-first century. It marks the birth of a new collective voice and consciousness—envisioning future works and volumes.

THE CASE OF SUSPECTED ADULTERY (NUM 5:11–31) IN LIGHT OF THE HITTITE INSTRUCTIONS FOR THE PRIESTS AND TEMPLE OFFICIALS (CTH 264)

Hannah S. An

Since its first publication in the early twentieth century, the Instructions for Priests and Temple Officials (CTH 264)[1] has been regarded as one of the significant extrabiblical texts that sheds insights into the priestly text of the Old Testament. Jacob Milgrom, for instance, noted that the Hittite text CTH 264 treats a wide variety of sancta trespasses occurring within the Hittite temple precinct, which helps us to grasp a "full range of biblical *ma'al*."[2] Milgrom's thematic survey of CTH 264 culminates in his proposal of "hierarchy of penalties for sancta trespass" within the Hittite cultic precinct.[3] Regrettably, scholarship since Milgrom's treatise on the Hittite sacrilege has not paid much attention to the nature of the Hittite legal proceedings in CTH 264, which encompasses various degrees of punishment, including a drinking ordeal in several cases. In this essay, I argue that the performative and prohibitive regulations regarding the sancta in CTH 264 illuminate one of the significant legal assumptions underlying the biblical laws that specifically address a suspected crime—the inescapability of the divine retribution in the Israelite jurisprudence in the case of a sancta trespass. I focus on the

---

This chapter is an excerpt from my PhD dissertation completed at Princeton Theological Seminary, NJ, USA in December 2014. The dissertation is accessible via ProQuest (UMI 3688103).

[1] Edgar H. Sturtevant and George Bechtel, *A Hittite Chrestomathy*, WDWLS (Baltimore: Waverly Press, 1935), 149–74; Albrecht Goetze, trans., "Instructions for Temple Officials," in *ANET*, 207–11. See also Jared L. Miller, *Royal Hittite Instructions and Related Administrative Texts*, ed. Mauro Giorgieri, WAW 31 (Atlanta: Society of Biblical Literature, 2013), 244–65 (No. 20), 389–97; Ada Taggar-Cohen, *Hittite Priesthood* (Heidelberg: Universitätsverlag, 2006), 33–139; Aygül Süel, "Hitit Kaynaklarinda Tapinak Görevlileri ile ilgili bir Direktif Metni" (PhD diss., AÜDTCFY 350, Ankara Üniversitesi, 1985).

[2] Jacob Milgrom, *Leviticus 1–16: A New Translation with Introduction and Commentary*, AB 3 (New York: Doubleday, 1991), 353–56.

[3] Milgrom, *Leviticus 1–16*, 349–56; Milgrom, *Cult and Conscience: The Asham and the Priestly Doctrine of Repentance*, SJLA 18 (Leiden: Brill, 1976), 27–35.

case of a suspected adulteress in Num 5:11–31, the only full-fledged account of trial by ordeal in the Old Testament.[4]

THE CULTURAL TRIAL IN THE HITTITE INSTRUCTIONS FOR PRIESTS AND TEMPLE OFFICIALS (CTH 264)

The Hittite text of the Instructions for Priests and Temple Officials (CTH 264) covers various cases of sancta desecration that pertain to the temple personnel's conduct within the demarcated ritual space as well as their handling of the sacrifices and utensils. As may be expected, the type and the extent of penalty resulting from circumventing ritual mandate are a function of the gravity of the sancta trespasses, including one's misconduct in the temple precinct and misappropriation of cultic assets. What is most peculiar about CTH 264 is that the Hittite text remarks on "unknown sin" in adjudicating a suspected case beyond the general description of the sancta trespasses. Several cases involving the "unknown sin" invoke an oracular inquiry in the form of a potion ordeal. The text also discusses in detail the outcome with the specific expression that denotes the status of the alleged offender. In fact, the binary outcome of "known" sin as opposed to "unknown" sin detected in CTH 264 allows us to categorize apparently disparate casuistic regulations scattered throughout the instructions text and to trace a structured judicial reasoning that underlies the Hittite priestly laws.

A Crime That "Does Not Become Known"

CTH 264 covers a number of instances in which a temple worker willfully disregards cultic regulations. For example, the instructions in §§14 and 16 mention the case of an offender who deliberately attempts to cover up one's ritual misconduct (§14, iii 68–83) or misappropriation of temple possessions (§16, iv 12–23) which is later discovered, or "becomes known" (*iš-du-wa-a-ri*). Also, the instructions feature cases of sancta trespasses that are deemed as "unknown" through the medio-passive "it does not become known" (*UL/Ú-UL-ma iš-du-wa-a-ri*) in §§17 (iv 31), 18 (iv 46–47), and 19 (iv 68). Each of these sections comprises an independent case of infringement upon sancta that requires the suspect to come "before the

---

[4] Scholars often associate the trial by ordeal in Num 5:11–31 with the Hammurabi Code §§131 and 132. Whereas §131 prescribes an oath on the suspected wife and sends her home, §132 mandates the river ordeal for the suspected wife. Neither of these legal provisions, however, offers detailed instructions that would elucidate the biblical law of jealousy. See Martha T. Roth, *Law Collections from Mesopotamia and Asia Minor*, 2nd ed., WAW 6 (Atlanta: Scholars Press, 1997), 106.

god" (ʿnuʾ [DIN]ʿGIR^{LIM}-niʾ p[a-i]t-te-ni,^{5} iv 32; cf. iv 47, iv 68–69) to ascertain one's innocence.

In §18 a suspect regarding the theft of "the first fruits"^{6} (iv 40) of the flock or herd is required to bring the offering before the deity (iv 47) and take an oath to declare his innocence. The oath is essentially a plea of innocence to the charges directed at the suspect, "If we have given these first fruits for our own desires first, or given them to our superiors, or to our wives (and) children, or to some other person, (then) we have offended the will of the gods"^{7} (§18, iv 49–52). Afterwards, the suspect is required to "drain the ryhton of the god of life"^{8} (§18, iv 52–53), which will either prove his innocence or reveal his guilt to the detriment of his kindred.

§18 If you (are) innocent, (it is) your protective deity. If, however, you (are) guilty, you will perish together with your wives (and) children.^{9} (iv 32–33)

Similarly, in §19 a suspect of the missing "portion"^{10} of the meat offering is required to recite an oath that captures all the possible acts of transgression (iv 71–77). Then the suspect is to drink "the rhyton of the god of life" (BI-IB-RU DINGIR^{LIM} ZI-aš/ZI^{TI}, iv 52–53, 69) taken from "the offering stand" (^{GIŠ}iš-ta-na-az, iv 70). Should the outcome of an ordeal "prove" the guilt of the suspect, the sinner and his entire household is to be killed.

In this vein, the idea of sin "not becoming known" (UL/Ú-UL išduwa-) refers to a situation in which the suspect is not declared officially guilty of the alleged transgression because of either the outright denial of the suspect or the lack of counter-evidence to prove the guilt objectively. If this interpretation is valid, the notion of sin "becoming known" (išduwa-) may be understood by a similar logic. The statement, "And it afterwards becomes known, it (is) a capital sin for you" (EGIR-zi-an-ma-at iš-du-wa-a-ri nu-uš-ma-ša-at SAG.DU-aš wa-aš-túl, §18 iv 45–46) does not merely denote a circumstance in which the second party is aware of the wrongdoing but one in which there is assumed to be incontrovertible evidence that the accused party has violated the law.

---

^{5} In this paper, I adopt Taggar-Cohen's transliteration of the Hittite text. See Taggar-Cohen, *Hittite Priesthood*, 66. Also, compare the reading with Miller, *Royal Hittite Instructions and Related Administrative Texts*, 262 (ˌnu DINGIR-LÌ-ni pa-itˌ-te-ni).
^{6} Gregory McMahon, "Instructions to Priests and Temple Officials (1.83)," in *The Context of Scripture: Canonical Compositions from the Biblical World*, ed. William W. Hallo and K. Lawson Younger Jr. (Leiden: Brill, 1997), 1:221.
^{7} McMahon, "Instructions to Priests and Temple Officials," 221.
^{8} McMahon, "Instructions to Priests and Temple Officials," 221.
^{9} McMahon, "Instructions to Priests and Temple Officials," 221.
^{10} McMahon, "Instructions to Priests and Temple Officials," 221.

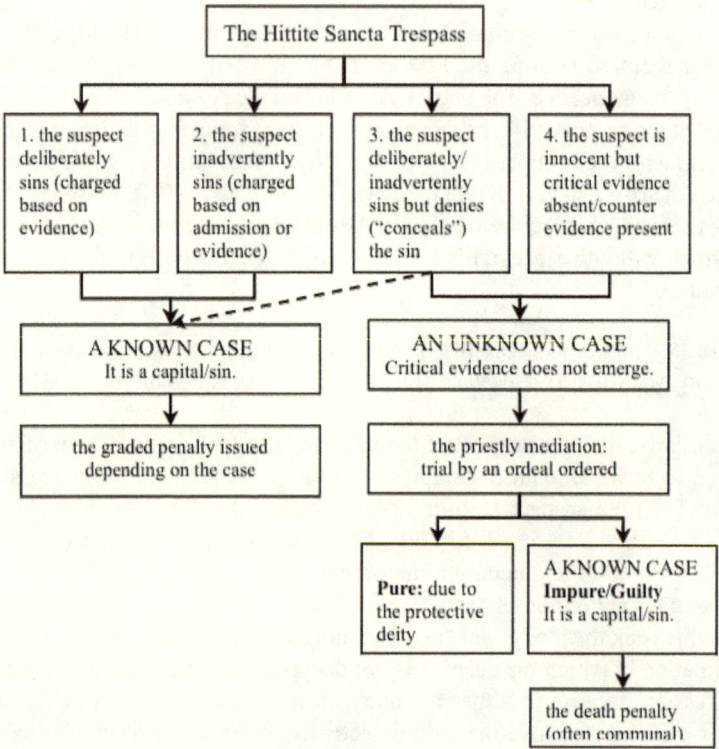

Figure 1. The Conceptual Flowchart of the Hittite Sancta Trespass[11]

---

[11] Briefly, the conceptual map of the Hittite legal logic may be represented as follows. The abbreviations are S_1 (a suspect who sinned intentionally), S_{-1} (a suspect who sinned unintentionally), S_0 (a suspect who is innocent), E_1 (incriminating evidence), E_0 (the absence of incriminating evidence), CE_1 (the presence of alleged evidence against the innocent suspect), A_1 (an admission of guilt), K_1 (a known case), K_0 (an unknown case), D_1 (a deliberate denial of the accused crime), $Pr(x)$ (the unknown case x that goes under the priestly mediation), P_0 (the declaration of guilt, impurity), P_1 (the declaration of innocence, purity).

Case 1: $S_1 + E_1 = K_1$

Case 2: (1) $S_{-1} + A_1 = K_1$; (2) $S_{-1} + E_1 = K_1$

From case 1 and 2, we can infer that $\{S_1 = S_{-1}$, where $K_1(E_1)\}$. The presence of the incriminating evidence merges both S_1 and S_{-1} into a single known case with provisions for the graduated penalty.

Case 3: (1) $S_1 + D_1 = K_0$; (2) $S_{-1} + D_1 = K_0$

From case 3, we can infer that $\{S_1 = S_{-1}$, where $K_0(D_1)\}$. As will be noted in the discussion of case 3, S_1 and S_{-1} collapse into a single unknown case when the suspect "conceals" the crime. The priestly mediation in the Hittite text involves $\{Pr(x) \to P_0, P_1\}$, where the outcome of the ordeal is theoretically binary, such as $\{Pr(S_1) \to P_0, P_1\}$ and $\{Pr(S_{-1}) \to$

Ritual Assumptions

When all of the affirmative and negative usages of the verb *išduwa-* ("to become known") in CTH 264 are considered, we can further infer that these expressions are indicative of legal reasoning within the Hittite cultic sphere (see fig. 1). The sancta trespasses in the Hittite temple precinct may be conceived in four general categories based on the case laws established in CTH 264:

(1) The suspect sins deliberately. The suspect is charged guilty by the evidence/testimony produced by another. The related cases would be §15 (iv 7–8), §16 (iv 12–22), §17 (iv 25–30), §18 (iv 43–46), and §19 (iv 61–66). For example, the temple worker who trespasses the cultic laws by stealing some of the temple property, such as grain or cattle, is to be apprehended (§15, §16, §17, §18, §19). The legal outcome of the indictment in these cases is labeled as "known" (*išduwa-*) and the verdict is formulated with the term "sin" (*wa-aš-túl*) or "capital sin" (SAG.DU-*aš wa-aš-túl*). The trespasser is expected to make prescribed restitutions (e.g., §15.10, an ox and ten sheep; §16.23, all the grain; §17.31, an ox). In certain cases, additional punishment is issued through the consultation of the oracles (e.g., §15.8–9).

(2) The suspect sins inadvertently (*karš-*). The suspect confesses one's sin voluntarily or is charged guilty by the decisive evidence/testimony produced by another. The related cases would be §10 (iii 15–16), §11 (iii 30–34), and §14 (iii 71–77). In the inadvertent case of §14, the temple worker who did not undergo ritual bathing is to admit his negligence to save himself from a worse predicament. By contrast, the negligent official who fails to fulfill the guard duty in the case of §10 is to be seized by the temple officials and charged guilty. As in the first category, these cases are to be considered as "known" (*išduwa-*) and the verdict is likewise formulated with the term "sin" (*wa-aš-túl*) or "capital sin" (SAG.DU-*aš wa-aš-túl*).

$P_0, P_1\}$. In view of the fact that the ritual must yield the ideal set of $\{S_1 = P_0; S_{-1} = P_0; S_0 = P_1\}$, the logical corollary is that $Pr(S_0) = P_1$, where $Pr(S_0) \rightarrow P_0, P_1$ (Case 4), although CTH 264 does not explicitly mention such a case. The potion ordeal in Num 5: 11–31 envisions this particular legal situation as will be discussed.

Case 4: (1) $S_0 + E_0 = K_0$; 2) $S_0 + CE_1 = K_0$

From case 4, we can infer that $\{E_0 = CE_1,$ where $K_0(S_0)\}$. In the Hittite ritual realm, the most unwanted combination of possibilities that would undermine the system are $Pr(S_1, S_{-1}) = P_1 \neq P_0$ and $Pr(S_0) = P_0 \neq P_1$. While the Hittite legal framers do not conceive the latter outcome as a possibility, they acknowledge the ritual outcome of $\{Pr(S_1, S_{-1}) = P_1\}$ and ascribes the favorable fate to one's "personal deity." On the other hand, Israelite ritual system does not admit such a loophole by upholding $\{Pr(S_1, S_{-1}) \neq P_1$ AND $Pr(S_0) \neq P_0\}$. Such a legal rationale is implicit in Num 5:31 as well as in Lev 5:1, especially in the particular usage of the phraseology נשא עון.

EXCURSUS: THE CASE OF NEGLIGENCE (§§ 10, 11, AND 14)

The scribe of §§10 and 11 does not appropriate or extend the ritual concerns of §§1–9 as other paragraphs do in part 1.[12] Rather, the paragraphs introduce new cultic provisions regarding the guarding duties of the temple, much reminiscent of the distinct roles of biblical priests and Levites.[13] Paragraph 10 reveals conspicuous divisions of custodial responsibilities among the high priest, temple officials, and guards:

> §10 Outside, let the guards keep their watch. But inside the temples let the temple officials make the rounds all night... Each night one high priest is to be in charge of the sentries. And further, of those who are priests, someone shall be (assigned) to the temple gate and shall guard the temple. (iii 9–14)[14]

Continuing the theme of paragraph §10, the scribe of paragraph §11 covers specifically the double duties of the guard, including accompanying the lay people entering the sacred realm and defending the temple precinct from unsuspected intrusions. What is distinctive about §§10–11 is that they contain the instructions on the case of neglect, a ritual situation not directly addressed in the earlier layer of §§2–8.

> §10 Whoever is a temple official—all [high] priests, lesser priests, anointing priests—whoever regularly crosses the threshold of the gods: let each not neglect (*kar-aš-ta-ri-ma*) to sleep up in the temple. (iii 3–6)

> §11 If there is some enemy idea that someone will attempt to cause damage, and those on the outer wall do not see him, (but) the temple officials inside see him, the guard must go after him. Let that (guard) not neglect (*kar-aš-ta-ri*) to "spend the night up in the temple."[15] If, however, he does neglect (to do so; *kar-aš-ta-*

---

[12] Nonetheless, §§10–11 evince similar ideas found in the earlier material. For example, the unique expression relating to "pardon" in §5.59 and §8.58 is echoed in §10.20; §5.59 = i 59 (EGIR-*pa wa-aḫ-nu-mar-ši li-e e-eš-zi*) "There is to be no pardon for him"; §8.58 = ii 51(EGIR-*pa wa-aḫ-nu-mar-ši li-e e-eš-zi*) "There is to be no pardon for them"; §10.20 = iii 20 (*li-e-ya-aš-kán ú-e-iḫ-ta-ri*) "And let him not be pardoned." All these instances conclude the section. See McMahon, "Instructions to Priests," 218–19 for translation. See also Sturtevant, "A Hittite Text," 401n58.

[13] Milgrom claims that the hierarchy in the Hittite case reflects the "class" division between the priests and the Levites in the Hebrew Bible. See his detailed exposition of §§10–11 in Milgrom, "Shared Custody," 204–9.

[14] McMahon, "Instructions to Priests," 219.

[15] Harry A. Hoffner Jr. and H. Craig Melchert, *A Grammar of the Hittite Language: Part 1 Reference Grammar* (Winona Lake, IN: Eisenbrauns, 2008), 336 (25.29); Hoffner and Melchert's translation is clearer than McMahon's "to sleep next to his god" in "Instructions," 219.

ri-ma), and they do not kill him, let them subject him to public humiliation. Naked—let there be no clothing on his body at all—let him carry water three times from the Larbarna's spring into the temple of his god. Let that be his humiliation. (iii 26–34)

The term *karš-* with the verb is to be defined as "to fail to (do something), neglect to (do something)."[16] The usage of the expression in both §§10 and 11 raises the question of what the scribe meant by "neglect": did it involve an intentional or unintentional trespass? In other words, is the scribe envisioning a case in which the temple officer intentionally ignores the rule or unintentionally break the rule? For one thing, what is clear from the context is that the scribe presumes the perpetrator's foreknowledge of the rules when articulating the injunctions. In §10, for example, the temple officials are enjoined not to disregard guarding the sacred precinct by night. That the prohibitive instruction, "let each not neglect (*kar-aš-ta-ri-ma*) to sleep up in the temple" (iii 5–6) is preceded by the specific reference to the status of the temple workers is a tell-tale sign. Specifically, the scribe addresses "whoever regularly crosses the threshold of the gods" (iii 4–5) among the three classes of the temple officials. Given such a particular emphasis, it is rather unlikely that the scribe would have envisaged a violation which any of the sacerdotal officials familiar with the temple precincts would commit due to outright ignorance of the rule. Still, the context of §10 is limited to deciding whether the prohibition of cultic oversight supposes deliberateness or inadvertency, even though the trespasser's awareness of the rule is apparent.

The instruction in §11, on the other hand, provides more contextual clues as it entails what kind of punishment is to be issued for the delinquent guard.

> Let that (guard) not neglect to spend the night up in the temple. If, however, he does neglect (to do so), and they do not kill him, let them subject him to public humiliation. (iii 30–31)

If the guard "does neglect" (*kar-aš-ta-ri-ma*, iii 30) to stay up during the night in the temple, he faces two possible outcomes: a death sentence or public disgrace. The lenient form of penalty should be imposed if the temple officials decide not to execute the negligent culprit. The scribe articulates that the guard, stripped of his clothes, is to undergo public "humiliation" (*lu-ú-ri-eš*, iii 34) by transporting water from the Larbarna's spring (*Labarnaš luliya-*) three times.[17] The accommodation for the less severe punitive measure itself suggests that the "neglect" at times may have involved an inadvertent case. Had the guard evidently violated

---

[16] McMahon, "Instructions to Priests," 336.
[17] The function of this particular spring or "basin" seems to have been closely related to the state cult of Ḫattuša. See Yiğit Erbil and Alice Mouton, "Water in Ancient Anatolian Religions: An Archaeological and Philological Inquiry on the Hittite Evidence," *JNES* 71 (2012): 53–74.

the command out of flagrant dereliction, he would have been apprehended and killed without exception.

Under what circumstances would "they" decide not to "kill" the unwitting offender and enforce a less harsh form of punishment? Perhaps the temple officials would have penalized the negligent guard depending on the extent of the consequential damage. They would have been especially tolerant in cases where no grievous consequences resulted from the guard's unintentional negligence—possibly from inattention or fatigue during the guard duties at night.[18] If this tentative consideration is acceptable, the allowance for a moderate form of punishment other than a capital penalty may be evidence that in certain instances "intentionality" served as a "mitigating factor" of the due penalty in the Hittite temple precinct (contra Milgrom).[19]

On the whole, the idea of "neglect" (*karš-*) in CTH 264 seems to be predicated on the assumption of the sinner's foreknowledge of the law coupled with the unwilful violation of the law. This observation is further affirmed in the only other instance in which the term *karš-* infinitive is used with the (§14). §14 (iii 71–83) appropriates §2 in a number of ways. The detailed instructions (see below a–b²) for the ritually defiled by sleeping with a woman are absent in the former layer. The scribe presents an intriguing development of purity rules where resolution of the desecration hinges on several circumstantial variables.

Rule	
	As soon as the sun (is) up, he must immediately bathe, and arrive promptly at the time of the gods' eating in the morning.
a	*If, however, he neglects (this; kar-aš-ta-ri-ma), it is a sin for him.*
a¹	*Whoever sleeps with a woman and his superior (or) his supervisor presses (him), let him say so.*
a²	*However, if he does not dare tell (his superior), let him tell a fellow servant. He still must bathe.*
b¹	*However, if he intentionally delays, and without bathing he forces his way near the gods' sacrificial loaves (and) libation vessel (while) unclean, and his fellow servant knows about him, and he appears to him (!):*
b²	*If he conceals (it), but afterward it becomes known, there (is) a capital penalty for them and both must die.*[20]

Figure 2. Paragraph 14: The Temple Worker's Purity Requirement after Intercourse

---

[18] Also note how the Hittite text entitled the Instructions to the Royal Guard (CTH 261) covers all types of contingencies for the royal sentinels. The instructions even address how to relieve oneself during the guard duty (§§6–8). See McMahon, "Instructions to Priests," 225–30.

[19] Milgrom, *Cult*, 42.

[20] McMahon, "Instructions to Priests," 220. The subject "he" refers to the "fellow servant."

First, the purity law stipulates that the kitchen attendant who sleeps with a woman the night before should not serve at the ritual table unless he bathes at the break of dawn and be ready to serve on time. The scribe follows up this injunction with a conditional sentence that addresses the case of neglect: "If, however, he neglects (this) it is a sin for him" ("a" in fig. 2; iii 73–74). The "neglect" (*kar-aš-ta-ri-ma*) of the ritual bathing is declared as "sin" (*wa-aš-túl*). This direct statement of indictment, however, does not specify what kind of punishment the unwitting trespass will entail.[21]

Instead, paragraph 14 makes further legal requirements for the defiled kitchen worker. When demanded, the man must confess his state of impurity to his overseer whether he was defiled intentionally or unintentionally (a^1 in fig. 2, iii 75). Otherwise, if the man dares not divulge his state of impropriety, he has an option of informing his fellow worker of the matter (a^2 in fig. 2, iii 77). It is important to note that these two contingent provisions (a^1 and a^2 in fig. 2) are subordinate to the case of unwitting neglect (a). The second instruction (a^2 in fig. 2) especially functions as a safety measure to prevent the impure kitchen attendant to commit potentially one of the blatant sancta trespasses out of sheer timidity. Once admitting the state of his ritual uncleanness, the worker will be appropriately kept away from having to handle the sacrificial food and utensils in the sacred area. He is commanded, nonetheless, to bathe to rid himself of the impurity.

Although the Hittite verb *karš-* is a neutral term that does not necessarily express the intentionality or unintentionality of an act of negligence, the concept of "neglect" (*kar-aš-ta-ri-ma*) in §14 may convey unintentional disregard as evinced by the subsequent legal prescriptions.[22] The scribe emphatically weaves the expression "if he intentionally delays" (*ma-a-an še-ik-kán-ti-it-ma* ZI-*it pa-ra-a da-a-i*, iii 78) into the protasis as he discusses the case of a glaringly defiant violation of the sancta (b^1 in fig. 2). If the kitchen worker, without having bathed, approaches the cultic table and his fellow worker does not inform the authorities of the trespass, both will face a capital penalty (SAG.DU-*aš* ÚŠ-*tar*) when it becomes known (*iš-du-wa-a-ri*). Again, the two conditional clauses (b^1 and b^2 in fig. 2) are in contrast to the preceding case of apparently unintentional neglect (a^1, a^2, and a^3 in fig. 2) in that they pertain to deliberate infringement of the sancta. The literal translation of the protasis of b^1 (*ma-a-an še-ik-kán-ti-it-ma* ZI-*it pa-ra-a da-a-i*) would be, "if with knowing will he puts forth,"[23] which helps illuminate the meaning of the expression "if he neglects" (*ma-a-an-ma-aš kar-aš-ta-ri-ma*) in a^1 (see fig. 2). The scribe's employment of the phrase "with knowing will" (*še-ik-kán-ti-it-ma* ZI-*it*, iii 78) in b^1 (see fig. 2) indicates that the incidence of "neglect" in a^1 must have been inadvertent rather than deliberate. The "intentional

---

[21] Such ambiguity may leave room for the legislative officials to determine what kind of corrective discipline the trespasser deserves.

[22] See *HED*, s.v. "*kar(a)s-, karass-, karsai-, karsiya-*."

[23] Also see Sturtevant and Bechtel, *Hittite Chrestomathy*, 173 (n. 3.78).

postponement" of bathing is not substantively different from the intentional "neglect" of bathing in this particular ritual situation. The scribe thus distinguishes between an unwitting trespass, on one hand, and a willful trespass, on the other, and ascribes the death penalty to the concealment of the latter case.

In this regard, we need to reconsider Milgrom's assertion that CTH 264 applies only to deliberate and intentional infringement in the cultic sphere.[24] The corollary to this claim is that the priestly source evinces a breakthrough within its own tradition (e.g., Lev 4–5), since its literary predecessors, including some of the earlier nonpriestly accounts, do not consider the lack of "intention" as a mitigating element in the sancta trespass.[25] Nonetheless, a detailed examination of the Hittite text reveals that the formulators do not entirely ignore the issue of inadvertency. The repeated stress on the scrupulous performance of the ritual tasks suggests that the framers of CTH 264 are duly mindful of the possibility of inadvertent infraction in the sacred sphere. For instance, the expression such as "be very afraid" ([*me-i*]*k-ki mar-ri na-aḫ-*[(*ḫ*)*a-an-t*]*e-eš e-eš-tén*, i 38) of the divine "will" or "word" (§3 i 38, §7 ii 29 and §8 ii 34), or "be very careful/cautious" (*me-ik-ki pa-aḫ-ḫa-aš-ša-nu-wa-an-te-eš e-ˀeš-tén*, ii 79) about observing the cultic regulations (§10 ii 79, §12–13 iii 43–44, §13 iii 54 and §14 iii 57) in turn reinforces the notion that neglect, be it intentional or unintentional, in the sacred realm is inadmissible.

In a broader scope, the instructions in §§9–19 which stress intentionality as a factor in the transgression are remarkable. Contra Milgrom, however, we cannot conclude confidently that the Hittite text does not make provisions for a mitigated penalty in the case of unintentional infringement. The framer of CTH 264 is especially careful to point out the gravity of the trespass that results from what appears as unintentional neglect of the sacerdotal duties by the temple personnel,

---

[24] Milgrom, *Cult*, 42. "Hittite trespass is deliberate; there is no equivalent to biblical *šggh*." In articulating the difference between the Instructions for Priests and Temple Officials (KUB 13.4) and the related biblical text, Milgrom claims that the Hittite text prescribes only "deliberate" cases of sancta trespass. He further proposes that this feature is indicative of the priestly innovation in Lev 4–5.

[25] According to Milgrom, the earlier traditions did not consider "inadvertency" as an ameliorating component in the sancta desecration (e.g., 2 Sam 6:6; 1 Sam 6:19; Num 4:15, 20): "Indeed, in positing inadvertency as a mitigating factor in trespass, P has broken with its own background in which intention is not a factor in trespass on the most sacred. But the glimmering of a tendency to alleviate the penalty for unintentional trespass is also detectable in older Egyptian law and perhaps in Hittite jurisprudence as well." Milgrom nonetheless acknowledges that the Instructions for Priests and Temple Officials does not necessarily represent the Hittite law at large and that the leniency exercised in the case of inadvertent infraction is not entirely absent from the Hittite legal tradition. As his own cautionary words may indicate, Milgrom's underlying premises are open to questions on several fronts. Milgrom, *Cult*, 42–43.

such as in §§10, 11, and 14. As already discussed, paragraphs 10, 11, and 14 employ the term *kar-aš-ta-ri* (med. pres. 3sg. √*karš-*) to cover the negligent misdeed in the cultic setting. These cases indicate some type of mitigated form of punishment less than the death penalty and serve as ancient evidence for "inadvertency as a mitigating factor" in the sancta trespass.

(3) The suspect sins either deliberately or inadvertently but denies involvement in the matter. The critical evidence or testimony is absent, or the counter-evidence or testimony is produced by the suspect. The cases treated in CTH 264 pertain to deliberate cases, such as in §§14 (iii 82–83), 17 (iv 31), 18 (iv 46–47), and 19 (iv 68). The case of the temple worker who intentionally defers bathing in the case of §14 is a unique case in that a passive party who is complicit in the crime is also indicted. It is logical to assume that both intentional and unintentional cases are collapsed into a single category of an "unknown" case should the offender deny the allegation.[26] In the absence of the offender's admission and material evidence to prove the case otherwise, the distinction between intentional and unintentional trespass is undecipherable. Such "unknown" legal cases proceed to a trial by ordeal unless critical evidence emerges to affirm or reverse the suspect's plea of innocence (see the dotted line in fig. 1). Through priestly mediation, the positive outcome of a potion ordeal will release the suspect from the alleged guilt whereas the negative outcome will charge the suspect (usually with his or her family) with the death penalty.

(4) The suspect is innocent but accused of the perpetration. The suspect cannot produce the critical evidence or testimony for the case or the counter-evidence is produced by the accuser. This instance is not mentioned in CTH 264. Nevertheless, the binary verdict of "pure" (*pár-ku-e[š-te]-ni*, iv 53) and "impure" (*pa-ap-ra-an-te-eš*, iv 54) through the potion ordeal presupposes the case in which the suspect is wrongfully alleged to have committed the violation. If the trial by an ordeal ratified by an oath turns out to uphold the plea of the innocent or the culprit, one's "protective deity" (ᵈLAMMA-*KU-NU*, iv 32, 54) takes the credit for the positive result. The resolution of the "unknown" legal cases necessitates priestly mediation through cultic means.

The four classifications of the sancta trespasses in CTH 264 on the basis of "known" and "unknown" cases of violations yield a coherent picture of the legal ramifications in the temple precincts. The most remarkable aspect is that if a trespass is deemed as "known," the objective declaration of judgment—"It is a capital/sin" (*wa-aš-túl* or SAG.DU-*aš wa-aš-túl*)—is expected to ensue. The legal scenarios of (1), (2), (3), and (4) eventually converge into the trespass that is to be made "known" through priestly arbitration except when the result of the ordeal proves to be affirmative. This is evidence that "to become known" (*išduwa-*) in Hittite jurisprudence does not merely connote the divulging of the previously unknown sin to the "public" (i.e., temple authorities). The trespass that "becomes

---

[26] See footnote 11, case 3.

known" (*iš-du-wa-a-ri*) signifies a judicial verdict of which the suspect is guilty by all accounts based on either forensic or cultic means of investigation.[27] Having assessed the significance of the term in the Hittite ritual realm, we will see whether the concept may be applicable to understanding the suspected transgression in Num 5:11–31.

THE BIBLICAL CASE OF A SUSPECTED TRANSGRESSION
THAT REQUIRES TO BE "KNOWN"

A Suspected Adulteress (Num 5:11–31)

This section examines the case of a suspected adulteress of Num 5:11–31 in light of CTH 264, given that both the biblical and the Hittite texts envision a suspected culprit who is subjected to trial by ordeal. In Num 5, the conditions set forth at the early part of the chapter contain the notion of "hiddenness" on the part of the accuser, the suspected woman's husband.

In this regard, the statement ונסתרה והיא נטמאה ונעלם מעיני אישה in Num 5:13 demands further investigation. The *nip'al* verb נעלם in the context of Num 5:12–14 does not merely connote the fact that the husband is not aware of his wife's affair. The semantic range of the syntactical unit נעלם+עינים+מן extends beyond the cognitive grasp of the suspicious incident on the husband's part in the context of Num 5. Rather, it stresses the legal situation in which there is no critical witness (Num 5:13, והיא נטמאה ועד אין בה), evidence or admission (Num 5:13, והוא לא נתפשה) to affirm the husband's suspicion out of the "spirit of jealousy" (רוח־קנאה). In fact, the conceptual arrangement of the legal exposition in Num 5:11–31 is remarkably consonant with the legal ramifications of CTH 264 in the case of the suspect who conceals one's trespass. In the Hittite realm, the trespass that does not "become known" (*išduwa-*) applies to the two possible legal circumstances where no concrete evidence or witness emerges for the suspect who either sins deliberately or inadvertently; but, conceals the case by denial (case 3) or is innocent (case 4).

Numbers 5:14 contain these two options. The woman who happens to be the object of her husband's "spirit of jealousy" is either guilty or innocent: she either defiled herself (והוא נטמאה, case A) or did not defile herself (והיא לא נטמאה, case B). As in the Hittite case, the suspects in any status—the deliberate, the inadvertent, or the innocent—are subject to trial by ordeal should there be no counter-evidence to invalidate the accusations on "legitimate" grounds. These include the suspect who sinned intentionally as well as the one who sinned unintentionally but both of whom that end up denying involvement in the illegal action, although

---

[27] The term *forensic* is derived from Bruce Wells' noteworthy article. Bruce Wells, "The Cultic Versus the Forensic: Judahite and Mesopotamian Judicial Procedures in the First Millennium B.C.E.," *JAOS* 128 (2008): 205–32.

the biblical law does not make the distinctions.[28] The violation of faithfulness which is "hidden from the eyes of the husband" (Num 5:13, ונעלם מעיני אישה) then necessitates priestly meditation through a potion ordeal. The ritual entails the ratification by an oath that features explicit curses (Num 5:22, ואמרה האשה אמן אמן), drinking of the potentially fatal potion, declaration of judgment and punishment based on the binary opposition of "pure" and "impure," and complete exoneration of the false accuser—all common to both the Hittite and the biblical ordeal. Based on the similarity between the Hittite and biblical legal ramifications (Num 5:11–31), we can infer the conceptual congruence between the biblical notion of the "concealed" sin (e.g., ונסתרה) that is "hidden from one's eyes" (e.g., ונעלם מעיני אישה) and the Hittite counterpart of the sin that "does not become known" (*UL/Ú-UL-ma iš-du-wa-a-ri*). It is also notable that Num 5:11–31 concludes with the definitive proclamation of the woman's guilty state at the end of presenting the ordeal laws which would presumably reveal the offense: ההוא תשא את־עונה.

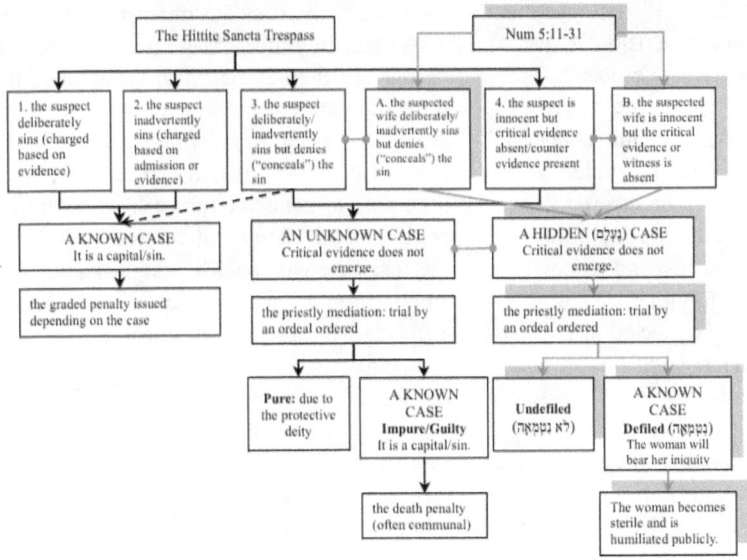

Figure 3. The Hittite and the Biblical Trial by Ordeal Compared

A further look at the final outcome of the trial by ordeal in the Hittite and the biblical texts may be helpful in defining the scope of the guilt and punishment in the trial of a suspected wife. In Num 5:31, the woman bearing her iniquity (והאשה ההוא תשא את־עונה, Num 5:31b) is placed in juxtaposition with the man being cleared from iniquity (ונקה האיש מעון, Num 5:31a). The significance of the statement והאשה ההוא תשא את־עונה, however, must be probed in the wider context of

---

[28] It is conceivable that the woman was inadvertently forced into a situation against her will but did not have recourse to make it known at the time of the transgression.

Num 5:11–31. The expression under investigation appears in the literary unit of Num 5:29–31, which succinctly recapitulates the trial by ritual in Num 5:12–28. As an exegetical addendum, the supplementation in Num 5:29–31 largely attends to the two lingering questions regarding the possible fate of the accusing husband and the suspected wife.

First, Num 5:12–28 does not clarify what would become of the husband whose "spirit of jealousy" turns out to be groundless. What would happen to the husband whose misleading accusation already has caused much psychological, if not physical, damage to the suspected wife whose innocence is affirmed through the trial by ordeal? The query is inferred from the conditional statement in Num 5:14, in which the arousal of the husband's "spirit of jealousy" (רוח־קנאה) equally applies to the defiled woman (והוא נטמאה) and the undefiled woman (והיא לא נטמאה). The verdict of the trial by ordeal, as described in Num 5:27 and 28, depends on the phenomenal impact which the "water of bitterness" (מי המרים, Num 5:18, 19, 23, 24)[29] will bring on the woman's body, such as "bitter pain" (למרים), "abdominal distension" (וצבתה בטנה), and possibly miscarriage (ונפלה ירכה).[30] If the suspected wife was defiled (אם־נטמאה) and thereby betrayed the faith of her husband (ותמעל מעל באישה), she will become an execration (והיתה האשה לאלה בקרב עמה) among the people. If the suspected wife was not defiled (ואם־לא נטמאה האשה)—as will be evident by her unharmed state—she is said to be clean (וטהרה הוא). She will be cleared (ונקתה) and be able to conceive the child (ונזרעה זרע). The law of the trial by ordeal concludes in Num 5:28 without commenting on the status of the husband who wrongfully accused the woman. More significantly, the first unit of Num 5:12–28 does not mention the defiled woman who could have escaped the expected physiological suffering from the potion ordeal. To the contrary, such a legal possibility is lucidly stated in the Hittite law of the trial by ordeal and considered as a sign of favor from the personal "protective deity."[31] It is not far-fetched to assume that the priestly legislators would have been well aware of such an exceptional legal loophole in the polytheistic ancient Near Eastern milieu. In Num 5:29–31, these issues are reconsidered with the slightly revised wording of the original conditional statement in Num 5:14, 15.

---

[29] The most recent discussion of the difficult term מי המרים is cogently presented by Eve L. Feinstein, who upholds the traditional translation, "bitter waters." E. L. Feinstein, "The 'Bitter Waters' of Numbers 5:11–31," *VT* 62 (2012): 300–306. See also J. Sasson, "Numbers 5 and the 'Waters of Judgment,'" *BZ* 16 (1972): 249–51; Herbert Chanan Brichto, "Case of the *Sōṭā*," *HUCA* 46 (1975): 55-70, 59.

[30] The "falling of her thigh" is probably a euphemistic reference to the gynecologic condition of uterine prolapse. Frymer-Kensky correctly points out the fact that ירך is often a metaphoric expression for the male genitalia in the Bible (e.g., Gen 46:26; Exod 1:5; Judg 8:30). So Tikva Frymer-Kensky, "Strange Case of the Suspected Sotah (Numbers V:11–31," *VT* 34 (1984):11–26.

[31] See CTH 264 iv 32, 54 for ᵈLAMMA-*KU-NU*, "your protective deity."

The "law of jealousy" (זאת תורת הקנאת) in the appendix to the main section (Num 5:29–31) is restated under two assumptions: (1) the suspected wife strays (תשטה אשה) and defiles herself (ונטמאה) as described in Num 5:29 *or* (או) (2) the husband is overcome with the "spirit of jealousy" (תעבר עליו רוח קנאה) and is "jealous of his wife" (וקנא את־אשתו) as in Num 5:30. In the previous unit of Num 5:12–28, the "spirit of jealousy" is unequivocally related to either a defiled or an undefiled case. In the latter unit, the first part of the conditional statement (Num 5:29) presumes that the law applies to the defiled wife. The premise following the coordinating conjunction "or" (או) is dubious nonetheless. In Num 5:30, the description of the husband who is filled with the "spirit of jealousy" refers to the one who is rightfully jealous of his wife rather than the one who is being suspicious of an innocent wife. The repetition of the clause, "He is jealous of his wife" (וקנא את־אשתו), intensifies the cause of the suspecting husband. With the presence of "or" (או) connecting verses 29 and 30, the condition stated in verse 29 is posed as an alternative to that in verse 30. According to the priestly writer of verse 30, the husband will be naturally overwhelmed with the "spirit of jealousy" only if the wife defiles herself. Under this rearranged conditional statement, the husband has every right to bring his suspected wife before YHWH for the priestly mediation (והעמיד את־האשה לפני יהוה, Num 5:30).[32] The ensuing final statement in Num 5:31 captures the diametrically opposed outcome of the trial in starker relief: the husband is to be cleared from iniquity (ונקה האיש מעון), but the wife is to bear her iniquity (והאשה ההוא תשא את־עונה).

The final verdict on the suspected wife in Num 5:31 appears to be a supplementary exposition of 5:27 and an inverse case of 5:28. If the suspected wife is defiled (אם נטמאה, Num 5:27), she is not clean (*הוא לא טהרה, cf. Num 5:28) as she has betrayed the faith of her husband (ותמעל מעל באישה, Num 5:27). She will not be cleared (*לא נקתה, cf. Num 5:28) but bear her iniquity (והאשה ההוא תשא את־עונה, Num 5:31). It is worthwhile to explore the theoretical apposition of the suspected wife's state of "defilement" (נטמאה, Num 5:27) and "impurity" (* הוא לא טהרה, cf. Num 5:28), or her breach of husband's faith (ותמעל מעל באישה, Num 5:27), on the one hand, and her state of "undefilement" (לא נטמאה, Num 5:28) and "purity" (וטהרה הוא, Num 5:28), on the other. In view of the counterpart "She has acted unfaithfully against her husband" (ותמעל מעל באישה) in Num 5:27, the emphatic statement "She is pure" (וטהרה הוא) in Num 5:28 is a ritual declaration of the suspected wife's innocence after the trial by ordeal.[33] The following statement "She will be cleared and will be able to bear children" (ונקתה ונזרעה זרע, Num 5:28) is a confirmation that ensures the inculpable wife's immunity from the consequential suffering of the suspected guilt. In this vein, the closing remark

---

[32] In CTH 264, the suspect is also required to be brought before the god. CTH 264 iv 32, 48.

[33] Compare the statement with the Hittite declaration of "pure" (*parkui-/parkueš-*) and "impure" (*paprant-/papreš-*).

"But as for the woman, she shall bear her iniquity" (והאשה ההוא תשא את־עונה, Num 5:31) theoretically follows a ritual declaration that she is "impure" (* הוא לא טהרה, cf. Num 5:28) and defines the limits of her consequential suffering from the guilt she incurred.

The final indictment of the jealous husband and the adulterous wife in Num 5:29–31 reckons with the ambiguity in the legal provisions of Num 5:12–28. On the one hand, the notion of the man's being "cleared from iniquity" (ונקה האיש מעון, Num 5:31) presumes his status in all conceivable cases. It naturally covers the case in which the suspected wife proves her innocence through the trial by ordeal and her husband's "spirit of jealousy" turns out to be groundless. Without further qualification, the declaration of the husband's "freedom from iniquity" may even apply to the wretched case in which the husband, based on his misleading intuition, wrongfully accuses the innocent with the dire consequence of a cultic trial. In this case, the wife is certainly undefiled but, nonetheless, suffers the unfortunate consequences of the potion ordeal. On the other hand, the notion of the woman's "bearing her iniquity" (והאשה ההוא תשא את־עונה, Num 5:31) pertains to the defiled wife's eventual suffering from the ordeal, including permanent sterility and social stigma. In addition, the concept logically supposes—as can be predicted from the Hittite ritual framework—for the extraordinary case in which the woman is undoubtedly defiled and yet, emerges from the potion ordeal intact.[34]

By contrast, CTH 264 has no mention of the punitive measures against the accuser who erroneously instigate a trial by ordeal. The Hittite cultic system, however, acknowledges the possibility of the guilty suspect surviving the potion ordeal and being declared innocent (§§17 and 18). In such a case, the favorable turnout is ascribed to the gracious protection of one's personal deity.[35] Unlike the Hittite legal precursor, the priestly legislation of Num 5:29–31 specifies that the "jealous" husband will be deemed exempt from any legal liability (Num 5:31). Moreover, under no circumstances is the suspected wife guilty of adultery able to

---

[34] The early rabbinic discourse regarding the probable outcome of the ordeal on the woman suspected of adultery (סוטה) sheds some light on this line of interpretation. Although the sages did not envision one's "protective deity" to get involved as in the Hittite example, they raised the possibility that the guilty may emerge from the ordeal unscathed and remain unharmed for a limited time because of some kind of merit on the woman's part. See m. Sotah 3:4 c–d; Danby, 296. Danby, trans. and ed., 296; Haim S. Horovitz, ed., *Siphre d'be Rab: Siphre ad Numeros adjector Siphre zutta* (Jerusalem: Wahrmann Books, 1966).

[35] In §17 the alleged perpetrator is to present himself "before the god" ([DIN]' GIR^{LIM}-ni' p[a-i]t-te-ni, iv 32; cf. iv 47). The preceding instructions in §17 regarding the misappropriation of a plow ox with the explicit examples of a culprit's possible excuses indicate that the instruction assumes a legal loophole in which the culprit manages to escape the punishment. In case the individual is deemed innocent, the scribe attributes the favorable verdict to his "protective deity" (^{d}LAMMA-*KU-NU*, iv 32). Otherwise, he will be declared guilty of a "capital sin" (SAG.DU-*aš wa-aš-túl*).

escape the due punishment in God's jurisprudence. In the priestly outlook of Num 5:11–31, the execution of the trial by ordeal "before YHWH" (והעמיד את־האשה לפני יהוה, Num 5:30) will dole out the just retribution to the guilty suspect. The curt statement והאשה ההוא תשא את־עונה concluding the legal prescription in Num 5:31 therefore functions to reinforce the inevitability or the inescapability of the divine punishment on the guilty (cf. Lev 5:1, ונשא עונו).[36] It can be inferred from the formulaic expression (תשא את־עונה) that the adulterous wife would not be able to avert the suffering of her guilt's consequences even if she survives the ordeal at the moment. The phrase ultimately evokes the sense of a dreadful divine intervention which may manifest itself in various forms of physical or psychological suffering in due time.

---

[36] This observation is also validated in the case of in Lev 5:1, in which the similar expression ונשא עונו is attested. According to the priestly rationale, the "hidden" witness (והוא עד או ראה או ידע אם־לוא יגיד) who deliberately violates "a public oath to testify" (קול אלה) will by no means escape the divine punishment.

DIVINE JEALOUSY, HUMAN ZEAL: SELF-PSYCHOLOGY AND THE KENOTIC SPIRITUALITY OF קנא IN NUMBERS 25

Hee-Kyu Heidi Park

In establishing the Yawhist cult, the Torah preserves emotionally charged religiosity in its ancient form. Numbers 25 is an example, charged with violent emotion and religious zeal. This emotion, namely, the jealousy "for" or "of" God, invites an interpretation that allows an analysis of the psychodynamics of the community behind this text. Drawing from Heinz Kohut's self-psychological understanding of leadership as a hermeneutic lens, my interpretation engages in a psychoanalysis of zealous spirituality. I argue that a powerful monotheistic-centered zeal can form during times of uncertainty and existential threats real or imagined, when a group's desperate desire for a powerful parental imago aligns with the emergence of a charismatic leader. Furthermore, when a religious leader projects his or her grandiosity on the divine rather than on the self, that grandiosity translates into religious kenosis, a phenomenon that requires careful examination. To build this argument, I describe and interpret the context of Num 25 and the central emotion that dominates this context. Then, I move to psychoanalyze and interpret Yahweh, Phinehas, and the community.

In the book of Numbers, chapter 25 is textually located in an interstitial space. The two censuses lists from which the book of Numbers takes its name marks the structure of the book that divides it into the narratives of the first and second generations.[1] The first census in chapter 1 lays the ground for the story of the first generation that came out of Egypt and the second census in chapter 26 marks the beginning of the second generation's activity. The narratives about the first generation and second generation overlap in chapter 25, where all remnants of the first generation except for Moses, Caleb, and Joshua pass away as a result of the plague, fulfilling the prediction of the death of the first generation in Num 14:30. As a chapter that marks the end of the first generation with the transition into the next, Num 25 provides a literary bridge to the second half of the book.

In Num 25, the Israelites find themselves in Shittim, a Moabite territory, across the Jordan river from Jericho. They are familiar with this location. Forty

---

[1] Dennis Olson, *The Death of the Old and the Birth of the New: The Framework of the Book of Numbers and the Pentateuch* (Chico, CA: Scholars Press, 1985), 83.

years ago, they all arrived on the banks of the Jordan, on the edge of the promised land (Num 13–14). They sent spies over the land of milk and honey. They and their parents stood there, trembling with fear because of the inhabitants of the land. The report from the spies rendered them inferior and fearful of the indigenous inhabitants. As a result of their refusal to enter the land, they faced the anger of YHWH, who felt betrayed by the people's anxiety and lack of trust in the promise. Here, that compromised generation was forbidden from entering the promised land. The newly freed slaves of Pharaoh failed the God-ordained task of turning into invader-warriors. After forty years, a new generation was retasked. They stood at the boundary, on the edge of that wilderness, looking at the land they were about to enter. Their parents' generation was filled with anxiety, ambiguity, and fear, which they expressed by outbursts of complaints. The new generation knew the consequences of new complaints.

Under such circumstances, some turned to a divine presence. Others searched for something more tangible, readily available or near to fill the space dominated by fear and anxiety. In a parallel manner, at Baal Peor, like the incident in Exod 32, the worship of the golden bulls or calves, in the name of Baal, the people turned to participate in religious sacrifices, a communal meal, and "prostituted themselves."[2]

Scholars have suggested that Num 25 is a compilation of two different stories, a JE account focusing on the apostasy of the Israelites with the Moabite deity, Baal Peor, and the P account, a narrative about a plague that inflicted the community when a leader had sexual intercourse with a prominent Midianite woman. These two stories are emotionally tied and joined together, to express YHWH's emotional outburst, responding to erotically charged religious actions. The emotion that YHWH expresses is pure jealousy.

Jealousy describes YHWH's desire for an exclusive relationship with the people of Israel (and Judah). The Hebrew term קנאה, translated as jealousy, describes emotions that are best rendered as envy and zeal. This term is a characteristic of YHWH, often a theonym itself. For example, Exod 34:14 states: "For you shall not worship another god, because YHWH, whose name is jealousy [יהוה קנא] is a jealous God [אל קנא]." The term repeats in Deut 4:24 and again in Deut 6:14–15. As a part of the Decalogue, Exod 20:5 and Deut 5:9, the stipulation, "You shall not worship them, and you shall not serve them, for I, YHWH your God, am a jealous God [אל קנא]," clearly expresses an emotional state of YHWH. In Deut 4:24, an additional clause is added, "a consuming fire," expressing anger. Because emotions are charged and linked to exclusive relationship, the jealousy

---

[2] Katharine Sakenfeld, *Journeying with God: A Commentary on the Book of Numbers* (Grand Rapids, MI: Eerdmans, 1995), 136. While it is often speculated that this may point to a ritualized form of sexual activity of fertility, Sakenfeld notes that evidence is lacking. She suggests that regular sexual activity led the Israelite men to participate in intercourse with non-Israelites as a form of union/worship.

of YHWH is described metaphorically, in marriage terms, a union between a husband and wife; as in the prophets (Ezek 16:38, 42; 23:25; 36:6; Joel 2:18; Nahum 1:2; Zeph 1:18; 3:8; Zech 1:14; 8:2). The other metaphor that is used is a parent-child relationship. According to the *Theological Dictionary of the Old Testament*, אהב, the Hebrew word for love, functions as an antonym or prerequisite of קנא.[3] But in translating Zech 1:14 and 8:2, the *Revised New Korean Standard Version* translates jealousy as "burning love [*yeolryeolhan sarang*]." The Korean translation could not effectively capture the Hebrew nuisance simply with jealousy. Given the context, the nuance of hot temperature nature is fitting. Whether love is love or love is laden with jealousy, the core quality of this emotion is correctly captured. This flaring jealousy is like a consuming fire, displaying YHWH's destructive and violent rage that leads to destruction. Most prophets call for Judah and Israel to return to YHWH, using jealousy of God as the rationale for their warning. In Num 25, we have a detailed narrative account of what this jealousy looks like, resulting in death by direct punishment and death by a plague.

Because of YHWH's jealousy, Moses was commanded to "Take all the chiefs of the people, and impale them in the sun before the LORD, in order that the fierce anger of the LORD may turn away from Israel" (Num 25:4). But Moses narrows and limits the punishment exclusively on the guilty. The kindled anger sets a plague in motion, and twenty-four thousand die.[4] During the plague, a prominent Israelite man and a prominent Midianite woman[5] enter a tent. When Phinehas sees this, he goes after the couple and pierces them with a spear. This zealous act stops the plague. YHWH says to Moses:

> Phinehas, son of Eleazar, son of Aaron the priest, has turned back my wrath from the Israelites by manifesting such zeal among them on my behalf that in my jealousy I did not consume the Israelites. Therefore say, "I hereby grant him my covenant of peace. It shall be for him and for his descendants after him a covenant of perpetual priesthood, because he was zealous for his God, and made atonement for the Israelites" (25:11–13).

---

[3] E. Reuter, "קנא," *TDOT* 13:49.
[4] Stephen Sherwood, *Leviticus, Numbers, Deuteronomy* (Collegeville, MN: The Liturgical Press, 2002), 181. Sherwood highlights the turning point of story, namely, the transition of the generations. The plague condemns the older generation. This fulfills the death of the first generation in the wilderness. More importantly, anxiety of space is intensified, leading to mass death.
[5] Sherwood, *Leviticus, Numbers, Deuteronomy*, 181. A reference, naming, the Midianite woman is significant. Sherwood notes and traces the root of the name Cozbi, כזב to mean, "to lie, deceive, disappoint" or "to be voluptuous." A parallel reference in Akkadian is attributed to Ishtar and Asherah. The commentator on Numbers in the *HarperCollins Study Bible: Fully Revised and Updated* notes that this story of the Midianite woman is used to elevate Aaron's family over Moses, who had married the daughter of a Midianite priest.

A grotesque violence committed in God's name and religious zeal is rewarded with peace and a covenant that legitimizes his family's permanent priesthood—in the order of Zadok.[6] It is a defining moment in the book of Numbers, when an ensuing generation becomes zealous for YHWH by establishing a boundary of what is permitted and what is not. The census in the ensuing chapter offers a new group identity for the whole,[7] highlighting the zeal, which brought deaths to a halt through an act of religious violence.

This passage disturbs me. I am not alone. Jacob Milgrom notes that similar discomfort is already found in the Hebrew Bible. In Ps 106:30, "Then Phinehas stood up and interceded, and the plague was stopped," the psalmist avoids the attribution of קנאה to Phinehas and "instead, utilizes the verb פלל (יפלל), which, as its occurrences elsewhere attest (e.g., 1 Sam 2:25), can only signify mediation by prayer."[8] The Jewish philosopher and rabbinic scholar Maimonides (1135–1204) interprets this jealousy of God as a mere anthropomorphism that stems from human limitation in depicting God through terms of human experience. In such limitation, humans are to describe God according to what they perceive as God's action. He writes in the *Guide of the Perplexed* that such seemingly emotional reactions are there "because those that are punished thereby have deserved them, not in consequence of any affection—far be it from us to impute to Him such lack of perfection."[9] Such effort to save God from this disturbing emotion of jealousy has persisted in past thoughts and scholarship.

In the Septuagint, the root קנא is consistently rendered with *zēl*-root, distinguishing it from another Greek term for envy, which is φθόνον. Thus, the *zel*-root words, jealous and zeal, are sanitized as a term attributed to God by distinguishing them from negative human emotion, like of envy; which is often associated with the evil eye, or a damaging emotion.[10] Nevertheless, violence provoked by jealousy is troubling.

---

[6] Sakenfeld notes that this covenant sets the theological rationale for the Zakodite lineage. See Sakenfeld, *Numbers*, 137.

[7] James Dunn argues that Phinehas's zeal "was not a concern for personal standing with God. It was much more provoked by concern to maintain and protect Israel's identity as a people set apart to God, a concern, in other words, for Israel's identity as a people set apart to God, a concern, in other words, for Israel's holiness over against other nations." James Dunn, *The New Perspective on Paul* (Grand Rapids, MI: Eerdmans, 2008), 478. For a contrary view, see Dane C. Ortlund, *Zeal without Knowledge: The Concept of Zeal in Romans 10, Galatians 1, and Philippians* 3, LNTS 472 (London: T&T Clark, 2012).

[8] Jacob Milgrom, *Numbers*, The JPS Torah Commentary (Philadelphia: The Jewish Publication Society, 1990), 215.

[9] Moses Maimonides, *The Guide of the Perplexed*, trans. Chaim Rabin (Indianapolis: Hackett, 1995), 75.

[10] See John Elliott, "Envy, Jealousy, and Zeal in the Bible: Sorting out the Social Differences and Theological Implications—No Envy for YHWH," in *To Break Every Yoke: Essays in Honor of Marvin L. Chaney*, ed. Robert Coote and Norman Gottwald, Social

In the Korean and Korean American church contexts, such zeal is reframed or read closer to the original intent of the text. Such zeal has led to a powerful spiritual energy behind religious revival movements in the twentieth century. Such evangelism has been fueled by a monotheistic exclusionism tendency. Such thoughts have generated a powerful experience for followers which contrarily led to terrible anxiety for those who did not. The slogan: "Jesus leads to heaven, non-believers (disbelief) to hell [예수천당 불신지옥]" is an example.

Such slogans mimic the Hebrew Bible's zeal, which is unapologetic about this self-identifying character of God. The jealous God appears as a theological construct and center of the Decalogue. God seems to be saying, "This is me, deal with it." But how do humans respond when God becomes so jealous? Once that anger and passion is kindled, the text in Num seems to be suggesting that Phinehas had the solution—match zeal with zeal, passion for passion.

Numbers 25:11 uses קנא to describe both zeal and jealousy: the Hebrew (קנאתי-את בקנאו) translates "my jealousy with his jealousy." Phinehas channels God's jealousy through his own jealousy. In other words, Phinehas's emotion was the same emotion expressed by God. With no additional description in the text of Phinehas other than his lineage, he is characterized and best remembered for the emotion he carried out. Technically, how are we to understand what happened to Phinehas's psyche? What made him carry out and transfer God's emotion? How are we to understand Phinehas's action and leadership style that gave way to the permanent priesthood? To further explore these inquiries, we turn to self-psychology developed by Heinz Kohut.

To better understand the psychodynamics of leadership formation, Kohut explores the psychohistory of individuals who demonstrated extraordinary leadership in difficult and challenging times. As a secular Jew who was in exile in the United States from Vienna during World War II, Kohut used introspection to observe outstanding leadership styles that resisted. People like Franz Jaegerstaetter, Hans Scholl, and Sophie Scholl were carefully observed and studied. Through his reflection on these personalities, I intend to follow similar suite and find insights into the spiritual dynamic that we see in Phinehas, projecting an image of God's image.

Kohut's predecessors in psychoanalysis would have noticed how this text is erotically charged, hinted by the language of "prostituting," sex, and the dominating language of jealousy, which is libidinally charged. Sigmund Freud, in his observation of men's love for women, notes that jealousy functions as the "necessary condition for loving." The passionate feeling for the woman increases as

---

World of Biblical Antiquity 2/3 (Sheffield: Sheffield Phoenix, 2007), 344–64; Elliott, "God-Zealous or Jealous but Never Envious: The Theological Consequences of Linguistic and Social Distinctions," in *The Social Sciences and Biblical Translation*, ed. Dietmar Neufeld, SymS 41 (Atlanta: Society of Biblical Literature, 2008), 79–96.

"another man claims the object of possession as her husband, fiancé or friend,"[11] thus resulting in his love injuring the other man. Conversely, his passion increases when the woman "is in some way or other of bad repute sexually" and thus her "fidelity and reliability are open to some doubt,"[12] which eventually enlist the urge of the man "to rescue the woman they love"[13] as he is convinced that "she is in need of him."[14] For Freud, this stems from the Oedipal complex, which is the infantile longing for the mother, who gets frustrated when the boy realizes that his mother inseparably belongs to his father. In this process, the boy's love for the mother injures his father, while his mother becomes unique and irreplaceable. Thus, the intricate dynamic of jealousy realizes the psychodynamics of such primal processes, becoming a necessary condition for love, the process of internalizing external object.

For Melanie Klein, a pioneer of object relations theory, often called "more Freudian than Freudians,"[15] this process of internalizing external object is present and intense in an infant's relation to the mother's breast. The mother's breast—a part object rather than a whole object (the personhood of mother)—is a good object, satisfying the infant's need. The early emotional life of the infant is characterized by how the infant internalizes and identifies this part object, which eventually fails to live up to the expectation of the infant. What it seeks is the unity that it had in the womb. Klein notes that along with libidinal desires and hunger, there is something more in the infant's craving for the mother's breast. In that moment of frustration, in failing to achieve the womb-like unity with the object raises anxiety, which marks the desired object as bad. Using Freud's notion of the death instinct, Klein explains that the infant experiences destructive impulses that persecute the bad breast and thus threatens the infant's own life source, which in turn generates the primary guilt and primary persecutory anxiety.[16]

Primary envy is felt when the breast that in the infant's fantasy can inexhaustibly satisfy the infant—keeping the goodness from the infant's reach. Such envy has the impetus to attack and destroy the object, which the infant desires to overcome. Klein sees the capacity for love (and eventually gratitude, which is a major derivative of the capacity to love) of the good object that withstands the temporary state of envious attacks to be the positive developmental process.[17] As an emotion

---

[11] Sigmund Freud, "A Special Type of Choice of Object Made by Men (Contributions to the Psychology of Love I)," in *The Freud Reader*, ed. Peter Gay (New York: Norton, 1989), 388.
[12] Freud, "Special Type of Choice," 388.
[13] Freud, "Special Type of Choice," 389.
[14] Freud, "Special Type of Choice," 389.
[15] Dave Hiles, "Envy, Jealousy, Greed: A Kleinian Approach" (paper presented at the Centre for Counselling and Psychotherapy Education, London, UK, November 2007).
[16] Melanie Klein, "Envy and Gratitude (1957)," in *Envy and Gratitude and Other Works 1946–1963: The Writings of Melanie Klein Volume III* (New York: The Free Press, 1975), 180.
[17] Klein, "Envy and Gratitude," 187.

based on envy, jealousy happens in whole-object oriented relationship that reflects the Oedipal relationships as Freud has articulated. Again, projecting the existential anxiety prompted by the death instinct in envy, jealousy prompted by the fear of losing the loved object aims to destroy the rival that threatens to take away the loved object. Thus, jealousy in this analysis, is a primarily object-oriented process.

Reading Num 25 with Klein, the text's anxiety begs for analysis. The situational context of Shittim across the Jordan contributes to the anxiety of space. As Dennis Olson notes, in this space, the older generation that had repeatedly failed to follow God's instruction is transitioning out of the scene, as the plague and killing function as the punishment to that generation.[18] The God we face in this chapter is blazing with destructive emotions. There is persecution and God's envy, jealousy, or wrath destroys God's love-object, the Israelites. The subject of envy and jealousy is God, who is supposed to feel persecutory anxiety, but in reality, it is the Israelites who experience this intense persecutory anxiety—not God. This reveals that we are dealing with a projection and psychodynamic lens of self-psychology is helpful in better understanding the psychological projection of the community.

In Kohutian language, scripture can function like a group's cultural self-object,[19] a projection of the group's narcissistic need.[20] Kohut's term, self-object, resolves the tension that Freud later noticed between object-libido and ego-libido,[21] sick persons or those with megalomania, which Freud noticed in withdraw of their libido cathexes from the objects to reinvent in the self. Freud has postulated the primary narcissism of a child, in which "he was his own ideal,"[22] gets frustrated by cultural and ethical biases and gradually yields its way to invest in object love. Understanding narcissism as a self-preservation mechanism, he acknowledges megalomania as possible health preserving process, leaving the door open for self-psychology to see grandiosity as part of healthy self-formation process. Freud regards ego-libido and object-libido as antithesis, as "the more of the one is employed the more the other become depleted."[23] However, Kohut notes that the reality pointing to two separate yet parallel developmental lines in narcissism. This parallel development is closely related to the way parents interact

---

[18] Dennis Olson, "Negotiating Boundaries: The Old and New Generations and the Theology of Numbers," *Int* 51.3 (1997): 229–40.
[19] Peter A. Lessem, *Self Psychology: An Introduction* (Oxford: Rowman & Littlefield, 2003), 26–62.
[20] Heniz Kohut, "On the Continuity of the Self," in *Self Psychology and the Humanities: Reflection on a New Psychoanalytic Approach*, ed. Charles Strozier (Markham, Ontario: Penguin Books Canada, 1985), 240–41. Kohut talks about how the creativity of the New Yorker magazine or science fictions functions as a testing ground of a group's sense of self.
[21] Sigmund Freud, "On Narcissism: An Introduction," in *The Freud Reader*, ed. Peter Gay (New York: Norton, 1995), 548.
[22] Freud, "On Narcissism," 558.
[23] Freud, "On Narcissism," 547.

with their child(ren). In other words, the self is formed by keeping tension between the libidinal investment in idealizing the perfect parental objects and the investment in one's own grandiosity. In this formation process, the self experiences the parental imago as one's extension: the object becomes a self-object, resonating with the part object experience of the breast by infants in Klein. Cultural self-object is the cultural object that a group of people experience as an extension of itself, fulfilling the unconscious need of the group to hold together a group's disintegrating self.[24] Many elements in our given text points to the experiences of the group behind the text who had embedded much of their unconscious processes.

If the text is the cultural selfobject of the community, and behind the text and community is their selfobject transference on God, revealing their own emotional reality, we then have enough psychological information about the community behind the text. To arrive at such an outcome, we take two steps: first analyze God's emotion(s) in the text, and second, analyze the projections found behind such analysis.

First, we find that God's emotion of jealousy resembles a narcissistic rage provoked by disobedient Israelites, who function as God's selfobject. Narcissistic rage is provoked when a selfobject fails to fulfill the will, desires, and projection that the self casts on the selfobject. In the text, God struggles with the narcissistic injury caused by the Israelites' failure to mirror God's grandiosity to the fullest, namely, the first generation that had failed to mirror God's grandiosity—failing whole-heartedly at the banks of Jordan river forty years ago. This time, the second generation fails to mirror God's grandiosity by turning to another deity attempting to seek assurance facing anxiety uncontrollable by the rational measures Moses implemented. The death-dealing jealousy is a full-blown expression of the narcissistic rage. Phinehas' action calms down the rage enacting another extreme effect, allowing God to idealize him as the twinship self-object, a priest who acts according to God's heart. אל קנא as the jealous God (or God of jealousy) is a deeply narcissistically injured God, whose whim should be carefully watched for and tiptoed around, as narcissistic injury generates narcissistic rage, which, according to Kohut is best characterized by "the need for revenge, for righting a wrong, for undoing a hurt by whatever means, and a deeply anchored, unrelenting compulsion in the pursuit of all these aims, which gives no rest."[25] Klein would add that this God has not fully integrated the splitting object of his beloved Israelites to form a healthy self. Kohut would say that this God has not resolved God's primary narcissistic needs, resulting in a fragile self that is desperately held together through this narcissistic rage and idealized transference on Phinehas.

---

[24] Heinz Kohut, "On the Continuity of the Self and Cultural Selfobjects (February 26, 1981)," in *Self Psychology and the Humanities: Reflections on a New Psychoanalytic Approach*, ed. Charles Strozier (New York: Norton, 1985), 235.

[25] Kohut, "Thoughts on Narcissism and Narcissistic Rage (1972)," 143.

However, because all of this is happening in a text, written not by God but by the communities of JE and P, this interpretation gets flipped and turned upside down. Because the sacred text of the community is the self-object of the community, their projection of the narcissistic need, the narcissistic injury probably belongs to the community struggling to keep their fragmenting selves together through an extreme measure. The ambiguity and anxiety that disintegrated their parent's generation into null is very much alive in this space. Shittim is a place of critical transition, a place of persecutory anxiety, filled with the deadly threat of the plague. The Israelites were in desperate need of grandiosity to overcome their anxiety, but the outcome of their effort only increased the shame, as exemplified in the description, "they prostituted themselves." In Kohut's leadership analysis "historical crisis influences group regression.... There is a first stage of painful increase of narcissistic tension with propensity toward shame, hypochondria and depression."[26] From self-psychology, the interaction with Baal Peor and the Midianites is the group's painful attempt at maintaining their narcissistic tension. Such narcissistic tension reveals the deeply seated narcissistic injury of the group that they would take at any distance to compensate for.

This compensation requires a strong projection of their narcissistic need of idealizing and grandiosity. Their dilemma is that God on whom their most omnipotent parental imago could be projected is currently mad at them, burning with plague-inducing jealousy. The projection needs someone else as a target. This someone needs to rise up with a grandiosity that can be idealized as the omnipotent parental imago. Kohut notes:

> the unconscious fantasies of the group's grandiose self, expressed in the transference upon the image of an appropriate leader figure, thus can play at times a crucial role in its cohesion. The leader of such a group is not primarily the focal point of shared values, as Freud suggested, but self-righteously expresses the group's ambitions and extols its greatness and power.[27]

This cohesion is centered around YHWH with the grandiosity of this leader, Phinehas, to channel the omnipotent parental imago of God as his grandiosity. Phinehas channels the jealousy of God as his own grandiosity and thus converges the groups' grandiosity projection and the idealizing parental imago.

This form of leadership that channels a group's desperate projection needs requires some commenting. Kohut compares several forms of leadership that manifested during the Third Reich. According to this form, Phinehas's leadership resembles that of Hitler's, rather than others that courageously protested against Hitler's regime. Unlike the anxiety driven projection of grandiosity of the group

---

[26] Heinz Kohut, "On Leadership," in *Self Psychology and the Humanities: Reflection on a New Psychoanalytic Approach*, ed. Charles Strozier (New York: Norton, 1985), 57.
[27] Kohut, "On Leadership," 57.

that we see in Phinehas, Kohut notes, when a person has a very clear understanding of the value and need of the self, which he calls nuclear self, this person can generate a decisive action. Jaegerstaetter, a Catholic peasant who was a conscientious objector to the Third Reich, had such a nuclear self. For Jaegerstaetter, his sense of self was continuous in time "with cohesive configuration in depth,"[28] which allowed him to have clarity during contentious times. Kohut notes that individuals who are able to demonstrate courageous clarity have three common features. However, none of them are noticeable in Phinehas: "The presence of a fine sense of humor; the ability to respond to others with subtle empathy; and, generally at the time when the ultimate heroic decision has been reached and the agonizing consequences have to be faced, the suffusion of the personality with a profound sense of inner peace and serenity—a mental state akin to wisdom."[29] These were interestingly and noticeably absent in Hitler. While he had shown some cynical humor when he joked, Hitler was deadly serious about himself, as the narcissistic injury he carried grandiose fantasies that fed into the need of the ego-ideal of narcissistically injured others. His leadership falls into the category of a paranoid leader. Kohut observes:

> The groups which are formed around the personality of paranoid leader, however, are not tied together by the convergence of their idealizing love, by an ego-ideal held in common. They are principally united by their sharing of an archaic narcissistic conception of the world that must destroy those who are different and the identity of their grandiose fantasies embodied in their leader. They are held together by a common grandiose self.[30]

The idealized grandiose self of the leader has the effect of creating group cohesiveness, mutual identification, and diminution of aggression between the members of the group, which is accomplished in Phinehas. The community, on the border of the wilderness overlooking Jericho, experiences a leadership transition at Shittim. Cohesion is sought but unachieved through their own autonomous effort. The jealousy of God, a projection of the state of the group, reveals the paranoia of the group, which was acted upon by Phinehas.

In spite of the similarity between the paranoid leadership of Phineas and Hitler, there is a clear distinction between the two: the omnipotent parental imago in Hitler was his own personality while in Phinehas, it was God. One thing that we need to note here is the absence of any other information about Phinehas's personality, while for Hitler, his personality was the very hook of grandiosity by which the group self-object was formed. For Phinehas, he is entirely defined by the emotion he carries: the jealousy of God. Phinehas as a person is empty, and by his

---

[28] Kohut, "On Leadership," 9.
[29] Kohut, "On Leadership," 15.
[30] Kohut, "On Leadership," 54.

zealous action, the text notes he "made an atonement for the Israelites." The grandiosity of the group in Phinehas also has the characteristic of *kenosis* (Phil 2). This direct and ironic connection of kenosis (self-emptying) and grandiosity is significant. The outcome in Num 25 suggests a self-emptying, manifested in graphic violence, to sanctify a community, which ultimately justified its priesthood. Violence further sanctified the religious community with spiritual endorsement. Kenosis sanctions religious violence. In other words, Kohut's warning that "human aggression is most dangerous when it is attached to the two great absolutarian psychological constellations: the grandiose self and the archaic omnipotent object,"[31] is realized in Phinehas's kenosis.

To conclude, we can see that the kindled jealousy of God channeled through the self-emptying Phinehas is the projection of fragmenting a group's narcissistic need for grandiosity and idealizing parental imago fermented when examined from a self-psychology perspective. This projection is poignantly needed for a group to maintain their sense of cohesion, when deeply threatened as they stood in the anxious space of Shittim. They were overwhelmed by traumatic history, transition, and plagues. Such projection, "can play at times a crucial role in [group's] cohesion."[32] Given a psychological profile of a paranoid leader on whom the groups' grandiosity is projected, Phinehas's priesthood may have attempted to justify the use of force of violence by priests in later historical periods. But the self-emptying spirituality that was described speaks to the activation of a group's grandiosity in Phinehas. That signals a danger in claiming spiritual kenosis, which can translate into religious violence.

In Korea, social, economic, and political turmoil after the Korean War (1950–1953) created much psychological vulnerability that propelled a need for religious enthusiasm. This was the real fuel that fostered Christianity's rapid growth on foreign soil. Put another way, there was an ambivalence to Western influence, which was separated out of Korean Christianity. The religiosity that exudes from fundamental monotheism echoes the jealousy of God and the zeal of Phinehas.[33] As we have examined, the psychodynamics behind such religious zeal has much to do with the projection of a group's narcissistic need for grandiosity, which is sometimes veiled behind kenotic spirituality—as was the case in Phinehas. When powerful leadership is formed in anxious space, a need for reflection on narcissistic wounds of those who line up behind such grandiose leaders are truly needed. After all, such powerful irrational presentation of grandiosity in society signals the presence of fragmented, injured selves whose narcissistic needs need to be tended to. The manifestation of the jealousy of God may signal the presence of the injured and hurt.

---

[31] Kohut, "Thoughts on Narcissism and Narcissistic Rage," 141.

[32] Kohut, "On Leadership," 54.

[33] For further study on monotheism and zeal, see David Lochhead, "Monotheistic Violence," *Buddhist-Christian Studies* 21 (2001): 3–12.

STATE, WAR, AND WOMEN

Kyungmi Park

In December 2015, the Korean government and the Japanese government came to an agreement regarding the comfort women issue. It is reported that in the agreement, the Japanese government expressed an apology to the Korean government for the comfort women. They offered compensation of one billion yen under the condition that the Korean government no longer raise the comfort women issue to the international community. Further, the Japanese government and its media requested that the Girl (Soneo) statue, built in memory of the victims in front of the Japanese Embassy in Korea, be removed as a condition for the proposed compensation. Not surprisingly, the comfort women survivors, along with the Korean Council for the Issue of Comfort Women, and other advocacy groups opposed the agreement, contesting such a humiliating compromise. Notwithstanding, the Korean government has yet to offer a reasonable explanation.

The then Korean government said that it made major diplomatic breakthrough on the issue beyond efforts made by previous administrations. But what we hear from the Japanese government is ambiguity, deep feelings of mixed emotions, betrayal, and half-hearted acknowledgement of responsibility. The Japanese government maintains the position that the forced conscription of Korean and others by the Japanese government or its army is not attested in any of its official documents. They say, the language of "volunteer" is used. Furthermore, the Japanese government avers that if the Korean government continues to raise the comfort women issue, it will not find itself in good standing with the international community. Japan wants to close the issue "irreversibly." In spite of the fact that Japan says it has made an apology, the nature, gravity, and sincereity of Japan's apology is still wanting. It is clear that the Korean government has not received an appropriate apology. Instead, Japan has humiliated the Korean people once again.

This is nothing new. It has happened repeatedly. Quite often, we in Korea, hear Japanese high-ranking officials justify Japan's colonization of Korea without a word of apology. Whenever this occurs, the Korean government delivers a public statement criticizing such speech. However, it seems that the Korean government only makes such public gestures to momentarily appease the Korean people's anger since the Korean government has never fully demanded reparation from Japan. Ironically, (past and present) Korean governments have been cooperating with Japan's ambition to become a military super power, again. How can this be? How can we explain this phenomenon? Scholars in the field of the modern history of Korea argue that the starting point goes back to the San Francisco Peace Treaty (1951), where all the victors of World War II gathered to discuss major postwar matters.

According to Dong-choon Kim, in the San Francisco Peace Treaty, the United States sought "to elevate the status of Japan as an anti-communist crusade to defend against the USSR and establish a major partnership with Japan in the liberal side of the world."[1] "With such self-interests in mind, the US tried to make Japan responsible only for causing the Pacific War, not for Japan's colonial domination of the people of Chosun, intending to reinstate Japan to the status of a peace-loving state whose action of invasion is prohibited."[2] The San Francisco Peace Treaty gave plenty of room for Japan to avoid an official apology and reparation to Korea and other concerned countries for crimes of invasion and colonization. Japan was subjected to make reparations to countries such as the Philippines and Vietnam, which were members of the Allied Forces that fought against Japan in the Pacific War. The case was different for Korea and Taiwan. They were not even invited to participate in the San Francisco Peace Treaty, and thus, they had no claim to demand reparation from Japan. Speaking strictly, both the United States and the United Kingdom were in the least favorable position to demand that Japan take responsibility for its colonial domination, since they were also imperial powers ruling over colonies. Relying on support from the United States, Japan refused to be responsible for its brutal colonial domination of the Korean people. Still worse, Japan now dares to raise itself as a powerful military state. Cultural differences may explain the different actions that Germany and Japan took after the war, but it should not be overlooked that their different actions were determined by the postwar US hegemonic strategies to dominate the world.

In this geopolitical context, what position did the South Korean government take? The first President of South Korea, Seung Man Lee, announced that he would support the position the United States took in the San Francisco Peace Treaty. He accepted and took the lenient position toward the past history of Japanese imperialism. In February 1950, President Lee made the statement that the two nations, Korea and Japan, would cooperate to fight communism—a common enemy. Such a statement was exactly what the United States wanted him to say, especially when the United States was seeking to place Japan at the center of the US anticommunist front in Northeast Asia. This weakened the status of the South Korean government in claiming Dok-do as its own territory and demanding reparation for the Japanese colonial domination.[3]

---

[1] Dong-choon Kim, *Why, South Korea* [Korean] (Seoul: Sakyejul, 2015), 188.
[2] Kim, *Why, South Korea*, 187.
[3] Kim, *Why, South Korea*, 189.

Later, the Park Jong Hee military regime, having seized governing power through a military coup and thus lacked legitimacy, set out grand economic developments in Korea. In order to finance the projects, the Park regime hastily proceeded to normalize relations with Japan. After normalization through diplomatic relationship, the Park regime received an aid fund of 500 million dollars from Japan as property claims against Japan. He used the funds to build industrial infrastructure projects. Consequently, the Park regime, just like the Lee regime, complied with the United States's East Asia policy to integrate South Korea as hinterland and sub-base for economic growth and expansion of Japan—in accordance with the Park regime's political drive and economic ambition. Such a move made it exceedingly difficult for individual victims of Japanese colonization to take legal actions and further proceedings against the Japanese government or Japanese companies. The fact that the Park regime accepted monetary aid from Japan implied that South Korea and Japan had provisionally resolved the unresolved matter of Japanese colonization of Korea. Shortly thereafter, the issue of reparation for the victims was transferred to the hands of the South Korean government. The South Korean government, however, has not taken appropriate action for the surviving comfort women, the Atomic Bomb victims, and the Sakhalin survivors.[4] Consequently, Korean economic advancement and development were made possible only though the sacrifices of those victims. Indeed, they were used in the name of the "state."

The historical sequence from independence, the division into South and North Korean governments, the San Francisco Peace Treaty, to the South Korea-United States Joint Defense Treaty all moved in accordance with the US East Asia policy. South Korea became a security point for the anticommunist front. In the meantime, those who collaborated with the colonizer transformed themselves into anticommunists and took hegemonic power in South Korean society. The South Korean collaborators and the Japanese war criminals undertook the mission of reconstructing South Korea and Japan under the banners of anticommunism and US political interests. Such a course, instead of promoting peace, accelerated conflict and violence, which led to the Korean War (1950–1953). Thus, the life of the colonial victims, including the comfort women survivors, was disregarded and abandoned. As in the past, the comfort women who were trampled down and sexually exploited by the Japanese imperial army, were once again abandoned and forgotten by their own country after liberation. With the demise of the old USSR, we now live in a post-Cold War era. But the United States has now shifted the target of its anticommunist front to China. Within this international geopolitical context, the continuing US opposition against North Korea and North Korea's development of nuclear weapons and tests of ballistic missiles has caused escalating tensions and crises on the Korean peninsula and East Asia. A case in point

---

[4] Kim, *Why, South Korea*, 194–95.

is the recent shutdown of the Kaesung Industrial Complex, the last symbol of inter-Korean economic cooperation.

STATE VIOLENCE AND WAR

Certain actions or behaviors contradictory to human dignity, common sense, morality, and justice are said to be justified when acted in the name of the "state." Terrible and horrible things are done and justified in state sponsored violence. Otherwise, the existence of war would be truly inexplicable. Essentially, the agent of war is the "state." Waging war involves killing and slaughtering. It seems that the central role of armies and soldiers is to kill, regardless of whether they are actual killers or not. States have the power to force soldiers not only to kill against their own will, but also to needlessly sacrifice their own lives for the state.

Violence and war are integral in the formation of the state. This may well explain why most nation-founding myths contain stories of killing and murder. For example, the founding myth of the ancient Babylon (Enuma Elish) has Marduk murdering his mother Tiamat. The founding heroes such as Yamato Takeru of Japan, Romulus of Rome, and Hodur of Scandinavia are known examples of fratricide and violence. These stories reflect that the founding of a state necessitates political sacrifice, that is, the elimination of existing or potential political enemies. Furthermore, a founding myth functions as an ideology. It encourages its people to regard the state as an indispensable institution in human society in spite of its involvement in enormous violence. Accordingly, the myths serve to justify the murder of mothers or brothers and violent actions in the name of and for the sake of the state.

Today we notice a similar ideological assumption implicit in the international judicial laws and diplomatic relations, including the United Nations. The underlying logic is that peace can be achieved by means of national violence, that is, by the deployment of peace keeping troops. According to this logic, peace is identified with a social state protected by the army, the police, and other institutional apparatus.[5] Here, "peace" means "negative peace," that is, a state cannot exist without war. The two salient examples of negative peace are the first-century "Pax Romana" and the contemporary "Pax Americana." According to this understanding,

> peace can be achieved when a powerful organization is given a right to wage war, that is, a legitimate right to kill. If an organization within a certain region gains enough power to defend against other organizations or groups, then violence will be dwindled. Therefore, while domestic peace will be attained by means of national violence, international peace will be maintained through mutual dread or balance of power (through balance of fear in the nuclear era).[6]

---

[5] C. Douglas Lummis, "Positive Peace?," in *Gandhi's 'Dangerous' Peace-law*, trans. Jongchul Kim (Seoul: Greenreview, 2014), 146.
[6] Lummis, "Positive Peace?," 149.

This logic is an illusion. Suffice to say, the countless wars and violence the Roman Empire in the past and the United States in the present have brought about in order to maintain what they call peace is an understatement. The task of the army is not confined to what is prescribed by international and military law. In the case of the comfort women, it is evident that Japan violated international law. Japan and its army were the very agents of violence against women through sex slavery. Whether in the East or in the West, countless numbers of rapes and sexual violences are committed during wars. Today, international law and military law in many countries prohibit killing of noncombatants, including plunder and rape. Nonetheless, such atrocities are deeply grounded in military tradition and culture. Potential threats become effectively real in times of war. Stories of Korean soldiers who killed innocent civilians, including those who were sexually assaulted during the Vietnam War, and the recent US torture of prisoners in Guantanamo are examples.

Although warfare law restricts killing to enemy combatants, the telling truth is that more civilians than soldiers are killed in any war. It is reported that during the twentieth century, the number of foreigners killed by states is 68,452,000, while that of the domestic people killed is 134,756,000.[7] It certainly raises the question that an army exists to protect its people from foreign enemies. In reality, the army, in most countries serves to consolidate the power of the state by keeping it away from the people.

No matter how lawful and justifiable it may be, war is synonymous with terrible violence. Although philosophers and theologians in the past have tried to justify (just) wars with ethical theories and moral rationales, war cannot embrace human dignity when its brutal savageness remains intact. According to international laws on the rules of engagement, there are prohibitions against aggressive wars. On the one hand, the ancient Roman Empire invaded and conquered states under the pretext of civilizing the barbarians. On the other hand, modern imperialist states have justified invasions and occupations in the name of democracy, human rights, and even peace. There is no legitimate war. Any and all wars involve devastating murder and slaughter. The presumption that an army and war will bring peace is illusion. It is imperative for Christians to take seriously this radical definition of positive peace—a peace without war.

WAR-VIOLENCE AGAINST WOMEN

The surviving comfort women's demand for Japan's apology exposes the utter immorality of the culture of war. Their demand for legitimate reparation emphasizes the war crimes of Japan. Again, Japan is attempting to become a military super power for the purpose of building a peaceful East Asia. What a shame! What

---

[7] Lummis, "Positive Peace?," 164.

a contradiction! Japan still does not want to acknowledge its brutal colonial domination and outrageous war crimes, including the war crime committed against the comfort women and yet, it wants to return to its former-like state?

In the book of Judges, we read stories of women who were sexually abused and exploited in the context of war during the period of the formation of ancient Israel and its settlements into Canaan. The deaths of two women, the daughter of Jephthah (11:1–40) and the concubine of a Levite (19:1–30) are implicated in the context of war. Both women had nothing to do with the actual battles, but they became victims of violence. The daughter of Jephthah was offered as a sacrifice to celebrate her father's victory. On the other hand, the death of the concubine became the catalyst for a new war.

Jephthah, born of a humble woman, was cast out by his step-brothers but became a leader of worthless fellows (11:3). Before fighting against the Ammonites, he made a vow to God. Actually, he proposed a deal with God, saying "If you will give the Ammonites into my hand, then whoever comes forth from the doors of my house to meet me, when I return victorious from the Ammonites, shall be the Lord's, to be offered up by me as a burnt offering" (11:29–31). When Jephthah returned home victoriously from war, it was his daughter who greeted him first.

In the story, we see Jephthah and his daughter stand against each other in remarkable contrast. Jephthah fought against the Ammonites to become the head of Gilead. In order to secure his victory, he made a deal with God at the cost of another's life, which resulted in the death of his own daughter. By contrast, the daughter was willing to sacrifice her life and self worth to fulfil her father's vow to God. She accepted the fate that otherwise another person would have to face. Her deed somehow uncovers unfairness and violence implicated in her father's vow.[8] Isaac, though intended to be presented as a burnt offering by his father in Gen 22, was saved. But the daughter of Jephthah was not. She went to the mountain, wandering on the mountain with her friends to bewail her virginity for two months. Her death tells and reminds us about the tragedy and inhumane sacrifice of young women due to war. It is said that the daughters of Israel went out every year to lament the death of the daughter of Jephthah for four days (11:40). In Judg 5, the song of Deborah "retells" the victory of Yahweh, repeatedly. The story of the daughter of Jephthah, however, tells a hidden story. The death of a helpless daughter in which even God was silent bring us to bear the truth of what war really is.

Judges 19 tells a story of a woman and her horrible death. A Levite sojourning in the hill country of Ephraim took to himself a concubine. For unknown reasons, the concubine went away from him to her father's house at Bethlehem in Judah. Although what happened between the two is not clear, an act of sexual abuse cannot be precluded. In fact, the Levite was the kind of man who was able to divide

---

[8] Danna Nolan Fewell, "Judges," in *Womens' Bible Commentary*, enl. ed., ed. Carol A. Newsom and Sharon H. Ringe (Louisville, KY: Westminster John Knox, 1998), 76–78.

the body of his concubine into pieces, limb by limb, is telling. At any rate, the Levite decided to visit his father-in-law in order to persuade his woman back to his home. His father-in-law granted unusual hospitality to him. The Levite and his wife left her father's house. On their way home, they stayed at an old man's home in Gibeah, which belonged to the Benjaminites. Then, the men of the city, base fellows, beset the house and demanded the man bring out the Levite so that they might "know him," that is, to sexually assault him. Instead, the old man offered his virgin daughter and the concubine. But when the men were so persistent, the Levite seized his concubine and put her out to them. The men raped her all night long till the early morning. She laid her trampled body at the door of the house. The Levite rose up in the morning to go on his way. He found her lying at the door of the house, with her hands on the threshold. He said to her, "get up, let us be going." But there was no answer. Then, he put her on his ass, returned to his house, took a knife, divided her body, limb by limb, into twelve pieces, and sent them to all the territories of Israel to assemble the people of Israel for a battle against the Benjaminites.

This story is told in relation to the origin of the battle against the Benjaminites. This intertribal battle was so devastating that it resulted in the utter destruction of the Benjaminites. Allegedly, only six hundred men survived, with all the women and children killed. Violence indeed incurs further violence. War gives rise to other wars. In order to satisfy their male desire, the men of the Benjaminites seized the daughters of Siloh and took them as their wives. What a horrible story.

This story reveals how female sexuality, especially in the extreme situation of the war, is used, abused, and disused by male power.[9] Many nameless and voiceless women were taken, raped, and murdered. No one helped them. There was no place for them to rest. Nevertheless, their stories were passed on. Their stories were remembered and retold in the Bible and other memories. Their stories are not about the prosperity of Israel, but about wars among men which involved women. These wartime stories relay the life and death of women. Stories of women are also remembered in the New Testament.

The Gospel of Matthew begins with Jesus's genealogy. Although we cannot take the Matthean genealogy as historically accurate, it is not difficult to understand why the author intended to have it as a prologue. Matthew links the birth of Jesus to the patriarchs and the Davidic kings. The genealogy suggests that Jesus is a direct descendant of King David whose reign brought prosperity to Israel. Within a carefully constructed patrilineage of Jesus, 1:16 is striking. It says, "and Jacob the father of Joseph the husband of Mary, of whom Jesus was born, who is called Christ." Given the patterned repetition in the genealogy, we would expect to read "Jacob the father of Joseph, and Joseph the father of Jesus." Instead, verse 16 reads "Mary, of whom Jesus was born." A phrase like "and Joseph the father

---

[9] Fewell, "Judges," 80–82.

of Jesus" would better suit the purpose to designate Jesus as a descendant of David. But verse 16 describes Joseph as the husband of Mary, not as the father of Jesus. Matthew 1:1–15 describes the birth of Jesus by tracing the patrilineal descent of David. But, verse 16, the climax of the genealogy, is divergent from the previous verses. Jesus is described as the son of Mary. Matthew 1:16 seems to insinuate a conflict between two traditions regarding the birth of Jesus: the tradition of Davidic descent and that of the virgin birth.

Another noticeable feature that breaks the convention in the Matthean genealogy is the inclusion of four women in the first section of the genealogy, that is, against the patrilineage in the genealogy: Tamar, Rahab, Ruth, the wife of Uriah, and Mary. The four women from the Old Testament are not the kind of women who deserve respect and honor. Rather, these four women in each peculiar way defame the ancestry of David. For the purpose of linking Jesus to the David, it would have been better not to include them. They were not from noble families, or beautiful and intellectual daughters-in-law, nor good wives of powerful husbands. Rather, these four women respectively remind us of scandals, particularly, sexual scandals.

Tamar, with her husbands deceased, disguised herself as a harlot to have intercourse with her father-in-law; and bore a child to Judah. Rahab, a harlot, played a crucial role in the midst of the military campaign of Israel against the land of Canaan, but she is not in the most noble profession. Ruth, a young widow and a foreign woman from Moab, chose to return with her mother-in-law, Naomi to Judah. She in the end is described as faithful and obedient to her mother-in-law. Ruth marries kin of her deceased husband, Boaz. The fourth woman we meet in the Matthean genealogy is Bathsheba, the wife of Uriah. She becomes the wife of David who murdered her husband, Uriah, and then becomes the mother of Solomon (see Ahn's essay in this volume). While these four women respectively represent sexually anomalous relations against the patriarchal family structure, these women took the initiative to act for themselves in their prevailing patriarchal culture. The inclusion of these women breaks into the royal tradition of the genealogy of Jesus. These women in the broadest sense represent women who were sexually abused and humiliated in the patriarchal history of Israel—as a story of "state" formation. The Matthean genealogy reveals that Jesus is the descendent of these women. These women were not forgotten. This is their subversive story. As in the case of the comfort women, the women in the genealogy of Jesus were endangered and humiliated, but they stood up against the patriarchal family structures of ancient Israel. Victimization of women by state violence almost always has a sexual aspect.

These four Old Testament women are also linked to Mary, the mother of Jesus. Jesus is not only the child of Mary, but also the child of these four women. God chose the very child of women who suffered from the power of Israel as a state and its patriarchal system as the Messiah. The subversive nature of God's action is reflected in the tradition of the virgin birth of Jesus. The tradition which excludes the role of the male in the birth of Jesus, brings to light, the errors committed by the patriarchal rulers, including pronouncements of judgment in (salvation) history. The lives of the four women in the genealogy of Jesus clearly exemplify the distorted history of the patriarchal and royal history of ancient Israel. The four women in the genealogy of Jesus and the two women in Judges as well as the comfort women represent the victims of past history and at the same time point to the source of life-sustaining history. They were sacrificed, vindicated to an extent, but surely remembered, and not forgotten as women.

A "Dialogic" Hero David from the Perspective of "Internally Persuasive Word" in the Narrative of Samuel

SuJung Shin

This study discusses the long-standing questions of David as a "hero" for Israel's experiment with kingship, examining a dialogic understanding of the hero's relations to the author and the reader. My work attempts to provide a dialogic, rather than monologic, way of understanding the interrelations of author, character, and reader in the Samuel narrative in light of the Bakhtinian theories of dialogue and novelness. Illustrating the usefulness of the Bakhtinian theory, this study utilizes a narrative-critical understanding of the prose that can help one see how to "continue" and develop an alternative discussion on the narratives of Samuel.

Narrative criticism in biblical studies provides us with investigative tools for the relations of author, character, and reader. For example, the roles of the implied author and the narrator, and their relationships to the characters, have been key elements to understanding biblical narrative. Traditionally, however, the author(s) has been generally conceived of in "monologic" terms, especially in terms of the relation of the author to the reader. Rather than depending on the traditional understanding of the author as monologic, and rather than reading the Samuel narrative as a monologic text from the point of view that the narrator predominates over other characters, we seek to reconceive the interrelations of author, character, and reader through the process of "dialogization."[1]

Dealing with the issues related to the complexity of the hero of David in the narrative of Samuel, I ask who David is (i.e., what kind of hero is David). According to the "multi-languagedness" of 1 and 2 Samuel, David is a shepherd in the field and a musician at the royal court; a little boy and a grown-up warrior; a young man who fights to defend Yahweh's honor and fights to promote himself and his ambitions; the anointed of Yahweh and "a man of blood"; the man after

---

[1] *Dialogization*, in this study, means the process of dialogue which takes place among the "plurality of consciousnesses" of "highly heterogeneous and incompatible material." See Mikhail M. Bakhtin, "Dostoevsky's Polyphonic Novel and Its Treatment in Critical Literature," in *Problems of Dostoevsky's Poetics*, ed. and trans. Caryl Emerson (Minneapolis: University of Minnesota Press, 1984), 14–17.

Yahweh's own heart and the man who speaks to his own heart; a quasi-Philistine refugee in exile and an Israelite king in return; the saver (savior) of his people and the killer of some of them, including his soldier Uriah (and his son Absalom?); the sinner and the innocent; the virile and the impotent; the crowned and the decrowned; the praised and the ridiculed; and et cetera.

This study examines David's complex interrelationships with supporting characters focusing specifically on the stories of crowning and decrowning (discrowning) of David in 2 Samuel and investigates how and why the character of David can be represented as the kind of hero who is *not* determined and finalized by "monologic" authoritative conclusion. From a Bakhtinian perspective of "internally persuasive discourse,"[2] I argue that the character of David does not remain in an isolated and static condition; based on the "internally persuasive discourse" in Samuel, the words and actions on the hero David are *not finite*, but *open* to (re)interpretation especially in a context(s) where hierarchical dominance and the authority of the monarchy have been lost.

From narrative-critical and postnarrative critical perspectives, I ultimately attempt to reveal how the Samuel text can be reread as dialogic, rather than straightforwardly monologic, when it speaks specifically to the questions of crowning and decrowning of David in the narrative of Samuel, and how rereading the text as dialogic affect and shape our understanding of the complexity of the character of David in the Samuel narrative.

MONOLOGIC VS. DIALOGIC

Narrative criticism in biblical studies is a useful tool for investigating what a Bakhtinian perspective can offer to a rereading of the narrative of Samuel. From the narrative-critical perspective, the roles of the implied author and the narrator, and their relationships to the implied reader, have been key elements to understanding biblical texts. From the point of view of traditional narrative criticism, investigations into the relationship between the implied author and the competent reader can result in the implied reader being suppressed.[3] In developing the concept of the implied author, Wayne Booth famously argued that "the author creates,

---

[2] According to Bakhtin, in internally persuasive discourse, as will be examined in detail in the next section, an utterance(s) becomes contested, disputed, and reaccented, having participated in more than one value system. Bakhtin, "Discourse in the Novel," in *The Dialogic Imagination: Four Essays by M. M. Bakhtin*, ed. Michael Holquist, trans. Caryl Emerson and Michael Holquist (Austin: University of Texas Press, 1981), 332.

[3] Stephen Moore identifies the problem of Iser's concept of the implied reader, noting that "the undifferentiated, prescriptive side of Iser's implied reader ... relegated its individualistic, actual-reader side to the margins." According to Moore, although Iser attempted to present a reading process that "balances text and reader," he ended up presenting the reader "in the firm grip of the text." Stephen Moore, *Literary Criticism and the Gospels: The Theoretical Challenge* (New Haven: Yale University Press, 1989), 102.

in short, an image of himself and another image of his reader; he makes his reader, as he makes his second self, and the most successful reading is one in which the created selves, author and reader, can find *complete agreement*."[4] In relation to the reader, the implied author is intended to "impose" a story world upon the reader (e.g., the author's point of view).[5] As David M. Gunn points out, "narrative criticism ... has tended to be relatively conservative in its methodology, concerned with observing the mechanics or artistry of literary construction ... and often still haunted by historical criticism's need to know the author's 'intention' and the text's 'original' readership if it is to speak legitimately of the text's meaning."[6]

Traditionally in narrative-critical method, the narrator is said to be "immanent" in the text, along the lines of a character who tells the story.[7] The narrator is considered "omniscient" or "reliable": the narrator knows the truth and tells accurate knowledge about the characters and events within the story line. For example, Meir Sternberg, in his study of *The Poetics of Biblical Narrative*, claims that "the Bible always tells the truth in that its narrator is absolutely and straightforwardly reliable."[8]

From the traditional understanding of the narrator as reliable, the text of Samuel is likely to be read as more monologic than dialogic. The Samuel prose can be easily read as a monologic text from the point of view that the narrator predominates over other characters and provides the reader with *the* point of view of authorial intention. Robert Polzin's prominent study of Samuel emphasizes the

---

[4] See Wayne Booth, *The Rhetoric of Fiction* (Chicago: University of Chicago Press, 1961), 138 (emphasis mine).

[5] Cf. The Bible and Culture Collective, "Reader-Response Criticism," in *The Postmodern Bible*, ed. Elizabeth A. Castelli, Stephen D. Moore, Gary A. Phillips, and Regina M. Schwartz (New Haven: Yale University Press, 1995), 33; The Bible and Culture Collective, "Structuralist and Narratological Criticism," 85.

[6] David M. Gunn, "Narrative Criticism," in *To Each Its Own Meaning: An Introduction to Biblical Criticisms and Their Application*, ed. Steven L. McKenzie and Stephen R. Haynes (Louisville: Westminster John Knox, 1999), 201–2.

[7] David M. Gunn and Danna Nolan Fewell note that the "narrator is a character who tells the story while other characters enact it.... And it is, in fact, the narrator who determines how other points of view emerge." David M. Gunn and Danna Nolan Fewell, *Narrative in the Hebrew Bible* (New York: Oxford University Press, 1993), 53. Cf. Moore, *Literary Criticism and the Gospels*, 46.

[8] Meir Sternberg, *The Poetics of Biblical Narrative: Ideological Literature and the Drama of Reading* (Bloomington: Indiana University Press, 1985), 51; Robert Alter, influenced by Sternberg, says that "the narrators of the biblical stories are of course 'omniscient,' and that theological term transferred to narrative technique has special justification in their case, for the biblical narrator is presumed to know, quite literally, what God knows, as on occasion he may remind us by reporting God's assessments and intentions, or even what He says to Himself." Robert Alter, *The Art of Biblical Narrative* (New York: Basic Books, 1981), 195.

role of the author (i.e., the Deuteronomist) and that of the reliable narrator in constructing diverse voices with diverse narrative ideologies. When Polzin uses Bakhtin's theories of dialogue in reading the narratives, he posits the Deuteronomistic History (DH) as a monologue, quite distinct from Bakhtin's definition of a true dialogue.[9] Polzin's reading of the Books of Samuel, in specific, and the DH narrative, in general, is heavily influenced by Bakhtin's perspectives on the monologic novel, in which "the author's [the Deuteronomist's, for Polzin] ultimate semantic authority is realized."[10] Even though he does not entirely leave out the possibility of DH's "hidden dialogue" that may reveal competing voices of God,[11] Polzin argues that the word of the narrator is subordinate to the utterance of God, in a way in which the monologic rather than dialogic construction is unveiled.[12] From Polzin's viewpoint, the narrator's reliability is dependent upon the "LORD's omnipotence."[13] Polzin shares Sternberg's view on the narrator. That is, Polzin reads DH with the "unifying ideological stance of a work's 'implied author' ... found in the words of the narrator or in the words of God found in the narrative."[14]

Polzin's structuralist understanding of the implied author and the narrator in the text of Samuel influences his appropriation of Bakhtin's theories of dialogue in his analyses of the narratives. For Polzin, the ideological voice of the Deuteronomist controls and predominates over the construction of other diverse ideologies in DH. In attempting to read this "ultimate semantic authority" of the

---

[9] Robert Polzin states, "Bakhtin summarizes the characteristics of a novel that is basically monologic in structure; his words are equally valid for a work such as the Deuteronomic History." See Robert Polzin, *Moses and the Deuteronomist: A Literary Study of the Deuteronomic History: Deuteronomy, Joshua, Judges* (Bloomington: Indiana University Press, 1980), 21.

[10] Bakhtin, "Discourse in Dostoevsky," in *Problems of Dostoevsky's Poetics*, 203, quoted by Polzin, *Moses and the Deuteronomist*, 21.

[11] Polzin, *Moses and the Deuteronomist*, 21–24, writes, "For clearly even a monologue may contain a variety of ideas and viewpoints that may or may not compete with one another with equal weight or authority.... Therefore the possibility exists that, whatever may be the obvious monologic composition of the Deuteronomic History taken as a unity, a closer reading of the text may reveal a hidden dialogue between competing voices within the various utterances of God both in themselves and as interpreted by the Deuteronomic narrator."

[12] Polzin, *Moses and the Deuteronomist*, 22.

[13] Polzin argues for the narrator's omniscient and prophetic qualities through the "very contract between narrator and reader that makes up the Israelite narrative convention." According to Polzin, "this omniscient power, belonging by right of convention and ideology to the Israelite narrator, is very much like a predictive power.... Like the Israelite prophet's knowledge, the Israelite narrator's omniscience is always and everywhere constrained by the LORD's omnipotence." See Polzin, *Samuel and the Deuteronomist: A Literary Study of the Deuteronomic History: 1 Samuel* (San Francisco: Harper & Row, 1989), 96–97.

[14] Polzin, *Moses and the Deuteronomist*, 20–21.

author and that of God, Polzin does not entertain the possibility the text of Samuel may be understood as dialogic in the Bakhtinian sense of the term.

In contrast to Polzin's argument, I argue that it is possible, even necessary, to open up an alternate Bakhtinian reading of Samuel, reconceiving the roles of and interrelationships among the author, hero, and reader, especially in terms of their dialogic nature: one can reread the text from the perspective of dialogue from which Bakhtin developed his theories on "novelness" and "prosaics."[15] I argue that the dialogic nature of the text becomes unmistakably perceptible when the author/narrator yields his/her "ultimate semantic authority" to others, that is, characters and readers, while he/she participates in the dialogue, in this case, on questions of David's identity and location and that of the Davidic monarchy. From that viewpoint, the Samuel text is then no longer considered the monologic word of the reliable narrator, the author, and, therefore, God. The core of my analysis discusses how the language of Samuel becomes fundamentally dialogic when it speaks to the character of David as a dialogic hero, focusing specifically on the ambivalent act of his crowning and decrowning as described in the narrative of Samuel.

THE AUTHORATIVE WORD VS. AN INTERNALLY PERSUASIVE WORD

One of Polzin's main contributions to the study of the books of Samuel might be his use of Bakhtin's distinction between "authoritative word" and "internally persuasive word." Bakhtin makes a sharp distinction between "authoritative discourse" and "internally persuasive discourse" as the opposed categories of ideological discourse. According to Bakhtin, the authoritative word represents the authority of "religious, political, moral" discourses and "the word of the father, of adults and of teachers, etc."[16] The authoritative word is "located in a distanced zone … connected with a past that is felt to be hierarchically higher. It is, so to speak, the word of the fathers. Its authority was already *acknowledged* in the past. It is a *prior* discourse.… It can be profaned. It is akin to taboo, i.e., a name that must not be taken in vain."[17] On the other hand, internally persuasive discourse is "a contemporary word, born in a zone of contact with unresolved contemporaneity," which enters into "an intense interaction, a *struggle* with other internally

---

[15] For this matter, Polzin's remark is helpful: "the Deuteronomist's work is fundamentally novel, that is, without sufficiently obvious literary progenitors." By novel, Polzin means a "real text rather than a hypothesized pre-text." Importantly, Polzin observed DH as providing "the more prosaic mystery of a new kind of narrative," clearly distinct from the texts of epics and myths from the ancient Near East. Here Polzin is, of course, seen as greatly influenced by Bakhtin's definitions and distinctions of the genres between prose and poetry. See Polzin, *Samuel and the Deuteronomist*, 148, n. 38.

[16] Bakhtin, "Discourse in the Novel," 342.

[17] Bakhtin, "Discourse in the Novel," 342 (emphasis original).

persuasive discourses."[18] According to Bakhtin, the semantic structure of an internally persuasive word is "*not finite*, it is *open*; in each of the new contexts that dialogize it, this discourse is able to reveal ever newer *ways to mean*."[19] In the authoritative word, one would encounter a single and unitary language containing a monologic ideological thought. In internally persuasive discourse, on the other hand, one discovers various available ideological points of view and values that become "contestable" in each of the new contexts that dialogize the discourse.

In analyzing this distinction between authoritative discourse and internally persuasive discourse, Polzin insightfully suggests that the successful integration of the authoritative word with what Bakhtin calls the internally persuasive word might have constituted the significant novelistic feature represented by the Books of Samuel. In Polzin's view, the representation of the Samuel text becomes "profoundly contemporaneous words about the past."[20] Polzin suggests that the Samuel narrative can be viewed as a contemporary word providing complex profundity for its present. In Polzin's view, however, this rich complexity of the internally persuasive word in Samuel does not defeat the authoritative nature of the Deuteronomist throughout the DH. That is, the author/narrator is considered to be the "master" in uniting both categories of discourse—externally authoritative word and internally persuasive word—as deliberate authorial activity.

The question on the reliability of the narrator has been raised by some recent literary studies in reading the narratives of the Hebrew Bible: David M. Gunn and Danna Nolan Fewell suggest that the "narrator is less than straightforwardly reliable, perhaps sometimes unsure of the 'facts', and perhaps, too, prone to use conflicting facts and evaluations ironically against the reader, as a device to shake the reader's assurance."[21] This observation on the narrator as "less than straightforwardly reliable" is an important key to understanding the role of the narrator for my rereading of the prose concerning David.

Of importance is the fact that the author/narrator may not have intended to fully control the reader's activity, as Polzin observes. From this new perspective, the ideological omnipotence of the narrator can be challenged, and its influence on the reader's role diminished. The narrator is no longer seen as the "master" of deliberate storytelling, located outside the reader, always giving accurate knowledge or instruction and admonition to the reader. Considering that the Samuel text is open to "contemporaneity," that is, to the realities of crisis for the generations living in/after a catastrophic event(s),[22] the narrator then loses the assurance of reliability against various available ideological points of view,

---

[18] Bakhtin, "Discourse in the Novel," 346.
[19] Bakhtin, "Discourse in the Novel," 346 (emphasis original).
[20] Polzin, *Samuel and the Deuteronomist*, 148.
[21] Gunn and Fewell, *Narrative in the Hebrew Bible*, 56.
[22] In this essay, when I read the Samuel prose as a "real text" (i.e., the present form of the text, whatever its pre-texts) or artful text from a narrative critical perspective, I do not

approaches, directions, and values. The narrator does not know everything and does not make a final decision for the reader regarding the identity and location of a Davidic hero and the Davidic monarchy particularly in a context(s) of social events of catastrophe and crisis.

A "Crowned/Decrowned" Hero David

One could ask, how and why can the character of David be represented as the kind of hero who is not subject to authorial control or determined by monologic conclusion, but remains open to interpretation? I explore below, from the perspective of internally persuasive word, how, according to the prose of Samuel, David can be perceived as a dialogic hero in the ambivalent act of his crowning and decrowning.

Bakhtin states that, when appearing as a distanced figure, a hero is an object of seriousness;[23] in a dialogic work, however, the seriousness inherent in hierarchical distance is destroyed, and a hero is brought to the world of open-endedness, indecision, and indeterminacy.[24] A dialogic hero acts and speaks "in a zone of familiar contact with the open-ended present."[25] In other words, the hero is presented not in the seriousness of the absolute and complete past, but in the realm of the present and in immediate contact with living contemporaries.[26]

Bakhtin describes this image of a hero's close contact with living contemporaries as "uncrowning" or "decrowning," which equates to the hero's removal from the "sacred and sacrosanct" plane of the past and the destruction of hierarchical distance.[27] The hero comes into proximity; in light of this image of a hero in proximity, a dialogic reading of Samuel underscores the very human characterization of David in Samuel—his fears, his mistakes, his foibles, etc. The hero's close contact with the reader in Samuel becomes readily apparent when one compares the depiction of David in Samuel with his portrayal in Chronicles. In Chronicles, the reader would not find a hero who comes in close proximity to them; rather, he/she may look up to an idealized and almost perfect figure of David, for example, the Chronicler's account does not introduce the audience to a David who sins against Bathsheba and Uriah.

---

endeavor to trace the history of the text's composition, e.g., via reference to redactional layers. This essay, methodologically speaking, does not attempt to ask the matter of historical issues, although I take seriously the prose's language as a product of particular social settings and historical traditions.

[23] Bakhtin, "Epic and Novel," in *Dialogic Imagination*, 23.
[24] See Bakhtin, "Epic and Novel," 16.
[25] Bakhtin, "Characteristics of Genre and Plot Composition in Dostoevsky's Works," in *Problems of Dostoevsky's Poetics*, 108.
[26] See Bakhtin, "Characteristics of Genre and Plot Composition in Dostoevsky's Works," 108.
[27] Bakhtin, "Epic and Novel," 23.

In such a "serious" representation of a character, David would remain forever "crowned" and "sacrosanct." That is, in a monologic text, crowning a hero is "single-leveled, absolute, heavy, and monolithically serious."[28] On the other hand, in a dialogic text, crowning is inseparable from decrowning and, therefore, becomes two-leveled and ambivalent. Thus, the crowning and decrowning of David can be perceived as inseparable: David's crowning already includes the idea of his immanent decrowning.[29]

A dialogic reading of 2 Samuel shows how the crowning of David is ambivalent and double-leveled from the very start as David is crowned twice, *before* and *after* civil war between the houses of Saul and David. In 2 Sam 1, David is informed that Saul has died in battle against the Philistines and, in the next chapter, David is crowned by the people of Judah at Hebron (2 Sam 2:4). Yet David's decrowning glimmers immediately in unresolved political tensions: he confronts the rift with the house of Saul and the people of Israel (2 Sam 2:8–11). In 2 Sam 2–4, Joab's brother Asahel is killed by Abner, Saul's army commander (2:23); Abner is killed by Joab, David's army commander (3:27); Ish-bosheth, son of Saul and king of Israel after Saul's death, is killed by Baanah and Rechab, Ish-bosheth's army commanders (4:7); and Baanah and Rechab are killed by David's men (4:12).

David is crowned again, this time by the elders of Israel in 2 Sam 5:1–3. Through this process, David, indeed, grows stronger, while the house of Saul grows weaker, as the narrator comments in 2 Sam 3:1. Yet although David becomes king over both Judah and Israel, his decrowning always lurks alongside his crowning,[30] which is felt in the unceasing and unresolved tension between the people of Judah and the people of Israel. One could even argue that a decrowning lurks throughout David's entire reign. After Saul dies in battle (in accordance with David's wishful prediction in 1 Sam 26:10), the undying threat from the house of Saul will distress David for most of his reign (cf. 21:12–14).

In fact, as soon as David is anointed by Samuel in 1 Sam 16, "the anointed one" of Judah submits to the house of Saul and becomes Saul's "servant" (1 Sam 16:14ff). But, David ultimately departs from the house of Saul: Saul's jealousy and fears estrange him from the house of Saul (1 Sam 18:9, 12–13). David plays the enemy of (the house of) Saul from that moment forward (cf. 18:29; 19:17). In so doing, David has to convince others (including Saul) of the "invincible" nature of being "the LORD's anointed" and kill those who fail to acknowledge it (especially after Saul's death).

The tension-ridden cycle of killing and crowning which foreshadows David's decrowning actually transpires through his son Absalom (2 Sam 15). After Saul's death, the one who "wins away the hearts of the people of Israel" (2 Sam 15:6) is

---

[28] Bakhtin, "Characteristics of Genre and Plot Composition," 124.
[29] See Bakhtin, "Characteristics of Genre and Plot Composition," 124.
[30] See Bakhtin, "Characteristics of Genre and Plot Composition," 125.

not Ish-bosheth, the king of Israel of two years; nor Abner, Saul's army commander; nor even Mephibosheth, Saul's grandson and the last of Saul's line. Rather, it is Absalom, the third son of David and killer of firstborn Amnon. The prose's description of Absalom's physical attractiveness (14:25) followed by Absalom's actions to "win away the hearts of Israel" in chapter 15 draws the reader's attention to Absalom and highlight his desire for kingship.[31] Michael Avioz argues that Absalom's beauty, especially his growing hair, is intended to "signal Absalom's intentions for kingship to the people, since long hair was related to beauty and was characteristic of kings."[32] This detail reminds the reader of earlier physical descriptions of Saul (1 Sam 9:2), Eliab (1 Sam 16:6–7), David (1 Sam 16:12), and Adonijah (1 Kgs 1:6). Each man, who is a kingly figure or a possible candidate for the role, is described as physically good-looking. Even more significant, both Absalom and Saul are described as *more beautiful* than any other men in Israel (1 Sam 9:2 and 2 Sam 14:25). If beauty is recognized as a trait of kingship in 1 and 2 Samuel,[33] and noting the consonance with Saul, it is highly likely that the mention of Absalom's beauty anticipates his role as a competitor of his father David.

The detail regarding Absalom's beauty is preceded by the story of Tamar and Amnon and the report of Absalom's return to Jerusalem after his murder of Amnon. The reader does not, of course, hear from the narrator that kingly ambitions motivated Absalom's murder of Amnon (cf. 13:32). Bar-Efrat claims that "it was family affairs, not political objective which according to the narrator, led to Amnon's murder."[34] However, if the narrator does not tell or does not know everything, then the reader is left to suspect that Amnon, the crown prince and the eldest son of David, might have been Absalom's intended target for more than one reason.

After Absalom flees upon Amnon's murder, Joab orchestrates his return to Jerusalem through the mediation of a disguised wise woman of Tekoa (14:1–24). The "widow" presents a fictitious analogue to the case of avenging of royal blood: "Your maidservant had two sons ... one of them struck the other and killed him. Then the whole clan confronted your maidservant and said, 'Hand over the one who killed his brother, that we may put him to death for the slaying of his

---

[31] Michael Avioz argues that Absalom's beauty, especially his growing hair, is intended to "signal Absalom's intentions for kingship to the people, since long hair was related to beauty and was characteristic of kings." See Michael Avioz, "The Motif of Beauty in the Books of Samuel and Kings," *VT* 59 (2009): 352.

[32] Avioz, "Motif of Beauty in the Books of Samuel and Kings," 352.

[33] Avioz notes that Samuel deals with the subject of beauty somewhat extensively, whereas Kings does not describe the beauty of Solomon, Hezekiah, and Josiah, "although such a casting could have contributed to their ideal description" ("Motif of Beauty in the Books of Samuel and Kings," 352, 359).

[34] Shimon Bar-Efrat, "The Narrative of Amnon and Tamar," in *Narrative Art in the Bible* (Sheffield: Almond, 1989), 274.

brother'" (vv. 6–7); "You have planned the like" (v. 13).[35] She continues to reveal her story, with some parallel to the case of the king: "Let your Majesty be mindful of the LORD your God and restrain the blood avenger bent on destruction, so that my son may not be killed" (v. 11); "your Majesty condemns himself in that your Majesty does not bring back his own banished son" (v. 13).

Following the king's favorable response to her plight, she exposes that "the king"[36] has "devised [חשב *chashab*] a thing" (v. 13), unlike God who "makes plans [חשב *chashab*] so that no one may be kept banished" (v. 14). In revealing tensions between the imminent danger of her son and the banished situation of the king's son, the disguised woman indeed draws upon the controlling images of killing and being killed by one's own family. She overtly uncovers the issue of life and death: "We all must die; we are like water that is poured out on the ground and cannot be gathered up. [But] God will not take away a life" (v. 14). Claudia V. Camp underscores the nature of the "incisiveness and authority" of her argument by suggesting that this verse reflects an "identificational proverb" that creates an image similar to the one found in Prov 17:14: "The beginning of strife is like letting out water; so stop before the quarrel breaks out."[37]

Interestingly, the woman of Tekoa likens David to "an angel of Elohim" twice (vv. 17, 20). In the books of Samuel, there are two more instances where David is called an angel of Elohim: the Philistine king Achish says David is as pleasing in his sight as an angel of Elohim (1 Sam 29:9), and Mephibosheth compares David to an angel of Elohim when he claims Ziba slandered him (2 Sam 19:28).[38] In both circumstances, David is ostensibly prevented from killing his enemy: Achish, heeding warnings from his commanders, withdraws David from the battle against Israel; similarly, Mephibosheth's story and appearance of mourning cast doubt on Ziba's claim and probably save his life.

In line with these instances where David is called an angel of Elohim, the situation presented by the woman of Tekoa also involves David making a life or death decision. The wise woman urges David to make a decision like an angel of Elohim who understands everything, good and bad (v. 17). The image of a "killing" angel in 2 Samuel is significant: when an angel is mentioned again in 24:16–17, the angel is destroying the people in Jerusalem as punishment for David's census-taking. Revealed as "an angel of Elohim," David the king is trapped by the wise woman in swearing the oath that "as the Lord lives, not a hair of your son

---

[35] All bible quotations are from the Tanakh (TNK) by the Jewish Publication Society (1999), unless otherwise noted.

[36] The prose of ch. 14 never mentions the name David.

[37] Claudia V. Camp, "The Wise Women of 2 Samuel: A Role Model for Women in Early Israel?," *CBQ* 43 (1981): 16, 20–21.

[38] Jeremy Schipper observes that in texts such as 2 Sam 14:20 and 19:28, one hears "traces of texts involving deception and disloyalty," arguing that David is deceived when called by "the angel of God." Jeremy Schipper, "'Why Do You Still Speak of Your Affairs?': Polyphony in Mephibosheth's Exchanges with David in 2 Samuel," *VT* 54 (2004): 350.

shall fall to the ground" (v. 11) and in exercising it as he has Joab bring Absalom back to Jerusalem (v. 21).

The one ultimately deceived in the prose, however, is not David but his son Absalom. It would take Absalom a few more years to learn that David's recalling him to Jerusalem did not equate with reconciliation. Based on a misled oath, Absalom's return is conditioned by a ban against seeing his father's face (v. 24). Essentially, Absalom spends two years in Jerusalem as David's "enemy" (v. 28) until he orchestrates a reunion through Joab (vv. 32–33). Although the prose does not tell exactly when Absalom begins to desire the throne, the two years that Absalom hated Amnon (13:23), his three years in exile from the king, and two more years in Jerusalem excluded from the king's palace add up to a substantial period for Absalom to make up his mind to stand against David.

Absalom finally exposes the tension of life and death between him and his father even more clearly: in 2 Sam 14:32, Absalom says, "If there is guilt in me, let him kill me!" (NRSV). Hearing that from Joab, David would kiss Absalom rather than kill him (in v. 33). Interestingly, from this moment of Absalom's reinstatement (14:33), Absalom "plays" an enemy of David, as one sees in and after 2 Sam 15:1ff. Eventually, Absalom becomes a "stench in his father's nostrils" by following Ahithophel's advice to lie with his father's concubines "before the eyes of all Israel" in 16:21–22. This incident is predicted by Yahweh through Nathan after David killed Uriah: in 12:10–11, Yahweh speaks through Nathan, "you spurned me by taking the wife of Uriah the Hittite and making her your wife.... I will take your wives and give them to another man before your very eyes and he shall sleep with your wives under this very sun." Thus, Absalom becomes the agent who fulfills Yahweh's retributive words against David.

In filling this role, Absalom culminates the process of decrowning David. David becomes the only king in the Samuel prose, in particular, and the DH narrative, in general, who flees from his own city and kingship, as one reads in 15:14. The people weep for David in verse 23, and the decrowned David weeps too, and walks barefoot with his head covered in verse 30. The contrast with Saul is noteworthy: it would be fair to say that Saul's kingship finally ends with his death, as is typical of most kings in DH. Saul is not really decrowned by the people in the seventeen chapters in Samuel that tell of a reign that overlaps with David's rise. Rather, Saul always plays a crowned king, even after he is rejected by Samuel and by Yahweh, until he dies in battle. Saul sustains his kingship with his people. In his death, Saul is beheaded and his body is dishonored by the Philistines but, once again, Saul's body is retrieved by people who risk their lives to give Saul an appropriate burial at Jabesh (1 Sam 31:9–13).

On the other hand, David is decrowned, in large part, because the people (with Absalom) reject him. At one point, the spirit of Yahweh leaves Saul and comes upon David in 1 Sam 16:13–14. Later, the hearts of the people leave David and veer toward Absalom in 2 Sam 15:6, 13. In the ambivalent act of David's crowning and decrowning, David's own son Absalom becomes his father's enemy and remains so until the son dies by the hands of Joab in 2 Sam 18. Trapped by his "hair" (2 Sam 18:9), his "crowning glory" (2 Sam 14:26), Absalom ends his life as an enemy of David and "completes" Yahweh's retributive words and Nathan's judgment against his father: "you [David] shall not die. However, since you have spurned the enemies of the LORD by this deed, even the child about to be born to you shall die" (2 Sam 12:13–14). David, once again, risks and loses his own child in saving himself and his kingship.

David is ultimately decrowned by Absalom. What makes the decrowning of David unique and quite different from the process of Saul's crowning and end of his kingship, is that David may return to Jerusalem to be crowned again in the future. A dialogic perspective on the ambivalent act of crowning and decrowning highlights this facet of the prose. David deliberately plans his return to Jerusalem with his friend Hushai the Arkite in 15:37; 16:16 (cf. 16:17). At the moment of his decrowning, David presents the idea of returning to Jerusalem and tells Zadok to take the ark back into the city (15:25). What the reader will unfailingly read is that the hero David himself presents the idea that he may return in the future: "If I find favor with the Lord, he will bring me back and let me see it and its abode" (15:25).

David separates his destiny from that of the ark momentarily in an attempt to send Zadok and Abiathar back to Jerusalem. David risks his life to protect the ark and kingship from being ultimately "decrowned" (15:26). David continues by telling Zadok, "I shall linger in the steppes of the wilderness until word comes from you to inform me [to return]" (15:28). Clearly, David "lingers" between the moments of crowning and decrowning. Through this lingering, David, as a dialogic hero, wavers between decrowning and (re)crowning in the loss of a good measure of his authority and of conclusiveness and finality.

At the point of his decrowning, "a new crowning already glimmers."[39] A dialogic hero, David is in his return to Jerusalem in 2 Sam 19. However, in typical seriocomic style, David returns to Jerusalem in "profanation," that is, in the midst of "carnivalistic blasphemies" and "bringing the hero to the plane of laughter."[40] In his return, David meets Shimei, whom Abishai recalls as the one who cursed rather than praised "the LORD's anointed" (19:22). David also confronts Mephibosheth, who asserts that Ziba betrayed him and lied to David (19:27–28); in listening to Mephibosheth, David realizes that he is being deceived (and, perhaps, ridiculed) by the one or the other. In his return to Jerusalem, David is also caught between the people of Judah, who claim to be David's "own flesh and

---

[39] Bakhtin, "Characteristics of Genre and Plot Composition," 125.

[40] Bakhtin points out that "profanation" is the significant aspect of the carnival sense of the world: "carnivalistic blasphemies, a whole system of carnivalistic debasings and bringings down to earth, carnivalistic obscenities linked with the reproductive power of the earth and the body, carnivalistic parodies on sacred texts and sayings, etc." ("Characteristics of Genre and Plot Composition," 123).

blood," and the people of Israel, who insist that they were the first to suggest bringing David back (19:43–44). Moreover, David encounters Sheba, whom he later refers to as the one who "will cause more trouble than Absalom" (20:1–2, 6). Furthermore, when David returns to his palace in Jerusalem, he finds his raped concubines, whose presence would continually remind David of his shameful defeat rather than his triumph and victory (20:3). The returned king faces the "ridicule" of others (i.e., both author and reader), who may laugh at the ambivalence of his crowning and decrowning,[41] and ridicule the "profanation" in his return. In a dialogic text, one does not expect "conclusiveness" or "absolute closedness" in the return of the hero.

Conclusion

In the Samuel prose, as a dialogic hero, David is crowned and decrowned; David escapes from Jerusalem and returns to Jerusalem. In his return to Jerusalem without Absalom, David may be praised as a victorious king but abused as a defeated father (cf. 2 Sam 19:1). David the king is ambivalently elevated and degraded; as a returned king, David is drawn into a zone of "familiar and crude contact" with others in the text of "dialogics."

The significant point here is that the dialogic act of a crowning and decrowning hero is perceived as sharply distinct from a "theatrical performance"; from that perspective, the hero does not perform, as though on stage, any act of "heroization."[42] David as a dialogic hero does not show to the audience a performance of any heroic action at a distance, such as the presentation of David's grand vision in Chronicles to build a house of Yahweh in the service of praise and thanksgiving; rather, he exposes himself to risks, dangers, and life crisis, and thus reveals to the audience his trials, goofs, and foibles. The reader laughs at and with David's ambitions and failures, not entirely unfamiliar with and dissimilar to one's own. This understanding illuminates how the reader, in facing the historical events of catastrophe and crisis, may see the serious, monologic treatment of a Davidic hero and Davidic monarchy with a parallel "comic double," such as in the process of crowning and decrowning David in the prose of Samuel.

If a monologic reading of Samuel is walled off from the audience's free contact with the open-endedness of the prose in the world of hierarchical seriousness

---

[41] For example, Bakhtin recalls the "scene of crowning and decrowning the 'King of the Jews' in the canonical Gospels," when he explains a defining influence of the "menippea" and "carnivalization" on ancient Christian literature. He argues that "carnivalization is even more powerfully present in apocryphal Christian literature," although he does not mention the (canonical) texts of the Hebrew Bible ("Characteristics of Genre and Plot Composition," 135).

[42] For Bakhtin's discussion of "epic heroization" and its parodic reworking, see Bakhtin, "From the Prehistory of Novelistic Discourse," in *Dialogic Imagination*, 51–68.

and determinacy, then a dialogic reading of DH is freely opened to the audience in the situation of contemporaneity. Through a dialogic reading, one can see how the figure of David comes close and is drawn into a zone of "crude and familiar contact" with the contemporaries. Such a representation of a dialogic hero who is both crowned and decrowned functions to create communal identity in relation to the polemical nature of a monarchical institution.

If readers live without the hierarchical structure of kingship in the midst of uncertainty, they may probe questions regarding David and/or a Davidic hero, especially in relation to promises made in 2 Samuel about his kingship. Given such a circumstance, a question arises: how would the ordinary people "without rank," that is, without grammar and structure, who are the audience for the prose of Samuel and DH, deal with the destruction of the kingship in the world of open-endedness and indeterminacy? The end of the Davidic monarchy (in DH) could have provided the audience, facing the realities of no kings, with images of both the destruction of hierarchy and of the return of a dialogic hero. In this respect, there exists no straightforwardly monologic word, but only a dialogic word—a double-voiced word[43] on a dialogic hero. A nonauthoritative but internally dialogized reading of the text, therefore, liberates from any dogmatic seriousness, from didacticism, from the illusion of the single meaning, the single level, the single monologic truth.

---

[43] Bakhtin argues that "for any and every straightforward genre, any and every direct discourse—epic, tragic, lyric, philosophical—may and indeed must itself become the object of representation, the object of a parodic travestying 'mimicry.' It is as if such mimicry rips the word away from its object, disunifies the two, shows that a given straightforward generic word—epic or tragic—is one-sided, bounded, incapable of exhausting the object.... Parodic-travestying literature introduces the permanent corrective of laughter, of a critique on the one-sided seriousness of the lofty direct word, the corrective of reality that is always richer, more fundamental and most importantly *too contradictory and heteroglot to be fit into a high and straightforward genre.*" Bakhtin, "From the Prehistory of Novelistic Discourse," 55 (emphasis original).

MURDER, ADULTERY, AND THEFT

John Ahn

The Laws of Ur-Nammu (2100–2050 BCE; Sumerian), Laws of Eshnunna (tell abu harmal, Bagdad, Iraq, 1800 BCE), Code of Hammurapi (1792–1750 BCE), Middle Assyrian Laws (1400–1000 BCE), and Hittite Laws (1650–1100 BCE) all have references to adultery, those suspected of committing adultery, falsely accusing another man's wife of committing adultery without proof, and laws pertaining to a contractually engaged or betrothed reassessed for breach of contract because the virginity of the woman was compromised.[1] These adultery codes are generally casuistic in form and style, covering a wide range of social, economic, and legal matters. The Decalogue's prohibition against adultery, however, is apodictic, without any additional clause or for that matter, no immediate infraction for breaking the law.

The vetitive לא תנאף (do not commit adultery) in an initial reading appears to be straight forward. It is this simplicity that concerns us. Since each of the other previous codes or stipulations in the Decalogue all have some extended modifiers or clauses that enumerate or expand, including a preamble at the outset, the commandments: לא תרצח, לא תנאף, and לא תגנב are markedly different. They appear to be an abridged, contracted, or possibly an original form of something more complex.

Following this introduction, I begin with ancient Near Eastern (con)texts focusing on adultery codes to help situate the text before us. We move into the Israelite context and then to modern social settings' dealings with the issue, raising new possibilities. After examining the possible source of לא תנאף, לא תרצח, and לא תגנב (Exod 20:13–15; Deut 5:17–19) that is, the narrative of David and Bathsheba's adultery (2 Sam 11–12), we reframe both sets of texts through the lenses of Anthony Giddens's work on self-identity.[2]

An abridged version of this paper was delivered in Seoul, South Korea (2016).
[1] James B. Pritchard, *Ancient Near Eastern Texts Relating to the Old Testament*, 2nd ed. (Princeton: Princeton University Press, 1955).
[2] Anthony Giddens, *Modernity and Self-Identity* (Stanford: Stanford University Press, 1991).

The Problem

Beyond the works of Dennis McCarthy[3] and others,[4] a review of the syntax and style of the codes in Exod 20:13–17 beginning with verse 16, לא תענה (literally "do not answer," rendered "do not bear false witness" [NRSV]) is immediately followed by a coordinating or subordinating prepositional phrase ברעך עד שקר (against your neighbor as a false witness). The resultative clause may be understood as how not to respond, namely, in deception or falsehood. It is a prohibition against perjury. Verse 17 follows the same pattern: לא תחמד, "do not covet" is followed by an expansion of what is not to be coveted: בית רעך לא־תחמד אשת רעך ועבדו ואמתו ושורו וחמרו. But immediately following the construct chain or bound form, "house of your neighbor," "do not covet" is repeated and further qualified with "the wife of your neighbor." Likely an interpolation, whoever inserted the phrase may have sought to remind the reader that not coveting a neighbor's wife was worth repeating, perhaps to reinforce לא תנאף or conversely, this particular segment of the covet code developed independently. The interpolation לא־תחמד אשת רעך has a different function altogether. The wife or woman is listed primary in a string of human and animal properties that occupy the house with: manservant, maidservant, ox, and ass—all affixed with a third person masculine singular pronominal suffix. These items, including the wife, all have ownership (indicated by the pronominal suffix). Such properties suggest an association with the wealthy, not the poor. The second half of the Decalogue concludes with a recapitulation of what is not to be coveted—namely, "everything that is your neighbor's."

Those without a wife, servants, and goods, as well as those with such acquired subjects and objects, are kept at a distance. The code also functions to keep equal among equals in check and attempts to prevent envy or jealousy from getting out of control. A cursory reading of the second-half of the Decalogue engages at least two socioeconomic classes. When we strip away all the conditional and emended

---

[3] Dennis J. McCarthy, *Treaty and Covenant: A Study in Form in the Ancient Oriental Documents and in the Old Testament*, 2nd ed., Analecta Biblica (Rome: Biblical Institute Press, 1978); Klaus Baltzer, *The Covenant Formulary: In Old Testament, Jewish and Early Christian Writings*, trans. David E. Green (Philadelphia: Fortress, 1971).

[4] Calcum M. Carmichael, *The Origins of Biblical Law: The Decalogues and the Book of the Covenant* (Ithaca: Cornell University, 1992); Innocent Himbaza, *Le Décalogue et l'histoire du texte: Études des formes textuelles du Décalogue et leurs Implications dans l'histoire du texte de l'Ancient Testament*, OBO 207 (Göttingen: Vandenhoeck & Ruprecht, 2004); David H. Aaron, *Etched in Stone: The Emergence of the Decalogue* (London: T&T Clark, 2006); Henning Graf Reventlow and Yair Hoffman, eds., *The Decalogue in Jewish and Christian Tradition*, LHBOTS 509 (London: T&T Clark, 2011); Dominik Markl, *The Decalogue and its Cultural Influence* (Sheffield: Sheffield Phoenix, 2013); Esias E. Meyer, "The Reinterpretation of the Decalogue in Leviticus 19 and the Centrality of the Cult," *SJOT* 30 (2016): 198–214.

clauses, we are left with a wooden set of codes that are more universal in scope. Perhaps, as traditions have noted, the original form of the secod half of the injunctions were:

you shall not murder	לא תרצח
you shall not commit adultery	לא תנאף
you shall not steal	לא תגנב
you shall not answer	לא תענה
you shall not covet	לא תחם

In contrast to all the other stipulations in the final form of the text, "Do not murder, do not commit adultery, and do not steal" are preserved in their short (original) form. How did this materialize, that is, what measures were used to prevent expansions or additions without any future qualifications? Among the three codes, "do not commit adultery"[5] appears to be seminal, offering a clue.

First, because all adultery is a form of stealing with possibility for murder from uncontrolled behavior (anger), the injunction against adultery keeps an individual or community safeguarded from all three. Second, this stipulation is the first commandment to (in)directly reference marriage, divorce, and the family.[6] Third, in Rabbinic Judaism, according to Hananiah b. Gamaliel, there is a parallel between the first five and second five: "On the one was written, 'I am the Lord your God' and opposite it: 'You shall not murder'… On the one was written: 'You shall have no other gods' [above me] and opposite it: 'You shall not commit adultery.'"[7] Idolatry and adultery have often been read side by side, especially in the prophets. Fourth, there are independent narratives (bordering) on the central theme of adultery in the Hebrew Bible and New Testament (1) Tamar and Judah (Gen 38), (2) David and Bathsheba (2 Sam 11), (3) Hosea and Gomer (Hos 1–2; 3), and (4) the Woman Caught in Adultery (John 7:53–8:11).[8] Finally, the subject matter of adultery was and continues to be socially and legally relevant, especially if it involves persons with power and authority.[9]

---

[5] Raymond Westbrook, "Adultery in Ancient Near Eastern Law," *RB* 97 (1990): 542–80.

[6] Bernard Jackson, "The 'Institution' of Marriage and Divorce in the Hebrew Bible," *JSS* 56 (2011): 221–51.

[7] See Jacob Neusner, "The Ten Commandments," in *Common Ground: A Priest and a Rabbi Read Scripture Together*, ed. Andrew M. Greeley and Jacob Neusner (Cleveland: Pilgrim, 1996), 157–58. See also, Edward Fram, "Two Cases of Adultery and the Halakhic Decision Making Process," *AJS Review* 26 (2002): 277–300.

[8] Larry J. Kreitzer and Deborah W. Rooke, eds., *Ciphers in the Sand: Interpretations of the Woman Taken in Adultery (John 7:53–8:11)*, Biblical Seminar 74 (Sheffield: Sheffield Academic, 2000).

[9] See, William David Spencer, "Cyber-Marriage, Virtual Adultery, Real Consequences, and the Need for a Techno Sexual Ethic," *Africanus Journal* 2 (2010): 14–23; Stanton L.

In modern context, notes Deborah L. Rhode, the Ernest W. McFarland Professor of Law and Director of the Center on the Legal Profession at Stanford University:

> Society's condemnation of adultery has increased rather than decreased over the last two decades. What has changed, however, is the public's increased respect for privacy and its decreased confidence in law as a means of policing marital fidelity. The preceding discussion makes clear why courts should get out of the business of monitoring extramarital conduct altogether. Adultery in this age seems to be nobody's business but that of the players in these family dramas.[10]

On February 26, 2015, South Korea overturned a law of sixty-two years, which criminalized anyone who committed adultery. Article 241 of the criminal code was deemed unconstitutional. Human dignity was highlighted. The outdated economic leverage used by women to weigh on cases of adultery was dismissed. Seven judges signed the decision and two dissented. In the dissent, adultery and fornication were referenced to go beyond a person's rights. It was noted that they intrude on people and community, including the fundamental value to protect the family and society.[11]

ANCIENT NEAR EASTERN CONTEXT AND ADULTERY

Moshe Weinfeld points out that the negative confessions in chapter 125 of the Egyptian *Book of the Dead* and the Mesopotamian incantation "*Šurpu*" include adultery (among murder, robbery, false oaths, talebearing, hypocrisy, wrongful acquisition, counterfeit weights and measures, boundary encroachment and failure to clothe the naked) as a serious offense.[12] In case 4 of Ur-Nammu, the wife of a man who entices another man, the consequence is death for the woman whereas the man is set free. In this particular case, the explanation is that a man is sexually helpless under a woman's charm. In case or law 26 of Eshnunna, a betrothed woman who loses her virginity to another man, the consequence and legal outcome is death for the male offender. In law 28 of Eshnunna, if the woman is a homemaker or housewife (stemming from law 27) and she is caught with another man, the housewife will die without any consequence for the man.

Jones, "My Genes Made Me Do It: Evolutionary Psychology May Explain Why We Commit Adultery—But Not Why We Don't," *Christianity Today* 39.5 (1995): 14–18.

[10] Deborah L. Rhode, *Adultery: Infidelity and the Law* (Cambridge: Harvard University Press, 2016), 88.

[11] https://www.nytimes.com/2015/02/27/world/asia/south-korea-strikes-down-adultery-law.html, accessed Jun 10, 2018.

[12] Moshe Weinfeld, "The Uniqueness of the Decalogue," in *Ten Commandments in History and Tradition*, ed. Ben-Zion Segal and Gershon Levi (Jerusalem: The Magnes Press; The Hebrew University of Jerusalem, 1990), 19 especially notes 63 and 64.

There are wider ranges of legislations and consequences on adultery in Middle Assyrian Laws. If charged and convicted of adultery, the punishments ranged from: the death penalty to mutilation of the body, flogging of one hundred lashes, pitch [tar] over the head, tearing out the eyes, or water torture. Although scholars point to a contractual aspect of the law of adultery—business tort or transactional law—the alternative is family law. Many of the laws resulting from adultery may have been in place to preserve the family and society.[13]

In Hittite Laws 197, the physical location of where the adultery took place is significant. If the incident took place in the mountains, that is, no one heard the woman cry for help, the perpetrator is at fault. However, if the adultery took place in her house, then, the woman is legally liable. Interestingly, if the husband finds both of them, he has the legal jurisdiction to kill both his wife and the adulterer without any self-infringement or consequence to himself. It would have been extremely rare for a woman to go outside her home, to the home of the adulterer to commit adultery. In law 198, if the husband decides to spare his adulteress wife, then legally, he is mandated to pardon the male adulterer as well. However, the male adulterer receives a mark on his forehead—a true precursor to Hester Prynne's scarlet letter. If the husband chooses to have them executed, the actual death decree has to be authorized by the king. If the king finds the parties guilty, the execution moves forward. But if the king decides against the death penalty and shows mercy and compassion, it is in the prerogative and legal jurisdiction of the king to grant clemency or absolution to both.

Laws of Ur-Nammu

> 4. If the wife of a man, *by employing her charms*, followed after another man and he slept with her, they (authorities) shall slay that woman, but that male shall be set free.
>
> 11. If a man had accused the wife of a man of fornication, and the river (-ordeal) proved her innocent, then the man who had accused her must pay one-third of a mina of silver.

Laws of Eshnunna

> 26. If a man gives bride-money for a(nother) man's daughter, but another man seizes her forcibly without asking the permission of her father and mother and deprives her of her virginity, it is a capital offense and he shall die.

---

[13] Lawrence Stager, "The Archaeology of the Family in Ancient Israel," *BASOR* 260 (1985): 1–35.

27. If a man takes a(nother) man's daughter without asking the permission of her father and her mother and concludes no formal marriage contract with her father and her mother, even though she may live in his house for a year, she is not a housewife.

28. On the other hand, if he concludes a formal contract with her father and her mother and cohabits with her, she is a housewife. When she is caught with a(nother) man, she shall die, she shall not get away alive.

Code of Hammurapi

129. If the wife of a seignior has been caught while lying with another man, they shall bind them and throw them into the water. If the husband of the woman wishes to spare his wife, then the king in turn may spare his subject. (// Deut 22:22)

130. If a seignior bound the (betrothed) wife of a(nother) seignior, who had had no intercourse with a male and was still living in her father's house, and he has lain in her bosom and they have caught him, that seignior shall be put to death, while that woman shall go free. (// Deut 22:23–27)

131. If a seignior's wife was accused by her husband, but she was not caught while lying with another man, she shall make affirmation by god and return to her house. (// Num 5:11–31)

132. If the finger was pointed at the wife of a seignior because of another man, but she has not been caught while lying with the other man, she shall throw herself into the river for the sake of her husband (// Num 5:11–31)

Middle Assyrian Laws

9. If a seignior laid hands on the wife of a(nother) seignior, thereby treating her like a young child, when they have prosecuted him (and) convicted him, they shall cut off [one] finger of his. If he has kissed her, they shall draw his lower lip along the edge of the blade of an ax (and) cut (it) off.

12. If, as a seignior's wife passed along the street, a(nother) seignior has seized her, saying to her, "Let me lie with you" since she would not consent (and) kept defending herself, but he has taken her by force (and) lain with her, whether they found him on the seignior's wife or witnesses have charged him that he lay with the woman, they shall put the seignior to death, with no blame attaching to the woman.

14. If a seignior has lain with the wife of a(nother) seignior either in a temple-brothel or in the street, knowing that she was a seignior's wife, they shall treat the adulterer as the seignior orders his wife to be treated. If he has lain with her without knowing that she was a seignior's wife, the adulterer is guiltless; the seignior shall prosecute his wife, treating her as he thinks fit.

15. If a seignior has caught a(nother) seignior with his wife, when they have prosecuted him (and) convicted him, they shall put both of them to death, with no liability attaching to him. If, upon catching (him), he has brought him either into the presence of the king or into the presence of the judges, when they have prosecuted him (and) convicted him, if the woman's husband puts his wife to death, he shall also put the seignior to death, but if he cuts off his wife's nose, he shall turn the seignior into a eunuch and they shall mutilate his whole face. However, if he let his wife go free, they shall let the seignior go free.

16. If a seignior [has lain with a(nother) seignior's] wife at her invitation, no blame attaches to the seignior; the (married) seignior shall inflict such punishment on his wife as he thinks fit. If he has lain with her by force, when they have prosecuted him (and) convicted him, his punishment shall be like that of the seignior's wife.

17. If a seignior has said to a(nother) seignior, "People have lain repeatedly with your wife," since there were no witnesses, they shall make an agreement (and) go to the river (for the water ordeal).

18. If a seignior has said to his neighbor either in private or in a brawl, "People have lain repeatedly with your wife; I will prosecute (her) myself," since he is not able to prosecute (her and) did not prosecute (her), they shall flog that seignior forty (times) with staves (and) he shall do the work of the king for one full month; they shall castrate him and he shall also pay one talent of lead.

Hittite Laws

197. If a man seizes a woman in the mountains, it is the man's crime and he will be killed. But if he seizes her in (her) house, it is the woman's crime and the woman shall be killed. If the husband finds them, he may kill them, there shall be no punishment for him.

198. If he brings them to the gate of the palace and declares: "my wife shall not be killed." And thereby spares his wife's life, he shall also spare the life

of the adulterer and shall mark his head. If he says, "Let them die both of them!"... The king may order them killed, the king may spare their lives.

Israelite Context and Adultery

Henrik Bosman notes that "adultery in ancient Israel referred to any coitus between a married or betrothed female and a male who was not married or betrothed to her.... Adultery is also used as a metaphor for Israel's idolatry and infidelity in the prophetic books of the Old Testament."[14] Bosman offers a historical development of adultery law from early Israel to late Wisdom Literature.[15] Discussions on the prophets and post-exilic influences are additionally referenced. He closes the discussion by noting that there can be little doubt that the prophetic tradition(s) influenced the final form of the Decalogue. More will be noted below.

Anthony Philips[16] argues that because Israelite's adultery law was a great sin against God, the husband did not have the power or means to forgive his wife. Accordingly, the execution of an adulterous wife is deemed justifiable in its ancient Israelite context.[17] What is noteworthy is his point that the "Deuteronomic legislation on adultery and seduction is not to be understood as mere repetition of ancient laws somehow without any concern or regard for the Book of Covenant."[18] For him, the stipulation reflects the interest of the Deuteronomists' legal action, bringing women into the courts of criminal law concerning adultery.

Philips describes early stages of ancient Israel's dealing with adultery: Sarah (Gen 12:10), Rebekah (Gen 20:1), and Bathsheba (2 Sam 11–12). In today's scholarship, the stories of Sarah and Rebekah are deemed later than the story of Bathsheba. The sister-wife narratives are read as stories of "suspected adultery." In the case of Abraham and Sarah, the Genesis Apocryphon (1QapGen)—reworked or an exercise in scripturalization or Midrash, more appropriately closer to the targum—clearly sought to avoid the implication that Sarai was sold into adultery (or prostitution) to Pharaoh for Abram's profit.

Philips argues that only when the biblical authors arrive in the late seventh or early sixth century BCE, that true Deuteronomic reform occurred with respect to

---

[14] Henrik Bosman, "Adultery, Prophetic Tradition, and the Decalogue," in *Wünschet Jerusalem Frieden: Collected Communications to the Twelfth Congress of the International Organization for the Study of the Old Testament, Jerusaelm 1986*, ed. Marrhias Augustin and Klaus-Dietrick Schunk (Frankfurt am Main: Lang, 1988), 21.

[15] Mark Sneed, ed., *Was There a Wisdom Tradition? New Prospects in Israelite Wisdom Studies* (Atlanta: SBL Press, 2015); Will Kynes, ed., *An Obituary for "Wisdom Literature": The Birth, Death, and Intertextual Reintegration of a Biblical Corpus* (Oxford: Oxford University Press, forthcoming).

[16] Anthony Philips, "Another Look at Adultery," *JSOT* 20 (1981): 3–25; Philips, *Ancient Israel's Criminal Law: A New Approach to the Decalogue* (New York: Schocken, 1970).

[17] Philips, "Another Look at Adultery," 19.

[18] Philips, "Another Look at Adultery," 14.

women's accountability for their crimes.[19] He suggests that the Josianic reform brought religious and political adultery into consciousness. The collapse and eventual forced migrations of the Southern Kingdom of Judah[20] is underscored by religious adultery. He uses the language of Jer 7:9 that, because the land was full of those who "steal, murder, and commit adultery" (Jer 3:8, 9; 5:7 see also 23:14; 29:23), the kingdom collapsed. There is a strong Deuteronomic tie to David's theft, adultery, and murder, which resulted in the loss of the initial ten tribes. This, then, becomes the precursor to the eventual loss and downfall of the Southern Kingdom of Judah.

In the postexilic or return migrations period, the death penalty for adultery is replaced by excommunication from the community. For Philips, unlike McKeating who argues that the death penalty was not practiced, the most severe form of punishment would have been a public stripping of the adulteress,[21] execution for adultery continued down into the first century CE. The story of the woman caught in adultery is his case in point (John 8:3–4).

In the Gospel of John, the adulteress is brought before a crowd of men—young and old. The men are described as holding stones to publicly execute the woman. In the meantime, Jesus is writing something on the ground—the subject of comments. In keeping with ancient androcentric legal (literary/scribal) tradition, only the woman is criminalized. She is already found guilty at her trial and execution. Jesus is put on the spot to take legal responsibility for proclaiming her death sentence or conversely, take the fault for releasing someone who has committed a crime. The male adulterer is not in the scene nor is her husband. But, the husband may have been among the men in the crowd since judgment was already rendered. Jesus's words to be the first to cast the stone if one is without sin (and he goes back down to write again), possibly telling her husband to cast the first stone, is portrayed by the Johannine author as the "king" who has the power to say "yes or no" to the public execution. One by one, the men depart. She is left alone with Jesus. According to the Johannine text, she is pardoned by the king. A redactor has added: "sin no more." By her acquittal, the unnamed male adulterer is also forgiven.

But what if the adulterer was the king? Who has the power to indict the king? It is with this background that we reexamine the story of David and Bathsheba as the *Sitz im Leben* for the apodictic codes: "do not murder, do not commit adultery, and do not steal." But before doing so, some reflexivity from modern social contexts.

---

[19] Philips, "Another Look at Adultery," 16.
[20] John Ahn, *Exile as Forced Migration*, BZAW 417 (Berlin: de Gruyter, 2011).
[21] H. McKeating, "Sanctions against Adultery in Ancient Israelite Society, With Some Reflections on Methodology in the Study of Old Testament Ethics," *JSOT* 11 (1979): 57–72.

Modern Social Contexts

African Context

For Gerald West, Isaiah Shembe's (a prominent first-generation African interpreter of the Bible in southern Africa) teaching on adultery, focusing on "re-membering," an oral tradition of hearing, remembering, and retelling of texts from pastors in African Independent Churches like the Ibandla lamaNazaretha, offers a unique perspective. During the early 1990s when the HIV/AIDS pandemic was at its heights, Shembe squarely placed the blame of adultery on men. In a predominately patriarchal African context, his teaching and position created a precedence.

Shembe emphasized spiritual and economic refuge for widows, orphans, and women previously held in polygamous marriages. The husbands who converted to (mission) Christianity's monogamous relationship on marriage were charged to live accordingly. Shembe systematized his views on adultery from archaic Nguni and biblical teachings on women, virgin girls, and their bodies.[22] Shembe's instruction on adultery comes from his exegesis of Gen 2 and Rom 7, summarized as: "Keep hold of yourself so that if [God] has already given the rib to another of your spiritual brethren, don't trouble it by saying 'Come my flesh,' don't cause that rib to sin before God (1 Cor 7:39). The law should be obeyed (Rom 7:4)."[23] For him, each husband has one wife, like Eve who is from Adam's rib. The responsibility is placed before the man not to commit adultery. "It is men who must control themselves. The woman's body, her shape, and her softness are not declared to be a problem—an occasion for sin, as they are in so many patriarchal texts, including the Bible. The problem is the man's inability to control his adulterous nature, calling to women who are not his rib."[24]

In a modern study by Daniel Jordan Smith on "Promiscuous Girls, Good Wives, and Cheating Husbands: Gender Inequality, Transitions to Marriage and Infidelity in Southeastern Nigeria," not surprisingly,

> women are made to feel that their sexuality belongs to their husband and his patrilineage. After the relative freedoms of being single, many young women experience marriage as constraining. But it is imperative to recognize that women are trading some forms of independence for a status that they themselves value, perhaps above all else: namely, the identity and the experience of being a married woman and a mother. While southeastern Nigerian society has relatively strict expectations regarding the sexual behavior, mobility, and overall independence of married women compared to single women, the same society also richly rewards women socially and symbolically for being wives and mothers. It would

---

[22] Gerald West, "Reading Shembe 'Re-Membering' the Bible," *Neotestamenica* 40.1 (2006): 163.
[23] West, "Reading Shembe," 176.
[24] West, "Reading Shembe," 175.

be inaccurate to suggest that young Nigerian women are somehow forced to marry against their will, reluctantly giving up the freedom and autonomy of being single. To the contrary, the overwhelming majority of young women seek marriage and parenthood as the ultimate expression and fulfillment of their ambitions for themselves as persons.[25]

Economics play a role:

Economically, the factors shaping young women's premarital and married men's extramarital sexual behavior are complex. While it would be a mistake to assume that all men's extramarital sexual behavior takes the form of so-called sugar daddy relationships, where young women are perceived to participate in sexual relationships with older married men for economic gain, or to suppose that young unmarried women's sexual relationships can be completely subsumed under this label (Luke 2005), it is certainly the case that such relationships are common in southeastern Nigeria. Some of the dynamics which are typically glossed in both academic and popular Nigerian interpretations under the label of the sugar daddy phenomenon accurately characterize features of the relationships between younger unmarried women and older married male lovers. Age and economic asymmetry feature prominently in both Nigerian discourse about women's premarital sexuality and married men's infidelity and in the actual sexual landscape. But even in sugar daddy arrangements, the motivations of both young women and married men are frequently multifaceted. Although married men who cheat on their wives with young single women are certainly seeking sex, my interviews and observations suggest that men's motives are connected to a range of aspirations related to the performance of social class and the enactment of socially rewarded masculinity for male peers (Smith 2007a, 2008).[26]

Bangladesh Context

In Southeast Asia, adultery is viewed as a serious offense.

In 2011, an Imam of a local mosque delivered a fatwa to lash a 14 year old girl 101 times in public for adultery with a married man. She dropped after 70 lashes and later died in the hospital (Ahamed & Basu, 2011). The male perpetrator of the crime was given no punishment. Hence, pre- and extra-marital sex is still considered a serious offence in rural society and punishment is severe for women than men.[27]

---

[25] Daniel Jordan Smith, "Promiscuous Girls, Good Wives, and Cheating Husbands: Gender Inequality, Transitions to Marriage and Infidelity in Southeastern Nigeria," *Anthropology Quarterly* 83.1 (2010): 124.
[26] Smith, "Promiscuous Girls," 128.
[27] Abul Hasnat Golam Quddus, "Behind the Myth of Puritan Bangladesh: Pre- and Extra Marital Sexual Reality among Lower-Class Urban Men," *Journal of Comparative Family Studies* 46.4 (2015): 454.

In urban slums, there is almost no reporting of pre- and extramarital affairs. Abul Hasnat Golam Quddus attributes this fact to peoples' individualistic, selfish, rational, and less sense of communal responsibility. In society, no matter what the norms of traditional or cultural practices may be, if a law causes harm and danger to children, in this particular case, the practice of child-brides, such norms need to be redressed and/or eliminated. Such practice has no justification and place in a world that seeks human dignity. Society needs to speak against and end such antiquated practice of marrying and impregnating children as young as eleven and fourteen.[28]

Chinese Context

In Na Zhang et al., "Sexual Infidelity in China: Prevalence and Gender-Specific Correlates," the authors begin with a series of research inquiries.

> For example, do women attempt to "trade up" in social and economic status …? Is men's impetus infidelity motivated more by sexual deficits in their stable sexual relationship while women are motivated more by a search for love and affection …? Or, are men and women more similar than different in their extra-relational quests …?[29]

The findings by the authors confirm economic and social upward mobility. In other words, there are markers that sexual infidelities among the married rise with an economic upswing and development. With striking conclusions that measure extramarital affairs in China with Norway, Britain, France, Switzerland, United States, Cameroon, Tanzania, Ivory Coast, Ethiopia, Peru, and the Philippine, the study shows that men with relatively higher or more stable income tended to exert a greater propensity toward extra-sexual activities, including adultery. Why is this significant for this study? It relates to David's newly acquired wealth and position.

Aboriginal Australian Context

Observations by three generations of anthropologists of an aboriginal community in Australia reveal fascinating social factors for adultery and other forms of extramarital affairs. "In the foreword to Meggitt's (1962) *Desert People*, Elkin characterizes the Warlpiri as a 'virile people' who 'are loyal to their social order, with 91 per cent of marriages conforming to the ideal rules; and they believe in stable marriages, particularly in the interest of their children (Elkin in Meggitt

---

[28] https://www.nytimes.com/2018/07/29/world/asia/malaysia-child-marriage.html, accessed Jun 10, 2018.

[29] Na Zhang, William L. Parish, Yingying Huang, and Suiming Pan, "Sexual Infidelity in China: Prevalence and Gender-Specific Correlates," *Arch Sex Behav* 41 (2012): 861.

1962:xii)."[30] In Meggitt's discussion, two different aspects of marriages are analyzed: first, how to get married, and second, to whom. In the explanation on how marriages occur, three forms are relayed: "the levirate," "private negotiation with the women's kinsmen (= matriline negotiations)—including the bride's price," and "promised or arranged marriage," which takes place through the practice of circumcision by the man who becomes the husband's father-in-law.[31]

In the Warlpiri language, there are terms to describe sexual activity, partners, and even desires inside and outside of marriage:

> *Warrura* = marriage partner or lover not in the correct kin relation. Often translated as 'slut' (used both for males and females)
> *Wingki* = wrong, antisocial, unlawful, uncompliant, immoral, heedless, disobedient
> *Vaninja* = throat, being in love, feeling sexual desire, yearning, lustful, amorous, lover, girlfriend, boyfriend.[32]

According to Musharbash, any woman or wife in a marriage can be identified as a *warrura* (in a marriage, in a boyfriend/girlfriend relationship, or when running around). She notes that the sexual act does not render this naming or title, but the kin relationship that is broken because of the woman/man and the sexual partner. Moreover, *wingki* describes sex between "wrong" partners resulting in a collapse of social order and decorum.

> In summary, "right and wrong" do not refer to the kind of relationship (marriage, affair, or casual sex) but to the (classificatory kin) relations between the partners concerned. Such a morality is quite censorious in terms of decorum defined by the social (kinship) norms of how people should relate to each other but extremely tolerant of the intense force of emotions such as love, lust and desire in people's lives. This does seem to be a fairly straight forward continuation from Meggitt's times. What has changed, however, is that in the past, marriages seem to have withstood the turbulences caused by adultery much better. In the past, marriage was a contractual arrangement between matrilines. There was further investment in the marriage by the husband's patriline with the advent of children, who were initiated into and carried on the patriline's rights and responsibilities in regard to land.... While potentially economically independent, genders combined their subsistence forays, and nuclear (and extended) families were tight economic units with clearly gender-defined rights and responsibilities. Love appears to have been an added bonus, and its potential absence in a marriage was one reason behind the numerous liaisons Meggitt described.[33]

---

[30] Yasmine Musharbash, "Marriage, Love Magic, and Adultery: Warlpiri Relationships as Seen by Three Generations of Anthropologists," *Oceania* 80 (2010): 279.
[31] Musharbash, "Marriage, Love Magic, and Adultery," 279.
[32] Musharbash, "Marriage, Love Magic, and Adultery," 279.
[33] Musharbash, "Marriage, Love Magic, and Adultery," 280–81.

American Context[34]

In "Religion, Infidelity, and Divorce: Reexamining the Effect of Religious Behavior on Divorce Among Long-Married Couples," Joshua D. Tuttle and Shannon N. Davis note that

> One key finding on U.S. couples is that religiosity promotes strong marital bonds and preserves traditional marital and sexual norms. Religious couples are characterized by higher levels of marital happiness and marital stability compared to nonreligious couples.... Married religious individuals are less likely to cheat on their spouses than nonreligious, married individuals.... Furthermore, marriages characterized by a high level of religiosity commitment are less likely to dissolve through separation or divorce than those characterized by a low level of religiosity.[35]

Yet, according to Alfred DeMaris (2013),[36] religious couples that have been marriage together for quite some time, when confronted with a martial affair often end in divorce as well. "What these new researches have provided in measuring the relative level of happiness in marriage—sexual relationship—is significant. The processes through which religious behaviors influence marriage, and subsequent divorce, are more subtle than previously thought."[37]

In American politics, former President Bill Clinton's affair with Monica Lewinsky drew much attention, especially by those who focused on the family. The starting point in family circles was: Did Bill Clinton commit adultery? Recall what the former president said: "I did not have sexual relations with that woman." He created and attempted to parse out a legal definition of what sexual relations is. But the simple question repeated: Did or did he not commit adultery? The fact of the matter is, Ms. Lewinsky was not married (still is not) at the time of her rendezvous. Thus, according to biblical definition, Bill Clinton technically did not commit adultery.[38] However, let's reverse the role and create a subjunctive-hypothetical. Should Hillary Clinton have won the election in 2016, and she was in the

---

[34] Jenna Weissman Joselit, *Set in Stone: America's Embrace of the Ten Commandments* (Oxford: Oxford University Press, 2017); Michael Coogan, *The Ten Commandments: A Short History of an Ancient Text* (New Haven, CT: Yale University Press, 2014).

[35] Joshua D. Tuttle and Shannon N. Davis, "Religion, Infidelity, and Divorce: Reexamining the Effect of Religious Behavior on Divorce among Long-Married Couples," *Journal of Divorce and Remarriage* 56 (2015): 475–76.

[36] Alfred DeMaris, "Burning the Candle at Both Ends: Extramatrial Sex as a Precursor of Martial Disruption," *Journal of Family Issues* 34.11 (2013): 1474–99.

[37] Tuttle and Davis, "Religion, Infidelity, and Divorce," 487.

[38] In English common law, adultery was a felony. According to the State of New York, adultery is defined as: a person who engages in sexual intercourse with another person at the time when he has a living spouse, or the other person has a living spouse. In 2001, the

oval office and decided to have her own rendezvous, she would be guilty of adultery regardless of whether the man is married or unmarried. By virtue of her marriage, according to the biblical definition, she would be liable.[39]

Summary

In the case studies presented above, the African and Chinese contexts point to economic advancements. With the rise in the economic status of men, engagements in adultery or other forms of sexual activity outside marriage increases. Over the observation of three generations by anthropologists, the Warlpiri society carefully demarcates and highlights the role of social and kin relationships that are equally important if not more than economic (land) and passing down the inheritance. These insights may offer something new beyond past examinations in the story of David and Bathsheba.

DAVID AND BATHSHEBA'S ADULTERY[40]

In Lev 20:10 and Deut 22:22, adultery is deemed a serious offense. If a man commits adultery with the wife of his neighbor, both the adulterer and the adulteress deserve death (Lev 20:10). In the Deuteronomy passage, however, the language is more technical: "If a man is found lying with a married woman who has a husband," clearly not a widow, "then both of them shall die—the man who slept with her and the woman" (Deut 22:22). In the book of Hosea, the subject matter of adultery is complicated by the identity of the women in Hos 1–2 and Hos 3.[41] If Hosea took a married woman (another woman besides Gomer in Hos 3), he is liable for adultery and even possibly death. But the text makes it clear that Hosea

---

State of Virginia prosecuted John Bushey for adultery, resulting in a guilty plea and a fine of $125. The United States military law has provisions prohibiting adultery.

[39] In the United States, adultery is outlawed in twenty-one states. In the State of New York, adultery is a misdemeanor, punishable by a fine of $500 or ninety days in jail.

[40] David Bosworth, "Faith and Resilience: King David's Reaction to the Death of Bathsheba's Firstborn," *CBQ* 73.4 (2011): 691–707; Anne Létourneau, "Beauty, Bath, and Beyond: Framing Bathsheba as a Royal Fantasy in 2 Sam 11, 1–5," *SJOT* 32 (2018): 72–91; Chichang Li, "Doing Theology in Chinese Context: The David-Bathsheba Story and the Parable of Nathan," *East Asia Journal of Theology* 3.2 (1985): 243–57; Alexander Izuchukwu Abasil, "Was It Rape? The David and Bathsheba Pericope Re-Examined," *VT* 61.1 (2011): 1–15; Jong-Hee Son, "'אני אמלך': 다윗왕위 계승순위의 뒤틀림," 구약논단 22.2 (2016): 98–131; Sandra Shimoff, "David and Bathsheba: The Political Function of Rabbinic Aggada," *JSJ* 24.2 (1993): 246–56; Moshe Garsiel, "The Story of David and Bathsheba: A Different Approach," *CBQ* 55.2 (1993): 244–62.

[41] Tchavdar Hadjiev, "Adultery, Shame, and Sexual Pollution in Ancient Israel and in Hosea: A Response to Joshua Moon," *JSOT* 41.2 (2016): 221–36.

and the woman in chapter 3 did not have sexual relationship, at least for the appointed period of time that Hosea purchased her. But the rumors and charges of the situation would have been scandalous and incendiary, casting doubt and suspicion, charging Hosea with adultery, even if he claimed his innocence: the prophet who committed adultery. As surprising or shocking as that may or may not be, the original sex-lies-and-video tape belongs to David and Bathsheba. Charging the king with adultery would have been difficult, if not impossible. How could a subordinate implicate the king of wrong doing? "Uriah could hardly have been a real threat to David, unless the legal implications were more serious than those described above, and if only the husband (not the community) was entitled to bring the charge (Num 5:11–15)," writes Arnold A. Anderson.[42]

In "Gaps, Ambiguity, and the Reading Process," Meir Sternberg suggests three possibilities: "David thinks that Uriah does not know," "Uriah knows what David knows," and "David does not know like the reader." Sternberg's reading of David is that his feelings toward Bathsheba was not "fire with love."[43] Rather, it was a one-night stand, a "young and the restless" moment. In a staccato of fast paced verbs, David "sent and inquired, then he took her, she came to him, he lay with her, and she returned" (2 Sam 11:3–4)[44]; may have been consensual, at least as Larry Lyke reads the text.[45] But victims are often without voice in the Hebrew Bible (e.g., Judg 19). In Lyke's reading, however, the entire plot and ploy was a grand seductive plan of Bathsheba to become the Queen mother. Her words: "I am with child" reveal her true intent. However, Sternberg sees David's action as "a man who regrets his involvement and is now trying to evade the consequences. An intoxicated lover and a king at that, would not have given up Bathsheba so readily,"[46] unless, even as the king, the charges of adultery was something that was of serious threat. Sternberg says that Bathsheba's beauty was mentioned only by the narrator (and not by David).

In my reading, it would have been virtually impossible for David not to have known the wife of one of his mighty thirty, Uriah the Hittite, a member of his inner circle of fellow warriors. Rhetorical features are at work in the text. Indeed, there are uncertainties and gaps in the narrative. But one thing is clear, adultery was committed between a married man (David) and a married woman (Bathsheba) with a husband (Uriah the Hittite). The adulterer is the king. In the conclusion of 2 Sam 11, the editor remarks: "The *thing* (word/matter/deed) that David had done was evil in the eyes of the LORD" (2 Sam 11:27). This evil casts more ambiguity

---

[42] A. A. Anderson, *2 Samuel*, WBC (Dallas: Word Books, 1989), 155–56.

[43] Meir Sternberg, *The Poetics of Biblical Narrative: Ideological Literature and the Drama of Reading* (Bloomington: Indiana University Press, 1987), 210.

[44] Sternberg, *Poetics of Biblical Narrative*, 197.

[45] Larry L. Lyke, *King David with the Wise Woman of Tekoa: The Resonance of Tradition in Parabolic Narrative*, LHBOTS 255 (Sheffield: Sheffield Academic, 1997).

[46] Sternberg, *Poetics of Biblical Narrative*, 210.

and legal questions: "Was the evil: murder, adultery, or stealing?" Or, all of the above?

The sexual encouter took place in David's home. According to laws that define and limit where the sexual encounter took place, there are hardly any regulations denoting a king's residence. The episode occurred during the day time. The information that Bathsheba bathed, perhaps in full purview and knowledge of David walking on the roof of his house is an understatement. An editor has inserted the comment that she was bathing after her period, which makes clear that the child that David and Bathsheba would conceive belongs to David and not Uriah. Later in the chapter, when David is confronted by Nathan the prophet, a משל is used to tell a story of a rich man stealing an ewe-lamb from a poor man.[47] We immediately hear the bifurcation of socioeconomic class. If the poor man represents Uriah the Hittite (or Bathsheba's father), this would suggest either Bathsheba came from a lower socioeconomic class or had married up to get closer to the inner circle, in close proximity to the palace (geographically). There is suspect in the words, "she came to him." David is angered and proclaims that the perpetrator should die; then offered financial recompense. Again, a reference to a possible payment for taking a woman's virginity. David's emotional outburst permits Nathan to sustain the tension and infamously utter the words: אתה האיש. Nathan never directly charges David of adultery or for that matter, murder; though he is charged with stealing—kidnapping a woman—or kidnapping a married woman. Only by the work of another (later) editor does the text add the two additional crimes: the LORD was angry at the murder and taking "his wife" (2 Sam 12:7–12).

David acknowledges his iniquity: "I have sinned against Yahweh" (2 Sam 12:13). However, he never says he sinned against Uriah or Bathsheba. The words "adultery" and "murder" are never mentioned in the text. Ironically, David is shown mercy. He does not die. Neither does Bathsheba. At some point, the reader must reconstruct that even if Bathsheba cried out for help in the palace, her outcry went unheard. Or conversely, she brilliantly played David into an incredible trap that would eventually make her and her son the heir of the kingdom. The story closes with two deaths or killings/murders—that of Uriah the Hittite and the child of David and Bathsheba (in place of David and Bathsheba).

Hittite Law 198 (see above) sheds light on Uriah the Hittite's decision to sleep at the gate of the palace. He does not have direct evidence that something isn't right. It's all circumstantial. However, when the king repeatedly says, "go down and wash your feet," a euphuism to have sex with his wife, Uriah understood the implication of what may have transpired. It is in this context that I see Uriah making a claim through his action to spare the life of his wife and that of the adulterer, his neighbor and commander in chief, King David. Uriah never goes down to

---

[47] John Ahn, "Ezekiel 15: A משל," in *The Prophets Speak on Forced Migrations,* ed. Mark Boda et al., AIL 21 (Atlanta: SBL Press, 2015), 101–19.

wash his feet. This was his subaltern way of saying, if you are with child, I am not the father. He is making a powerful point that the king and his wife are both guilty; and though deserving death, he was saving them. Uriah offers forgiveness. David plots murder. Indeed, there is ambiguity and complexity, as in any twisted relationship. In my view, this narrative acts as the backdrop and text against the prohibitions: "do not murder, do not commit adultery, and do not steal." The authors or tradents did not have to enumerate or expand. What is brilliantly remarkable is that these three codes in the Decalogue were preserved and passed down in its short-final protected form without any future emendations by succeeding generations of scribes.

The Decalogue

The Decalogue is understood as "fundamental principles which give its special quality to the concept of the sanctity of life."[48] In general, the first five stipulations relay a relationship between the suzerain and the individual or community. The second five relates to the community or humanity respecting the rights and dignity of fellow humanity. If the first five are specific to Israel, the second set is universal in message.[49]

Moshe Greenberg notes that the personal and ethical message of the decalogue (addressed to you, second person masculine singular pronoun) finds home in an Egyptian text (names of deities omitted), which highlights correct ethos and praxis of living an honorable life. The following first eleven lines are from "Protestation of Guiltless" of the dead a New Kingdom (sixteenth-century text):

(1) I have not committed evil
(2) I have not stolen
(3) I have not been covetous
(4) I have not robbed
(5) I have not killed men
(6) I have not damaged the grain measure
(7) I have not caused crookedness
(8) I have not stolen the property of a god
(9) I have not told lies
(10) I have not taken away food
(11) I have not committed adultery[50]

---

[48] Shalom Albeck, "The Ten Commandments and the Essence of Religious Faith," in *Ten Commandments in History and Tradition*, 282.
[49] Moshe Greenberg, "The Decalogue Tradition Critically Examined," in *Ten Commandments in History and Tradition*, 112.
[50] Greenberg, "Decalogue Tradition Critically Examined," 110–11.

Moshe Weinfeld echoes Philo of Alexanderia (*Dec.* 39) and Martin Buber, saying that the personal characteristic of the Decalogue is unique because if a dictum is merely addressed to a small or large group, then, the individual gets lost in the crowd. However, if the address is individualized, even in a large crowd, the person who hears those words cannot evade the commandment and cannot use the crowd as an excuse.[51]

With respect to adultery, Greenberg notes that the seventh commandment was defined as a sexual relationship between a man and a married woman. Greenberg makes a distinction between נאף ("to commit adultery") and זנה traditionally rendered "to fornicate" but described it as a willing participation in sexual intercourse with a man not one's husband.[52] Rashi, using Exod 23:13 and Deut 5:17 expressed the view that adultery was between the woman who was the wife of a married man and any man. Ibn Ezra disagreed and pressed for a coterminus understanding of נאף and זנה.[53] Although every case of adultery is considered fornication, not every act of fornication is considered adultery. Ezra Melammed consider a reference to such practice not only in the the Decalogue but also the shema:[54]

Decalogue	Shema
You shall not commit adultery	do not follow heart and eyes in your lustful urge

Brevard Childs notes that the commandment against adultery was employed to maintain the union of marriage and that the subject of the verb נאף could be both man and woman. Childs outlines differences between שכב "to lie down," זנה "to commit harlotry," and נאף "to commit adultery;" while providing examples of adultery narratives and other passages in the Old Testament.[55] Sarna notes that in the social setting of Israel, polygamy was accepted but not polyandry. Adultery is mutually consented sexual intercourse between a married woman and a man who was not her husband. Adultery is deemed a severe crime since it is situated between murder and theft. If one takes these commandments as divinely inspired, the aftereffects have even more weight.[56]

At the social level, marriage is considered an important institution, forming social adaptability. The prohibition against adultery serves to protect the family

---

[51] Moshe Weinfeld, "The Uniqueness of the Decalogue and Its Place in Jewish Tradition," in *Ten Commandments in History and Tradition*, 10.
[52] Greenberg, "Decalogue Tradition Critically Examined," 104–5.
[53] See Shalom Albeck, "The Ten Commandments and the Essence of Religious Faith," in *Ten Commandments in History and Tradition*, 280.
[54] Ezra Zion Melammed, "'Observance' and 'Remember' Spoken in One Utterances, in *Ten Commandments in History and Tradition*, 213.
[55] Brevard S. Childs, *Exodus*, OTL (Louisville: Westminster, 1974), 422.
[56] Nahum M. Sarna, *Exodus*, JPS Torah Commentary (Philadelphia: JPS, 1991), 114.

and society.⁵⁷ Since the days of Emile Durkheim, family sociology has functioned to protect against anomie.⁵⁸

Terence Fretheim states that this commandment serves to protect the family. He adds that there has been an androcentric bent in which women are always guilty whereas men are deemed not guilty if the woman was not married.⁵⁹ According to John Durham, adultery is read as a breach of covenant between Yahweh and Israel.⁶⁰ Walter Harrelson's interpretation of the adultery code is noted below:⁶¹

> Indeed, it might be possible to say that this commandment, perhaps more than any other in the list, must be set aside today, as persons have learned a new joy and fulfillment in life through the adoption of much freer relations between human beings sexually. Many a person today—indeed many a Christian theologian today, may want to urge the Christian community to avoid at all costs any narrow code of sexual conduct, since such narrow teachings in earlier times have done grave damage to individuals and to families and to the larger human community.... Marriage may itself be a somewhat outmoded institution today.... The two partners may by open decision agree that sexual relations with others are acceptable, perhaps within agreed-upon bounds. Why not? Sometimes it is said, sexual relations outside marriage improve the marriage, as one or other partner learns what is enriching and fulfilling in sexual relation.⁶²

Without going into a diatribe, in my view, Harrelson is wide of the mark. The institution of family and the economic unit, bound in a covenantal relationship, which extends to children and the land, is the cornerstone of society's belonging, boundary, and group/self-identity. In the holiness code of Lev 20:10, adultery is defined as *a man* who has a sexual affair with his neighbor's wife, the repetition or dittography in the text emphasizes the *man* who commits the adultery. Nathan charged David, the man, with stealing a neighbor's wife, which led to adultery. The implications of adultery are revealed in the unfolding description of Nathan's משל concerning the poor man: who took care of and loved the ewe—as it used to eat out of his hand, it (she) was family to him. Notwithstanding, Nathan represents a prophetic tradition, which according to Bosman is said to have influenced the Decalogue. Major prophetic texts that deal with adultery include the following:

---

⁵⁷ Scott Coltrane and Randall Collins, *Sociology of Marriage and the Family: Gender, Love, and Property*, 5th ed. (Belmont, CA: Wadsworth, 2000); Raymond Westbrook, *Property and the Family in Biblical Law* (Sheffield: JSOT Press, 1991).

⁵⁸ Peter Berger and Hansfried Kellner, "Marriage and the Construction of Reality: An Exercise in the Microsociology of Knowledge," *Diogenes* 46 (1964): 1–23.

⁵⁹ Terence Fretheim, *Exodus*, IBC (Louisville: John Knox, 1991), 234–35.

⁶⁰ John I. Durham, *Exodus*, WBC (Waco, TX: Word Books, 1987), 293–94.

⁶¹ Walter J. Harrelson, *Ten Commandments and Human Rights* (Macon, GA: Mercer University Press, 1997), 178–79; see notes 35 and 37.

⁶² Harrelson, *Ten Commandments and Human Rights*, 109–10.

Isa 57:3	adultery = man who commits adultery + (woman who commits harlotry)
Jer 3:8–9	adultery = idolatry + sexual infidelity against Yahweh
Jer 5:7–8	adultery = idolatry + sexual lust for another's wife
Jer 7:9	adultery = adultery (// decalogue Exod 20:14 or Deut 5:18)
Jer 9:1	adultery = adulterers (participle- committing adultery), band of traitors (//Ps 50:18 [9:2 in English])
Jer 23:10	adultery = land full of adulterers
Jer 23:14	adultery = prophets commit adultery, walk in lies
Jer 29:23	adultery = Zedekiah and Ahab roasted in fire for committing adultery with neighbor's wives in exile
Ezek 16:32	adultery = adulterous wife, strangers instead of husband
Ezek 16:38	adultery = woman who commits adultery
Ezek 23:37	adultery = adultery (fornication) + idolatry
Ezek 23:43	adultery = adultery, sexual acts, harlotry
Ezek 23:45	adultery = whore, adultery, bloodshed
Hos 3:1	adultery = woman with a lover + idolatry
Hos 4:2	adultery = adultery (//decalogue)
Hos 4:13	adultery = idolatry + adultery/sexual
Hos 4:14	adultery = daughters-in-law commit adultery with men
Mal 3:5	adultery = adulterer and adulteress
Ps 50:18	adultery = friends with thief and keep company with adulteress (//Jer 9:1 {9:2})
Prov 6:32	adultery = No sense, one who destroys himself
Prov 30:20	adultery = sexual intercourse and no guilt or wrong doing
Job 24:15	adultery = at twilight in disguise + oppression/ violence

Based on these and other texts, it is difficult to assess fully, or arrive at a conclusion that prophets influenced the prohibition against adultery or for that matter, stealing and killing or murder. Prophets reflect society.[63] However, in these texts, the prophets have employed and even abused adultery for their own textual and political/religious gains. The personal and private are exploited. These texts or traditions do not appear to add any inventiveness, imagination, or voice in the summation of "do not murder, do not commit adultery, and do not steal." Rather, the Jeremanic text's threefold echo of the Decalogue (Jer 3:8, 9) appears to be an act of scripturalization or inner biblical exegesis of David and Bathsheba. The prophets read adultery as a metaphor. There is nothing metaphoric about a king who abused his power to sleep with the wife of his subordinate, and then, had him killed. Although no one was above the king, the Deuteronomist reminds the king that the law is above the king; and the law judges the king. There is much social and self-reflexivity in our narrative and the Decalogue.

---

[63] See Robert R. Wilson, *Prophecy and Society in Ancient Israel* (Philadelphia: Fortress, 1984).

Anthony Giddens

Anthony Giddens notes in his *Modernity and Self-Identity* that: (1) The self is reflexive—"we are not what we are, but what we make of ourselves."[64] (2) The self is a trajectory of the past to guide the future—"awareness of various phases of the lifespan ... becomes the dominant 'foreground figure' in the *Gestalt* sense." (3) Self reflexivity is on-going and at key moments forces us to pause and ask: What is happening right now? What am I thinking? What am I doing? What am I feeling? How am I breathing? (4) Self-identity has a narrative—the self is made explicit through the narrative. (5) Self-actualization suggests that time is being controlled—"'Holding a dialogue with time', is the very basis of self-realization."[65] (6) Awareness of the body is as an extension of self-reflexivity (How am I breathing?). (7) Self-actualization is a balance between opportunity and risk— letting go of oppressive emotions and creating opportunities for self-development. (8) Moral thread of self-actualization is being true to oneself, disentangling the true from the false self. (9) Life is seen as a series of "passages."[66]

When we analyze 2 Sam 11–12 through Giddens (1) both David had his own reasons for the affair: he has amassed economic prosperity, unified the kingdom, others can go out to war on his behalf while he stays home, felt he could do whatever he pleased, including sexual boredom. As for Bathsheba: she may have been unsatisfied in her (inter)marriage to Uriah the Hittite, desired greater status and power, including economic advancement, wanted to be in the palace, etc. Both are made out to be who they wanted to be as the fientive verbs denote: "he took her and she came unto him" (ויקחה ותבוא). Because of the adultery, Bathsheba benefits and becomes the Queen Mother. For David, his future line would be from Bathsheba—Solomon. (3) In the immediacy of the events following David's adultery: What is happening right now? What am I thinking? What am I doing? What am I feeling? How am I breathing? David's initial request to Joab ("Send me Uriah the Hittite"; 2 Sam 11:6) to his last "Set Uriah in the forefront of the battle and retire from him" (2 Sam 11:15) are juxtaposed with his several unsuccessful attempts, including getting Uriah drunk, to go down to his house and sleep with his wife. When his plan to have Uriah appear to be the father of the child fails, David's anxiety level rises to the point of premediated assassination, exposing a killer's instinct, which he suppressed against King Saul—an upper class—but not against a Hittite. After Uriah's death, David takes Bathsheba in, but such a deed does not rectify or justify the wrong. The child born to David and Bathsheba stops breathing. And during the illness of the infant, all the feelings and emotions of David are on full display. Only after the infant's death, David once again eats,

---

[64] Giddens, *Modernity and Self-Identity*, 75.
[65] Giddens, *Modernity and Self-Identity*, 77.
[66] Giddens, *Modernity and Self-Identity*, 79.

anoints himself, and goes to worship. (4) This narrative is one of the most recognized cultural memory stories in the Hebrew Bible. Embedded in the text are themes of loyalty, honor, shame, faithfulness, and love for God mixed with murder, adultery, and theft (2 Sam 11–12).

(5) Time is a relevant factor as time is needed for the birth of another child, Solomon. In due course, it would be Bathsheba, Nathan and others (Zadok, Benaiah, Shimei, Rei, and Solomon) who are left out of the coronation ceremony of Adonijah (1 Kgs 1). It would be Nathan and Bathsheba who would appear before David's death bed and usurp the throne. (6) As Giddens expands on the body and food consumption, he says: "Fasting, and the self-denial of various kinds of foodstuffs, have obviously long been part of religious practices, and are found in many different cultural frameworks."[67] Anorexia mirabilis (distinctive from anorexia nervosa) is a form of protest and it raises urgency and strength. David fasted while the child was alive. "He said, I fasted and wept; for I said: who knows whether the Lord will not be gracious to me, that the child may live?" (2 Sam 12:22).

(7) In opportunity and risk, David's confession: חטאתי ליהוה casts him as a model for excellence, that is, even after doing something wrong, to acknowledge that serious mistake, and for God to offer David a second chance, has become the hallmark in religious societies. Moreover, Bathsheba's calculated risk paid dividends. (8) David's moral thread is finally untangled in his reflection and reflexivity when he hears about Absalom who pitched a tent on the rooftop of the king's house and had sexual intercourse with his father's ten concubines (2 Sam 15:16). A heightened replay of David's affair is repeated by his own son. (9) Finally, the entire court narrative of David, including his final request to Solomon concerning Joab and Shimei but showing kindness to the sons of Barzillai (1 Kgs 2) are series of passages.

Giddens explains that "control" is a key factor in modernity. I would extend that into an ancient society that was emerging into a nation or city-state, toward "an internally referential system of knowledge and power"[68] or to use Gidden's language, "uncontrol" resulted when the last Davidic king and his royal family were displaced and resettled to Babylonia in 597 BCE. The underclass would follow in 587 and 582 BCE.

Conclusion

In his chapter on "Sequestration of Experience," Giddens explains that sequestration is necessary for establishing security in day to day life. "Ontological security, in other words, is sustained primarily through routine itself."[69] "Sequestration is not a once-and-for-all phenomenon, and it does not represent a set of frictionless

---

[67] Giddens, *Modernity and Self-Identity*, 104.
[68] Giddens, *Modernity and Self-Identity*, 144.
[69] Giddens, *Modernity and Self-Identity*, 167.

boundaries.... The frontiers of sequestered experience are faultiness, full of tensions and poorly mastered forces; or to shift the metaphor, they are battlegrounds, sometimes of a directly social character, but often within the psychological field of the self."[70]

For David and Bathsheba, the five-fold sequestration of experience (madness, criminality, sickness and death, sexuality, and nature) are a fitting conclusion. (1) The social incorporation of madness: "(the expression of traits of personality and behavior which touch on experiences 'bracketed out' by ordinary attitudes of ontological security),"[71] initially attributed to God's will in an ancient setting reveals the forces of a bifurcated world—those of the dominant being protected from the minority. David's madness rests on his personality and behavior, which acted and resulted in "stealing, adultery, and murder." (2) Criminality "(the expression of traits of personality and behavior which many represent 'alternatives' to routine concerns and involvements)" was so significant that the Deuteronomist created a triad of laws to keep a king or future kings in check. (3) Sickness and death (connecting points between social life and external criteria concerning mortality and finitude) cannot have been scripted any better to highlight these finite markers of humanity. (4) The sexuality (eroticism as a form of connection between individuals and the continuities of the generations) of David and the wife of Uriah, echoes in the text and subtly, behind the commandments "do not kill, do not commit adultery, and do not steal." "Sexuality has then become, as Luhmann might put it, a 'communicative code' rather than a phenomenon integrated with the wider exigencies of human existence."[72] And finally (5) nature (the natural environment as constituted independently of human social activity) is demarcated from built environments like a city. In our narrative, the incident took place in a recently acquired city, Jerusalem. In an urban setting (as referenced in the Bangladesh's case),

> the very routines that provide such security mostly lack moral meaning and can either come to be experienced as "empty" practices, or alternatively can seem to be overwhelming. When routines, for whatever reason, become radically disrupted, or where someone specifically sets out to achieve a greater reflexive control over her or his self-identity, *existential crises are likely to occur.*[73]

It is this existential crisis that has been captured and preserved in Nathan's parable but also reproduced as a communicative code in the Decalogue to remind the community that the only way to check a king's abuse of power was through legal precedence, ironically without consequences. In closing, what is noteworthy is relationships, the preservation and proper maintenance of David's kin relationships as well as Bathsheba's in a natural sense were both compromised (Warlpiri

---

[70] Giddens, *Modernity and Self-Identity*, 168.
[71] Giddens, *Modernity and Self-Identity*, 168.
[72] Giddens, *Modernity and Self-Identity*, 164.
[73] Giddens, *Modernity and Self-Identity*, 167 (my italics).

society). Yet, a new remarkable relationship developed and continued, from one generation to another, across the ages, which suggests that the unconditioned apodictic laws that guard against such fissures, would give rise to not only future canonical consciousness governing murder, adultery, and theft, but also mercy, forgiveness, and grace.

ETHICS OF REMEMBERING: SCAPEGOATING MANASSEH AFTER THE SEWOL FERRY TRAGEDY

Koog-Pyoung Hong

On April 16, 2014, a ferry carrying 476 lives sank in the southwestern sea of Korea. Two hundred ninety-nine died with five still missing. The incompetence and indifference in the South Korean government's management of the disaster was striking to the point of arousing public fury. The government's reaction to criticism was equally disappointing. Rather than admitting to mismanagement and showing contrition, the government's reaction was denial, excuses, and attempts to cover up. The public outrage, after a series of related scandals, led to the impeachment of President Park Geun-hye on March 10, 2017, three years later.

The Sewol Ferry tragedy reminded Korean theologians of an age-old theological quandary, evoked repeatedly in human history when an unimaginable event like the Holocaust occurs.[1] Why is there evil and suffering in this world that was created by a benevolent God? Where was God when hundreds of innocent lives were sinking underneath water? These questions often lead to the denial of the existence of an omnipotent, omniscient, and benevolent God, which induces theologians, in turn, to defend God. The question and challenge are readily attested in the Bible. The Hebrew Bible is replete with literature that struggles with the problem of evil and suffering.[2] One of them is the Deuteronomistic History (DtrH). DtrH struggles with the fall of Judah. Facing the subsequent theological question, the historian(s) offer an answer from the perspective of theodicy. It is not because of the incapability or negligence of Yhwh but the result of Israel's

---

This is a revised version of an article originally published in Korean in *Theological Forum* 79 (2015): 69–103. It is used here with permission.

[1] A number of theological works have been published after the Sewol Ferry tragedy. See, e.g., NCCK Sewol Disaster Task Force, ed., *Theology of the Remnants: The Memory, Fury, and Thereafter* (Seoul: Dongyeon, 2015); The Society of Korean Cultural Theology, ed., *Theology after Sewol: Weep with Those Who Weep* (Seoul: Mosinunsaramdeul, 2015); Yungsik Park, *Where Was God on That Day? Sewol and the Task of Christian Faith* (Seoul: Holy Wave Plus, 2015).

[2] See James L. Crenshaw, ed., *Theodicy in the Old Testament* (Philadelphia: Fortress, 1983); Crenshaw, *Defending God: Biblical Responses to the Problem of Evil* (Oxford: Oxford University Press, 2005).

infidelity to the covenant they made with their God. This historical perspective, based on theodicy, salvages their God from accusations in the wake of the devastation of God's temple, land, and people. Yet, this rescue came with heavy cost. Israel, a victim in historical fact, was victimized again by a theological discourse.

This essay addresses a particular scapegoat mechanism inherent in a discourse of theodicy.[3] Justifying God requires a sacrifice. I address this question in relation to the Sewol Ferry tragedy because a scapegoat mechanism has been utilized in post-Sewol social discourse in Korea. In the wake of the Sewol sinking, Koreans were swept by the question of *who is responsible for this*? The usual targets include Yoo Byung-un, the owner of the ferry company, Lee Joon-seok, the captain of the crew, corrupt government officials, and President Park. Both Yoo Byung-un and Lee Joon-seok have been the targets of harsh media coverage. Yoo's strange career as a founder of a cult responsible for a mass suicide in 1987,[4] and Lee's irresponsible behavior in abandoning the ship and passengers while saving his own life, made them savory targets for the media. Yoo was later found dead,[5] an incident that remains a mystery, and Lee has been sentenced to life in prison.[6]

There is no question that these people are utterly responsible for the incident. I have no intention in defending or exonerating them. The question is who benefits from this scapegoat mechanism. There is no doubt that scapegoating these individuals played a significant role in diverting attention from others who shared responsibility for the disaster.[7] That is why so much attention has been given to President Park's "seven missing hours."[8] The focus of this essay is about the similar dynamic between the absence of the divine or human leader in the wake of

---

[3] For a theoretical discussion on scapegoating, see René Girard, *The Scapegoat* (London: Athlone, 1986).

[4] http://time.com/74967/south-korea-ferry-sewol-chonghaejin-investigation/, accessed Jun 10, 2018.

[5] https://www.washingtonpost.com/news/morning-mix/wp/2014/07/22/the-strange-saga-of-now-dead-billionaire-south-korean-ferry-owner-yoo-byung-un/, accessed Jun 10, 2018.

[6] https://www.nytimes.com/2015/11/13/world/asia/south-korea-ferry-captain-conviction-sewol.html, accessed Jun 10, 2018.

[7] See Poong-In Lee, "The Sewol Ferry Disaster and the Scapegoat Mechanism," *Presbyterian Theological Quarterly* 319 (2014): 87–112.

[8] After the incident, President Park failed to make a public appearance for seven hours, which led to a probe on the negligence and all sorts of conspiracy theories on the president's whereabouts and private life. See https://www.koreatimes.co.kr/www/news/nation/2016/11/116_217395.html, accessed Jun 10, 2018. It has been only recently revealed that Park was meeting with her private counsel, Choi Soon-sil. Choi's inappropriate influence on Park over many important official decisions was a major cause for Park's impeachment. See http://koreajoongangdaily.joins.com/news/article/article.aspx?aid=3046205, accessed Jun 10, 2018.

the people's suffering and the way the scapegoat mechanism is employed to divert attention from the negligence.

When the text engages in a discourse of violence, how should modern readers deal with it? I tackle this question by reassessing the Deuteronomist's evaluation of Manasseh. Manasseh is an intriguing figure, so far as he is blamed for the fall of the kingdom of Judah. It is unusual that a single person is blamed for a national calamity, but the extreme nature of the claim makes one wonder whether Manasseh is being scapegoated by the text, and for what purpose. I ask this question not from a historical perspective in terms of the formation of DtrH or the reconstruction of the historical Manasseh,[9] but from a theological and ethical perspective. How should we read this scapegoating from the post-Sewol Korean context?

DEUTERONOMISTIC IDEOLOGY AND SCAPEGOATING OF MANASSEH

It is no secret that the Deuteronomist (Dtr) has a distinct theological perspective that is imbued in his historical project. There is no objective history free of the historian's perspective. This means that the past memories or traditions, are unwittingly censored through an ideological lens. What fits the perspective is preserved, what does not fit is discarded. Then, we face an uncomfortable question. To what extent can we trust Dtr's distorted memory?

The degree of influence of a historian's perspective may vary. Suppose that there is a Korean history written according to the pro-Japanese colonial perspective. Even though the history is based on a colonial perspective, not every bit of its account can be declared as fabrication. There are certain aspects, however, that colonial perspectives tend to highlight: negative descriptions of Korea and positive appraisals of Japanese regime. If so, a healthy and responsible way of reading the colonialist history of Korea would be to read them with due reservations, or with *hermeneutics of suspicion*.

How about DtrH then? As noted above, one may characterize DtrH as a history from the perspective of theodicy.[10] It advocates God who remained silent during the national calamity and redirects the cause of the fall elsewhere, in defense of God. This reflects the theological struggles and challenges that the exiled

---

[9] It is difficult to restore the historical Manasseh due to the paucity of the hard evidence from biblical and extrabiblical sources. For a recent discussion, see Ernst Axel Knauf, "The Glorious Days of Manasseh," in *Good Kings and Bad Kings*, ed. Lester L. Grabbe, LHBOTS 393 (London: T&T Clark, 2005), 164–88. Past studies on Manasseh tended to focus on the redactional issue of the passages that address Manasseh's sin. The composition of DtrH is a critical issue but evades the main focus of this study, which aims to tackle the role of the reader in the context of the present form of the canonical text.

[10] See Marvin A. Sweeney, *Reading the Hebrew Bible after the Shoah: Engaging Holocaust Theology* (Minneapolis: Fortress, 2008); Sweeney, "King Manasseh of Judah and the Problem of Theodicy in the Deuteronomistic History," in *Good Kings and Bad Kings*, ed. Lester L. Grabbe, LHBOTS 393 (London: T&T Clark, 2005), 264–78.

Judeans faced. The crux of the challenge is God's impotence and negligence. In the ancient near Eastern cultural mind, the fall of the Jerusalem temple most likely meant the defeat of *our* God Yhwh to *their* gods.[11] For many, the only logical solution is to submit to the stronger power and serve their gods.

Biblical writers of Judah refused to submit to this ideological tide that denied Yhwh's sovereignty. Yhwh is not incapable. The empirical sense of the lack of God's interference is the result of a divine plan to bring about repentance and restoration by temporarily allowing evil to inflict Israel. This theological tendency is replete in exilic literature, from prophecy, history, psalms, to lamentation. The prophetic literature reminds the people of the continued warnings of Yhwh's prophets, which Israel has repeatedly ignored. It thereby justifies Yhwh's wrath and the affliction as a necessary expression of frustration from God's part. On the other hand, psalms and lamentations represent the voice of petition on God, asking how long God's people will wait for divine help and suffer the atrocity caused by their enemies. These are outcries of God's people to awaken their slumbering God.[12] DtrH reflects the same message by a historical recollection as to how much Israel's history has been saturated by the sin against Yhwh, which justifies God's decision to finally bring about the punishment Israel deserves. Of course, both DtrH and prophetic literature aim for restoration. When Israel returns to the old covenantal relation with Yhwh, God will drive away the enemies and remove sufferings from Israel. This is a powerful ideology that interprets the past and prepares the future based on the covenantal structure of Deuteronomy. This ideology provides a strong logical scheme against which there are no circumstances—no matter how bad they are—that cannot be justified. If the situation gets better, one can attribute it to divine help. If it gets worse, one can blame the people for their failure to repent.

If one admits that DtrH has an ideological tendency to highlight the sins of Israel while covering up God's responsibility, it becomes clear which particular aspect we must be wary of potential exaggerating: the theological appraisal of figures whom Dtr identifies as culprits of the destruction of the covenantal relation. If the historian needed a scapegoat to salvage the fame of God, what do modern readers have to do with the violence the text wages in search of a scapegoat? Of course, one cannot say that Dtr's identification of the *bad* kings was absent of any grounds. Historians would not take a risk to introduce an entire fabrication in persuading readership. They do not have to. They can always pick

---

[11] Sweeney, "King Manasseh," 274.
[12] Carleen Mandolfo, *Daughter Zion Talks Back to the Prophets: A Dialogic Theology of the Book of Lamentations* (Atlanta: Society of Biblical Literature, 2007); Jon D. Levenson, *Creation and the Persistence of Evil: The Jewish Drama of Divine Omnipotence* (San Francisco: Harper & Row, 1988).

among usual suspects and aggrandize their sins. Think of Dtr's accusation on Manasseh then. On his shoulder, the entire fate of the kingdom has been posed.[13] Can we take the words of Dtr that Manasseh was the culprit of the fall of Jerusalem? Or did Manasseh happen to be chosen by Dtr as a scapegoat for Dtr's theological ideology?

DIVERGENT MEMORIES ON MANASSEH

Memory is multifarious and flexible. It exists in the space where people together recollect the past to reconstruct what happened. It is situational in that bits of the collective memory are chosen against others under the influence of the situation. Based on specific needs of the situation, it is chosen, edited, expanded, and reconstructed.[14] Thus, to read ancient history that is basically a collection of past memories, in whichever forms, one must pay attention to various voices hidden behind the text. Indeed, more than one version of memory is preserved in the biblical tradition on Manasseh.[15]

---

[13] Jeroboam ben Nebat is similar to Manasseh in that he takes all the blame for the sinfulness of northern Israel. Yet Jeroboam does not take as much blame as Manasseh. There are other kings who joined in the feat of treacherous behaviors for which Jeroboam set the path. Of course, Jeroboam's characterization also must be understood within the north-south rivalry in ancient Israel and Judah. For this traditional issue, see Frank Moore Cross, *Canaanite Myth and Hebrew Epic: Essays in the History of the Religion of Israel* (Cambridge: Harvard University Press, 1973), 198–200. For an attempt to reconsider the characterization on Jeroboam's sin, see Sweeney, *Reading the Hebrew Bible after the Shoah*, 67–72.

[14] The relation between memory and history and its implications on biblical studies have been actively discussed recently. See, e.g., Alan Kirk and Tom Thatcher, eds., *Memory, Tradition, and Text: Uses of the Past in Early Christianity*, SemeiaSt 52 (Atlanta: Society of Biblical Literature, 2005); Tom Thatcher, ed., *Memory and Identity in Ancient Judaism and Early Christianity: A Conversation with Barry Schwartz*, SemeiaSt 78 (Atlanta: Society of Biblical Literature, 2014).

[15] There are several studies that dealt with the divergent images of Manasseh in Kings and Chronicles. See, e.g., Stuart Lasine, "Manasseh as Villain and Scapegoat," in *The New Literary Criticism and the Hebrew Bible*, ed. J. Cheryl Exum and David J. A. Clines, JSOTSup 143 (Sheffield: JSOT Press, 1993), 163–83; P. S. F. van Keulen, *Manasseh through the Eyes of the Deuteronomists: The Manasseh Account (2 Kings 21:1–18) and the Final Chapters of the Deuteronomistic History* (Leiden: Brill, 1996); Philippe Abadie, "From the Impious Manasseh (2 Kings 21) to the Convert Manasseh (2 Chronicles 33): Theological Rewriting by the Chronicler," in *The Chronicler as Theologian: Essays in Honor of Ralph W. Klein*, ed. Matt Patrick Graham, Steven L. McKenzie, and Gary N. Knoppers, JSOTSup 371 (London: T&T Clark International, 2003), 89–104; Francesca Stavrakopoulou, *King Manasseh and Child Sacrifice: Biblical Distortions of Historical Realities*, BZAW 338 (Berlin: de Gruyter, 2004); Lester L. Grabbe, ed., *Good Kings and Bad Kings*, LHBOTS 393 (London: T&T Clark, 2005). For studies in Korean, see Joong-

Manasseh the Culprit of Judah's Fall

The final form of DtrH identifies Manasseh as the culprit of Judah's fall. In 2 Kgs 21, Manasseh brought about the end of Jerusalem despite the good deeds of Josiah. This point is manifested in the way the text is structured.

I.	Introduction: Regnal report on the beginning	1
II.	Body: The sin of Manasseh and the fall of Judah	2–16
	A. Cause: Sin of Manasseh	2–9
	B. Effect: Announcement of Judah's impending doom	10–15
	C. Appendix: more sins	16
III.	Conclusion: Regnal report on the end	17–18

The body of the regnal report of Manasseh is constructed in a cause-effect chain. It makes clear the causal relation between Manasseh's deeds and Judah's fall. The description on Manasseh's sin (vv. 2–9) is fraught with all kinds of accusation. It begins with a general remark that he has done evil before Yhwh (v. 2) and moves to more specific deeds. He followed foreign abominations (v. 2), rebuilt the high places that Hezekiah had destroyed (v. 3), built altars for Baal and erected an Asherah pole in the temple following the deeds of Ahab (vv. 3, 7), worshipped celestial deities (v. 3), and erected altars at the temple to worship celestial deities (vv. 4, 5). He also engaged in a child sacrifice (v. 6) and allowed all sorts of forbidden behaviors (v. 6).

No other Judean king is accused for such a dreadful litany of sins. However, one also senses that there is not much substance behind these conventional forms of accusation.[16] None of them is peculiar and episodic to his behavior, but they are all typical accusations used for other kings here and there.[17] It feels as if the historian musters some typical formulae for characteristic sins to make a case that Manasseh was the sinner. It is very rare that these formulaic expressions are gathered at one place. There is one exception: In 1 Kgs 17 Dtr's theological commentary is provided concerning the fall of Samaria. This is one of the texts where Dtr's

---

Ho Chong, "A Study on Manasseh's Religious Policy," *Studies in Religion* 17 (1999): 213–33; Taek Hyun Oh, "Manasseh in the Deuteronomistic History," *Theology and Ministry* 31 (2009): 63–76; Seokgyu Jung, "Dual Functions of Manasseh's Sin (2 Kings 21: 1–18) in the Deuteronomistic History," *Korean Journal of Old Testament Studies* 16.2 (2010): 30–52; Hakseo Kim, "A Re-evaluation on King Manasseh and the Theological Implications: 2 Kings 21:1–18 and 2 Chronicles 33:1–20" (Th.M. Thesis, Yonsei University, 2013).

[16] Lasine, "Manasseh as Villain and Scapegoat," 163–64.

[17] The only exception is to build the altars for celestial deities in the fields, which, one may argue, has been borrowed from the account of Ahaz who is known for building the altars after visiting Damascus (2 Kgs 16:10–16).

ideology is most evidently expressed.[18] What appears in both passages are remarks on high places (21:3 // 17:9, 11), Baal (21:3, 4 // 17:16), Asherah (21:3, 7 // 17:10, 16), celestial deities (21:3, 5 // 17:16), idols (21:11 // 17:12), child sacrifice (21:6 // 17:17), rejection of the law (21:8 // 17:13–15), and following foreign abominations (21:2, 9, 11 // 17:8, 11, 15).[19] In a word, the sin of Manasseh amounts to all the sins that all kings of Israel committed. The following section (vv. 10–15) is the core of the unit. Due to Manasseh's sins (vv. 2–9), it is declared, Judah will fall. By setting an unreasonable causal relation of his sin and the fall which does not happen until a half century later, the text attempts to put all of the burden of Judah's fall on one person.[20]

Note that the warning for the fall is modeled after the fall of northern Israel. Yhwh will "stretch over Jerusalem the measuring line of Samaria" (v. 13). This pericope adds two decisive accusations: Manasseh was more wicked than the nations "whom Yhwh destroyed before the people of Israel" (v. 9) and shed more innocent blood (v. 16). These are important because they are reminiscent of Ahab, a representative figure of Israel's religious apostasy. Ahab is also blamed for shedding innocent blood, and most notably known for the incident of Naboth's vineyard (1 Kgs 21:1–21). His sins are compared to the Amorites "whom Yhwh cast out before the people of Israel" (1 Kgs 21:26). Connecting Manasseh's sin to Ahab is evident. As many have observed,[21] Manasseh is connected to the sin of northern Israel so that it becomes clear that Judah also will not be able to escape from Yhwh's wrath and follow the path of Samaria.[22] Israelite kings followed the footsteps of Jeroboam ben Nebat that caused the fall of Samaria. Manasseh followed the sins that Israelite kings committed which brought the same fate to Jerusalem.

---

[18] Richard D. Nelson, *The Double Redaction of the Deuteronomistic History*, JSOTSup 18 (Sheffield: University of Sheffield, 1981), 55.
[19] For more details, see Jung, "Dual Functions of Manasseh's Sin," 40–43.
[20] Klaus Koch, "Is There a Doctrine of Retribution in the Old Testament?," in *Theodicy in the Old Testament*, ed. James L. Crenshaw (Philadelphia: Fortress, 1983); Joel S. Kaminsky, "The Sins of the Fathers: A Theological Investigation of the Biblical Tension between Corporate and Individualized Retribution," *Judaism* 46 (1997): 319–32.
[21] K. A. D. Smelik, "The Portrayal of King Manasseh: A Literary Analysis of II Kings Xxi and II Chronicles Xxxiii," in *Converting the Past: Studies in Ancient Israelite and Moabite Historiography* (Leiden: Brill, 1992), 132; Lasine, "Manasseh as Villain and Scapegoat," 167–70; Marvin A. Sweeney, *King Josiah of Judah: The Lost Messiah of Israel* (Oxford: Oxford University Press, 2001), 49–54.
[22] It has been claimed that his given name "Manasseh" reflects Hezekiah's interests in northern Israel and that such interests ultimately are part of the reasons that opened the door for northern Israelite syncretic influence to Judah. Stavrakopoulou, *King Manasseh and Child Sacrifice*, 70–72; Stavrakopoulou, "The Blackballing of Manasseh," in *Good Kings and Bad Kings*, ed. Lester L. Grabbe, LHBOTS 393 (London: T&T Clark, 2005), 253–54.

The import of Manasseh's sin within the framework of the DtrH is evident. In the wake of the fall of Jerusalem, Dtr needed to provide an explanation that justifies Yhwh's failure to protect it despite Josiah's heroic efforts to restore the covenantal relation with Yhwh (2 Kgs 23). According to the Deuteronomistic ideology, Josiah's model behavior must entail blessings from God's part. With Josiah's untimely death (2 Kgs 23:29–30), however, Judah's fate quickly tumbles into a havoc. Instead of prosperity, an utter destruction befalls God's people. For Dtr, Manasseh was the reason. Immediately after praising Josiah's reformation came the announcement of the impending doom of Jerusalem because of Manasseh's sins (2 Kgs 23:25–27). Evidently, this anticlimactic ending of Josiah's regnal report is inserted to make sense of the fall of Judah.[23] It is not Yhwh's lack of ability to save Judah. The magnitude of Manasseh's sin was so huge that even Josiah's efforts were insufficient to quiet God's wrath.

Manasseh a Repentant and Restored

The Chronicler's depiction of Manasseh is quite different being manifested in the way the Chronicler's version (2 Chr 33) is structured.

I.	Introduction: Regnal formula	1
II.	Body: Manasseh's sin and repentance	2–17
	A. Manasseh's sin	2–9
	B. Yhwh's punishment	10–11
	C. Manasseh's repentance	12–13
	D. Manasseh's good deeds and reformation	14–17
III.	Conclusion:	18–20
	A. Note on other sources	18–19
	B. Regnal ending formula	20

The body (II) of the text is composed of Manasseh's sin, repentance, and other virtuous deeds that follow. The description of Manasseh's sin (vv. 2–9) is no different from that of Dtr. Manasseh rebuilt the high places that Hezekiah had demolished (v. 3), worshipped Baal, Asherah and celestial deities (v. 3), built altars for celestial deities in the two courts of the temple (v. 5), engaged with child sacrifice (v. 6), and used necromancy and other forbidden customs (v. 6). Even the note that his sin is compared to the nations driven out by Yhwh is included. Yet the continuity between the two versions goes only thus far.

In DtrH, the list of Manasseh's sins serves as grounds for Judah's fall. In contrast, in the Chronicler's version, repentance and restoration follow, a *forgotten* part in DtrH. Yhwh punishes Manasseh for his sins, and in his distress during exile, Manasseh repents. The way he repents is described in a dramatic fashion. He "entreated" and "humbled himself greatly" before Yhwh. Yhwh is "moved by

---

[23] Cross, *Canaanite Myth and Hebrew Epic*, 274–89; Nelson, *Double Redaction*, 83–85, 123.

his entreaty" (vv. 12–13) and brings him back to Jerusalem. Moreover, Manasseh's repentance is followed by prosperity and reformation. The first is strengthening the military defense system. He revamped the city of David and strengthened the army in all the fortified cities in Judah (v. 14). The second is religious reformation. Manasseh removed foreign gods and idols from the temple (v. 14) and destroyed all the altars that he had built (v. 15). He also restored the altar of Yhwh and commanded the people of Judah to serve Yhwh (v. 16). Thus, in the Chronicler's version, Manasseh redresses most of the sins of which he had been accused.[24]

This variant tradition is of utmost important not only for Manasseh himself, but also to the reader of the Hebrew Bible. The Manasseh that the Chronicler remembers is not compared to Ahab. Above all, Manasseh in Chronicles is not blamed for the fall of Judah. Although he had been a bad king, he is an icon of a repentant king. Readers can easily empathize with a character of repentance and restoration. In this scheme, Manasseh's earlier grievous evil is utilized not as a cause for Judah's fall. Rather, it is a theological device to trigger and to highlight the importance of repentance and the magnitude of Yhwh's grace to those who return to God. If God accepts Manasseh back, there is none whose grace cannot embrace.

REREADING SCAPEGOATING MANASSEH

Manasseh is remembered as the most sinful king in Judah's history, the culprit behind the fall of Jerusalem and, at the same time, the role model of repentance and restoration.[25] Behind these divergent memories, scholars have focused on reconstructing the historical reality of the time of Manasseh. Naturally, they attempted to sift through the more objective memory among them. Chronicles has been considered less valuable in that regard. As far as Manasseh's accounts are concerned, one may have to rethink whether the traditional evaluation holds true. It is generally true that Chronicles betrays a certain *Tendenz* in its historical description. Yet, as noted above, the Dtr's description of Manasseh is equally saturated with its *Tendenz* for retribution theology. Recently, scholars have begun to realize that Manasseh was a scapegoat of Dtr's historical ideology. This point has been articulated most clearly by F. Stravrakopoulou as she indicates, "The

---

[24] See Grabbe, *Good Kings and Bad Kings*.
[25] In addition, there is another fragment of memory preserved in Jer 15:14, "I will make you serve your enemies in a land that you do not know, for in my anger a fire is kindled that shall burn forever." One may take this as a sign that a memory of the bad king Manasseh has been preserved until the time of Jeremiah. However, this short passage describes Manasseh's act as vaguely as DtrH. This statement does not cohere with Jeremiah's tendency to charge his contemporary rather than earlier generations. Given the close relation between Jeremiah and DtrH, it is more likely that this passage is influenced by DtrH. Stavrakopoulou, *King Manasseh and Child Sacrifice*, 254.

Hebrew Bible offers itself as a window into the past, yet the possibility that the glass is distorted is often overlooked."[26] Thus, she claims, "In blaming the Manasseh of history for these 'crimes', modern scholarship has all too frequently perpetuated the blackballing of Manasseh."[27] There are some grounds to support this observation.

First, Dtr's description on Manasseh is filled with formulaic expressions for bad kings but lacking any concrete and distinct episode on his crimes. Lasine speaks of the "faceless" description on Manasseh, "The chapter includes no quoted speeches of the king, let alone descriptions of his emotions similar to those reported of his fellow-apostate Ahab. Nor does the narrator describe any interaction between Manasseh and the 'people', opposition parties, specific prophets, or rival leaders, as he did for Jeroboam and Ahab."[28] Instead of the objective description, the historian's intent is more pronounced. Granted, one may suggest that the lack of concrete information may result from the intentional expunging by the later period. One can find cases in history when a historical record of a monarch is systematically wiped out for political reasons, like the case of the Pharaoh Akhenaten. In that case, however, what is targeted is either the positive achievements or the very existence of the king. That is hardly the case for Manasseh. It is difficult to imagine that the concrete records of his crimes are erased and replaced by formulaic descriptions. One may also argue in partial truth that descriptions of other kings in Dtr are similar to Manasseh in that their descriptions tend to be more typical than concrete. If a king holds little significance for the historian, the description can be substituted by typical expressions. Yet, it is different for a king who holds a critical position like Manasseh in Judah. Compare with Jeroboam ben Nebat or Ahab in northern Israel, who are comparable with Manasseh in the negative evaluation by Dtr. The accounts of Jeroboam and Ahab are filled with colorful episodes that distinguish these kings from others. The readers get the distinct impression on the character of these kings. They know Jeroboam as the one who built the golden calves at Bethel and Dan. The readers remember Ahab as a wicked king whose evil nature is epitomized in episodes like Naboth's vineyard. The accounts of Jeroboam and Ahab include some typical formulae used for other kings, but the characteristics expressed by them are substantiated by peculiar episodes. Likewise, if the historian wants to blame Manasseh for the fall of Jerusalem, it would be much more effective and persuasive if corroborated by concrete and striking episodes. If there are some, for what reason would the historian hide them from the reader?

Second, unlike the extremely negative appraisal of Manasseh by Dtr, he appears to be a successful king, who ruled Judah peacefully for fifty-five years,

---

[26] Stavrakopoulou, "Blackballing of Manasseh," 258. See also Knauf, "Glorious Days of Manasseh," 176.
[27] Stavrakopoulou, "Blackballing of Manasseh," 259.
[28] Lasine, "Manasseh as Villain and Scapegoat," 164.

longer than any other Judean king.²⁹ The longevity of reign is a virtue for any monarch as it indicates political stability. According to biblical historians, Judah grew exponentially during the period of Hezekiah and Manasseh.³⁰ Whether the stability and growth came from his successful rule or his pro-Assyrian stance is unclear. The success in political and economic areas does not necessarily translate into the success in religious aspects either. Still, one may question whether Dtr's evaluation of Manasseh, filled as it is with ideological rhetoric, is a just and objective appraisal of this king.

Third, recent discoveries indicate that there are some historical values in the Chronicler's version of history.³¹ Archaeologists point to the development of Jerusalem in the time of Hezekiah and Manasseh. This was the time when Jerusalem had undergone a significant westward expansion by building a great defensive wall to the West of the city.³² This information is featured in the Chronicler's version but is lacking from Dtr's. The Chronicler tells us that the growth of Jerusalem came as a divine reward for his sincere repentance. This causal relation makes us rethink on the Chronicler's remark on Manasseh's repentance. There may be some ground for his change, which one can take as an indication that, in the case of Manasseh, Dtr's version is more theologically distorted. Dtr had every reason to erase a positive memory on Manasseh to use him as a ground for the theological explanation for the fall of Jerusalem.³³

Given these, one may be able to say that Manasseh was probably not an important figure in the Josianic edition of DtrH. What made him important was the

---

²⁹ Knauf, "Glorious Days of Manasseh."

³⁰ Magen Broshi, "Expansion of Jerusalem in the Reigns of Hezekiah and Manasseh," *IEJ* 24 (1974): 21–26.

³¹ The prejudice against the historical value of Chronicles has a long history. See, e.g., Julius Wellhausen, *Prolegomena to the History of Ancient Israel: With a Reprint of the Article Israel from the Encyclopaedia Brittanica* (New York: Meridian Books, 1957), 206–7.

³² Broshi, "Expansion of Jerusalem in the Reigns of Hezekiah and Manasseh," 21–26. Scholars have debated what caused this expansion. Most noteworthy is a series of debate between Na'aman and Finkelstein. See, e.g., Nadav Na'aman, "When and How Did Jerusalem Become a Great City? The Rise of Jerusalem as Judah's Premier City in the Eighth-Seventh Centuries B.C.E.," *BASOR* 347 (2007): 21–56; Israel Finkelstein, "The Settlement History of Jerusalem in the Eighth and Seventh Century BC," *RB* 115 (2008): 499–515; Nadav Na'aman, "The Growth and Development of Judah and Jerusalem in the Eighth Century BCE: A Rejoinder," *RB* 116 (2009), 321–35; Israel Finkelstein, "Saul, Benjamin and the Emergence of 'Biblical Israel': An Alternative View," *ZAW* 123 (2011): 348–67. See also Philippe Guillaume, "Jerusalem 720–705 BCE: No Flood of Israelite Refugees," *SJOT* 22 (2008): 195–211.

³³ Steven L. McKenzie, *The Chronicler's Use of the Deuteronomistic History*, HSM 33 (Atlanta: Scholars Press, 1985), 163.

time following the fall of Jerusalem, when Dtr needed a reason for this anticlimactic ending after Josiah's earnest efforts to restore Judah's relation with Yhwh. This explains much of the earlier questioning. The reason that not much was preserved on Manasseh's fifty-five years of reign is because of the theologically insignificant position of Manasseh in the earlier setting in DtrH. He was one of the bad kings in the history of Judah and Israel who happened to enjoy political stability due to the international circumstances during his reign. In the exilic version of DtrH, Manasseh is identified as the reason for Jerusalem's fall. Why Manasseh? If he was one of the *ordinary* bad kings, we cannot tell.[34] What is important is the likelihood that Dtr is scapegoating Manasseh as the cause of the fall of Jerusalem for a theological purpose. I have no intention to argue that Manasseh was innocent. The point simply is that Dtr's accusation of Manasseh is exaggerated. The DtrH is a theological program in which theological necessity often takes precedence over historical veracity. In the name of salvaging God's fame in the wake of a historical calamity, Dtr needed Manasseh as a scapegoat.

Here lies the central issue of this essay. The Dtr historians may have resolved one of the thorny theological questions of the exilic time by scapegoating Manasseh. Yet, in doing so, they have left an indelible scarlet letter on the back of Manasseh. He has become demonized. The problem is that this scar continues to be reproduced in the reception of subsequent generations.[35] For instance, in the rabbinic tradition, the typical and impersonal Manasseh in DtrH has been personified as a true villain with several glowing episodes and blank accusations. The rabbis remember Manasseh as the king who despised the Torah. He attempted to cut out the divine name from the Torah (b. Sanh. 103b) and to prove the worthlessness of the Torah (b. Sanh. 99b). Other rabbinic traditions remember Manasseh as an idol maker, but their descriptions are more graphic than the Dtr version. Manasseh built an idol with faces on each side of the temple so that God (*shekinah*) can see the face in every direction (b. Sanh. 103b). Note how his malign intention is highlighted. Manasseh is also accused for violating his sister (b. Sanh. 103b).[36] Several rabbinic traditions, including the Midrash, Talmud, and The Ascension of Isaiah, identify Manasseh as the slayer of Isaiah (b. Sanh.

---

[34] As noted above, some scholars think that Dtr's choice of Manasseh has something to do with his name that alludes to a northern influence. Stavrakopoulou, *King Manasseh and Child Sacrifice*, 70–72; Stavrakopoulou, "Blackballing of Manasseh," 253–54. On the other hand, others consider the longevity of his reign as the reason for the choice. The length of his reign left an indelible mark in history that even Josiah's good deeds could not overcome. See, e.g., William M. Schniedewind, "The Source Citations of Manasseh: King Manasseh in History and Homily," *VT* 41 (1991): 451–55.

[35] The discussion in this paragraph owes to Stavrakopoulou, *King Manasseh and Child Sacrifice*, 122–33.

[36] Stavrakopoulou, *King Manasseh and Child Sacrifice*, 123, n. 11.

103b).[37] This certainly is an extension out of the textual reference on Manasseh's innocent bloodsheds (2 Kgs 21:16). Given that another tradition reports Manasseh as Isaiah's grandson, taken together, Manasseh's alleged crime is escalated to a patricide. It is hardly likely that these rabbinic traditions, produced centuries after the time of Manasseh, are based on hard evidence. The demonization of Manasseh in the text and the lack of concrete information on Manasseh's evil deeds, catalyzed rabbinic imaginations to produce several ideas to fill the gap in the text and justify the scriptural description of the wickedness of Manasseh.[38] In doing so, these imaginations are complicit in allowing violence in the text to grow.

To expand and reproduce the violence inherent in the text are not limited to ancient readers. Modern readers who take pride in the pursuit of an historical, objective reading reproduced the textual violence in their own way.[39] For a long time, modern scholars have taken for granted the evil nature of Manasseh without resisting the textual force of violence. Some have accused Manasseh's character as being innately evil.[40] Others attempted to prove the historical veracity of his engagement in foreign cults, such as necromancy and Ishtar worship.[41] Sticking to the text (!), critics attempted to reconstruct the reality behind the text in Manasseh's time based on the textual description. In doing so, they participated in Dtr's scapegoating of Manasseh.

The question I raise concerns the ethics of reading. The way one reads scripture cannot be separated from the way one lives. How one treats a distorted depiction on Manasseh affects how one addresses biased perspectives and discourses saturated in one's social life. This is the reason why I problematize the way we remember villains in history.

---

[37] This malicious reception has been widespread, which signifies its ancient origin. See Stavrakopoulou, *King Manasseh and Child Sacrifice*, 122, esp. n. 5; Betsy Halpern Amaru, "The Killing of the Prophets : Unraveling a Midrash," *HUCA* (1983): 153–80.

[38] On the other hand, there are more positive receptions of Manasseh as well, which most likely are inspired by the memory preserved in Chronicles. The most well-known is a late pseudepigraphal text the "Prayer of Manasseh." J. H. Charlesworth, "Manasseh, Prayer of," *ABD* 4:499–500. Also, the rabbis acknowledged both Manasseh's negative and positive depictions. For the latter, some rabbis claimed that Manasseh will have his share in the world to come. See Stavrakopoulou, *King Manasseh and Child Sacrifice*, 124.

[39] These are well examined by Stravrakopoulou and I am indebted to her analysis. Stavrakopoulou, "Blackballing of Manasseh," 257–58.

[40] T. R. Hobbs, *2 Kings* (Waco, TX: Word Books, 1985), 311–12; Mordechai Cogan and Hayim Tadmor, *II Kings: A New Translation* (Garden City, NY: Doubleday, 1988), 273.

[41] See, e.g., Brian B. Schmidt, *Israel's Beneficent Dead: Ancestor Cult and Necromancy in Ancient Israelite Religion and Tradition* (Winona Lake, IN: Eisenbrauns, 1996), 292.

Rereading by Intertextual Recontextualization

Scapegoating someone for the sake of God's name is not limited to the past. It very much continues today in Korean Christianity. An unfiltered reception of a violent text *as is* in the name of scriptural authority or the heavily abused slogan of *sola scriptura* may serve to prolong the textual violence in the present. The predominantly conservative climate in Korean churches rarely offers an occasion for an in-depth discussion on the ethics of reading. Then, pulpits can become a place where violence is reproduced in which victims continue to be blamed for suffering. Yet, some texts require an active involvement or even a resistance of the readers. The role of the reader is not merely to reproduce what is written, but to resist against generalizing its violent solution to the world outside the text. Interpretation is never about a mere reproduction of the meanings found in the text. Contexts change, and the changed circumstance requires one to seek the relevance of the text. When the seed of violence is sown in the text, the interpreter must deal with it even when the context no longer requires the exertion of that violence.

What I suggest in this essay is an intertextual recontextualization by reading a text with other related texts. One can never change the content of what is written, especially so when the text in question has been given communal authority. One must find a way to acknowledge the content while moderating the degree of its potential violence. A good way to achieve this is to relativize the message by highlighting the contextual nature of the text. Every text is read against a background, and without a background, there is no meaning. If so, altering the background can provide a means to deal with an alleged violence in a passage. In the book culture, context is preset in the process of production. This immediate literary context serves as the primary background against which the meaning of the text is produced. This contextual fixation prevents a passage from being read against other, far-removed contexts. However, one must remember that the fixation of context is not necessarily an absolute and invariable norm. Before the emergence of book culture, the notion of context was a much more flexible one. The sense of contextual fixity may well be a byproduct of book culture. In the pre-literate culture in which the text operated within the space of human mind, a text's position was not necessarily fixed in a tangible, linear space of book. This means that the scribe/performer could freely access, rearrange, and transform the text. Then, one can also say that the way oral text has operated may be similar to the way post-structural theories envision how a text operates in a reader-oriented reading.[42] In this reading, text is not governed by the printed form, but by the active participation of the reader.

---

[42] John Miles Foley, "Plenitude and Diversity: Interactions between Orality and Writing," in *The Interface of Orality and Writing: Speaking, Seeing, Writing in the Shaping of New Genres*, ed. Annette Weissenrieder and Robert B. Coote, WUNT 260 (Tübingen: Mohr Siebeck, 2010), 116–17.

One must realize, then, that to read a text within the fixed literary context is also a part of modern readers' decision over against other freer ways of reading the text. Hans Frei has demonstrated well how setting the boundary of a reading affects the meaning production of the text. When Old Testament texts are read in conjunction with the New Testament, their potential meanings are reframed according to Christian interpretation. They become the shade, type, or prototype of what is to come. What Frei coins the "eclipse of biblical narrative" has been kindled by the modern recognition of the literary boundary of the Old Testament and by critical scholars' decisions to sever the literary connection to the New Testament. Indeed, Old Testament texts have been read in conjunction with the New Testament for a long time before the advent of modern critical studies. Important, at this point, is what forced early Christians to read the Old Testament *together with* the New Testament? One may think that it was the material production of the Christian Bible that included both Old and New Testaments. Yet, we also know that the decision on the canonical boundary came only after serious internal struggles and debates. Ultimately, it was early Christian's collective agreement to accept both parts as their authoritative texts that gave rise to a material form of a combined codex of the Old and New Testaments. That means, before they were put together, the *space* between the Old Testament and the New Testament may not have been a *continuous* one. What I take away from this observation is that for a long time, before the finalization of the canonization,[43] Christians have read the Old Testament in light of the New Testament that was a separate literary entity from the Old Testament.

The potentially violent nature of Dtr's account of Manasseh justifies the proposed intertextual recontextualization. The Deuteronomistic scapegoating of Manasseh is part of a PTSD (posttraumatic stress disorder) symptom after a traumatic experience of national calamity. If that is so, today's readers must take into account how the traumatic experience of Dtr affected the way Manasseh was depicted. In this perspective, one may take Dtr as an object that requires a healing procedure. Rather than merely accept what this historian has to say on Manasseh, one may question the potential distortion of reality. Dtr needed Manasseh to answer the difficult question of Yhwh's silence and inability to redeem. Yet, we also know that the biblical answer to suffering does not end there. There are texts that intend to overcome the destructive side effect of the abuse of the Deuteronomistic ideology. The other most well-known solutions are represented in the book of Job and John 9.[44] These texts provide divergent perspectives on suffering than DtrH and, thereby, may serve well as a second lens *with* which the Manasseh account can be read.

---

[43] Of course, I acknowledge the impractical assumption behind the notion of the *finalization* of the canon debate.

[44] The intertextuality among these texts is well recognized. See, e.g., Raymond B. Dillard, *An Introduction to the Old Testament* (Grand Rapids: Zondervan, 1994), 208–10.

It has been long recognized that the book of Job is directed against abuses of the Deuteronomistic ideology of retribution.[45] It questions the universal value of retribution theology by setting up a situation that the legendary "blameless and upright" figure suffers apparently for naught. The reader knows where Job's suffering comes from, but Job and his friends do not. Thus, a tantalizing debate is set up between an innocent sufferer, Job, and the doctrinal advocates, his friends. Elipaz's remark captures the position of Job's contestants. "Remember: who that was innocent ever perished? Or where were the upright cut off?" (Job 4:7) Theologically speaking, all their words may be *correct*. Yet, their correct words lose their explanatory power against Job's particular situation. Neither Job nor the reader is persuaded. Thus, Job's innocent suffering provides an ideal setting to discuss the generalization of retribution theology. The innocent can suffer in reality. The reason for suffering remains in the realm of mystery. Even after the eventual encounter with Yhwh out of the whirlwind, Job is given no direct answer for his suffering. His life is restored to normal, but he dies without knowing the reason why. There is suffering that humans can never decipher.

John 9 provides another perspective to the problem of suffering. Concerning the man blind from birth, the disciples ask an interesting question: "Rabbi, who sinned, this man or his parents, that he was born blind?" (John 9:2). For us, this question functions as a hypertext that brings this episode right in the middle of the debate between Job and his friends. Whether present suffering is the product of the sins of the contemporary or the previous generation is contested in biblical literature (cf. Ezek 18). The disciples' question indicates that the Deuteronomistic perspective remained dominant during first century Judaism despite the efforts to overcome its abuses in the book of Job. Jesus's answer, however, represents a new way to overcome the Deuteronomistic retribution theology. "It was not that this man sinned, or his parents, but that the works of God might be displayed in him" (9:3). Jesus rewrites the past of this man to transform his present and future. Listening to this answer, one can see that a sense of hope arises inside the mind of this blind man. He realizes that his suffering perhaps is not the result of sin but part of the bigger plan of God. As he assents to this big picture, the miracle was unfolding inside his mind. Rather than digging into the reason for suffering, Jesus redirects his attention to divine providence. Like the book of Job, Jesus does not explain the reason for his suffering, but his suffering provides him an opportunity to become the hero in this important moment of Jesus's ministry.

Both Job and John 9 are intertextually tangled with DtrH within the canonical literature through the theme of suffering. This existing tie allows us to read DtrH in the context of the intertextual debate among these texts. Read against Job and John 9, the Deuteronomistic accusation leveled at Manasseh may be interpreted in a different manner. Read together with Job, Dtr's evaluation of Manasseh is put

---

[45] See J. L. Crenshaw, "Popular Questioning of the Justice of God in Ancient Israel," *ZAW* 82 (1970): 380–95.

into dialogue with Job's stringent refusal to accept the retribution framework. Given that the book of Job is meant to balance the abuses of retribution theology, Job's refusal to accept his suffering as punishment (and Yhwh's sanctioning of that view) affect the way Dtr's retributional evaluation of Manasseh is interpreted. If the book of Job contends with DtrH, Job's debate with his friends can be taken as a defense for Manasseh. Indeed, the crux of Job's friends' words was that there must be sins for Job that he needs to redress and repent. Note that this theological necessity is precisely what forced Dtr to search for sins in Manasseh. Thus, Dtr's reading of Manasseh very much mirrors the accusations of Job's friends. At the same time, this precise logic is the point Job cannot accept.

Granted, Manasseh is different from Job. The text hardly sanctions his innocence. Still, even for Job, one is not to accept that he was impeccable and infallible. The point is that Job did not commit sins that deserve the suffering of such scale and that there was no causal relation between his acts and his suffering. Then, even if one accepts the sinful nature and deeds of Manasseh, one may question if Dtr's judgment is justifiable. The violent nature of scapegoating does not depend on the chosen scapegoat's reputation. A scapegoat is rarely chosen among those who carry an exemplary reputation, but those with flaws make them vulnerable targets. One must equally value Manasseh's right to defend himself. The moral issue around Dtr's evaluation may become more serious if one accepts that Dtr deliberately forgot and expunged the memory of Manasseh's repentance and restoration. If so, reading DtrH with Job, one can say that in his tenacious dispute with his friends, Job is defending none other than figures like Manasseh, the victim of theological discourse.

John 9 problematizes Dtr's cursory evaluation of Manasseh. Jesus's answer devaluates Dtr's dogged pursuit for the reason for suffering. If the Jobban poet's position is characterized as agnostic, John's solution is teleological. In a suffering reality, one can find God's plan. The teleological explanation does not necessarily nullify the causal explanation. Whatever was the cause of the suffering, one can no longer change that which lies in the past. Rather than reside in the past, Jesus calls for a change in theological discourse that directs attention to the present and future. To be able to explain the reason does not remove the suffering. What it takes away is the pain of not knowing the reason. Note in this regard that Dtr's explanation does little in alleviating the pain of Judeans in the exile. Even if Dtr's explanation is true, Manasseh is a figure in history, and there is nothing one can do about his sins. What it does is to exonerate God, and only that. Either way, the ones who must learn from this explanation and carry the burden of the excruciating reality are Judeans in the exile. In light of John, Dtr's scapegoating of Manasseh cannot be the end of the story. Despite the tragic end of the Judean monarchy, one still needs to recover a sense of hope. In John's solution, on the other hand, the role of God is different. Instead of sacrificing Manasseh for the sake of God, God's role is to show a glimpse of the divine purpose that had been hidden thus far. This man was to be used as an agent to glorify God, through his handicap. Unlike Dtr who scapegoats Manasseh for the sake of God and exiled Judeans, John embraces the physical stigma of this blind man as a channel to invite others to identify with him. Through this man, others who struggle to find a value in their existence because of their flaws can change perspectives. If this man's defect can be used for a divine purpose, nothing may hinder others from seeing divine purpose in them. Note the continuity between this observation with those on Chronicler's depiction of Manasseh as a model repentant. Can we then say that when Jesus heals the blind man's stigma, what Jesus healed were none other than all who have been stigmatized by theological discourses, including Manasseh? If one realizes a possibility that John 9 can be read as a healing of Manasseh, or even the healing of Dtr who needed to scapegoat him, our reading of Dtr's evaluation of Manasseh can no longer be the same. When this path of intertextual connection is considered, one can no longer return to accept Dtr's accusation on its face value.

It is not proposed here that one alters a text's literary context at will. The proposed recontextualization is called for by the existing intertextual connection between texts around common themes. Some texts are inherently interwoven through common theme, language, and idea. My proposal is to seek out meaning within this intricate web of texture. DtrH, Job and John 9 are intertwined with each other through the common theme of suffering. By reading them together, one can maintain a balance on the problem of suffering, without altering the scale through a bias toward one text. By reading texts with other texts, one can relativize the Dtr ideology and direct attention to the polyphony of biblical text. One can thus escape the narrow view point of Dtr ideology and seek meanings from the broader canonical context.

Conclusion

Subsequent to tragic events like the Sewol Ferry disaster, the public tended to find an easy target to blame. What makes this uncomfortable is that after the scapegoating, we easily forget those incidents. After the Sewol Ferry tragedy, we Koreans pledged not to forget what happened by a continued participation in remembering, which is symbolized in the yellow butterfly ribbon.[46] Yet, already we are hearing some people say let us move on.

Though Manasseh is not entirely comparable to the owner or the captain of Sewol Ferry, what is similar is the scapegoat mechanism that hides others who are also responsible for the incident. Above all, the president and government officials cannot escape criticism for their mishandling of the event. Moreover, one cannot deny that all the members of Korean society share responsibility for the tragedy in that we all partook in the making of this sickening society of systematic

---

[46] https://edition.cnn.com/2014/04/24/world/asia/south-korea-yellow-ribbons/index.html, accessed on Jun 10, 2018.

flaws that failed to protect the lives of its own members. We all participated in fostering this lethal system in our greed, negligence, and impatience. Thus, perhaps all of us needed a scapegoat for fear of confronting the monstrous face of a society that we all have nurtured in the name of development and prosperity.

The Dtr escapes a difficult question of divine silence by scapegoating Manasseh. Theologians fear the revealing of God's incapability or indifference. They would rather find comfort in blaming someone else. Yet, in their seeking of a temporary relief, a seed is sown for pandemic violence. To the world that is fraught with pain, the least that theologians want to achieve is to add more pain by weaving a theological discourse of violence. I propose a way of alleviating the violence in the text by a contextual reframing of a text. By nurturing a reading community that is sensitive to the polyphony of the text, we can together build a believing community that is wary of abuses of theological languages. Equipping the believers with the courage to stand up against the scapegoating in the text, my hope is to contribute in the communal making of a society that is immune to prolonging and reproducing the violence of scapegoating. There are times when we humans are left with no answers. We must learn to withstand together the excruciatingly painful silence of God, because these are part of human reality. We have already made so many Manassehs in seeking an answer.

HALF SPEAK ASHDODITE AND NONE CAN SPEAK JUDEAN: CODE-SWITCHING IN EZRA-NEHEMIAH AS AN IDENTITY MARKER FOR REPATRIATE JUDEANS AND KOREANS

Roger S. Nam

Ezra 4–7 narrates the reconstruction of the house of the Lord during the Judean repatriation under the Persian Empire. In the narration, there is a linguistic alteration between Hebrew and Aramaic for an extended portion of the narrative. The first Aramaic portion occurs in Ezra 4:8–6:18, beginning with the royal letter to King Artaxerxes, which would naturally be composed under the standard lingua franca of Aramaic. Similarly, the second Aramaic portion in Ezra 7:12–26 begins with the Artaxerxes Rescript, giving imperial support for the reconstruction. The contents of these passages befit the Aramaic language. Although the shift between the languages is rare in biblical text, it is not entirely unwarranted as Aramaic was the official language of Persian correspondence. Yet, what is puzzling is the deployment of Aramaic beyond the royal epistolary texts to include significantly substantial portions in the narrative.

In critical studies of these texts, scholars often turn to the composite nature of Ezra-Nehemiah to explain the insertion of the Aramaic sections.[1] Traditional historical-critical theories, in the spirit of Wellhausen, construct a schema of sources with the Persian imperial correspondence in Aramaic.[2] More recently, critical scholars have considered a more gradual traditional historical approach to reconstruct the textual development of Ezra-Nehemiah. Reinhard Kratz suggests that the Aramaic portions of the narrative form the inspiration for Ezra 1–4.[3] Others suggest that these Aramaic sources were reordered for the purposes of a

---

This is an expanded version of a paper delivered at the 2016 International Meeting of the Society of Biblical Literature in Seoul, Korea. I am grateful for the sponsorship of the Korean Biblical Colloquium.

[1] This paper assumes the compositional unity of Ezra-Nehemiah in line with much critical scholarship; for a summary of the issues, see Roger S. Nam, *The Theology of the Books of Ezra and Nehemiah* (Cambridge: Cambridge University Press, forthcoming).

[2] For a basic overview of diachronic issues, one may consult Thomas Bolin, *Ezra-Nehemiah* (Collegeville: Liturgical Press, 2012), 5–16.

[3] Reinhard Kratz, *The Composition of the Narrative Books of the Old Testament*, trans. John Bowden (London: T&T Clark, 2005), 49–86.

positive portrayal of the rebuilding.⁴ One of the clues to these diachronic theories is the *Wiederaufnahme*, or resumptive repetition of the phrase "Darius King of Persia" (vv. 5, 24) that signals insertion at a latter period.⁵ The authenticity of the Aramaic letters have recently come under heavy assault, with the argument that the Aramaic is a stylized literary inclusion.⁶ Regardless of the questions over authenticity, these diachronic theories of textual development do not account for the final form of the Ezra text including the Aramaic framing throughout the narrative, such as Ezra 4:8–11, 24, or even Ezra 5:1–2, which draws from the Hebrew sources of Haggai and Zechariah.

In addition, scholars have continued to examine rhetorical features and explanations for the bilingualism in Ezra-Nehemiah. In other words, the usage of Aramaic is not merely an accident of the composite nature of the text, but it is a deliberate rhetorical intention by the author-compilers. Daniel Snell suggests that the framing marker of Ezra 4:7 signals such intentions:

וכתב הנשתון כתוב ארמית ומתרגם ארמית
The letter was written in Aramaic and translated

Snell identifies this statement as an indication of a new viewpoint that signals authority against the preceding Judean perspective.⁷ Similarly, Gary Rendsburg does not specifically refer to the Aramaic portions of Ezra, but he argues for the presence of a "foreign factor," in that the biblical texts may utilize lexical elements from Canaanite languages for rhetorical effect.⁸ Bill Arnold draws on Boris Uspensky to argue that the alternating usage of Aramaic and Hebrew represents shifting points of view from the internal repatriates and the other.⁹ Arnaud Sérandour argues that the bilingualism carries a direct theological contrast between the

---

⁴ Joseph Blenkinsopp, *Ezra-Nehemiah* (Louisville: Westminster John Knox, 1988); Hugh Williamson, *Ezra, Nehemiah* (Waco, TX: Nelson, 1985); also see C. C. Torrey, *The Composition and Historical Value of Ezra-Nehemiah* (Giessen: J. Ricker'sche Buchhandlung, 1896).
⁵ Blenkinsopp, *Ezra*, 115; Williamson, *Ezra*, 57; cf. D. A. Clines, *Ezra, Nehemiah, Esther* (Grand Rapids: Eerdmans, 1984), 82.
⁶ For a representative article defending the historical authenticity of these documents, see Hugh Williamson, "The Aramaic Documents in Ezra Revisited," *JTS* 59 (2008): 41–62; for representative works challenging this historical authenticity, see Lester Grabbe, *Ezra-Nehemiah* (New York: Routledge, 1998), 6; and Sebastian Grätz, *Das Edikt des Artaxerxes: Eine Untersuchen zum religionspolitischen und historischen Umfeld von Esra 7,12–26* (Berlin: de Gruyter, 2004).
⁷ Daniel Snell, "Why Is There Aramaic in the Bible?," *JSOT* 18 (1980): 32–51.
⁸ Gary Rendsburg, "Linguistic Variation and the 'Foreign' Factor in the Bible," in *Language and Culture in the Near East*, ed. Shlomo Iz'real and Rina Drory (Leiden: Brill, 1995), 177–90.
⁹ Bill Arnold, "The Use of Aramaic in the Hebrew Bible: Another Look at the Bilingualism in Ezra and Daniel," *JNSL* 22 (1996): 1–16.

sacred, exclusive language of Hebrew and the universal, gentile language of Aramaic.[10] Joshua Berman gives one of the most complete analyses on the narrative perspective of Aramaic as an external point of view of the Samaritans, who slowly come to understand the efficacy of the repatriate group.[11] Berman argues that the string of independent pronouns and pronominal suffixes indicate that the Aramaic narrative sections assume an outsider group against the exclusivist repatriate Judeans. Ezra 5:1–4 is particularly illuminating to this outsider perspective for the Aramaic portions:

- In 5:1, Haggai and Zechariah are said to prophesy "to the Judeans who were in Judah and Jerusalem" (and not "to us").
- In 5:2, the temple is identified as "the house of the God who is in Jerusalem."
- In 5:3, Tattenai and the associates come "to them" and speak "to them" (and not "to us").
- And in 5:4, the Samarians are identified in the first person: "So then we asked them" (rather than "they asked us").[12]

The avoidance of the second person pronominal endings alongside the Aramaic indicates a perspective of the Samaritans, distinct from the Judean insider language (Ezra 1–4) and the first-person accounts of the so-called Ezra memoir (Ezra 7). These studies by Snell, Arnold, Rendsburg, Sérandour and Berman benefit from the growing research surrounding bilingualism arising from both sociolinguistics and applied linguistics. They account for a more sophisticated and richer understanding of the Aramaic portions beyond source analysis.

I add that bilingualism of Ezra-Nehemiah has unexplored possibilities. My investigation does not intend to supplant the theories that the bilingualism emerges from sociolinguistic rhetorical ideals, or the traditional understanding of a composite development of the Ezra-Nehemiah text. More specifically, I think through the phenomenon of code-switching as a further supplement to these earlier studies in ways that are not mutually exclusive. The alternating languages in Ezra-Nehemiah are analogous to modern-day code-switching. Namely, the shifts

---

[10] Arnaud Sérandour, "Hébreu et Araméen dans la Bible," *Revues des Études juives* 159 (2000): 345–55; cf. A. Sérandour, "Remarques sur le Bilinguisme dans le Livre d'Esdras," in *Mosaïque de Langues, Mosaïque Culturelle: Le bilinguisme dans le Proche-Orient Ancien*, ed. F. Briquel-Chatonnet (Paris: Librairie d'Amérique et d'Orient, 1996), 131–44.

[11] Joshua Berman, "The Narratorial Voice of the Scribes of Samaria: Ezra iv 8–vi 18 Reconsidered," *VT* 56 (2006): 313–26; more recently, Berman expands his argument to place Aramaic portions within a greater narrative flow; see J. Berman, "The Narratological Purpose of Aramaic Prose in Ezra 4:8–6:18," *Aramaic Studies* 5 (2007): 165–92.

[12] Berman, "Narratological," 165–92; cf. Gary Knoppers suggests that the divide between Samaritans and Judeans is overstated in Ezra-Nehemiah, *Jews and Samaritans: The Origins and Histories of Their Early Relations* (Oxford: Oxford University Press, 2013).

between Aramaic and Hebrew signal an expression of a complex identity maker that encapsulates the self-perceived origins of Ezra's repatriate community. By alternating between Hebrew and Aramaic, Ezra portrays the Judean community as an adapting community within the dynamics of the Persian empire while simultaneously with zeal, preserving their own heritage as the Lord's people. In doing so, code-switching in Ezra contributes to a subversive message that Judeans can maintain their identity as the people of God in the midst of colonization. Because code-switching is a modern sociolinguistic phenomenon, I offer observations on how code-switching can be a point of dialogue between the text of Ezra-Nehemiah and diasporic Koreans in ways whereby language signals our own negotiations within the larger worlds.

Code-Switching

Code-switching suggests that the change from one language to another is not mechanically rote, but deliberate and intentional.[13] It does not depend so much on competencies, but on social intentions. Bilinguals have the choice to shape a social context though language selection. Admittedly, the vast majority of research on code-switching is through modern spoken language, particularly in secondary language acquisition, and not through written texts. Formal studies in code-switching has its inception with John Gumperz and Jan-Petter Blom through studies of dialect-switching on a Norwegian fishing village.[14] Consequently, code-switching research largely assumes cognitive duality that emerges somewhat subconsciously. For the biblical comparison, scribal systems would be much more deliberate and intentional through written bilingual activity. Observations connect the phenomenon of code-switching to be activated by shared language structures, driven by the bilingual's linguistic competency and revealed through phonology and morphology, limited in observation compared to modern settings.[15] Also, code-switching is primarily used to alternate between languages within the same utterance, thus being more applicable to the insertion of two Aramaic words in Gen 31:47 than the extended narrative sections in Ezra 4–7.[16] Recent approaches

---

[13] Penelope Gardner-Chloros, *Code-Switching* (Cambridge: Cambridge University Press, 2009), esp. pp. 1–19.

[14] John J. Gumperz and Jan-Petter Blom, "Social Meaning in Linguistic Structures: Code Switching in Northern Norway," in *Sociolinguistics: Current Trends and Prospects*, ed. R. Shuy (Georgetown: Georgetown University Press, 1972), 407–34.

[15] Shana Poplack, "Sometimes I'll Start a Sentence in Spanish Y TERMINO EN ESPAÑOL: Toward a Typology of Code-Switching," *Linguistics* 18 (1980): 581–618; David Sankoff and Shana Poplack, "A Formal Grammar for Code Switching," *Research on Language and Social Interaction* 1 (1981): 3–45.

[16] Hedi M. Belazi, Edward J. Rubin, Almeida Jacqueline Toribi, "Code Switching and X-Bar Theory: The Functional Head Constraint," *Linguistic Inquiry* 25 (1994): 221–37.

to code-switching argue for complete linguistic data, and not just select portions, for a more holistic assessment of linguistic competencies.[17]

Despite these constraints, like other sociolinguistic theories and social-scientific approaches in general, the underlying hypotheses of code-switching can help explain the phenomena in Ezra's scribal bilingualism.[18] Timothy Hogue points out that scribal code-switching carries a greater conscious intent between the language alteration.[19] Code-switching may give insight on the governed intentions behind the final form of Ezra in two languages. The essential question behind code-switching, whereas not completely congruous to modern spoken registers, also serves the intent of biblical scholars: What drives bilingualism from the shared matrix of linguistic competencies and social factors? The matrix between language use would have been complex in the scribal world of Persian Yehud. Despite our lack of observable, empirical data, I contend that bilingualism within an ancient text, especially one so obsessed with written authority, reflects a complex social phenomenon behind the language switches.

In her analysis of bilingualism throughout the book of Daniel, Anathea Portier-Young suggests that code-switching can explain the Aramaic portions as a deliberate movement to forge identity in the midst of empire.[20] Portier-Young contends that the Hebrew opening in Daniel 1 provides a foundation for Judean identity, but the switch to Aramaic in Dan 2–7 reflects the reality of living in a vast empire. The return to Hebrew for Dan 8–12 parallels the narrative content of the triumph of colonial resistance over the hegemony of empire. This explanation for the bilingualism in Daniel is convincing, but one must resist the tendency to immediately draw direct parallels to the Aramaic portions of Daniel. The dating of the Aramaic literary genres is different. Most significantly, one must consider the broader social context of the Persian repatriation against the Hellenistic context of Daniel. Yet at the same time, as Portier-Young modeled, code-switching has potential as a methodological frame for Ezra-Nehemiah and its social context of bilingual Yehud under Persian hegemony.

---

[17] Jeff MacSwan, "Code Switching and Linguistic Theory," in *Handbook of Bilingualism and Multilingualism*, ed. T. K. Bhatia and W. Ritchie (Oxford: Blackwell, 2013), 221–37.

[18] Other examples of sociolinguistics in biblical studies, see William M. Schneidewind, *A Social History of Hebrew: Its Origins through the Rabbinic Period* (New Haven: Yale University Press, 2013).

[19] Timothy Hogue presents an additional point of alternation in the movements between Official Aramaic and Western Aramaic; see "Return from Exile: Diglossia and Literary Code-Switching in Ezra 1–7," *ZAW* (forthcoming); cf. Frank H. Polak, "Sociolinguistics and the Judean Speech Community in the Achaemenid Empire," in *Judah and Judeans in the Persian Period*, ed. O. Lipschitz and M. Oeming (Winona Lake: Eisenbrauns, 2006), 589–628.

[20] Anathea Portier-Young, "Languages of Identity and Obligation: Daniel as Bilingual Book," *VT* 60 (2010): 98–115.

The Aramaic Sections in Ezra

I suggest that bilingualism in Ezra manifests the repatriates' efforts to forge their own Judean identity in the midst of both adaptation and preservation during a crucial period of the repatriation events. Following Portier-Young's usage of code-switching as a methodological framework on the bilingualism in Ezra-Nehemiah, code-switching reveals an awareness and resistance of the political power of the Persian Empire. That resistance demonstrates a linguistic ability which makes Ezra capable of embodying that power but also using it subversively to promote Judean goals of proper worship and sociopolitical identity in Jerusalem.

Adaptation

The usage of Aramaic indicates the adaptive competencies of the repatriate community behind the composition of Ezra-Nehemiah. Because of their hyper-awareness of scribal communication, the ability to switch to Aramaic for both documents as well as narrative demonstrates a level of linguistic authority and power.[21] The usage of Aramaic establishes the community's access to writings and knowledge.[22] The prologue hints at the strategy of adaptation in Ezra 1:1:

> In the first year of King Cyrus of Persia, in order that the word of the LORD by the mouth of Jeremiah might be accomplished, the LORD stirred up the spirit of King Cyrus of Persia so that he sent a herald throughout all his kingdom, and also in a written edict declared." (NRSV)

In the opening verse, rather than relying on the reign of an Israelite or Judean king, the historical reference centers on the reign of King Cyrus. More significantly, the LORD stirred up the spirit of Cyrus and not a Davidic representative—as Zerubbabel is relegated to the background in Ezra-Nehemiah. Immediately, the text gives an outwardly favorable assessment of the Persian Empire, in line with Second and Third Isaiah, and other texts that espouse a viewpoint of adaptation to the empire. Strategically, the prologue boldly places the foreign king inhabiting

---

[21] Two recent doctoral dissertations investigate textual authority within Ezra-Nehemiah; Cameron Howard, "Writing Yehud: Textuality and Power under Persian Rule" (Emory University, PhD diss, 2010); Lisa Cleath, "Reading Ceremonies in the Hebrew Bible: Ideologies of Textual Authority in Joshua 8, 2 Kings 23, Nehemiah 8" (UCLA, PhD diss, 2016).

[22] Mark Leuchter, "The Aramaic Transition and the Redaction of the Pentateuch," *JBL* 136 (2017): 249–68.

a Davidic role within the returning community.²³ The Judeans do not need to fight the empire, but rather through it, they can return to God's favor.²⁴

Because of this outward recognition of Persian authority and power, Ezra-Nehemiah must turn to a more adaptive strategy. Along these lines, fluency in Aramaic demonstrates a powerful capacity by the repatriate community to communicate in the imperial language. The imperial mandate to unify scattered peoples through the language of Aramaic dates back to at least the eighth century BCE and the conquests of the Assyrian empire. By the time of the Persian period, epigraphic evidence overwhelmingly supports the widespread usage of the Aramaic script and language. Large Aramaic archives appear at multiple sites in Yehud (Arad, Beershaba) and surrounding areas (Wadi Daliyeh, Tell el-Kheliefeh). Extant examples of Hebrew are rare. They are limited to symbolically charged texts such as coins or sealings.²⁵ In contrast, almost all legal documents and economic texts are written in Aramaic signifying the permeance of Aramaic.

The Aramaic portions of Ezra exemplify that the command of Aramaic is significant, powerful, and ultimately can be harnessed in favor of the repatriate Judeans. The Aramaic letter to Artaxerxes and commentary in Ezra 4:8–6:18 show the adversaries making appeals to the Persian Empire to subvert the reconstruction project. This rhetorically powerful letter warns about the potential disobedience of Jerusalem through adjectives like "rebellious" (מרד; Ezra 4:12, 15, 19; cf. Hebrew cognate to describe Jerusalem in Neh 2:19; 6:6), "bad" (באיש; Ezra 4:12), "hurtful" (נזק; Ezra 4:15), and "seditious" (אשתדור; Ezra 4: 15, 19). These negative descriptors align with the primary accusation that the construction will allow Judeans to "not pay tribute, custom, or toll, and the royal revenue will be reduced" (Ezra 4:13). Rather than assert their own experiences of exclusion from the rebuilding in Ezra 4:2–3, the adversaries attempt to persuade the Persians against Jerusalem through financial threat. Authoritatively and legally, the language of the letter would be in Aramaic to appeal to the Persians. The argument is compelling. As a result of this letter written in Aramaic, Artaxerxes orders the stoppage of the rebuilding.

But the strategy of adaptation is effective, as the Judean Aramaic response from Ezra 5:8 reverses the stoppage. Inspired by prophetic activity, another letter

---

²³ Joseph Blenkinsopp, *David Remembered: Kingship and National Identity in Ancient Israel* (Grand Rapids: Eerdmans, 2013), esp. pp. 68–69, 104–7.
²⁴ Multiple commentators highlight this aspect of Ezra 1:1, most recently Lisbeth S. Fried, *Ezra: A Commentary* (Sheffield: Sheffield Phoenix, 2015), 47; cf. Antonius Gunnerweg, *Esra* (Gütersloh: Gütersloh Verlagshaus Mohn, 1985), 41.
²⁵ Ya'akov Meshorer, *Persian Period through Hasmoneans*, vol. 1 of *Ancient Jewish Coinage* (New York: Amphora Books, 1982); Nahman Avigad, *Corpus of West Semitic Stamp Seals*, rev. Benjamin Sass (Jerusalem: Israel Academy of Arts and Sciences/Israel Exploration Society/Institute of Archaeology, Hebrew University, 1997); for a sociolinguisitic analysis, see William M. Schniedewind, *A Social History of Hebrew: Its Origins through the Rabbinic Period* (New Haven: Yale University Press, 2013).

in Aramaic appeals to an earlier decree from Cyrus, and thus reassures the Persians. This response letter counters the adversaries' appeal to archives that record Jerusalem's former greatness to another set of written documents that validate the original edict of Cyrus for continued reconstruction. As a result, in a stunning reversal of fortune, not only is the reconstruction taken up again, but done so at the expense of the empire and the empowerment of Sheshbazzar as the (new) director of the rebuilding project (Ezra 5:14, 16). In addition, the usage of Aramaic exhibits Judean capability and credibility to arrive at the desired outcome—reversal to the stoppage.

The Hebrew/Aramaic bilingualism in Ezra 4–7 sharply contrasts with that of 2 Kgs 18:26. In the latter text, set during the siege of Jerusalem, the Judeans at the wall plead with the Assyrian invaders to speak in Aramaic in order to shelter the city dwellers from the verbal rhetoric. The verse implies that Aramaic is limited to official and high-level usage in contrast to the common vernacular of Hebrew.[26] But consistent with general knowledge of Assyrian war tactics, the invaders refute the request and continue their threats upon the people in Hebrew, portending an unprecedented level of starvation and doom. The Judeans were not asking for withdrawal, but rather request for mercy through spoken Aramaic to keep the Jerusalem dwellers from panic and threat. The Assyrian invaders, represented by the Rab-sheka, however, deliberately spoke in Hebrew to communicate to the masses, to intimidate the defenders to surrender or face perpetual doom. By departing from the lingua franca and speaking in the vernacular, the Assyrians' demonstration of linguistic competency displays a wide range of powerful weapons to incite fear on the Judeans. In this case, the echoed words that the wall cannot protect the Judeans and that they will face starvation and death is further mixed with mockery of Yahweh.

In Ezra 4–7, it is the repatriate Judeans who bypass Hebrew and demonstrate fluency in the lingua franca of Aramaic to counter the letter of the adversaries by pointing out that there is a Persian source that legitimizes their reconstruction project. The medium of written words goes beyond spoken words and further accentuates the power of complete control of bilingualism in Ezra-Nehemiah. This linguistic adaptation ultimately assures the continuation of the temple project and the continuation of YHWH worship after generations in exile.

Preservation

On the one hand, code-switching suggests an effort to preserve an inherited culture. And on the other hand, the aspect of *adaptation* in code-switching reveals acculturation and command of the dominant culture. In the prologue of Ezra 1:1,

---

[26] Avi Hurvitz, "Hebrew and Aramaic in the Biblical Period: The Problem of 'Aramaisms' in the Linguistic Research of the Hebrew Bible," in *Biblical Hebrew: Studies in Typology and Chronology*, ed. Ian Young (Sheffield: Sheffield Academic, 2003), 24–37.

the efforts in *preservation* reach a culmination at the end of the work in Neh 13 as the repatriates reach resolve over the problem of language selection. Persian Yehud was undoubtedly a multilingual society.[27] Aramaic was the language of the Persian Empire and the imposed tongue and lingua franca of the ancient Near East since the Assyrian Empire. The emergence of Aramaic in the ancient Near East was among multiple alphabetic languages including Phoenician, Moabite, and even Hebrew, which developed for political ideologies. Seth Sanders contends that the rise of alphabetic script in the Western Levant in the early first millennium is a direct reflex of defining their own political order as articulated through royal inscriptions.[28] Sanders states, "Their language and assumptions are performative, in that they entail the existence of the very things they are trying to create on the ground: a single people, language, territory, and god."[29] In other words, languages are created and utilized for political gains and aims. Thus, Aramaic served as colonial hegemon, as it represented continuity of several generations of political empire—from the loose Aramaean states to the Neo-Assyrians' desire to create a single unified language, passed down to the Neo-Babylonian and Persian Empires. Accordingly, within the repatriate community, Aramaic represents the language of outsiders, associated with false gods in Jeremiah, or Babylon in Daniel. In contrast, Hebrew was the heritage language of resistance. It had little usage for economic gain or international correspondence even with other displaced and marginalized Judean groups such as the community at Elephantine. But Hebrew was the sacred language of the people's texts, and later referred to as the "holy tongue" / לשון הקודש. The hyper-awareness of their own language reaches crisis in Neh 13:24:

ובניהם חצי מדבר אשדודית ואינם מכירים לדבר יהודית וכלשון עם ועם
And half of their children spoke the language of Ashdod, and they could not speak the language of Judah, but spoke the language of various peoples.

Although the specific linguistic classification of the "language of the Ashdod" is under dispute, the significance lies in the ideology of the children adopting the language of a Philistia state.[30] Ashdodite was a denigrated language of the others in contrast to Hebrew due to its association with pagan deities (1 Sam 5:5–6; Is 20:1; Jer 25:20; Amos 3:9; 2 Chr 26:6). Of particular note, the people of Ashdod are referred to as ממזר in Zech 9:6, specifically referring to those children of mixed marriage (Deut 23:3). In the repatriation, the children lost their heritage language, which was natural for the children and grandchildren of immigrants.

---

[27] Bernard Spolsky, *The Language of the Jews: A Sociolinguistic History* (Cambridge: Cambridge University Press, 2014), 30.
[28] Seth L. Sanders, *The Invention of Hebrew* (Urbana: Illinois University Press, 2009).
[29] Sanders, *Hebrew*, 118.
[30] Edward Ullendorff suggests that "Ashododite" is literary creation of a foreign/outsider language in contrast to Hebrew; "C'est de l'hébreu pour moi!," *JSS* 13 (1968): 125–35.

The occurrence is decried as the switch to Ashdodite demonstrates their pathway to assimilation.[31] Such a final statement to close the collective work of Ezra-Nehemiah repeats the earlier mixed marriage crisis of Ezra 9 and sets the repatriate community to ensure their protection from assimilation in the years to come. Of course, such a recourse of dissolving such marriages violates basic social norms in modern society. But within the social context of Ezra-Nehemiah, the liminal spaces of repatriation activate a preservation of Hebrew as a deliberate display of identity negotiation.

This preference for Hebrew is pronounced at different places in the narrative. One of significant examples is Ezra 6:19–21 when the narrative switches back to Hebrew in order to introduce the community's celebration of Passover.[32] Here, the usage of Hebrew is a natural switch for the celebration of a festival that symbolizes God's providence for an exclusive community in an escape from one land of bondage and entry to another land of promise. Other times, the Hebrew influence is likely unintentional, such as the Aramaisms within the Hebrew portions of Ezra-Nehemiah.[33]

The alternating languages between Hebrew and Aramaic present a parallel view of the repatriate community. They are able to adapt to the international lingua franca with enough facility to defeat the adversaries from their own satrap. Despite their diasporic situation with multiple displacements, Ezra-Nehemiah closes with a commitment to maintain their heritage language, even at the extreme cost of separating wives and children from the community. They remain Judeans at their core, and deeply committed to the preservation of their heritage, of which language is a crucial expression of said heritage.

Together, this adaptation and preservation also contribute to a subversion of empire. In *A Biblical Theology of Exile*, Daniel Smith-Christopher argues that Ezra-Nehemiah is ultimately a subversive text, one that openly acquiesces to Persian imperial authority, but within a deeper subtext, seeks to undermine the empire and empower the diasporic community to thrive in the midst of displacement.[34] Such subversion plays out in looking at some of the wider themes within Ezra-Nehemiah. Although the Aramaic epistolary letters help bring the reconstruction to completion, Ezra-Nehemiah recognizes another written document, the Torah, written in Hebrew.

---

[31] "The phrase, "but spoke the language of various peoples" is omitted in the LXX, as the phrase condemns the LXX audience of diaspora Jews"; Schniedewind, *Social History*, 165.
[32] Fried, *Ezra*, 285–96.
[33] The study of Aramaisms in Biblical Hebrew goes back to the seminal work by E. Kautzsch, *Die Aramaismem im Alten Testament. I: Lexicalischer Teil* (Halle), 1902; for a summary of Aramaisms in Ezra-Nehemiah, see Angel Sáenz-Badillos, *A History of the Hebrew Language*, trans. John Elwolde (Cambridge: Cambridge University Press, 1996), 121–22.
[34] Daniel Smith-Christopher, *A Biblical Theology of Exile* (Minneapolis: Fortress, 2002).

Whereas Ezra-Nehemiah begins with the somewhat surprising declaration of Cyrus's regnal formulation, it ends with a repentant spirit over assimilation. The banishment of foreign wives and children is set in tension with the purity of the preservation of an inherited language, Hebrew. Although epigraphic evidence suggests the pervasiveness of Aramaic during this period, the limited samples of Hebrew indicate that it is symbolically charged.[35] As Persian control of Yehud atrophied in the mid-fourth century BCE, Yehud coins began to reflect the Hebrew language instead of Aramaic. Torah would last beyond royal Aramaic decrees. And God's people would survive beyond the Persian Empire.

CODE-SWITCHING AND KOREAN AMERICAN INTERPRETATIONS

The concept of code-switching may elicit particular responses in the landscape of Korean and Korean American interpretation.[36] Because the vast majority of Korean families immigrated after the Immigration and Nationality Act of 1965, we begin to see the second and third generations of Korean Americans reaching adulthood in the masses. Bilingualism is a direct concern for Korean American communities, and consequently, the concept of code-switching may serve as a powerful prefigurative reading strategy.[37] In an earlier work, I argued for repatriation as an interpretive strategy for Ezra-Nehemiah, particularly for Korean communities.[38] Without essentializing the return migration experience, I suggest multiple parallels between the Judean and Korean repatriates, specifically, the centrality of blood purity in identity formation, as well as the effects of long term displacement. A repatriation hermeneutic is less of a methodology and more of a form of discourse that provokes discourse and imagination.[39] It is with hope that

---

[35] Schniedewind, *Social History*, 157–61.

[36] I categorize Korean American interpretation in broad terms, in applying a conscious Korean American lens to the study of biblical texts; for further discussion, see Hyun Chul Paul Kim, "Currents in Korean-American Biblical Interpretation" *Journal of Korean American Ministries and Theology* 5 (2012): 7–19.

[37] Tat-Siong Benny Liew distinguishes the terms of "prefigurative" and "prescriptive," by drawing on Sharon K. Han, "Cross-Discipline Trafficking: What's Justice Got to Do with It?," in *Orientations: Mapping Studies in the Asian Diaspora*, ed. K. Chuh and K. Shimakawa (Durham: Duke University Press, 2001), 81, 97–98; the prefigurative approach does not claim exclusivity, but rather intends to function as a complementary option; see Liew, *What Is Asian American Biblical Hermeneutics? Reading the New Testament* (Honolulu: University of Hawaii Press, 2008), 2.

[38] Roger S. Nam, "Unsettled Homecomings: A Repatriate Reading of Ezra-Nehemiah," in *Reading in These Times*, ed. Benny Tat-siong Liew and Fernando Segovia (Atlanta: SBL Press, forthcoming).

[39] Kwok Pui-Lan, *Postcolonial Imagination and Feminist Theology* (Louisville: Westminster John Knox, 2005).

the Korean perspective on repatriation can create avenues of engagement for the multivalent Korean reading communities and broader Asian American worlds.

All of these communities must confront the issue of language and bilingualism as central factors in identity formation. Thus, the concept of code-switching carries enormous hermeneutical weight for today's Korean American readers. Bilingualism is a reality that we navigate. Whether Korean biblical scholars attempt to foster dialogue in an international community, or second or later generation diasporic Koreans wrestle with heritage, the development of our own bilingualism of either Korean as our heritage language or English goes beyond mechanical communication that resonates with the individual and the broader community. Code-switching according to the linguists Bhatia and Ritchie:

> Language clearly intertwines powerfully with conceptions and definitions of allegiance and "belonging." It possesses more than instrumental value; it is the vehicle of tradition and culture, and the medium of group narrative.... when more than one language is involved, then, we should expect ramifications in terms of identity and "groupness."[40]

Because Korean interpretation is deeply embedded within social contexts, said interpretations are not merely geographic and cultural. The Korean perspective is also a "social and political designator."[41] The centrality of language in the Korean community may parallel the usage of code-switching that signals assimilation, preservation and subversion. Each of these three themes emerge for both the Korean American (or really, any diasporic Korean) interpreter as well as the Korean interpreter.

My place as a second-generation Korean American informs my own interpretation of the bilingualism of Ezra-Nehemiah. For my parents' generation, the mastery of English was elusive. The shedding of their Asian accents was impossible. Proficiency in English was a path to assimilation, and many of us grew up at the insistence of English at the expense of our mother tongue. Paradoxically, this emphasis on access, through English competence, accompanied deliberate efforts at maintaining Korean language. I had an evolving relationship with the Korean language. As a child, I dreaded mandatory Korean language classes held on Saturdays at the church. But as a young adult, I eagerly took two years of Korean language as an undergraduate and moved to Seoul upon graduation. Such a desire for heritage language preservation is not natural and often met with resistance by younger generations. John WcWhorter suggests that the next-

---

[40] Tej K. Bhatia and William C. Ritchie, eds., *The Handbook of Bilingualism and Multilingualism* (Oxford: Wiley Blackwell, 2012), 19.

[41] Mary F. Foskett and Jeffrey Kah-Jin Kuan, eds., *Ways of Being, Ways of Reading: Asian American Biblical Interpretation* (St. Louis: Chalice, 2006), xiii; cf. Jin Young Choi, "Asian/Asian American Interpretation," in *The Oxford Encyclopedia of the Bible and Gender Studies*, ed. Julia M. O'Brien (Oxford: Oxford University Press, 2014), 1–9.

generation often has little incentive to continue with the older language through a host of political and social reasons.[42] But these heritage languages arise in subversion. Long before the global rise of K-pop and K-drama, the desire to learn Korean was deeply tied to a sense of heritage preservation. For some like myself, this drive to cultural preservation led me to stay in Seoul for four years during my twenties, and the desire to instill this drive in my children, was a central reason behind a recent yearlong sabbatical in Korea.

The context for bilingualism is also subversive in political and social ways. With the rise of South Korea as the twelfth largest GDP in the world, a level unimaginable for the group of immigrants of the late 1960s, Korean is a legitimate language for business contacts. Korean language classes are now offered at every major university and even community colleges and high schools. On a social level, the efforts at bilingualism defies an American monoculturalism, and presents Korean-ness as a part of the identity. Code-switching presents a larger opportunity for both worlds, that allows one to assimilate into the language of privilege (English) while preserving the language of heritage (Korean).

Beyond all the linguistic theories and social-scientific approaches, bilinguals, whether from Persian Yehud or the Korean diaspora, all have an innate sense of the connection to a heritage language. Language connects, informs and expresses our own narratives and our own identity. The tenacity to protect such language runs deep and even nonsensical, but we understand that our articulation of self-identity begins with the language that we can self-select.

---

[42] John WcWhorter, *The Power of Babel: The Natural History of Languages* (New York: Harper, 2001), 271.

REREADING "A VIRTUOUS WOMAN" (*'ĒŠET HAYIL*) IN PROVERBS 31:10–31

Sun-Ah Kang

The "virtuous woman" (*'ēšet hayil*)[1] in Prov 31:10–31 has been used widely by various readers. Inasmuch as the text is read or sung at Jewish weddings, it functions to justify male dominance over women (in Yahweh's name). In Korean churches, this text is preached on Mother's Day to teach Korean Christian women on how to live motherly. I suggest that in the Korean context, this text requires redress and reexamination since the positive elements concerning the virtuous wife is misconstrued in light of Korean Confucianism.

I begin this essay by noting shared characteristics of *'ēšet hayil* in Prov 31:10–31 and the virtuous wife in the teachings of Korean Confucianism.[2] There are parallel views of woman established by the lenses of economic commodity, household manager, and warrior and husband's reputation. I then explain how and why, culturally, Korean women so easily identify themselves with the *'ēšet hayil* in Prov 31:10–31. At the outset, it may have something to do with early indoctrination and cultural understanding of the Confucian virtuous wife. Lastly, I conclude this essay with a fresh rereading of Prov 31:10–31, highlighting the *panopticon* developed by Michel Foucault in *Discipline and Punish*[3] as a

---

[1] I employ the term *'ēšet hayil* as "a virtuous woman" in order to compare with Korean Confucianism instead of the literal Hebrew bound form, אֵשֶׁת חַיִל. The *'ēšet hayil* is translated variously: "A virtuous woman (KJV)," "a good wife (RSV)," "a wife of noble character (NIV)," and "a capable wife (NRSV)."

[2] Here, when it comes to Korean Confucianism, technically, it refers to Neo-Confucianism that was introduced in the later thirteenth and fourteenth centuries in the end of the Koryò and Choson dynasties. Neo-Confucianism, as a ruling ideology of the Choson dynasty, has spread into different walks of people and especially, on women and they are bound by their father, husband, and son. See, John Duncan, "The Korean Adoption of Neo-Confucianism" and Wei-Ming Tu, "Probing the 'Three Bonds' and 'Five Relationships' in Confucian Humanism," in *Confucianism and the Family*, ed. Walter H. Slote and George A. De Vos (Albany: State University of New York Press, 1998).

[3] Michel Foucault, *Discipline and Punish: The Birth of the Prison*, trans. Alan Sheridan (New York: Vintage Books, 1995).

hermeneutical lens to encourage Korean women to "discipline" the Confucian view of the virtuous women.

Women in Korean Confucianism

At the outset, it may be helpful to note how *'ēšet hayil* has been translated in the Korean Bible. The Korean Revised Version[4] reads *'ēšet hayil* as a "wise and virtuous woman." This resonates with the "virtuous wife" in Korean Confucianism. This translation of the "virtuous woman" connotes a subtle but noticeable link between the biblical text and Korean Confucianism.

When we speak of Korean Confucianism, we are refering to Neo-Confucianism that arose in the later thirteenth and fourteenth centuries at the end of the Koryò and Choson dynasties. Neo-Confucianism, as a ruling ideology of the Choson dynasty, spread steadily throughout Korean society. It has had an enormous influence on the lives of women. Through education, which involves teaching women about moral behaviors and virtuous attitudes, correct behavior and attitude as well as self cultivation are underscored. As an example of Korean Confucianism, a text meant to instruct women called *Naehun* is consider. It is an anthology that consists of chapters on speech and behavior, filial piety, wedding, couple, mother's duty, affability, and frugality. Martina Deuchler translates the preface of the *Naehun* as follows:

> All human beings are born with the spirit of Heaven and Earth, and all are endowed with the virtues of the Five Relationships ... yet whether [a human being resembles] an orchid or a bitter smelling shrub depends entirely on the method of self-cultivation.... The rise or fall of the political order, although connected with the husband's character, also depends on the wife's goodness. She therefore must be educated.... Generally, men let their hearts wander in passions and amuse themselves with all kinds of subtleties, [yet] because they naturally distinguish between right and wrong, they are able to keep themselves [on the right track].... Women only concern themselves with the quality of their embroidering skills and are ignorant of the urgency of virtuous conduct. This is what worries me daily![5]

Here, it is assumed that women, by nature, are inferior to men and cannot choose what is right. Women do not care for higher education or desire to be a sage (or

---

[4] The Korean Revised Version (1962) is the most popular Bible in Korean churches, which is comparable to the grammatically rigid King James Version (1611). The KJV translates *'ēšet hayil* as "a virtuous woman" and accordingly, the Korean Revised Version reads *'ēšet hayil* as "a wise and virtuous woman."

[5] Martina Deuchler, "Propagating Female Virtues in Choson Korea," in *Women and Confucian Cultures in Premodern China, Korea, and Japan*, ed. Dorothy Ko, JaHyun Kim Haboush, and Joan R. Piggott (Berkeley: University of California Press, 2003), 147.

professor) but are only interested in amusing themselves with domesticated tasks such as embroidering. It constructs an androcentric ideal picture of womanly behavior:

> Moral conduct—women need not have great talents, but must be quiet and serene, chaste and disciplined ... proper appearance—women need not be beautiful but must be clean in dress and appearance; and womanly tasks ... must pay attention to such duties as weaving and entertaining guests.... She [married woman] had to serve her parents-in-law, be an obedient and dutiful wife, and a wise and caring mother.[6]

These teachings connect moral and appropriate conducts as womanly behaviors that all women should follow. They propagate what is supportive, obedient, and dutiful wife or daughter-in-law based on a rigid Confucian teaching of women, who by nature, are considered lower than men. The role of women in restoring the household suggests that women are encouraged to bear adversities for the good of the household. In order for her to play such a significant role, *Naehun* admonishes women to cultivate themselves to be virtuous and wise supporter of the household.

Consider the following story of Lady Chang (1598–1680), the exemplary wife who managed her household and practiced Confucian ideals in her daily life. Lady Chang faithfully followed what *Naehun* asserts by remaining silent and invisible while supporting her husband from behind the scenes. Through daily discipline, her cooking and management skills exceeded all expectations. She became renowned for her cookbook (1670) eventually becoming more famous than her husband. There are striking similarities between the imagery of the household manager in Lady Chang and the virtuous woman in Prov 31:10–31. Both are wives who faithfully performed their gendered labors by weaving and spinning textiles to advance their respective households. Their abilities were extraordinary, namely, in supervising female servants, treating them with dignity, and increasing economic prosperity. They also instructed children and others in wisdom. Thanks to them, their husbands gained recognition with reputation and success. These images illustrate how disciplinary power leads to unexpected results, producing powerful (autonomous) women in society.

REREADING '*EŠET HAYIL* FROM KOREAN WOMAN'S PERSPECTIVE

In contemporary Korean society, a Korean TV show called "(Cy)Borg-mom" has become popular in portraying the "ideal" Korean mother. The storyline fosters a scientist who creates a humanoid cyborg resembling his late wife to take care of

---

[6] Martina Deuchler, *The Confucian Transformation of Korea: A Study of Society and Ideology* (Cambridge: Harvard University Press, 1992), 257.

his kindergarten son. The show further sarcastically depicts overly involved Parent Teacher Assocation (PTA) moms at a prestigious school called "Buckingham." Characteristically, the Borg mom stands out among all other PTA moms because of her exceptional beauty, body shape, extraordinary skill set, cosmopolitan style, and her wisdom. The cyborg mom is depicted as the perfect supermom. Such caricatures invite a rereading of Prov 31:10–31 in a Korean Confucianized Christian society.[7] Without Korean Confucianism, the proper diagnosis of Korean women, especially as educative mothers, cannot be made in full.

Currently, in the west, the idea of the ideal Asian American mother is the "tiger mom," when in fact, it only pertains to Chinese, Korean, Japanese, and Taiwanese mothers, whose extraordinary zeal for their children's educational success, is unmatched. In Korea, on the day of the (comparable) Scholastic Assessment Test (SAT), Korean mothers pray (*Sunung* in Korean) at the gate of the schools where their children take the exam. Korean mothers habitually gather for specially called "prayer meetings" at churches or Buddhist temples on behalf of their children.

On the day of the SAT in Korea, literally, every major city at 8:10 AM embraces silence. Even military drills are banned. Every year, it is reported that some students attempt suicide due to the extreme pressure and stress related to this national college entrance examination. Starting around the age of seven, to gain advantages, parents often consider moving to neighborhoods with the best educational system, such as Gangnam, the area with the greatest number of exceptional schools and private after-school educational institutes called *hakwon* (Korean). Although the famous episode of Mencius's mother moving three times for Mencius's education is understood as ahistorical, this story is widely circulated and popularized in Korea. It finds a home in the Korean motto that Korean mothers will move anywhere for their children. This perpetuates the cultural stereotype of Korean mothers as *ajumma*, a married woman who is passing through her prime years without self-care. An *ajumma* is a liminal being, figuratively speaking, in-between the female and male sexes. She is an asexual being who is strong, aggressive, and even reckless – doing whatever it takes for the household, especially her children. An *ajumma* does not consider her beauty. She is no longer concerned about her clothes, make-up, hair, nails, and well being.

The portrait of the *ajumma* can be found in a contextualized reading of Prov 31:10–31 with Korean Confucianism: The *'ēšet ḥayil* is extraordinarily productive (vv. 18, 21, 27, 29, 31) in attaining food for her family (vv. 14–15), running her textile industry (vv. 13, 19, 22, 24), and going out to the field (v. 16). She possesses strong loins and arms (vv. 17, 25) from working all day (vv. 15, 18).

---

[7] Nam-Soon Kang, *Diasporic Feminist Theology: Asia and Theopolitical Imagination* (Minneapolis: Fortress, 2014), 286. Kang criticizes the Korean church as "ethically Confucianized Christianity." She additionally notes that church continues to oppress women.

She mulit-tasks (v. 19) and her attitude is beaming with confidence and bravery like a general (v. 25). She is far from beautiful, charming, sensual, or seductive, like her very opposite, Woman Folly in Prov 1–9 (v. 30).

Korean Confucianism teaches that such wife's name will be rewarded and remembered by later generations: "Her [wife's] reward was a posthumously granted honorific title commensurate to her husband's achievements in the outside world."[8] Korean women continue to endure difficulties by sacrificially serving men who aspire to become great scholars or government officials. In the history of Confucianism, these two occupations held the highest honor and notable achievements in society. Haejoang Cho introduces a tombstone of a scholar's wife:

> On one tombstone inscription, a poor *sonbi*'s (scholar's) wife was praised because she could "suspend the decline and prevent the breakdown of the family, managing an impoverished household, making three meals a day, preparing the ancestral rites, and making family gatherings happy and comfortable." It ends with "whose spirit will be nobler than hers!"[9]

The poor *sonbi* were typical Korean Confucian men who lacked economic astuteness and capability. They were dependent on the wife's odd jobs for sustatinence. The wife's management skills would navigate the family through financial impoverishment, while the husband studied diligently in order to save face. The women's labors (*naejo*) for husband and household are regarded as virtuous: "Equally, from behind the scenes (*naejo*), a woman [wife] could advance her husband's career as an official or a scholar."[10] The wife's supportive actions (*naejo*) enabled her husband to focus on work; and by doing so, he hoped to succeed. Without her *naejo*, however, he will not materialize or achieve succees.

In Proverbs, the husband and wife hardily ever find themselves in the same frame. The wife stays at home, or goes out to work, to the marketplace to sell her products, while the husband stays at the gate with other men and elders. This relationship mirrors the relationship between male and female in Korean Confucianism—man as heaven (*yang*) and woman as earth (*yin*). Heaven and the earth cannot be in the same place together. They are divided by hierarchy and cosmology, with heaven taking precedence over earth. The woman's work is the hard work of a housewife, a *yojangbu* better qualified as a woman commander:

---

[8] Deuchler, "Propagating Female Virtues in Choson Korea," 152.
[9] Haejoang Cho, "Male Dominance and Mother Power: The Two Sides of Confucian Patriarchy in Korea," in *Confucianism and the Family*, ed. Walter H. Slote and G. A. DeVos, SUNY Series in Chinese Philosophy and Culture (Albany: State University of New York Press, 1998), 197–98.
[10] Deuchler, "Propagating Female Virtues in Choson Korea," 152.

In order to be a successful and respectable *chongbu* [primary wife], she said that one had to be practical, hardworking, and skillful in managing economic and human resources. She must be strong and firm just like a *yojangbu*, a woman commander.... The image was further elaborated with descriptions of physical characteristics, usually ugly faces, strongly built asexual bodies, and vigorous activities such as horseback riding.[11]

This imagery of a woman warrior (*yojangbu*) alludes to Korean mothers who protect and attack on behalf of the family, especially for her children's wellbeing. With a Korean Confucian understanding of humanity, beginning with yang and yin, underscored by Korean Confucian's emphasis on education as the central path to success, naturally lends to supporting Korean Confucianized Christianity's teachings on the wise and good mother in Prov 31:10–31. In essence, in Korea, today's Korean women are encouraged to become militant supermoms. Yani Yoo writes:

> The superwoman in Proverbs 31 does all the work alone while her husband seems to be idle. She is praised because her works contribute to her husband's good name outside the home and because she serves as an ideal wife. This couple sounds quite Asian.[12]

As Yoo points out, regardless of her virtuous deeds, it is all for her husband. This Confucianized reading of Prov 31:10–31 engenders labor and idealizes women's labor as praiseworthy. This praise is further grounded in the fear of the Lord. Unfortunately, not only Korean Confucianism but also Korean Confucianized Christianity promotes "borg moms."

In current Korean society, there is a plethora of women workers in the following industries: cleaning, highway tollbooths, call centers, register counters at grocery stores, among other low end jobs. These jobs are poorly paid but women (mothers) make up the majority. They have been propelled to work to earn extra income for their children's *hakwon*. Their fervor and zeal for educational advancement is idealized as "superlative education and success" go hand in hand. In a highly competitive context, Korean women become militant *ajumma* for their children. Similarly, Korean women additionally experience the "empty nest syndrome" after their children go off to college, get a job, or get married. Women who have spent their entire life savings for their children's education have little return, as some grown children as adults, do not feel any obligilation to repay or take care of their aged parents. These Korean women are left with emotional and economic emptiness and bankruptcy. The teaching of the subordinate virtue, the

---

[11] Cho, "Male Dominance and Mother Power," 198.

[12] Yani Yoo, "Women's Leadership Fragmented: Examples in the Bible and the Korean Church," in *Korean Feminists in Conversation with the Bible, Church and Society*, ed. Kyung Sook Lee and Kyung Mi Park (Sheffield: Sheffield Phoenix, 2011), 106.

good mother and noble wife by the Confucianized Korean churches cannot offer redemption for those that promote such values. After all the selfless acts, through personal sacrifice on behalf of the family, Korean women are completely emptied. In this regard, rereading *'ēšet hayil* from a Korean woman's perspective offers redeeming insights on Korean women's agency and self-cultivation.

Acknowleding economic variance, Christine R. Yoder reads *'ēšet hayil* as a reflection of affluent women in the Achaemenid Empire. These women run their own businesses with confidence and agency. Yoder argues that women managed their own household economy:[13] "Women at Elephantine went about in the marketplaces, buying, selling, and bartering for various goods.... Women also tended to the preparation of wool and flax fibers, spinning, weaving, tailoring, and the cleaning of clothing."[14] Royal women were land owners, estate managers, employers of groups, and lenders to other business women:

> Among their [women's] responsibilities as managers of the household, women manufactured textiles, traded in the marketplaces, and might own and supervise slaves. Women also made and received deliveries, managed properties, and were parties to the purchase and sale of slaves and land. As workers in the royal economy, non-royal women engaged in a wide greater than men; women also worked at varying ranks and degrees of specialization. Moreover, women with sufficient amounts of capital might get into the credit business, making loans of cash and other goods at favorable interest rates.[15]

Yoder's descriptions of women's lives in the Achaemenid Empire are eye-opening. Women were neither passive housewives nor dependent and subordinate to their husbands. They had agency. Korean women must also acquire agency.

To read fairly and ethically from a woman's perspective is to see *'ēšet hayil* as a reflection of various images of women in real life. She is a professional who finds success in her field of work. She is an artisan of textiles (vv. 13, 19, 22), an international merchant (vv. 14, 17, 24), an entrepreneur (vv. 15, 18, 21, 24–25, 27), an adventurous investor (v. 16), euergetes and philanthropist (vv. 20–21), a human resource administrator for her husband (vv. 23, 27–29), a professor or guru (v. 26), an educator (v. 28), a deaconess (v. 30), and a celebrity (vv. 28–31). In today's terms, these imageries resonate with successful women. The text empowers those who are already successful, wealthy, and upper-class. We cannot simply evaluate Prov 31:10–31 as oppressive to women without acknowledging this variation. Instead, this text may be counterintuitive, in select cultural contexts, especially to Korean daughters-in-law who feel liberated, career-oriented yet feeling guilty about being away from home. Is there any way to be more subversive?

---

[13] Christine Elizabeth Yoder, *Wisdom as a Woman of Substance: A Socioeconomic Reading of Proverbs 1–9 and 31:10–31*, BZAW304 (Berlin: de Gruyter, 2001), 59.

[14] Yoder, *Wisdom as a Woman of Substance*, 59.

[15] Yoder, *Wisdom as a Woman of Substance*, 71.

Korean Confucianism and rereading of Prov 31:10–31 may lead to Nam-Soon Kang's understanding of autonomy: "Autonomy, in this feminist context, is not absolute self-sufficiency, as many too readily claim, but one's capacity for independent survival, thinking, and judgment. Autonomous persons recognize others' needs for freedom and their own lives."[16] In other words, it might be impossible for one—not only women, but also some men—to find absolute agency in this kyriarchal society. However, it is possible for one to attain and exert power to survive.

In the case of Prov 31:10–31, the *'ēšet hayil* is known for her deeds by her husband (vv. 10–11, 23, 29), children (v. 28), and even by YHWH (v. 30). Although her labors contributed to her husband and his family, it is uncertain whether she received dividends for her personal profit. Nevertheless, it is the *'ēšet hayil* whose name and deeds are praised rather than the deeds of her husband (v. 31). It is the *'ēšet hayil* who the narrator underscores in Prov 31:10–31 rather than her husband. Without her, the husband is worthless. She is thererefore, powerful and worthy in Prov 31:10–31.

Although both Korean Confucianism and Prov 31:10–31 partially praise and celebrate women's autonomous actions, there are limitations. Attempts to suppress women's talents and abilities cannot make women invisible. Under the limitations of time and societal structures, women have survived leaving legacy for future generations. Cho rightly evaluates:

> Korean women ... who survived rough and troubled histories as the stronghold of the family, naturally developed a sense of power and fortitude. This sense of power, as the major supporters of the family, made women even more aggressive about maximizing their own self-interest, which were, at least in appearance, predominantly familial.[17]

Indeed, women in the time of Korean Confucianism as well as in Proverbs, survived on the margins and centers. Women have practiced their roles greatly and sustained kyriarchy.[18] Today, in the form of *ajumma*, they survive and even expand their abilities and talents unexpectedly by kyriarchy. Women are not born into the notion of being strong but had to become strong in order to educate and protect their children and family. This cannot diminish the side effects of women's work that bring a generational crisis and bankruptcy of the family. It is worthwhile refocusing and rediscovering the true value of being a Korean woman.

Korean Confucianism emphasizes that everyone may reach Confucian human ideals through self-cultivation. That understanding begins with an acknowledgement of goodness in humanity. *Naehun* warns women to guard their speech and

---

[16] Kang, *Diasporic Feminist Theology*, 313.
[17] Cho, "Male Dominance and Mother Power," 198–99.
[18] Elisabeth Schüssler Fiorenza, *The Power of Naming: A Concilium Reader in Feminist Liberation Theology* (Maryknoll: Orbis Books, 1996).

urges them to remain silent. Yet, at times, it recommends that women advise their husbands. For example, Queen Sohye served as a royal advisor to her son, King Songjong. Her thoughts and speeches were influential. Women's roles as advisors were regarded as virtuous in *Naehun*. For instance, in the chapter on husband and wife, there are examples from the wives of the Chinese emperors who advise with sincerity, respect, and dignity.[19] Queen Sohye teaches that women are educated in order to educate their husbands as well as other women and men. Korean Confucianism teaches that through right woman behavior, women can become sages. This leads us to a rediscovery of the *'ēšet hayil* as a sage in Prov 31:26: "She opens her mouth with wisdom, and the teaching of kindness is on her tongue." Both Prov 31:10–31 and Korean Confucianism express discipline to navigate through a patriarchical system. A woman's service cannot be underestimated by her appearance, status, or role. Expressing appreciation for women's work is not enough. By rereading Prov 31:10–31 with critical awareness of women's situation, readers are invited to focus on (re)discovering women's agency and the necessity of women's self-cultivation.

Power of Observations

Reading the "virtuous woman" in Prov 31:10–31 through Michel Foucault's model of panopticon reveals a new perspective. In *Discipline and Punish*, through observation, Foucault examines how power is constructed and disciplined in modern society. Using Jeremy Bentham's panopticon model of the prison, Foucault suggests that the disciplinary force through observation can be a pedagogical training when applied to other institutions such as monasteries, schools, armies, and hospitals. Bentham's idea of the panopticon is as follows:

> At the periphery, an annular building; at the centre, a tower; this tower is pierced with wide windows that open into the inner side of the ring; the peripheric building is divided into cells, each of which extends the whole width of the building; they have two windows, one on the inside, corresponding to the windows of the tower; the other, on the outside, allows the light to cross the cell from one end to the other.... By the effect of backlighting, one can observe from the tower.[20]

The cadre of the panopticon fabricates the inmate to suspect that she or he is under surveillance leading one to control one's own behaviors, and thereby keeps attention to rule following. In order to make this possible, surveillance must be visible and unverifiable so that one cannot find out who is in the center tower. In an isolated cell, through repetition of daily schedule, the inmates are disciplined to follow rules – while punishment and praise foster discipline. Bentham argues

---

[19] Kyung-Ha Lee, "A Woman Intellectual in Fifteenth Century, Insu-Daebi," *Research of Korean Classical Women's Literature* 12 (2006): 165.
[20] Lee, "Woman Intellectual in Fifteenth Century," 200.

that this system effectively controls the state of inmates without having to invest in human supervisors in the central tower. Foucault adds:

> Hence the major effect of the Panopticon: to induce in the inmates a state of conscious and permanent visibility that assures the automatic functioning of power. So to arrange things that the surveillance is permanent in its effects, even if it is discontinuous in its action.[21]

This system manipulates the individual to a subservient position in a power differential. Power relations[22] produce discourses that construct what is normative and acceptable. For Foucault, power is not only repressive or negative, but productive and even positive: "In fact, power produces; it produces reality; it produces domains of objects and rituals of truth. The individual and the knowledge that maybe gained of him belong to this production."[23]

Actualizing Foucault's definitions on Prov 31:10–31 is a wife who is constantly under the gaze of the narrator, her husband, her children, and YHWH. The anonymous gaze of the narrator follows closely by describing how the wife's daily schedule goes and this gaze permeates her every behavior throughout her domestic and public spheres. Although her husband stays at the gate of the town (v. 23), he knows her daily schedule, as if he watches over her every action (v. 29).

In verse 28, her children praise their mother's contributions. But Yahweh, who is invisible, most effectively gazes on her actions. According to Foucault, the disciplinary gaze should be visible yet, unverifiable in order to control one's behavior. The wife does not spend any time for herself but rather, works for the benefit of her husband and the household. She becomes docile and submissive to the power of her husband. This is related to Foucault's understanding of how power controls the inmates by taking away their liberty.

By praising her works and contributions, this too becomes a discourse of God-talk that constructs a system of power over women, especially those who want to be faithful and wise. From Foucault's point of view, praise can function as a form of surveilling power over women. In this way, this text has disciplinary power to support norms for women to work hard for the household, suggesting that household work is to be identified with how women fear God. YHWH is the ultimate sovereign gazer in the text and the real power throughout the entire book of Proverbs. There is no tangible evidence of how she is to fear the Lord, so her contribution to the household is equated to fearing God. This is problematic. The only one who truly benefits from her activities is then, her husband. He, not she, becomes the one who enjoys the good reputation at the gate while she is outside the gates earning the living for her family.

---

[21] Lee, "Woman Intellectual in Fifteenth Century," 201.
[22] Michel Foucault, *The History of Sexuality*, vol. 1 (New York: Vintage Books, 1990).
[23] Foucault, *History of Sexuality*, 94.

Foucault's notion of observation opens space for resistance. Bentham's theory of the panopticon is meant to be a perfect system, but there are serious slippages that produce unintended consequences such as "the maintenance of delinquency, the encouragement of recidivism, the transformation of the occasional offender into a habitual delinquent, the organization of a closed milieu of delinquency."[24] In Prov 31:10–31, disciplinary power produces discourse about women that supports male power in the *'ēšet hayil*. The surveillance partially fails to make her entirely obedient and docile in the face of power. She does not fear but rather is strong and confident (v. 25), unlike other inmates under surveillance in Foucault's theory.

CONCLUSION

It should be noted that Prov 31:10–31 has been read as a text to encourage women to support their leadership in the household. Yet, it also has limitations. Since it is rare to find ample evidence of woman's leadership and praiseworthy performance in the Hebrew Bible without benefiting others, *'ēšet hayil* attempts to denote rediscovery and self-cultivation for Korean women. Foucault's notion of surveillance and observation as well as resources drawn from Korean Confucianism to interpret Prov 31:10–31, which has often been read to suppress and dominate women even in spite of efforts by scholars to read the text as a celebration for women's autonomous leadership in the household, is reassessed.

Through Foucault's critique, we see that this text can be used to create discourses of obedient and submissive women, which are convenient to maintain male-dominated power over women. Korean Confucianism shows how this text can further attempt to justify women's submission and sacrifice for the household as praiseworthy by YHWH. These approaches show that the text of Prov 31:10–31 can be read in light of androcentric anxieties regarding women, which require full redress and reappropriation. In a Korean context, reading the text in light of this kind of cultural consciousness is essential. Prov 31:10–31 may not have been intended as a threat to women, but the text continues to be interpreted and applied to oppress. By rereading Prov 31:10–31, Korean women will likely (consciously or unconsciously) identify themselves with the capable wife and will need to discipline themselves under the invisible and visible observations of Korean women, men, and YHWH. In this regard, in order not to be put the invisible prison of trying to emulate *the capable wife*, reading Prov 31:10–31 with Foucault and Korean Confucianism invite readers to be aware of the multiplicities of the text and meaning making. Indeed, the text is neither wholly oppressive to women nor totally subversive against patriarchy. This interpretation is a first step toward debunking discourses on patriarchy while attempting to liberate women readers from cultural and religious surveillance.

---

[24] Foucault, *Discipline and Punish*, 272.

JOB THE PENITENT:
WHETHER AND WHY JOB REPENTS (JOB 42:6)

Paul K.-K. Cho

על־כן אמאס ונחמתי
על־עפר ואפר

Therefore, I reject and I repent
concerning dust and ashes (Job 42:6)

Whether Job repents in Job 42:6 and, if he does, why are matters of ongoing debate. Since 42:6 is Job's final utterance in the book, coming at the end of the poetic core before the resumption of the prose narrative, much weight is placed on its translation and interpretation. The verse is understood as the crux for the entire book—having to do with the character of Job, the relationship between the poetic core and the prose frame, and the ethical and moral landscape of the book.[1] The perceived importance of the verse and the genuine difficulty of the Hebrew text have led to various translations and concomitant interpretations. Norman C. Habel helpfully summarizes a wide range of possibilities:[2]

- Job completely surrenders to the will of God, repents of his arrogant attitude and stands humble before his God.

I presented a version of this essay at the International Meeting of the Society of Biblical Literature in Seoul, South Korea in July 2016 and thank those who were present for their critique and engagement. I also thank Hyun Chul Paul Kim for his thoughtful comments on an earlier version of this paper.

[1] David J. Clines echoes the sentiment of most commentators when he writes, "this final reply by Job [Job 42:2–6] is hugely important for the understanding of the book as a whole, it is truly tantalizing that it is so cryptic and ambiguous." David J. Clines, *Job 38–42*, WBC 18B (Nashville: Nelson, 2011), 1212.

[2] Norman C. Habel, "The Verdict on/of God at the End of Job," in *Job's God*, ed. Ellen van Wolde (London: SCM, 2004), 27. For the wide range of proposed translations, see below.

- Job is reconciled to God, coming to an understanding of God's governance of creation and is once more a wise one who fears God.³
- Job's words reflect a comic irony. God's bravado from the whirlwind reflects God's attempt to handle Job's exposing of God's inconsistency. Job mollifies God with his "tongue and cheek" confession.⁴
- Job's speech is his final act of defiance. While Job recognizes his human limitations, he rejects a deity who answers human cries of despair with arrogant boastings from a tempest.⁵

The interpretations of Job 42:6 and, as we shall see below, translations are truly diverse—the Job who speaks ranges from "Job the Pious"⁶ to "Job the Defiant."⁷

In response to the wide range of renderings, William Morrow and others argue that ambiguity was deliberately "structured into 42:6 by the Joban author" and contributes to the variegated polyphony of the book.⁸ The rich history of scholarship on the verse seems to recommend Morrow's judgment that Job 42:6 is ambiguous. The issues of language alone—the meaning of the two verbs אמאס and ונחמתי, the matter of their (missing) object(s), the syntactic function of על, and the referent of עפר ואפר, et cetera that riddle the verse—multiply possible translations and interpretations.⁹ Morrow, for example, is able to provide three

---

³ Robert Gordis writes, "The beauty of His world constitutes an anodyne for his pain and serves as the basis for his renewed faith in the justice of God. This is more than submission—it is reconciliation." Robert Gordis, *The Book of God and Man: A Study of Job* (Chicago: University of Chicago Press, 1965), 304.

⁴ David Robertson writes, "In 42:2–6 he has to entreat his opponent; in order to calm God's whirlwinds he has to declare his guilt by his own mouth. He makes his confession, then, tongue-in-cheek." David Robertson, "The Book of Job: A Literary Study," *Soundings* 56 (1973): 466. Robertson elsewhere summarizes his reading of Job: "the irony in Job [is] all pervasive, encompassing the entire book in its arms, so that, for example, Yahweh's speeches are a joke on him, Job's replies tongue-in-cheek, and the ending ludicrous." Robertson, "The Comedy of Job: A Response," *Semeia* 7 (1977): 42. Along the same vein is Clines: "Job's speech … is a crafty and subtle speech that means more than it says" (*Job 38–42*, 1212).

⁵ See John Briggs Curtis, "On Job's Response to Yahweh," *JBL* 89 (1979): 497–511.

⁶ I take the epithet, "Job the Pious," from Michael V. Fox's insightful article, "Job the Pious," *ZAW* 117 (2005): 351–66. See also Athalya Brenner, "Job the Pious? The Characterization of Job in the Framework of the Book," *JSOT* 43 (1989): 37–52. On the "Joban tale" as an originally independent tradition, see the author's, "The Integrity of Job 1 and 42:11–17," *CBQ* 76 (2014): 230–51.

⁷ I derive the epithet "Job the Defiant" from Curtis's discussion in "On Job's Response to Yahweh" that Job loathes Yahweh and utterly rejects Yahweh as God.

⁸ William Morrow, "Consolation, Rejection, and Repentance in Job 42:6," *JBL* 105 (1986): 212, 223. So too Newsom, "Book of Job," 629.

⁹ Morrow writes "that each clause constituent in 42:6 is capable of (at least) two interpretations. Although perhaps not all equally likely, neither can any of them be ruled out unequivocally" ("Consolation," 212).

distinct translations of the verse.¹⁰ Even so, I do not agree with Morrow that ambiguity is deliberate and, with Ellen van Wolde and others, see it as possible to construct a more precise and circumscribed interpretation of the verse.¹¹ To borrow language from Job, we can put a hedge around the verse whose meanings burst out onto the pages of articles and commentaries (1:10).

In this essay, I argue that Job repents in 42:6.¹² First, I offer a methodological reflection on the art of translation and propose that, based on the work of Roman Jakobson, translation requires three steps: selection, combination, and alignment. Second, I reproduce the wide variety of proposed translations of 42:6 as a demonstration of the inadequacy of translation as an exercise primarily of selection and combination. Third, I offer a critique of John Curtis Briggs's translation and interpretation of 42:6 using the framework of selection, combination, and alignment and underline the importance of alignment. Finally, I situate my translation of 42:6 within a new literary context and offer the interpretation that Job repents of the blasphemous hubris that underlies his utterances in Job 29–31. Of special importance to the discussion will be the location of 42:6 within the compositional history of the book of Job. In particular, based on older and more recent works on the literary history of the book, I treat Job 29–31 and 38:1–42:10 as belonging to the same compositional layer.¹³ That is to say, Job's final words will be read as

---

¹⁰ Morrow, "Consolation," 211–12. Newsom outdoes Morrow and provides five translations. See below for the actual translations.

¹¹ Ellen van Wolde, "Job 42,1–6: The Reversal of Job," in *The Book of Job*, ed. W. A. M. Beuken (Leuven: Leuven University Press, 1994), 247; Charles Muenchow, "Dust and Dirt in Job 42:6," *JBL* 108 (1989): 598–99.

¹² David A. Lambert has recently challenged, leveling a Foucauldian critique, the traditional understanding of repentance as "an inner act or mental state," marked by "agency, interiority, and moral amendment." He goes too far in denying the ancients an interiority, but he has helpfully turned our attention to the ritualistic and sociostructural aspects of what has commonly been interpreted through an internal and penitential lens. There is a history, Lambert convincingly argues, to repentance, thus a time before repentance came to be considered natural and universal. David A. Lambert, *How Repentance Became Biblical: Judaism, Christianity, and the Interpretation of Scripture* (Oxford: Oxford University Press, 2016), 5, 187. Lambert has also taken up the topic of repentance in Job and defines נחם in 42:6 as indicating "a compelled change in the state of relations between a subject and an object, one of release, of letting go or disengagement"—with no reference to one's interiority ("Job in Ritual Perspective," 566). I am not convinced that we can void נחם of its emotional, internal content as confidently as Lambert proposes, but, however we understand the verb, I will argue that Job's repentance in 42:6 involves an aspect of regret, on the part of Job, "concerning dust and ashes." Repentance here, though not everywhere in the Hebrew Bible, is not only a matter of renouncing "a ritual stance of mourning" (559) but has to do with an internal transformation, corresponding to "a change in the state of relations" between God and Job.

¹³ See, for example, the author's article, "Job 2 and 42:7–10 as Narrative Bridge and Theological Pivot," *JBL* 136 (2017): 857–77.

part of the dialogue between Job and God (Job 29–31 and 38:1–42:6), uninterrupted by Elihu, and as forming a compositional unity with the following prose section (42:7–10) in which, God directly rebukes Job's friends for their folly and indirectly, but explicitly, affirms what Job said in the poetic core. In short, I argue that Job is penitent in 42:6 and that his repentance is far from representing an ultimate rejection of Job's anguish, given pained articulation in the poetry, on the part of Job or of the Joban poet. Rather, I argue that Job's repentance is far more qualified than some fear and that whom we might call Job the Penitent reconciles the two more famous Jobs, Job the Defiant of the poetic dialogue (Job 3–31) and Job the Pious of the traditional Joban tale (Job 1; 42:11–17).

The Work of Translation

Roman Jakobson, in an influential essay on language and aphasia, identifies the two aspects of language as "selection" and "combination."[14] He writes, "Speech implies a SELECTION of certain linguistic entities and their COMBINATION into linguistic units of a higher degree of complexity."[15] That is to say, a speaker *selects* phonemes from an available finite set and *combines* them to create words; words from a less finite set to create sentences; and sentences from an unlimited set to create an infinite variety of discourses—all according to the rules set out by a linguistic code. Communication takes place, within this framework, when the addressee decodes the addresser's message using the same—or at least approximate—code the addresser used to encode the message, such as ASL or *hangul*.[16] This means that communication breakdown can also occur:

> The separation in space, and often in time, between two individuals, the addresser and the addressee, is bridged by an internal relation: there must be a certain equivalence between the symbols used by the addresser and those known and interpreted by the addressee. Without such an equivalence the message is fruitless: even when it reaches the receiver it does not affect him.[17]

In short, the addressee must know how to decode the encoded message of the addresser in order for communication to take place. Otherwise, the chain of communication breaks down and the communication is fruitless.

---

[14] Roman Jakobson, "Part II: Two Aspects of Language and Two Types of Aphasic Disturbance," in *Fundamentals of Language*, ed. Roman Jakobson and Moris Halle, 2nd rev. ed. (Berlin: de Gruyter, 1975). First edition printed in 1956, 67–96.
[15] Jakobson, "Two Aspects," 72.
[16] Roman Jakobson, "Closing Statement: Linguistics and Poetics," in *Style in Language*, ed. Thomas A. Sebeok (New York: The Technology Press of the Massachusetts Institute of Technology, 1960), 350–77.
[17] Jakobson, "Two Aspects," 76.

Jakobson also recognized that, even when the addresser and the addressee share the same code, it is possible for the addressee to decode the addresser's message in multiple, alternate ways. The simple response, "Yes," for example, given variation in context and tone, can take on a variety of meanings, ranging from a gentle and welcomed agreement to annoyed and undesired reassertion. Jakobson writes, "there are two references which serve to interpret the sign—one to the code, and the other to the context, whether coded or free, and in each of these ways the sign is related to another set of linguistic signs, through an ALTERNATION in the former case and through an ALIGNMENT in the latter."[18] Put simply, given the code alone, the message can take on multiple, sometimes contradictory meanings: the reassuring *yes* versus the annoyed *yes*. It might be said that the function of the code, through the work of selection and combination, is to make it possible to construct alternate interpretations of a message. The work of alignment, on the other hand, leads to the elimination and honing of the interpretation in relation to the context. Decoding a message, in short, consists of three steps: selection, combination according to the code, and alignment to the context.

In addition, the work of translation is a kind of decoding and requires the work of selection and combination according to the code and alignment to the context. Allow me to offer an example involving *yes* within a hybrid cultural and linguistic context.

The setting is *Taekwondo* practice at Payne Whitney Gym in an adopted *dojang*.[19] The explicit culture is Korean against the background of an American university, but the dominant language is English punctuated by select Korean words and phrases familiar to most *Taekwondo* practitioners, such as *junbi sijak*. The master, *sabunim*, summons me in English. I respond, in English, "Yes," and scurry to him. The master, a second generation Korean American, reprimands me, a 1.7 generation Korean American, for having failed to show him proper respect and ask that, in the future, I answer him with "Yes, sir" or "Yes, Mr. H."

Had I responded in Korean to the master, I would have said *ye*, which is the honorific form of *yes*. That was the response I had intended to encode in my message, "Yes." For, given the explicit cultural context, I thought that *yes*—as opposed to *yea* or *okay*—would be the proper English equivalent of Korean *ye*. *Yes*, in my mind, had acquired an honorific inflection from the Korean cultural context. However, the master, though he too spoke Korean and English, did not decode my *yes* as a translation of *ye*. He heard the untranslated English *yes*, marked as neither informal nor formal, because relevant to him was the dominant linguistic context. For the master, the honorific internal to Korean *ye* must be externalized by English *sir/ma'am* or *Mr./Ms./Mrs.*[20] In short, communication had

---

[18] Jakobson, "Two Aspects," 75.

[19] *Dojo*, from Japanese, is the English equivalent of Korean *dojang*.

[20] I wonder if my and the master's different experiences with *Taekwondo* offers an explanation. I practiced *Taekwondo*, until joining this *dojang*, in exclusively Korean-speaking

broken down. According to the work of selection and combination according to the code, *ye* could be translated as *yes*; *yes sir/ma'am*; *yes Mr./Ms./Mrs.*, all legitimate alternatives. The work of eliminating and honing the translation takes the form of alignment to the context. For the master, the relevant context was the linguistic reality of English-dominance, resulting in the choice of *yes sir* or *yes Mr.* For me, the relevant context was that of Korean culture and so I chose *yes*—consequently showing lack of respect toward the *sabunim*. The above scenario demonstrates that the choice of context has a nontrivial consequence for the work of translation.[21]

As we shall see below, translations of Job 42:6 from Hebrew to English according to the code give us a dizzying array of alternatives, thanks to the numerous problems of selection and combination that riddle the verse. What will prove determinative for the important work of eliminating and honing the translation and interpretation, will be the choice of context and the work of alignment. The work of translation, as we shall see, takes at least three steps: selection, combination according to the code, as everyone recognizes, and, similarly important, alignment to relevant contexts.

Translation of Job 42:6 or Symptoms of Aphasia

The difficulty modern readers have translating and interpreting Job 42:6 arises from the fact that, separated by both space and time, we do not share an "internal relation" with the Joban poet; we do not hold in common the code he used to construct his masterpiece. We must, before we can decode the message, reconstruct the code itself, which is not only linguistic but also literary, cultural, and theological. However, even given the code, the work of selection and combination remains problematic. Our best reconstructed code sets before us, as we shall see, more than one alternative for each element of Job 42:6 and a number of combinatory possibilities. The difficulty is aggravated by the observation that the Hebrew text seems to elide a key element of the message, frustrating any desire for certainty. In sum, the issue of code and its deployment (selection and combination) makes it difficult for modern readers to decode the message of Job 42:6, a difficulty we share with ancient translators and commentators.[22]

In order to demonstrate the inadequacy of translation as an exercise primarily of selection and combination, I shall first schematize the proposed translations of

---

contexts, first in Korea, then in the United States, whereas the master, I presume, practiced in English-dominant *dojang*s in the United States. In the *dojang*, I was always translating from Korean to English, *ye* to *yes*, whereas the master operated within a linguistic landscape where the honorific *yes* was always already *yes, sir*.

[21] It also shows that power relations have a nontrivial impact on linguistic practices.

[22] See LXX; 11AQtJob; traditional Targum. See the discussion in Morrow, "Consolation," 212–15; Clines, *Job 38–42*, 1207–11.

42:6; and second, simply reproduce a range of translations proposed and defended in the scholarly literature. The schema treats each word individually and provides: (1) substitution options for each element of the verse (selection), (2) the other elements of the verse with which that element might be linked and how (combination), and (3) the translation I adopt. The schema will give us a representative data set out of which we can theoretically construct the full range of possible translations of 42:6: על־כן אמאס ונחמתי על־עפר ואפר.

The result will be something akin to a word heap, resulting from the difficulty of combination, or an idiolect, resulting from the difficulty of selection.[23] In short, something not unlike the speech of an aphasic.

- על־כן
    1. The adverbial word-group may be rendered as "therefore," "wherefore," or "so."
    2. The word-group posits a causal relationship between what comes before (X) and the statement that follows (Y): X; therefore, Y. Ambiguity about how much of what precedes is included in the causal relationship poses the central combinatory challenge. Does it link 42:6 minimally with the preceding verse or two only or maximally with all that Job has said since 3:1?
    3. "Therefore"—I argue that Job's dialogue with God in Job 29–31 and 38–41 is the reason that Job repents in 42:6.

- אמאס
    1. The problem of selection begins with the verbal root, whether the verb derives from מאס I or מאס II. The former means "reject, refuse" and is the easier reading of the MT. The latter is a biform of מסס and, in the *niphal*, means "run, flow" (BDB). Both options have modern adherents, and the LXX apparently avoided the selection problem by providing a double translation: ἐφαύλισα ... καὶ ἐτάκην, "I despise ... and I melted."[24]
    2. The selection of מאס I leads to two combinatory issues. First, it is possible that מאס I means absolutely, but we usually expect an object, which the MT does not supply.[25] Several options have been suggested as the unnamed object. The object may be Job himself ("I despise myself," NRSV), the words Job acknowledges he spoke without knowledge (42:3) ("I reject [my words]"),[26] life ("I despise my life"),[27]

---

[23] Jakobson, "Two Aspects of Language," 82, 85.
[24] See Morrow, "Consolation," 212.
[25] מאס I usually has an object. The exception of its absolute usage appears in Job 7:16; 34:33; Ps 89:39. Lester J. Kuyper ("The Repentance of Job," *VT* 9 [1959]: 94) writes, "The MT offers no object for this verb. Every translation must supply one."
[26] Kuyper, "Repentance of Job," 94.
[27] Clines notes that one MT MS (Kenn 601) supplies חיי as the object, probably taking cue from 9:21 (*Job 38–42*, 1207).

wealth ("I despise my wealth"),²⁸ or the legal suit Job has made against God ("I retract").²⁹ God has also been named as the elided object of Job's loathing.³⁰ It is also possible that עפר ואפר functions as the object for both אמאס and ונחמתי, giving us "I repudiate ... dust and ashes."³¹ In truth, the elision of the expected object renders translational and interpretive certainty impossible. The second combinatory issue is whether אמאס and ונחמתי should be taken together, as the Masoretic accentuation indicates.³² If so, it becomes more likely that על־עפר ואפר functions as the object of both verbs.³³

3. "I repeat"—I argue that Job rejects certain aspects of his speech in Job 29–31, namely, his blasphemous hubris.

- ונחמתי

  1. There are two issues of selection. The first is whether the *waw* is conjunctive ("and") or contrastive ("but," "yet," etc.).³⁴ Second, the verb may be understood as *piel* or *niphal*. In the *piel*, נחם means "comfort, console," though this option is seen as unlikely. In the *niphal*, it can mean (1) "regret, be sorry, repent, relent," (2) "be moved to pity, have compassion," or (3) "comfort oneself, be comforted, be consoled."³⁵ Recently, David A. Lambert has proposed that the verb refers to (4) "a compelled change in the state of relations between a subject and an object, one of release, of letting go or disengagement, and therefore an operation parallel to that of מאס."³⁶
  2. As noted above, the MT accentuation pairs the word with אמאס, separates it from על by means of an *'atnah*, and connects על to עפר ואפר with a *maqqef*. However, נחם על is idiomatic and may be read together. The idiomatic phrase means (1) "repent, change one's mind concerning" or (2) "console oneself, be comforted, be consoled concerning." The former meaning, almost always, has God as the subject with two

---

²⁸ Targum has עתרי.
²⁹ Norman C. Habel, *The Book of Job: A Commentary*, OTL (Philadelphia: Westminster, 1985), 575.
³⁰ Curtis, "Job's Response," 504: "there can be little doubt that the unexpressed object of the loathing is God."
³¹ Dale Patrick, "Job's Address of God," *ZAW* 91 (1979): 280–81. See below for selection options for עפר ואפר.
³² Daniel Timmer, "God's Speeches, Job's Responses, and the Problem of Coherence in the Book of Job: Sapiential Pedagogy Revisited," *CBQ* 71 (2009): 299.
³³ Timmer, "God's Speeches," 299; Michael V. Fox, "God's Answer and Job's Response," *Biblica* 94 (2013): 19.
³⁴ Thomas F. Dailey, "And Yet He Repents—On Job 42,6," *ZAW* 105 (1993): 205–9.
³⁵ Clines, *Job 38–42*, 1208.
³⁶ Lambert, "Job in Ritual Perspective," 566.

exceptions;³⁷ and fourteen of eighteen uses of the phrase with a human subject carries the latter meaning.³⁸

3. "I repent"—I argue that Job repents in the sense that he changes his mind about and regrets aspects of his speech in Job 29–31.

- על
  1. על may be vocalized as the noun עֻל, meaning "infant, child," which has the support of the Targum.³⁹ The meaning of the prepositional על varies significantly depending on the issue of combination.
  2. Connected to עפר ואפר, with a weak connection to ונחמתי, על may best be understood as locative: "upon dust and ashes." The common translation "in dust and ashes" (KJV, RSV, NAB, JB, NIV, NEB) is similarly locative but misconstrues the spatial relationship between Job and dust and ashes.⁴⁰ על understood idiomatically in connection to ונחמתי introduces the object of interest, however one translates the verb, and may be translated as "of," "for," or "concerning."
  3. "Concerning"—I take the preposition as introducing the object of interest of ונחמתי.

- עפר
  1. עפר literally means "dust" and by metonymy may refer to the mourning rite of throwing dust on one's head (Job 2:12; Ezek 27:30) or rolling in dust (Mic 1:10).⁴¹
  2. עפר is usually taken together with ואפר as a word pair. The referent is uncertain, and several options have been proposed: the ash heap on which Job sits (Job 2:8), mourning ritual,⁴² or the frailty of humanity (cf. Gen 18:27; Job 30:19).⁴³
  3. "Dust and Ashes"—I understand the idiomatic phrase, "dust and ashes," as referring to the lowly state of human being relative to the divine but not necessarily to humanity as frail.

---

³⁷ Exceptions where humans are subject can be found in Exod 13:17 (without על) and Jer 8:6 (with על). Verses in which God is the subject: Gen 6:6, 7; Exod 32:12, 14; Judg 2:18; 1 Sam 15:11, 29(2), 35; 2 Sam 24:16; Isa 1:24; 57:6; Jer 4:28; 15:6; 18:8, 10; 20:16; 26:3, 13, 19; 42:10; Ezek 24:14; Joel 2:13, 14; Amos 7:3, 6; Jonah 3:9, 10; 4:2; Zech 8:14; Pss 90:13; 106:45; 110:4; 1 Chr 21:15.

³⁸ Curtis, "Job's Response," 500.

³⁹ Al Wolters, "'A Child of Dust and Ashes' (Job 42,6b)," *ZAW* 102 (1990): 116–19.

⁴⁰ Clines, *Job 38–42*, 1209.

⁴¹ Clines, *Job 38–42*, 1209.

⁴² Clines, *Job 38–42*, 1209; Van Wolde, "Job 42,1–6," 247; Lambert, "Job in Ritual Perspective," 565; P. A. H. de Boer, "Does Job Retract? (Job xlii 6)," in *Selected Studies in Old Testament Exegesis*, ed. C. van Duin, OTS 27 (Leiden: Brill, 1991), 191.

⁴³ Edward L. Greenstein, "In Job's Face/Facing Job," in *The Labour of Reading: Desire, Alienation, and Biblical Interpretation*, ed. Fiona C. Black, Roland Boer, and Erin Runions (Atlanta: Society of Biblical Literature, 1999), 310–11; Curtis, "On Job's Answer to Yahweh," 500–501.

- ואפר
    1. אפר literally means "ash" and by metonymy may refer to the mourning rite of sitting on ashes (Job 2:8; Isa 58:5; Jer 6:26; Ezek 27:30) or putting ashes on one's head (2 Sam 13:19).[44]
    2. See under עפר above.
    3. See under עפר above.

The schematic summary of lexical and syntactic studies of Job 42:6 above shows that "each clause constituent of 42:6 is capable of (at least) two interpretations."[45] Consider:

Therefore/Wherefore I reject/despise/loathe/recant _____/my words/myself/you, O God/my lawsuit and/but/yet repent/am consoled/have compassion/am sorry on/in/concerning/of a child of dust and ashes/frail humanity/mourning ritual/dust and ashes.

Though the number of possible combinations is fewer in practice than in theory—since the translator, like the speaker, "is by no means a completely free agent in his choice"[46]—the range of alternate translations, nevertheless, remains daunting. The schema above is a veritable spider's web of associations that refracts and diffracts the sunlight in a myriad of ways. The result is—more than ambiguity—confusion. Following is a selection of actual proposed translations of the verse that concretizes that confusion:

그러므로 내가 스스로 거두어들이고
티끌과 재 가운데에서 회개하나이다 (NKRV)

Therefore I despise myself,
and repent in dust and ashes. (NRSV)

Therefore, I recant and relent
Being but dust and ashes. (NJPS)

C'est pourquoi je me rétracte et me repens
sur la poussière et la cendre. (Lévêque)[47]

---

[44] Clines, *Job 38–42*, 1210.
[45] Morrow, "Consolation," 212.
[46] Jakobson, "Two Aspects of Language," 72.
[47] Jean Lévêque, *Job et son Dieu: Essai d'exégèse et de théologie biblique*, 2 vols. (Paris: Librairie Lecoffre, 1970), 2:526.

Darum widerrufe ich und bereue
in Staub und Asche! (Fohrer)[48]

Therefore I have had enough of it all and leave dust and ashes behind. (de Boer)[49]

So I submit, and I accept consolation
for my dust and ashes. (Clines)[50]

Therefore, I feel loathing contempt and revulsion
    [toward you, O God];
and I am sorry for frail man. (Curtis)[51]

THEREFORE I (still) despise YET repent
concerning the (in)justice of this life. (Dailey)[52]

This is why I sink down and repent,
On dust and ashes! (Dhorme)[53]

Wherefore I repudiate (what I had said),
And repent, (sitting) upon dust and ashes. (Driver and Gray)[54]

Therefore I am disgusted and repent on dust and ashes. (Fox)[55]

Therefore I despise and repent
of dust and ashes. (Good)[56]

Therefore I abase myself
and repent in dust and ashes. (Gordis)[57]

---

[48] Georg Fohrer, *Das Buch Hiob*, KAT 16 (Gütersloh: Gütersloher Verlagshaus G. Mohn 1963), 531.
[49] De Boer, "Does Job Retract?," 194.
[50] Clines, *Job 38–42*, 1205.
[51] Curtis, "Job's Response," 510.
[52] Dailey, "Yet Job Repents," 208.
[53] Édouard Dhorme, *A Commentary on the Book of Job*, trans. Harold Knight (Nashville: Nelson, 1984), 646.
[54] Samuel Rolles Driver and George Buchanan Gray, *A Critical and Exegetical Commentary on the Book of Job, Together with a New Translation* (Edinburgh: T&T Clark, 1977), 373.
[55] Fox, "God's Answer," 18.
[56] Edwin M. Good, *In Turns of Tempest: A Reading of Job, with a translation* (Stanford: Stanford University Press, 1990), 375.
[57] R. Gordis, *The Book of God and Man: A Study of Job* (Chicago: University of Chicago Press, 1965), 305.

Therefore I retract
And repent of dust and ashes. (Habel)[58]

Therefore I despise myself,
and repent in dust and ashes. (Hartley)[59]

Therefore I recant and change my mind
concerning dust and ashes. (Janzen)[60]

I protest, but feel sorry for dust and ashes. (Purdue)[61]

Therefore I reject (my words), an[sic.] I repent in dust and ashes. (Kuyper)[62]

Therefore, I reject and have compassion
with dust and ashes. (van der Lugt)[63]

1. Wherefore I retract (*or* I submit) and I repent on (*or* on account of) dust and ashes.
2. Wherefore I reject *it* (implied object in v 5), and I am consoled for dust and ashes.
3. Wherefore I reject and forswear dust and ashes. (Morrow)[64]

Therefore I will have nothing more to do with (i.e., despise and reject) the sins of which you charged me which I committed by my speaking without understanding, and I repent upon dust and ashes. (Newell)[65]

1. "Therefore I despise myself and repent upon dust and ashes" (i.e., in humiliation; c. NRSV; NIV);
2. "Therefore I retract my words and repent of dust and ashes" (i.e., the symbols of mourning);
3. "Therefore I reject and forswear dust and ashes" (i.e., the symbols of mourning);
4. "Therefore I retract my words and have changed my mind concerning dust and ashes" (i.e., the human condition);

---

[58] John E. Hartley, *The Book of Job*, NICOT (Grand Rapids: Eerdmans, 1988), 575.
[59] Hartley, *Book of Job*, 342.
[60] J. Gerald Janzen, *Job*, IBC (Atlanta: John Knox, 1985), 251.
[61] Leo G. Purdue, *Wisdom Literature: A Theological History* (Louisville: Westminster John Knox, 2007), 125.
[62] Kuyper, "Repentance of Job," 94.
[63] Pietervan der Lugt, "Who Changes His Mind about Dust and Ashes? The Rhetorical Structure of Job 42:2–6," *VT* 64 (2014): 625. It must be noted that van der Lugt argues that God, not Job, is the speaker of 42:6.
[64] Morrow, "Consolation," 211–12.
[65] Lynne Newell, "Job Repentant or Rebellious?," *WTJ* 46 (1984): 315.

5. "Therefore I retract my words, and I am comforted concerning dust and ashes" (i.e., the human condition). (Newsom)[66]

Therefore I repudiate and repent
of dust and ashes. (Patrick)[67]

So I recant and repent
In dust and ashes. (Pope)[68]

Therefore I despise myself,
and repent in dust and ashes. (Rowley)[69]

Therefore I abhor and repent
[all my words].
[Let me die and go down]
to dust and ashes. (Tur-Sinai)[70]

Therefore I recant and repent,
a child of dust and ashes. (Wolters)[71]

Therefore, I reject and repent
concerning dust and ashes. (Cho)

How do you choose? The motley collection of translations showcases the difficulty of translating the verse and, in their diversity, demonstrates that interpretation is constitutive of translation—since some translations are more representations of interpretation than anything we might call a straightforward translation from one language to another. More than that, the collection of translations demonstrates that the lexical and grammatical code we possess is not sufficient for the task of selection and combination necessary to decode the message of the verse with precision. The code alone gives us too many alternatives, and, as noted above, what we must bring to bear on the work of translation to eliminate some alternatives and hone others, is the context with which the translation must be made to align.

---

[66] Carol A. Newsom, "The Book of Job," *NIB* 4: 629.
[67] Patrick, "Job's Address of God," 24.
[68] Marvin H. Pope, *Job*, AB 15 (Garden City, NY: Doubleday, 1965), 288.
[69] H. H. Rowley, *Job* (Melbourne: Nelson, 1970), 342.
[70] N. H. Tur-Sinai, *The Book of Job: A New Commentary* (Jerusalem: Kiryath Sepher, 1967), 578.
[71] Wolters, "A Child of Dust and Ashes," 117.

Whether Job Repents: No

That Job repents in 42:6 is no longer the presumed interpretation and has not been since at least John Briggs Curtis's provocative 1979 article, "On Job's Response to Yahweh," which argues that Job, far from repenting, repudiates Yahweh as God.[72] Curtis offers, as a translation of 42:6:

> Therefore I feel loathing contempt and revulsion
>   [toward you, O God];
> and I am sorry for frail man.[73]

Few today subscribe fully to Curtis's translation of 42:6, but the reasoning behind his interpretation and translation, most notably the assumption that the verse should be read first and primarily within the context of the poetic core, continues to exert influence. The assumed literary history and context are wrong, as I will argue below, but Curtis's argument bears review since it well demonstrates the importance of alignment in the work of translation.

Curtis argues that Job, in his final response to God, "is more insolent than repentant,"[74] and expresses loathing toward a "god so remote, so unfeeling, so unjust."[75] Job defiantly rejects Yahweh as god, is Curtis's thesis. In support of this radical conclusion and departure from the traditional reading of Job as penitent and contrite, Curtis signals that he will follow two lines of argumentation: one, what he characterizes as "purely literary considerations" and, two, the matter of the "language itself."[76] From the beginning of the article, Curtis downplays the importance of the "literary considerations," the rejection of which, he claims, "will not greatly affect the argument," and devotes most of the article to the discussion of the issue of language.[77] However, it will be his literary considerations, not his linguistic arguments (which have in any case won few adherents) that will prove enduring.

Curtis's translation of Job 42:6, if we understand translation as only a matter of Jakobsonian selection and combination, is a possible, if ultimately unconvincing, option. Each translation choice is somewhat suspect: "I feel loathing

---

[72] Fox, "Gods' Answer," 19.

[72] John Briggs Curtis, "On Job's Response to Yahweh," *JBL* 89 (1979): 507. Curtis writes, "Job in his final words to Yahweh has rejected the god who responds to the anguished plea of his most devoted worshipper with contemptuous and arrogant boasting.... There is not the slightest suggestion that he recants or in remorse grovels before the divine" (505).

[73] Curtis, "Job's Response," 510.

[74] Curtis, "Job's Response," 499.

[75] Curtis, "Job's Response," 510.

[76] Curtis, "Job's Response," 499.

[77] Curtis, "Job's Response," 499.

contempt and revulsion" is an over-translation of אמאס;[78] the translation of ונחמתי על as "and I am sorry for" relies on a subtle but important distortion of the evidence;[79] "frail man" is more an interpretation than a translation of עפר ואפר (lit., "dust and ashes");[80] and the supplied object of אמאס, "you, O God," is a possible yet questionable suggestion.[81] That said, Curtis capably weaves an interpretative framework in which his translation might possibly convince. Because Curtis paints the God of the poetic dialogue, building on Matitiahu Tsevat, as the callous and unfeeling God of a world utterly devoid of morality, it becomes imaginable that Job loathes this God.[82] In fact, it becomes unimaginable within Curtis's reconstruction of the Joban world that Job would repent and capitulate to his unsympathetic tormentor.

What bears underlining, at this juncture, is the critical, but unacknowledged, role the literary context plays in Curtis's overall argumentation. The body of Curtis's article, as noted, centers on the language of Job's response (Job 40:4–5; 42:2–6), that is, on the issue of selection and combination.[83] However, framing this discussion are brief—and I would argue revealing—notes about the assumed literary context. At the beginning is the discussion about what constitutes the original layer of God's speeches and Job's responses (Job 38:1–42:6). Curtis downplays the discussion, as noted above, as concerning "purely literary considerations" and claims that "the rejection of any or all of [the literary assumptions] will not greatly affect the argument."[84] What stands out and is worth noting is that, for Curtis, "the original," by which he means the oldest part of the Joban tradition, is of ultimate interpretative consequence.

A discussion of the literary context also brackets the end of the body of the article. Curtis, after offering his interpretation of Job as defiant and rejecting Yahweh as god, makes a telling observation concerning the composition history of Job: "it is clear that the character of Job himself as given in the prologue and epilogue is so different from that presented in the poetic dialogue that the prose sections and the poetical sections of the book cannot originally have belonged together."[85] He goes on to argue that, so different are the pious Job of the prose from the defiant Job of the poetry, "the poetry *must not* be interpreted in terms of the prose."[86] Underlying this interpretive prescription is the important literary assumption, not only that the prose frame and the poetic core stem from different hands but also that the composition of the poetry precedes that of the prose: the

---

[78] Curtis, "Job's Response," 501–3.
[79] Curtis, "Job's Response," 499–500.
[80] Curtis, "Job's Response," 500–501.
[81] Curtis, "Job's Response," 504.
[82] Matitiahu Tsevat, "The Meaning of the Book of Job," *HUCA* 37 (1966): 73–106.
[83] Curtis, "Job's Response," 499–510.
[84] Curtis, "Job's Response," 499.
[85] Curtis, "Job's Response," 510.
[86] Curtis, "Job's Response," 510 (emphasis added).

poetry is "original." The prose and the poetry do not "originally" belong together and, what more, the "prose ending [was] appended" at a later date to the poetic original.[87]

Now, though Curtis presents the theory of the belatedness of the prose frame, specifically of the epilogue, as a conclusion to his argumentation, it is no less an assumption than the "purely literary considerations" with which he begins the article. The difference between the two sets of literary assumptions at the head and the tail of the article is that Curtis cannot say about the latter that its "rejection ... will not greatly affect the argument," for it actually lies at the heart of his argumentation. A Job who loathes God and feels sorry for humanity in Job 42:6 may be consistent with the Job of the poetry—but he has no place alongside the Job of the prose frame.[88] In Jakobsonian terms, the interpretation of 42:6 as an expression of human defiance and rejection of God is not only a matter of translational selection and combination but crucially the result of an interpretive alignment with one literary context, namely the poetic core, over against another, the prose frame.[89] The assumed literary context—that of the poetic core taken alone—dictates for Curtis what to select and how to combine among the various translational options for elements of Job 42:6. In other words, alignment with a different context would have resulted in a different translation. That is the real reason that "the poetry *must not* be interpreted in terms of the prose," for that would produce a translation of 42:6 diametrically opposed to the one Curtis advances.

A simple counter example makes the above point clear. Michael V. Fox takes the opposite position from Curtis regarding the context in which to interpret 42:6. Fox argues that the prose frame, for a variety of literarily sensitive reasons, should be given hermeneutical priority when interpreting the entire book.[90] Predictably, Fox's translation and interpretation of Job 42:6 is diametrically opposed to Curtis's. Fox's interpretation is that Job genuinely repents in recognition of "God's omnipotence and his own ignorance," bringing the Job of the poetry—Job the

---

[87] Curtis, "Job's Response," 510.

[88] Note that Curtis's depiction of God as unconcerned about humanity has no place in the prose frame, in which the piety of a human individual is the topic of divine conversation and interest.

[89] The assumption that Job 42:6 should be read first and primarily, if not exclusively, within the literary context of the poetic core is an enduring assumption for antipenitential readings of the verse. Typical, for example, is Kember Fullerton, who writes, "if 42 1–6 is interpreted as an admission by Job that God is in the right and he is in the wrong, this conflicts in the most strident way with what we have seen to be the real meaning of the Dialogues." Kember Fullerton, "The Original Conclusion to the Book of Job," *ZAW* 42 (1924): 125.

[90] Michael V. Fox, "Job the Pious," *ZAW* 117 (2005): 351–66, esp. 356–58; see also Fox, "Reading the Tale of Job," in *A Critical Engagement: Essays on the Hebrew Bible in Honour of J. Cheryl Exum*, ed. David J. A. Clines and Ellen van Wolde, HBM 38 (Sheffield: Sheffield Phoenix, 2011), 145–62.

Defiant—into harmony with Job the Pious of the prose frame.[91] When 42:6 is read both as Job's final statement within the poetic core and as anticipating the prose epilogue—because one assumes that the poetry was written either after the prose or by the author of the prose—that is, when the entire book of Job is taken as the context for interpreting the verse, what Curtis finds inadmissible becomes quite defensible and even mandatory: Job repents.

To summarize, Curtis and Fox demonstrate with their divergent but complementary readings of Job 42:6 that context matters for interpretation and for translation. Alignment to context is constitutive of translation, and, in the case of Job 42:6, can be determinative. This makes it all the more critical that we get the literary context, including the literary history, of Job 42:6 correct.

A New Literary Context of Job 42:6

The compositional history of the book of Job continues to be a matter of scholarly debate. Important for our purposes are the relationship between the prose frame (Job 1–2, 42:7–17) and the poetic core (Job 3–42:6) and the status of the Elihu speeches (Job 32–37).

I hold to a three-stage history of composition of the book of Job in gross agreement with the majority view as represented in figure A (below). Where I differ from the majority view and is of critical importance to our discussion concerning the prose frame:

	Prose Prologue		Poetic Dialogue			Prose Epilogue	
	Outer	Inner	Job & Friends	Elihu	God & Job	Inner	Outer
Joban Tale	1						42:11–17
Joban Poet		2	3–27	28 ?	29–31	38:1–42:6	42:7–10
Later Additions				28 ?	32–37		

Figure A

---

[91] Michael V. Fox, "God's Answer and Job's Response," *Bib* 94 (2013): 18; Fox, "Job the Pious."

At the earliest literary stage of the Joban tradition lies the Joban tale, which in the canonical book makes up the outer prose frame (Job 1 and 42:11–17 only). The Joban tale is—as evidenced by its narrative, structural, and theological unity over against the inner prose frame (Job 2 and 42:7–10) and the poetic core (Job 3–42:6)—a compositional unity and originally constituted an independent tradition. The tale, literarily, is a ring composition and, theologically, teaches the high value God places on unmotivated piety.[92] The Joban tale features as its protagonist Job the Pious.

In the second stage of development, likely in the exilic or post-exilic period, a gifted poet took up the Joban tale as the trampoline for his own dramatic work. This poet split the Joban tale into two (Job 1 and 42:11–17), composed his own poetic masterpiece in dialogue form between Job with his friends and Job with God (3:1–42:6, minus the Elihu speeches and possibly the poem on wisdom), and composed the inner prose frame (Job 2 and 42:7–10) as a narrative and theological bridge between the Joban tale and the poetic dialogues.[93] To underline the details relevant for our presentation, the Joban poet who composed the poetic core—so 42:6—also composed the inner prose frame—so 42:7–10.

In the third stage of development, a young poet from a generation after the poet of the dialogues composed and inserted the Elihu speeches (Job 32–37) and possibly the poem on wisdom (Job 28). Disruption to the third cycle may have been introduced at this stage of development.

There are two implications of the proposed literary history for the interpretation and translation of 42:6. The first negative implication is that 42:6 should not be read as the conclusion of the work of the Joban poet, thus as the poet's final pronouncement concerning the Job of the poetry. This negative implication considerably diminishes the interpretative weight that might be placed on the verse. The second positive implication is that the verse should be read, on the one hand, as the conclusion to Job's dialogue with God and, on the other, as a part of the bridge, along with the inner prose epilogue (42:7–10), between the poetic core and the outer prose epilogue. That is, we should expect 42:6 to enact a transition from the poetry to the prose, as opposed to marking a disjunction between them. A Job who repents, as we shall now see, perfectly performs this *Brückenfunktion*.

---

[92] For detailed argumentation, see Paul K.-K. Cho, "The Integrity of Job 1 and 42:11–17," *CBQ* 76 (2014): 230–51. For the basis of the theological reading of the Joban tale, see Fox, "Job the Pious."

[93] For detailed argumentation, see Paul K.-K. Cho, "Job 2 and 42:7–10 as Narrative Bridge and Theological Pivot," *JBL* 136 (2017): 857–77.

WHETHER JOB REPENTS: YES

A penitential translation of Job 42:6, as we saw above, is a viable linguistic option. It now remains to show that a Job who repents aligns with the newly proposed literary context.

An oft repeated objection to a penitential reading of 42:6 is that, "if 42:1–6 is interpreted as an admission by Job that God is in the right and he is in the wrong, this conflicts in the most strident way with what we have seen to be the real meaning of the Dialogues."[94] It is unimaginable, the argument goes, that the Joban poet, who has given us a most pitiable Job and in him a voice to all who suffer without (adequate) reason, should betray all that he has written prior by having Job repent. To use the language developed in this essay, a Job who repents does not align with the rest of the poet's work. This objection assumes that the poet's work concludes with 42:6. However, according to the proposed literary history above, the inner prose epilogue (42:7–10) is also the composition of the Joban poet and the actual conclusion to his work. Does either a defiant Job or a Job who repents only tongue-in-cheek align with the inner prose epilogue?

No, a Job who does not repent genuinely does not align with the inner prose epilogue. In 42:7–10, God alone speaks and provides a summary judgment on Job and his three friends: God rebukes the friends for having committed folly (42:8) and for not having spoken "what is right" about God, unlike Job who has and whom God twice calls "my servant" (42:7, 8). If we maintain that Job does not repent in 42:6, then we would have a God who, after rebuking Job, affirms a still defiant Job. That is, the cost of holding on to a Job who does not repent—because for Job to repent would be tantamount to self-betrayal—is a God who betrays himself. However, betrayal either on the part of Job or God is not inevitable. Rather, the problem of betrayal, that is, the problem of false alignment disappears once we accept that Job repents of what he has said in dialogue with God and that God affirms what Job has said in dialogue with his friends.

Let us begin with God's affirmation. That God affirms Job for having spoken what is right does not mean that God affirms all that Job said in the poetry. It is important, in this light, that God's approval contrasts what Job said against the folly of the friends. God says to Eliphaz, "My anger burns against you and your two friends, for you have not said what is right about me as my servant Job has" (42:7b). The contrastive juxtaposition suggests that what God considers to have been right is what Job said in dialogue with the friends in Job 3–28 only.[95] In the "contest of moral imaginations" between Job and his friends, as Newsom put it, only one side could be right. And God with his final words names Job the victor. We might wonder whether God really affirms all that Job said in those three rounds of verbal boxing. It is clear, in any case, that God unequivocally restores

---

[94] Kember Fullerton, "The Original Conclusion to the Book of Job," *ZAW* 42 (1924): 125.
[95] Greenstein, "In Job's Face/Facing Job," 309.

Job to honor in 42:7–10 vis-à-vis his friends. The friends had questioned and attacked Job's honor throughout the dialogue, but God instead rebukes the friends and elevates Job, making him priest over them.[96] The friends can approach God but through the mediation of Job (42:8–9). And if they had lingering doubts about Job's righteousness, still holding on to a woodenly retributive understanding of justice, God provides proof of Job's righteousness by redoubling his blessings (42:10).

God's affirmation of Job's words in dialogue with his friends leaves open the possibility for repentance precisely of what Job says in dialogue with God in Job 29–31. We will turn to the detailed discussion of what Job repents of below. It suffices at present to note that a Job who repents in 42:6 does not turn his back on all that he has said but only on (a part of) what he said to God in this final speech. A repentant Job does not conflict "in the most strident way with what we have seen to be the real meaning of the Dialogues." Rather, just as the Joban poet's God reaches backward from the prose and grabs onto the defiant Job of the poetry and restores him to honor, the poet's Job reaches out from the poetry and grabs onto the God of the prose and restores him to honor. Job's final words of repentance (42:6) and God's final words of approval (42:7–8) are two interlocking hooks that link the poetry and the prose to each other. A God who approves of Job's words and a Job who repents of his words go together well and together resolve the problem of alignment. Where poetry meets prose, the human and the divine embrace.

WHY JOB REPENTS

Precision about what God considers Job to have said rightly and conversely of what Job repents is not possible. Even so, we can reasonably suggest that God affirms much of what Job says prior to his final speech in Job 29–31, for God contrasts the folly of Job's friends to the right things Job said in conversation with them. If we can agree, then, that God affirms what Job said in dialogue with his friends, then we must look elsewhere to find the cause of God's thunderous rebuke: "Who is this that darkens design with words without knowledge" (38:2). The remaining option is what Job says in Job 29–31. And, as I will now argue, that God rebukes and Job repents of what he said in these chapters make both narrative and theological sense.

First, a Job who repents makes good narrative sense within the thrust of Job's dialogue with God (Job 29–31, 39:1–42:6). Starting at Job 29, Job no longer addresses his friends but rather turns toward God. That God is Job's intended addressee becomes clear in Job 31. At one point, Job says:

---

[96] Job's friends assume that Job has sinned from the beginning of the dialogue. Their rhetoric is at first gentle but becomes increasingly acerbic (cf. Eliphaz's first and last speeches, Job 4–5, 22).

> If I walked with falsehood
> or my feet hastened to deceit,
> May he weigh me in scales of righteousness
> and may God know my purity. (31:5–6)

God is clearly the intended audience, and Job, with this and other self-imprecatory oaths of innocence, obligates God to respond. Edwin Good puts it forcefully:

> A curse was not a casual expression to be trifled with or tossed aside. It was the most powerful way people had of setting in train forces of action and reaction, and no one would take a curse lightly.... The curse is a way of forcing [the] god to respond, requiring his attention, because the curse cannot go unattended. It will work ineluctably through its end result, and [the] god himself is under its sway.[97]

When Job curses himself in making his oath of innocence, God must respond. That is the magico-logic of ancient oath making. In terms of plot, Job's oath sets in motion a train of events that will work itself out, either in Job's destruction or justification at God's hand.

So, as expected, God responds to Job and speaks out of the whirlwind. In YHWH's first speech (Job 38–39), God directly addresses Job but seems to sidestep Job's concerns.[98] God does not address the matter of Job's righteousness but instead describes creation, from the great cosmic boundaries to the details of faunal life. In any case, God concludes with a demand that Job responds (40:2b), and Job in his first response to YHWH, while not without its ambiguities, appears to adopt a posture of humble silence without retracting his previous statements:

> Look, I am small. How can I answer you?
> I put my hand on my mouth.
> Once I spoke, and I did not answer;
> And twice, but I will not again. (40:4–5)

Job acknowledges that he has spoken ("Once I spoke ... twice ...") and that what he has said is inadequate as a response to God ("I did not answer"). He at the same time refuses to say more ("How can I answer you? I put my hand on my mouth.... I will not [speak] again"). Job humbly refuses to add to what he has already said, realizing perhaps that he cannot properly respond to God. But Job also courageously, even defiantly, stands by what he has already said. He does not say more, but he also does not recant.

---

[97] Good, *Tempest*, 314.

[98] On the ways God provides an apt response to Job's speeches, see Paul K.-K. Cho, "'I Have Become a Brother of Jackals': Evolutionary Psychology and Suicide in the Book of Job," *BibInt* (forthcoming).

YHWH is not satisfied with Job's first response of silent resolution and demands that Job again answers him (40:7; cf. 38:3). In the second divine speech (40:6–41:26), YHWH briefly touches on the issue of ruling over the proud and the wicked (40:12–14) but mostly describes with apparent pride the fabulous Behemoth and Leviathan. The reason for the focus on Behemoth and Leviathan is elusive, but a part of the purpose seems to be to compare Job to these near-mythic creatures. God states, "Behold Behemoth whom I made as I made you," before going on to describe its monstrous strength (40:15). The point seems to be that Job is as fabulously powerful as Behemoth. Furthermore, God uses Leviathan as a negative measure of Job's strength: "Can you draw out Leviathan with a hook / or keep its tongue down with rope?" (42:25). YHWH will not let Job off the hook, so to speak. Job, comparable to Behemoth and even to Leviathan, is not too small to answer God. Refusal to speak further without addressing what he has already said will not do.

Thus, Job responds a second time and repents, and his repentance makes narrative sense. In Job 29–31, Job systematically reviews his life and makes a confident claim to innocent righteousness. After God's first speech, Job speaks in order to say that he will not speak further in 41:4–5. After God's second speech, Job goes further and speaks to take back (some of) what he has said. The drama moves from open expression to silence, finally to retraction. What does Job retract and, more than that, repent of? Not, as we saw above, of all that he has said in the poetic dialogue but only of what he has said in Job 29–31.

It remains to show that God rebukes Job for what he says in his final speech and that Job repents make theological sense. Job repents, I shall argue, of his blasphemous hubris.

The key to the following argument is to recognize that there are two different Jobs in Job 29–31. There is, on the one hand, the Job of utter ethical and moral integrity, the Job we meet in the prose prologue. On the other, there is the Job who, from that earthly summit of ethical perfection, looks haughtily down on fellow humanity and blasphemously on divinity with pride and arrogance. God affirms the former Job, both in the prologue (1:8, 2:3) and the epilogue (42:7–8). But God puts the latter Job on trial and rebukes him. God says to the second Job:

> Gird your loins like a man.
> I shall ask you, and you will tell me. (Job 40:7)

It is this second Job who repents in Job 42:6.

Job 29–31 is more than Job's summation of his life. It is rightly understood within a legal framework as a closing statement in which Job makes a claim for a certain kind of future he believes he deserves as recompense for his past life. In brief, in Job 29, Job provides a nostalgic remembrance of things past: "O that I were as in the days of old" (29:2). Job presents himself as a revered member of society who exercised his considerable authority with equity and compassion and without regard to social standing or self-interest. Job 30 is an anguished plaint of his lamentable present: "But now they make sport of me" (30:1). Job bemoans the radical social demotion, the resulting shame, his physical death-like suffering, and God's mysterious antagonism. Thus, he concludes, "And my lyre has become mourning, / and my flute a weeping call" (30:31). In Job 31, Job makes a bold wager for the future in the form of an oath of innocence. It is an effort to regain the honor he has lost, as Charles Muenchow has shown, by forcing God to recognize him and, beyond that, to recognize his righteous innocence.[99]

In these three chapters, we find two different Jobs: Job the Pious and Job the Defiant. We find the righteous Job of Job's self-understanding primarily in Job 29 and 31. In Job 29, Job celebrates God's beneficent presence (29:3–6), his revered status at the city gate (the ancient hall of justice)—as indicated by the induced silence among the young, the old, and the noble (29:7–10)—and describes himself as savior to the poor, the orphan, the wretched, and the widow, eyes to the blind, feet to the lame, a father to the fatherless, defender of the weak, and the scourge of the wicked. To suggest a modern analogy, Job presents himself as Bruce Wayne and Batman in one: philanthropic billionaire and righteous vigilante.

If we meet in Job 29 the outward form of the righteous Job, we peer inside him in Job 31. The chapter contains questions (e.g., 31:2–4, 14–15), statements (31:5, 7–8, 9–10, 13), exclamation (31:35), and curses (31:5, 7–8, 9–10, 13).[100] In Job 31, Job claims that in deed and in thought he has been faultlessly righteous. In fact, he defends his righteousness in the strongest way possible. "He wishes disaster on himself not only for overt actions like withholding food from the starving (vv. 16–17) but also for inward attitudes."[101] So certain is he that he has been utterly pure, Job demands that God punishes him should he be found lacking even in the least.

Two examples of Job's self-imprecatory oaths of innocence stand out. First, Job says:

> If I rejoiced at the ruin of those who hate me
> Or was excited when evil found them. (31:29)

The celebration of the downfall of one's enemy is almost an involuntary reaction. One might say it is a nonmoral and altogether natural response. But Job is certain that he has not allowed himself even this small pleasure and calls unspecified curses on himself in swearing that he has not "rejoiced at the ruin of those who hate me."

---

[99] Muenchow, "Dust and Dirt in Job 42:6."
[100] Good, *Tempest*, 311.
[101] Good, *Tempest*, 313.

The second example that stands out is his treatment of slaves:

> If I rejected the cause of my male or female servant
> When they had a suit against me,
> Then what shall I say when El stands up?
> Or when he comes in judgment, what shall I answer him?
> Did not the one who made me in the belly make him,
> and the one fashion us in the womb? (31:13–15)

Job connects here a simple, if noble, act of equity to a profound and revolutionary principle: masters should treat slaves justly because God is equally the creator of both. In a culture that considered slaves property, the idea that master and slave might stand on equal footing at the city gate—because they are equally created by God—is without question a high moral achievement. Thus, Georg Fohrer and others rightly heap the highest praise on Job: "It cannot be disputed that the Job who utters the oath of purity in chapter 31 stands almost alone upon an ethical summit."[102] What more, there is no reason to doubt the integrity of Job's self-presentation as a blessed and honored man and as an impossibly just, ethical, and moral man. Job represents himself as the best of humanity. And so he is. He need not—and does not—hide his transgressions like Adam, for he has none (31:33). Job is perfect. What the narrator has told us (1:1) God has assured to Satan (1:8, 2:3), and now Job himself confesses. In conclusion, we can be certain that, if Job repents in 42:6, it is not this Job who does.

Georg Fohrer, who places the righteous man in Job 31 alone on the summit of ethical perfection, also finds in this chapter the very opposite of a model of piety. He finds also "a Promethean and Titanic man from whom God had torn away prosperity and happiness, who confronts God boldly with the conviction that he is perfect in order to triumph over Him, and who wants to force Him to acknowledge his innocence by means of his undisputed righteousness."[103] Fohrer finds a second Job in the concluding speech and characterizes him as heretical because Job "considers himself to be righteous before God."[104] I would put it more boldly. Job is not only heretical but, in his blasphemous arrogance, displaces God and imagines the world alright without God. As Norman Habel aptly notes, "Job virtually usurps the functions of God when he reaches the conclusion of his speech."[105] We find traces of this second, blasphemous Job throughout Job 29–31.

In Job 29, Job presents himself as a revered citizen who exercises just authority with righteous compassion in his community. But, as Edwin Good has pointed

---

[102] Georg Fohrer, "The Rightoues Man in Job 31," in *Essays in Old Testament Ethics (J. Philip Hyatt, In Memoriam)*, ed. James L. Crenshaw and John T. Willis (New York: Ktav, 1974), 19.
[103] Fohrer, "Rightoues Man in Job," 31.
[104] Fohrer, "Rightoues Man in Job 31," 21.
[105] Habel, *Job*, 406.

out, the very language Job uses not so subtly undermines his explicit claims about himself.[106] Consider:

> Lads saw me and hid;
> And elders rose, stood;
> Nobles restrained words
> And placed their hand on their mouths;
> The voices of princes hid,
> And their tongue stuck to their palate. (29:8–10)

When Job appears, people hide, refrain from speaking, and their tongues stick to the roof of their mouths. Good rightly notes, "Job describes respect there, but also terror."[107] Job's fellow citizens more than respect Job; they are terrified of him. And Job, blinded by pride, does not pause to consider whether silence is a sign of respect or fear, whether what he remembers as having been benevolent rule was not experienced by others as tyranny. Job may very well have been a just judge, but, by his own admission, was not a beloved judge.

Job's pride and boasting reverberates throughout Job 29 and crescendos at the end in which he explicitly compares himself to a king. In 29:11–17, Job describes the ways in which he exercises justice in the community: he champions the cause of the poor and needy (29:11–13, 15–16) and terrorizes the wrongdoer (29:17). In the middle of this passage, Job slides into a self-panegyric Habel has helpfully compared to Lady Wisdom's panegyric in Prov 8.[108] Job says:

> I put on righteousness and it clothed me.
> My justice was like a robe and a turban. (29:14)

This is language belonging to the praise of God or, short of that, of kings and priests. For example, Isaiah celebrates God as the one who puts on "righteousness as a breastplate" (59:17). Isaiah also says that God is the one who clothes human beings with "the robe of righteousness" (61:10)—in contrast to Job's claim here that he himself puts on righteousness as a robe—and, when God does, it is usually kings and priests who are so robed (Lev 8:7; Ps 132:9).[109] Job here is engaged in a not so subtle act of self-coronation, if not self-deification. He, not God, clothes himself with righteousness. In Job's world, God is no longer needed to carry out justice, because Job is enough.

Job takes his self-aggrandizement a step further toward the end of the chapter when he compares himself to rain and to light. First, Job says that he is rain for the people:

---

[106] Good, *Tempest*, 294–303.
[107] Good, *Tempest*, 298.
[108] Habel, *Job*, 406.
[109] Good, *Tempest*, 299; Clines, *Job 21–37*, 989.

> They waited for me as for rain
> And they opened wide their mouth as for spring rain. (29:23)

Kings were likened to rain in the Hebrew Bible, for example, in Ps 72: "May he [the king] be like rain that falls on the mown grass, / like showers that water the earth" (72:6). More often, rain is associated with the power and beneficence of deities. In Ugaritic mythology, for example, Baal the storm deity is the consummate giver of rain without which the earth withers and life languishes. Recall that, when Baal dies, even El the high god is powerless to rejuvenate the withering earth. And this mytheme finds echoes in biblical portrayals of YHWH as the giver of rain, for example, in the Elijah narratives (1 Kgs 17; see also Deut 11:14; Hos 6:3; Jer 3:3; 5:24). In comparing himself to rain, therefore, Job demonstrates the utmost hubris and in effect claims royal authority and divine power.

Job takes yet another step further into arrogance when he likens himself to light:

> I smiled on them when they had no confidence;
> And the light of my countenance they did not extinguish. (29:24)

Job declares himself light that delights the people and at which they fall in worship. He has taken the place of God, the creator of light.

At the end of Job 29, Job does away with suggestive metaphors and explicitly claims kingly status:

> I chose their way and I sat as head,
> And I dwelled like a king among the troops. (29:25ab)

Like the gods of the ancient Near East, Job determines the destinies of the people and sits king-like, indeed god-like, in the midst of his fawning subjects. Job claims for himself even more than God can say about himself in the book of Job—total authority and unquestioned honor—for God has defined Job as his favored servant and the questioning Satan as a permanent member of his divine council. Job presents his authority and honor as more absolute than the authority and honor God possesses in the world of Job.

In Job 30, under the cover of lament, Job gives full expression to his disdain for other people and makes another claim of superiority over God. In 30:1–8, Job lays out the primary reason for his complaint: Those whose fathers he disdains even to keep with the dogs of his flock make sport of him (30:1–2; cf. Ps 104:26). Job laments the calamities that have befallen him (30:15, 16–19). But the height of his suffering is not the destruction of his property, the death of his family, or the suffering of his body. Rather, it is that "they" the worthless "sons of fools" mock him. It is social humiliation that irks him most profoundly. Good writes, "Job's contempt [for the people] has dropped its mask of double meaning and appears on the surface."[110] He considered the people less than his equal and finds it insufferable that these nobodies now jeer and mock him:

> I have become a brother of jackals,
> And a friend to ostriches. (30:29)

Next, Job attacks God's administration of justice. Job declares that it is unthinkable that anyone would refuse pity to one who cries out for help (30:24); that he has shown appropriate pity for those who suffer (30:25); but that God has refused to answer him when he cried out for help (30:20), instead redoubling cruelty and deathly torment (30:21, 23). God, Job implies, is less than human; failing to do justice, God also refuses compassion—unlike Job. Job claims that he is more just and equitable than God.

In Job 31, Job presents the strongest case possible for his innocent righteousness. He makes a self-imprecatory oath of innocence in which he curses himself should his claims prove false. We find analogies to this type of oath in funerary texts from Egypt, in Mesopotamian legal codes (e.g., Code of Hammurabi), and elsewhere in the Hebrew Bible (Exod 22:6–10).[111] That God answers Job but does not bring on him the curses Job places on himself indicates that, at one level, Job is as righteous as he claims to be. We established this above. At the same time, the blasphemous arrogance Job perhaps unconsciously but for that no less clearly airs in the previous chapters continues in his final speech.

Job, in his opening speech in the poetic dialogue in Job 3, mimics the language of creation from Genesis 1 to rhetorically undo creation.[112] Echoing God's sublime first words: "Let there be light" (יהי אור, Gen 1:3), Job, declares: "That day, let it be darkness" (היום ההוא יהי חשך, Job 3:4) and from there continues to strip away created orders one by one. He even attempts to arouse Leviathan and Sea, primordial forces of chaos God defeated at creation (3:8). Job's anticreation lament gives expression to his deep despair. It also, now in retrospect, demonstrates not a little hubris. Job directly opposes God, his יהי חשך ("let it be darkness") pitted against God's יהי אור ("let there be light").

The allusion to Genesis 1 in Job 3 also demonstrates that the Joban poet was familiar with the Priestly Genesis. This means that the poet was also familiar with Gen 2–3, the Yahwistic story of Adam and Eve. This is significant because, just as the poet revisits Gen 1 in the first of Job's speeches, he returns again to Genesis, this time to Gen 2–3, in Job's final speech. And whereas Job attempts to rewrite cosmic history by undoing creation in his first speech, Job concludes his defense in his final speech with an allusion to Adam and an attempt to rewrite human

---

[110] Good, *Tempest*, 303.

[111] Fohrer, *Hiob*, 428–31; Good, *Tempest*, 309; Habel, *Job*, 428–29.

[112] Michael Fishbane "Jeremiah IV 23–26 and Job III 3–13: A Rediscovered Use of the Creation Pattern," *VT* 21 (1971): 151–67, esp. 153–55.

history. Job contrasts himself to Adam: "If I hid my transgressions like Adam [אִם־כִּסִּיתִי כְאָדָם פְּשָׁעָי]" (31:33a).

For Job, Adam represents the typical sinner who, in order to avoid public shame, conceals his sin, and Job says that he is nothing like Adam: "Though Adam, the first human being, sinned and hid his sin, I do not. In fact, I have no sin to hide. Where Adam failed, I succeeded," Job seems to say. The Joban poet thickens the connection to the primordial story of creation by alluding to the curse that results from Adam's sin. As Adam's disobedience led to the ground being cursed so that "thorns and thistles it shall bring forth for you" (Gen 3:17–19), Job concludes his oath by cursing the ground:

Let thorns grow instead of wheat,
And foul weeds instead of barley. (Job 31:40)

In his conclusion, Job returns once again to the beginning. He returns to primordial history and rewrites that history. Adam sinned and the ground was cursed. In contrast, Job says that he has lived a life worthy of prelapsarian Eden, that he is primordially pure, perfect not only as a creature of history but as a cosmic archetype of humanity—like Adam but unlike Adam. Thus, he challenges God, his adversary at law, to write an account of his life which he claims he will carry on his shoulders and proudly wear like a crown (31:36). Job will not hide in fig leaves when he hears God approaching as Adam did (Gen 3:7–8). Rather, he welcomes, indeed demands, that God confront him. When God does, Job says that he will confidently approach God like a prince (Job 31:37). Job knows that, if he is found guilty, he might die. But he is willing to risk his life, willing to die, because he believes with total confidence that he is in the right. He claims to be a second Adam, the perfect human being who can redeem the impugned reputation of humanity. If Job imagined himself as God and king, ruling over a perfect world without God in Job 29, in Job 31, he seems to want to rewrite human history without God, with Job—not Adam whom God created—at the beginning.

The accumulated meaning of Job 29–31 is the pride of humanity. Job is a man who, with a clear conscience, can stand before God and declare himself righteous and innocent, a man who has reached the apex of human ethical and moral excellence. But that is only half of the story, for he is also a man who, from upon that summit of human excellence, looks down on creation and finds no evidence of God, no need of God, finds that he has been not only God's ambassador but in fact God's replacement, God's better. God-like. In presenting himself as righteous, Job has imagined—put more forcefully, created with words—a world without God, a world with Job as the all-sufficient king. And that world, in Job's moral imagination, is good. In fact, it is better than the world created and ruled by the God who unjustly afflicts the innocent with suffering and whose Adam is but a typical sinner. And so, at the end of his speech, Job begins to fantasize about a history in this godless world with him as a second, true Adam.

It is in response to this second Job, no less real than the first, pious Job, that God responds with rebuke. In the first speech, God describes creation, from the great cosmic boundaries to the details of faunal life, and challenges Job whether he was there at their creation and can control cosmic or even wild faunal phenomena. Job had dared to imagine himself the anticreator, Shiva to God's Brahma. God shows Job what it means to be Brahma and Vishnu, creator and sustainer, to one who dares imagine himself Shiva, destroyer. In the second speech, God questions whether Job has exercised just rule, especially over the proud and the wicked, as a king should. God acknowledges that Job is a wondrous creation, not unlike Behemoth (40:15), but reminds Job that Leviathan is the "king over all the children of pride" (41:26). There are creatures, human and otherwise, that live beyond Job's sphere of authority—and who do not and need not acknowledge his honor.

That is, God does not challenge Job's claim that he is innocent and righteous or his complaint that he suffers though having done no wrong. God addresses primarily Job's understanding of the world without God and himself at its center and his claim that such a godless world might be good, that it may be even better than the real-world God created. God rebukes Job for claiming too much for himself and for humanity by graciously, though not without terrifying clarity, showing Job that he does not know what it means to have created and to rule over the world in which Behemoth and Leviathan—and Job—are a reality. Job's understanding of the world, it turns out, is more than caricature but less than true—comparable to the utopian dream of a tyrant. Job had imagined himself a goodly king, a godlike figure in his miniature world. God shows him the entire world and compares him to terrifying beasts, Behemoth and Leviathan, who are as real as Job but more powerful. God shows Job that he has darkened "design with words without knowledge" (38:2).

Thus, Job repents. He does not repent for having claimed innocence or for complaining of the injustice of his suffering, as he does throughout his dialogue with the friends (Job 3–28). Rather, he repents for having claimed too much for himself. He realizes, finally, what it means for him to be "dust and ashes" (42:6; cf. 30:19).

Allow me to bring my argument that Job repents with a consideration of the meaning of the idiomatic phrase "dust and ashes" (עפר ואפר). "Dust and ashes," as seen above, is not without ambiguity. But, as has been noted, the phrase can refer to "the composition of the human frame (Gen 18:27; Ecclus 10:9; 1QH 18:5; 4Q266 [4QD^a] fr. 1 a–b.22–23; 4Q227 [4QpsJub^c] fr. 7.ii.16)"[113] and can be used to underline humanity's relative humble state in relation to the divine. This is the way Abraham uses the term in Gen 18:27 when he addresses the divine visitors: "And Abraham responded and said, 'Please allow me to speak to the Lord, though I am but dust and ashes.'" Abraham assumes a position of relative humility—"I

---

[113] Clines, *Job 38–42*, 1211. See Curtis, "On Job's Response to Yahweh," 500–501.

am but dust and ashes"—but one of sufficient honor to address God—"Please allow me to speak to the Lord." That is, the phrase "dust and ashes" is not a term of abject humility but of humanity's relative humility in relation to creator God.[114]

What, then, does it mean for Job to "reject and repent concerning dust and ashes"? Job rejects what he had claimed for himself in his final address to God and repents concerning what he, as a human being and as an Adam, had claimed for himself. Job had thought that he, a mere mortal, could replace God—as king and judge in the world. But Job has learned, thanks to God's terrifyingly clear and graciously revelatory speeches, that he is but "dust and ashes" in comparison to God who made humanity, as he made Behemoth. Job arrives at a new understanding of his relation to God, and thus to the world in which he lives. Job had blasphemously begun to imagine a world without God and with himself in power and found it to be utopic. But then God expands the horizon of his vision, and Job realizes that he is small and his world all too small. Thus, he changes his mind and repents—and agrees with God.

In sum, a Job who repents concerning "dust and ashes" in 42:6 aligns with Job who claimed too much for himself, who is "dust and ashes" (30:19), before God. Job does not repent of what he said in conversation with his friends. In fact, God affirms Job in relation to his friends and restores him to honor in human society (42:7–10). But Job does repent of what he said in conversation with his God.

Conclusion

Recent commentators have found it uncomfortable that Job repents and so have taken advantage of the linguistic ambiguities of the verse to argue that Job does not repent, at least not genuinely. The most provocative suggestion has been that of John Briggs Curtis who argues that Job expresses loathing for God and sorrow for the human condition. I have argued that Curtis and others who reject that Job repents genuinely, while standing on plausible linguistic grounds, have failed to take the literary context into sufficient account. When we align Job 42:6 to the proposed literary context, we find that the linguistic ambiguities that arise from the exercise of selection and combination according to the code dissolve. We find that Job repents for his apparent haughty arrogance and the blasphemous pride he expresses in dialogue with God in Job 29–31. Job does not repent, as feared by those who oppose a penitential reading, of all that he has said. Indeed, it is important to remember that God commends Job for having said what is right about God in dialogue with the friends. In short, the work of the Joban poet reveals itself as a work that reconciles humanity and God: Job in repenting restores God to honor; God in affirming Job restores humanity to honor.

---

[114] The phrase occurs only in Job 30:19 in addition to Gen 18:27 and Job 42:6. There also, the phrase occurs in Job's speech directed toward God: "He [God] has thrown me into the mud, / and I have become like dust and ashes."

An Invitation for Postcolonial Reading of the Prophetic Tradition Claiming Imperial Powers as God's Agents in the Context of American Colonialism in Korea

SungAe Ha

The problem of "scriptural colonialism" has been widely discussed in postcolonial biblical studies' and critical scholarship's relation to Western colonialism.[1] R. S. Sugirtharajah and others have written much on the subject matter.[2] Rethinking missionary activities, especially colonialism and the Bible, this essay explores select prophetic traditions that claim imperial powers as God's agents—reflected in America's colonial influence on Korea in particular—reexamining and reinterpreting Jer 27:1–15 and Isa 44:28–45:13 through the lenses of postcolonial biblical criticism.

Consciously speaking, an understanding of imperial power as an agent of God for God's judgment plays a significant role in prophetic literature.[3] In particular, Jeremiah clearly attributes his prophecies to God (e.g., Thus says the Lord) and explains that God has given all the lands, even the wild animals of the field, into the hand of the Babylonian emperor Nebuchadnezzar, "God's servant," so that all the nations might serve him and his son and grandson until their time ends (Jer 27:6–7). Jeremiah goes further by saying, "But if any nation or kingdom will not

---

[1] For details, see Michael Prior, *The Bible and Colonialism: A Moral Critique* (Sheffield: Sheffield Academic, 1997); Edward E. Andrews, "Christian Missions and Colonial Empires Reconsidered: A Black Evangelist in West Africa, 1766–1816," *JCS* 51.4 (2009): 663–91; Elsa Tamez, "The Bible and the Five Hundred Years of Conquest," in *Voices from the Margin: Interpreting the Bible in the Third World*, ed. R. S. Sugirtharajah (Maryknoll, NY: Orbis Books, 2006), 13–26; R. S. Sugirtharajah, *The Bible and Empire: Postcolonial Explorations* (Cambridge: Cambridge University Press, 2005).

[2] R. S. Sugirtharajah, *Asian Biblical Hermeneutics and Postcolonialism: Contesting the Interpretations* (Maryknoll, NY: Orbis Books, 1998); Sugirtharajah, *The Bible and Asia: From the Pre-Christian Era to the Postcolonial Age* (Cambridge: Harvard University Press, 2013).

[3] In prophetic literature, various imperial powers act as agents of God's punishment of Israel: Assyria (Isa 10:1–7), Babylon (Deut 28–30; Jer 25:1–11), and Persia (Isa 45:1–13).

serve this king, Nebuchadnezzar of Babylon, and put its neck under the yoke of the king of Babylon, then I will punish that nation with the sword, with famine, and with pestilence, says the Lord, until I have completed its destruction by his hand" (Jer 27:8). As an emphasis, any nation that remains in its own land to till it and live there, must bow its neck under the yoke of the emperor (Jer 27:11–12).

The redactor or pro-Babylonian ideology, or for that matter, any pro-empire influence on a text, sets a jaundiced religious-plitical agenda (as being from God and agent of God). For example, Cyrus is deemed the liberator of the peoples according to Deutero-Isaiah (Isa 40–55).[4] In Second Isaiah, Cyrus is God's shepherd and anointed[5] who carries out God's purpose, including the rebuilding of Jerusalem and the temple. Cyrus liberates and returns the forced Judean migrants from Babylonia to Yehud. It is for this and other reasons that God anointed him and gave him treasures and riches to fulfill these and other tasks on behalf of God's chosen people (Isa 44:28–45:4, 13).

As difficult it is to hear that a foreign ruler and power like Cyrus the Persian, who conquered and subjugated nations, is rendered as messiah to carry out YHWH's mission, like Pharaoh in Egypt, is not surprising. As parts of the Torah predate the sixth century BCE, old vestiges of an earlier tradition that centered on a national god[6] is made more visible. The covenant between the Israelites and their God through the exodus event helped foster the identity of a national god.

In Second Isaiah, however, a new ideology on God is fostered. The new construct is monotheism. The new notion, which promulgates and crosses over from an individual-local or national to universal god, claims supremacy, sovergnity, and validity of god in the broadest sense possible—a political reflection of the

---

[4] See the Cyrus Cylinder, which records Cyrus's propaganda that he is a chosen instrument by the supreme god (Marduk) to liberate Babylon. He respects the citizens of the city, their gods, and also the gods of their slaves. "I am Cyrus, King of the globe, ... when my numerous soldiers in great numbers peacefully entered Babylon.... I did not allow anyone to terrorize the people of the lands.... I kept in view the needs of the people and all their sanctuaries to promote their well being.... As to the inhabitants of Babylon who against the will of the gods were enslaved, ... I freed all slaves.... Marduk, the great lord, was well pleased with my deeds, ..." Samuel Willard Crompton, *Cyrus the Great* (New York: Chelsea House, 2008), 78–81.

[5] The title of God's "anointed" (messiah in Hebrew) had previously been given only to priests, prophets, and kings of Israel. Cyrus receiving the title messiah is striking. See John N. Oswalt, *The Book of Isaiah: Chapters 40–66*, NICOT 16 (Grand Rapids: Eerdmans, 1998), 201.

[6] Mark S. Smith, *The Origins of Biblical Monotheism: Israel's Polytheistic Background and the Ugaritic Texts* (New York: Oxford University Press, 2001), 155–63. The idea of territorial limitation of the deity underlies texts like Deut 32:8–9; 1 Sam 26:19; 2 Kgs 3; 5; Judg 11:24. Bob Becking et al., *Only One God? Monotheism in Ancient Israel and the Veneration of the Goddess Asherah* (Sheffield: Sheffield Academic, 2001), 192–93.

monopolar political landscape of the Near East during the Iron Age.[7] The development of the "one-god" worldview found in Deutero-Isaiah seems to be a response to the claims of hegemonic Mesopotamian "one-god" ideology of the time.[8] While the God of Israel eventually came to combine all the traits and associations of major deity, such as El, Baal and Asherah, who offer fertility and nourishment,[9] the deity YHWH was associated with the event of the exodus and the people's struggle over the land of Canaan. This YHWH is characterized mainly as a warrior deity,[10] represented by his titles: "man of war (*ish milhama*)" (Exod 15:3) and "the Lord of Hosts."'

The concept of a warrior god connected to a national god presumes that gods fight one another in the heavens, just as their subjects fight one another below.[11] The idea of gods fighting one another is relevant to the God of Israel. YHWH as a warrior deity directly battles with human enemies of Israel.[12] This is exemplified in the exodus events, where YHWH fights for Israel against Pharaoh (a diety) and the Egyptians (Exod 14:14), the people of the Canaan (Joshua and Judges), and other enemies: "When the Ark was to set out, Moses would say: Advance, O Lord!

---

[7] For details about the process in which the notion of national gods began to give way to emerging monotheism during the Iron Age, see Smith, *The Origins of Biblical Monotheism: Israel's Polytheistic Background and the Ugaritic Texts*.

[8] Mark S. Smith, *God in Translation: Deities in Cross-Cultural Discourse in the Biblical World* (Tübingen: Mohr Siebeck, 2008), 19.

[9] Archaeological evidences suggest that in the premonarchic and early monarchic period features belonging to deities such as El, Asherah, and Baal were absorbed into the Yahwistic religion of Israel, as is evident in poetic compositions including Gen 49; Judg 5; 2 Sam 22 (// Ps 18); 2 Sam 23:1–7; Ps 29; 68. Mark S. Smith, *The Early History of God: Yahweh and the Other Deities in Ancient Israel*, 2nd ed., BRS (Grand Rapids: Eerdmans, 2002), 19–64.

[10] Patrick D. Miller, *The Divine Warrior in Early Israel* (Atlanta: Society of Biblical Literature, 2006); Millard Lind, *Yahweh Is a Warrior: The Theology of Warfare in Ancient Israel* (Scottdale, PA: Herald Press, 1980). In ancient Canaan, there were warrior gods with characteristics that parallel some of the martial characteristics of the biblical God of Israel. For example, the god Yam of Ugarit (broadly, in Canaan) had messengers who appear as flaming warriors with flaming swords, parallel to the cherubs and flaming turning sword put in place by the God of the Hebrew Bible in Gen 3:24 (see also Num 22:31; Josh 5:13; 2 Sam 24:16–17; 1 Chr 21:27–40), and the image of the God of Israel as warrior (Exod 15:3), storm god (Gen 7; Exod 14:21) and king (1 Sam 8) parallel Baal.

[11] According to Sa-Moon Kang, in the Hittite context the defeat of one god by another is symbolized by the carrying of the divine statue from the defeated nation and to the temple of the victorious nation. See Sa-Moon Kang, *Divine War in the Old Testament and in the Ancient Near East*, BZAW 177 (Berlin: de Gruyter, 1989), 71.

[12] Millard Lind, *Monotheism, Power, Justice: Collected Old Testament Essays*, TRS 3 (Elkhart, IN: Institute of Mennonite Studies, 1990), 184–90.

May Your enemies be scattered and may Your foes flee before You!" (Num 10:35);[13] "So may all Your enemies perish, O Lord!" (Judg 5:31).

The God of Israel, a warrior and national god, in covenant with the people, is remembered for God's abilities in Exodus and the conquest but contrasted against the collapse of the Southern Kingdom of Judah in 597, 587, and 582 BCE. The experience of forced migration with the losses of the political and religious systems and symbols, and the enslavement of peoples as prisoners of war, raise deep theological tensions, inevitably questioning and damaging the view of a mighty warrior God.

National disaster likely reversed the belief in the omnipotence of their God. The fact of the matter was, their people, not their enemies, were scattered (Ps 68:1, 12). Their defeat was best understood as their God's defeat; their national god deemed inferior to the gods of the Babylonians, and their God gave them up and let them be enslaved before their enemies.

The difference between the exodus from Egypt and the new-exodus from Babylonian captivity may be found in the Deuternomistic theology of retribution.[14] The principle of divine retribution uses empires: Assyria, Babylonia, and Persia for the purpose of divine judgment (and restoration) (Isa 40:2; 50:1; 51:17–23; Jer 25; Ezek 23; 39:21–24). The prophets defend the God of Israel who employed this ideology and called on the people to return so that they might be restored. However, if they did not return, then, those enemies were used by God as retribution.

The theological interpretation of the destruction of Jerusalem and the forced migrations of Judeans to Babylonia is often expressed as God's judgment on the nation. This requires redress. In the exodus event, there was no need for God to make the Egyptian emperor or pharaoh, a true servant of God. All that God had to do was: fight against pharaoh and liberate the people. However, in God's plan to punish then restore, God needs agents, someone else to fight and defeat God's own people. Thus, agency becomes determinative, foreign nations that have a purpose in carrying out God's plan. According to the Dtr, then, Israel's "one-God" controls and subjects all nations to God-self rather than being a national god who solely fights as a warrior god against the enemies to prove supremacy.

Consequently, the Babylonian and Persian emperors are God's instruments. God in exilic and postexilic Yehud can be read as a claim to hegemony of the imperial forces, including a claim for universal supremacy (against the national

---

[13] The Ark of the Covenant is the symbol and banner of God's presence in battle (1 Sam 4:4; 2 Sam 11:11).

[14] The Deuteronomistic theology of retribution explains that the destruction of the Kingdom of Israel by the Assyrians (721 BCE) and the Kingdom of Judah by the Babylonians (586 BCE) are punishment for national sin and disobedience of Yahweh, which led to the disastrous exile or forced migrations of the people. Steven L. McKenzie, *Covenant*, UBT (St. Louis: Chalice, 2000), 26.

god of the Babylonian empire, Marduk). In the Book of Isaiah, the ruler of the peaceful kingdom is described as God's agent—filled with the spirit of wisdom, power, and justice—to judge the world, bring justice to the poor, and destroy the wicked. The prophecy about the peaceful kingdom is quite radical in the sense that it focuses on the restoration of justice for the poor and weak, which was perhaps intended to offer hope for the colonized peoples of Judah. It even includes peaceful coexistence of people with wild animals (Isa 11:6–9).

From a modern perspective, taking power to control all things (as necessary to realize the ideal of a just world) attempts to justify autocracy and communist dictatorship. As often heard in colloquial talk, "Power tends to corrupt, and absolute power corrupts absolutely. Great men are almost always bad men." What matters is not whether power, including divine power, is exercised justly or not, but simply, absolute power corrupts. As long as absolute power is ascribed to the one God, absolute corruption is also attributed to the same one God (who could be described as a dictator). Overcoming oppressive power by the colonized when they have no power can offer a message of hope. Conversely, taking power to establish a just world could support imperialism, as attested in the history of communism and Christianity. It should be noted that both started out as a sect, a voice of the oppressed minority, but in due time, became communist imperialist or Christian imperialist, respectively.

Ironically, the two power-oriented imperial forces, the Soviet Union representing communist imperialism and the United States, representing capitalist and Christian imperialism,[15] are directly responsible for Korea's South and North conflict,[16] including the years of war.[17] The Korean War caused immense destruction,

---

[15] American imperial interest in East Asia went along the lines of American evangelical enthusiasm and movement for foreign mission activities between 1880s and 1920s. Many foreign mission advocates claimed that an expansion of trade, through the missionaries' creation of demand, was one of the desirable results of foreign missions. It encouraged economic expansions. See William Appleman Williams, *The Tragedy of American Diplomacy*, 2nd rev. and enl. ed. (New York: Dell, 1972), 63. Francis E. Clark of the United Society of Christian Endeavor claimed that foreign missions brought increase of exports and the "widening of our empire." See Francis E. Clark, "Do Forgien Missions Pay?," *NAR* (March 1898): 280. For detailed discussions of Christian imperialism and American foreign missions, see also Emily Conroy-Krutz, *Christian Imperialism: Converting the World in the Early American Republic* (New York: Cornell University Press, 2015).

[16] The South Korean state was founded in a maelstrom of decolonization, national partition, and the rise of the Cold War. After Japan surrendered to the victorious Allies at the conclusion of the Pacific War, American administrators divided the peninsula along the thirty-eighth parallel, with US military forces occupying the southern half and Soviet military forces occupying the northern half. Donald W. Boose Jr., "Sideshow: The Korean Occupation Decision," *Parameters: USAWCQ* 25.4 (1995–96): 112–29.

[17] The Korean War (1950–1953) between the Republic of Korea (supported primarily by the United States of America, with contributions from allied nations under the aegis of the

generating more than four million casualties. A nation divided after the Korean War, separated ten million families across the border. Many died without ever being reunited.

The division of Korea caused by external powers fighting for colonial expansion and military hegemony is generally considered the main cause of the suffering experienced by Koreans.[18] The sharp national division has been fertile grounds for ideological similarities and differences. For example, both supported dictatorships (in the North and the South). The north depends on China and Russia, whereas South Korea depends on the United States and its imperial anticommunist ideology.[19] The tool that has been utilized as a powerful ideological and institutional constraint to suppress political opposition to authoritarian regimes and even liberation movements are the laborer's or worker's movement, democratic movement, women's movement, among others.[20] The division of the Koreas and its stance on anticommunism in South Korea are reinforced by a patriarchal ideology promoting militarism and Confucianism—reframed as patriarchal ethics—loyalty to the king and one's father, the head of state and family, which serves to secure the people's obedience to authoritarian regimes.[21] This

---

United Nations) and the Democratic People's Republic of Korea (supported by the People's Republic of China, with military and material aid from the Union of Soviet Socialist Republics) was primarily the result of the political division of Korea by an agreement of the victorious Allies at the end of World War II. With both North Korea and South Korea sponsored by external powers, the Korean War was a proxy war. Bruce Cumings, *The Origins of the Korean War*, 2 vols. (Princeton: Princeton University Press, 1992), 770.

[18] World Council of Churches, "Statement on Peace and Reunification of the Korean Peninsula" (statement filed under the World Council of Churches 10th Assembly, Busan, Republic of Korea, 8 November 2013); United Methodist Church, "Korea: Peace, Justice, and Reunification," in *The Book of Resolutions of the United Methodist Church 2016* (Nashville: United Methodist Pub. House, 2016), 650–57.

[19] The anticommunist national identity remained hegemonic in the context of the bloody Korean War and prolonged military confrontation between the two Koreas. Crucial to the making of this national identity was the political dynamic during the period of the US Army Military Government in Korea (USAMGIK; 1945–1948). At the outset of the Cold War, rivalry between the United States and the Soviet Union, the USAMGIK attempted to establish a friendly regime in Korea, serving its own political and strategic interests, with heavy reliance on coercive means. The United States's intention was to bring Korea under US tutelage after delinking it from the Japanese Empire, which was part of the US's imperial plans to make the former colonial territories, once free of their masters, politically and economically dependent on the United States. Anthony Eden, *The Reckoning: The Memoirs of Anthony Eden, Earl of Avon* (Boston: Houghton Mifflin, 1965), 593.

[20] For historical trajectory of anticommunism in South Korea since 1945, see Kwang-Yeong Shin, "The Trajectory of Anti-Communism in South Korea," *AJGES* 2.3 (2017): 1–10.

[21] Anti-Communism has played a significant role in producing an official nationalism that contains a strong militaristic strand and, therefore, has implications for gender hierarchy in

division further implicates women who suffer even more because of and beyond the bifurcation.

In my postcolonial reading of the prophets of exile: Deutero-Isaiah, Jeremiah, and Ezekiel, their hopeful message, oracles or announcements of salvation, the fall of the Babylonian empire, and the release and return of the peoples to their homeland parallel Korean Christians who sought for a message of hope and liberation after the Japanese colonization in 1910–1945. When reading the Old Testament, Koreans can easily identity with ancient Israel who suffered under the rule and regimes of Egypt, Assyria, Babylon, Persia, and the Greeks. Since the Japanese knew these stories, they prevented these prophetic messages of restoration of Israel and their contextual salvation history to be read and proclaimed in the Korean church. Simply, the Japanese prohibited Koreans (Christians) from reading the Old Testament.[22]

The same exploitation is rendered by US imperial forces, which took shape and power on the Korean peninsula. God's agent to liberate the Koreans from Japanese colonization was none other than the Americans. With Japanese retreat from the Korean Peninsula after the atomic bombings of Hiroshima and Nagasaki in 1945, the United States entered Korea and occupied the land with its forces. Throughout its occupation (1945–1948), the US Army Military Government in Korea militantly suppressed the indigenous grassroots political movements organized around the Korean People's Republic and the peoples' committees.[23] The USAMGIK collaborated with the conservative landed gentry class and bureaucrats in South Korea who had served the Japanese colonial government.[24] This

---

Korean society. The anticommunist national identity was crucial to disciplinary control over members of the nation in that it provided ruling regimes with ideological justification for the surveillance, normalization, and repressive violence exercised over the people. Seungsook Moon, "Begetting the Nation: The Androcentric Discourse of National History and Tradition in South Korea," in *Dangerous Women: Gender and Korean Nationalism*, ed. Elaine H. Kim and Chungmoo Choi (New York: Routledge, 1998), 37; Seungsook Moon, *Militarized Modernity and Gendered Citizenship in South Korea* (Durham: Duke University Press, 2005), 18.

[22] Especially, this atmosphere was further strengthened by the alliance between Japan and the German Nazi regime with hostility toward the Jews in the Second World War. Chŏngmin Sŏ, 일본기독교의 한국인식 [서정민, 일본기독교의 한국인식 [*Japanese Christianity's Recognition of Korea*] (Seoul: Hanul Akademi, 2009), 109.

[23] Bruce Cumings, *The Origins of the Korean War*, 2 vols. (Princeton: Princeton University Press, 1981–1992), 1:441–43.

[24] As the Japanese colonial rule, especially after 1931, was characterized by a fusion of colonial and Fascist orders, and hence was fiercely anticommunist, the struggle against anticommunism and the struggle against colonial rule got inextricably interlinked. The Communists and Leftists came to dominate the Korean nationalist movement after 1925 and "Leftism" became almost synonymous with opposition to Japan. See Bruce Cumings, "American Policy Towards Korean Liberation," in *Without Parallel: The American-Korean Relationship since 1945*, ed. Frank Baldwin (New York: Pantheon Books, 1974), 51.

privileged minority was equally threatened by the mass based movement aiming to redistribute land and other resources. The conservative Korean elites and the USAMGIK shared anticommunist sentiments—to the point of equating any autonomous local movement in the South with communist insurgency sponsored by the Soviet Union.[25]

Heavily influenced by American missionaries, those who held and advanced conservative theology with Christian imperialist tendencies[26] (South Korean protestants under the rule of the USAMGIK) cooperated with the US military government receiving benefits and preferential treatment.[27] A majority of South Korean Protestant churches supported and took advantage of the anticommunism and pro-Americanism positions, which helped them achieve tremendous growth in numbers and hegemony in South Korean society.[28] As a result, conservative anticommunist and pro-American biblical interpretation has been at the center of Korean Protestant churches, whereas only a small number of Minjung churches have struggled against dictatorship and oppression offering emancipated biblical

---

For more discussion on the nature and character of Japanese colonial rule, see Gregory Henderson, *Korea, the Politics of the Vortex* (Cambridge: Harvard University Press, 1968), 72–112; Harold Hakwon Sunoo, *Korea: A Political History in Modern Times* (Columbia, MO: Korean-American Cultural Foundation, 1970), 255–95.

[25] Cumings, *Origins of the Korean War*, 349, 80.

[26] American missionaries accounted for 69.3 precent of the total of 1529 foreign missionaries who came to Korea before 1945. Sŭng-t'ae Kim and Hye-jin Pak, eds., 내한선교사총람 [*A Comprehensive Survey of Missionaries in Korea*] (Seoul: The Institute of Korean Christian History, 1994), 4. For further discussions of early American missionaries' activities based on their conservative theology and imperialist perspective, see Dae Young Ryu, "Understanding Early American Missionaries in Korea (1884–1910): Capitalist Middle-Class Values and the Weber Thesis," *ASSR* 46.113 (2001): 93–117. For discussions on how the foreign missions in colonial Korea established controlling power over Korean Christians by relying on colonial privileges such as extraterritoriality and financial wealth, which perpetuated their power over local Christians through Church and mission schools, see Motokazu Matsutani, "Church over Nation: Christian Missionaries and Korean Christians in Colonial Korea" (PhD diss., Harvard University, 2012).

[27] Chŏng-min Sŏ, 건국대통령 이승만 [*Syngman Rhee, the First President of South Korea*] (Seoul: Institute of Korean Church History Studies, 2013), 211–14; In-ch'ŏl Kang, 한국기독교회와 국가, 시민사회 [*Church, State, and Civil Society in Korea: 1945–1960*] (Seoul: The Institute of Korean Christian History, 2003), 162–89.

[28] For more discussions of anticommunism and pro-Americanism of South Korean protestant conservatives and their political activities, see Dae Young Ryu, "Political Activities and Anti-Communism of Korean Protestant Conservatives in the 2000s," *AJGES* 2.6 (2017): 1–18; Ju Hui Judy Han, "Contemporary Korean/American Evangelical Missions: Politics of Space, Gender, and Difference" (PhD diss., University of California, Berkeley, 2009), 27–38.

interpretation that is indigenous.²⁹ Consequently, while biblical prophets announced and waited for the coming of the next emperor of Persia, those who liberated the colonized Koreans continued to suffer under the new regime of Japanese colonialism or US neocolonialism.

Even though prophetic voices that announce liberation for the oppressed can be exploited to serve the oppressor, God on top as the real emperor who controls worldly powers through agency requires deconstruction and reframing–through a reconstruction of power where God's agents are genuinely qualified.

A theology of retribution based on divine judgment and restoration, and punishment and reward, was used to subject colonized peoples. Indeed, obedience to the authority of the imperial power is another form of God's agency. As Spanish conquerors and missionaries justified their invasion of the Americas, a contextual representation of "the conquest of Canaan," they saw themselves as "divine instruments" of punishment and liberation from indigenous "idols." They caused much suffering on the indigenous peoples. This was explained as a form of God's punishment.³⁰ As an extension, it has been an afterthought, a primal seduction in the United States to imagine that "the United States is the New Israel, God's anointed carrier of freedom and justice to the rest of the world."³¹

Any mindset to dominate is truly problematic. Any mission activity to remove and replace indigenous life and all cultural spheres of influences is unquestionably oppressive. The mindset of conqueror and domination in Christian theology or biblical interpretation underscores this missional point.³²

Ironically, Christian imperialism has its origins as an oppressed minority group within Judaism and the Roman Empire. It was a persecuted religion of slaves and others. Christianity sought legitimacy and power to raise the voices of

---

²⁹ Korean Minjung theology privileges the readings of historically dominated groups. For more discussion of how Korean Minjung Christian communities have interpreted the Bible, see Choi Hyung muk and Cho Ha mu, "한국 그리스도교 민중공동체의 성서해석" ["Methods of Biblical Interpretation in Korean Minjung Christian Communities"], *Theological Thought* 63 (1988): 811–45.

³⁰ Tamez, "Bible and the Five Hundred Years of Conquest," 14–16.

³¹ Walter Brueggemann, "Faith in the Empire," in *In the Shadow of Empire: Reclaiming the Bible as a History of Faithful Resistance*, ed. Richard A. Horsley (Louisville: Westminster John Knox, 2008), 37. According to Brueggemann, this US Christian imperial seduction becomes even more dangerous and more problematic in contemporary society when the United States has emerged as the dominant superpower, with a readiness to impose its will everywhere by the mobilization of limitless economic and military resources (37).

³² To articulate "the complex inter-structuring of domination" and to underscore the political matrix of "a broader range of networks of power" underlying discrimination ideologies like sexism and misogyny, Schüssler Fiorenza uses the term *kyriarchy*, deriving from the Greek *kyrios* (the Lord). Elisabeth Schüssler Fiorenza, *Rhetoric and Ethic: The Politics of Biblical Studies* (Minneapolis: Fortress, 1999), 5.

the oppressed minority. However, once it became normative and powerful, its exclusivism and power-orientation functioned just like its previous imperal oppressors.

Korean Christianity also started out as the voice for the oppressed. It experienced heavy persecution in its early periods by Confucian institutions. Gradually, Korean Christianity grew and became a powerful institution to oppose colonial and post-colonial powers in society. Korean Christianity's aspiration for power is well represented and documented. Today, those that once freed the many have become the oppressors by demanding total obedience to God and especially its leaders. The aspirations and repetitions of its own form of retribution theology is alarming, but not surprising.

South Korean churches have adapted the colonial narrative: the "benevolence" of American dominance in Korea and South Korea's capitalist development under the umbrella of American dominance are the result of God's providence for the nation. As exporters of missionaries,[33] Korean Christianity produces the largest number of Christian missionaries behind the United States. What underlies these triumphant missionaries' predictions are the new landscapes of Korean Christianity's understanding that a new era of south-to-south mission activities are well underway because of South Korea—a chosen nation that progressed from poverty to prosperity in part, due to the coupling of Christianity with capitalism. Missionaries showcase South Korea's achievements and cast this reality to expand and influence its status to poor and non-Christian nations.[34] South Korean churches' enthusiasm for world missions is tied inextricably to the affinities and alliances between Korea and a particular form of Christianity espoused in the United States. Conservative Korean Christians' eagerness to stand second in command to the United States in a "new world order"—as the second most highly and globally connected nation to support and send missionaries—has heralded the managerial role of "global Christian leadership" with the United States. By doing so, South Korean churches also manifest imperial ambitions.[35]

As enacted by American missionaries in Korea, Korean missionaries are now dedicated to the expansion of their conservative theology abroad. Without giving any careful consideration of the diverse forms of Christianities, oppressive systems that reinforce imperialism, colonialism, and power-orientation, these old-new seeds are resown.

Inasmuch as God's relationships with others are divinely sanctioned, and God is the source of all creation, creation, however, should be modeled after the

---

[33] Melissa Steffan, "The Surprising Countries Most Missionaries Are Sent from and Go To," *Christianity Today*, 25 July 2013, https://www.christianitytoday.com/news/2013/july/missionaries-countries-sent-received-csgc-gordon-conwell.html, accessed Jun 10, 2018.

[34] Han, "Contemporary Korean/American Evangelical Missions: Politics of Space, Gender, and Difference," 10.

[35] Han, "Contemporary Korean/American Evangelical Missions," 123.

Minjung God—not the imperial God of the missionaires. The understanding that God is the all-powerful ruler, who justifies power-centric attributes, and total subjugation of all creation, is thoroughly questioned and challenged. Again, how the Minjung God who relates to others in creation should be the model for creation. A hierarchical human relation presupposes a hierachial view of the God-human relationship. Conversely, I invite a postcolonial reading, reimaging and offering a subversive decentered, redistributed powerlessness of God.

While the prophets' visions for liberation of the colonized are confined in a hierarchical power structure, the colonized peoples' aspirations for power begins with an understanding of God who has decentered and self-emptied. In the book of Job, there is a reversal, an antiprophetic stance by God in the very position of decenteredness (27:2). God is held accountable. Job's lawsuit against God reflects this distortion of power.[36] This perspective in Job places God in the position of the covenant breaker, read in the oppressive and exploitative context of Babylonian imperialism and colonization of Judah. God ended the nation. God broke the Davidic convenant. Thereby, God has to provide an important interpretative insight into a new religious and ethical mechanism for justifying power. Power and control serve the powerful and condemn the powerless. But when divine retribution is exercised, it further increases oppression on the colonized by blaming them rather than the colonizers.

The image of God who is all powerful, like an emperor who exercises absolute power over subjects or uses US imperial force as an agent against the colonized Koreans, truly perpetuates oppression. An all-powerful God reinforces a system of hierarchy, domination, and control. In Minjung theology, God is colonized, oppressed, and powerless, like the people.[37] God and people struggle together to confront abusive power. Here lies a paradigm for new hope and reading.

---

[36] Carol A. Newsom, "The Book of Job: Introduction, Commentary, and Reflections," in *The New Interpreter's Bible* (Nashville: Abingdon, 1996), 336.

[37] Korean Minjung theology sees Jesus in the oppressed in their struggles for liberation, like the attacked by the robbers in the parable of the Good Samaritan. Yong-Yeon Hwang, "The Person Attacked by the Robbers Is Christ: An Exploration of Subjectivity from the Perspective of Minjung Theology," in *Reading Minjung Theology in the Twenty-First Century: Selected Writings by Ahn Byung-Mu and Modern Critical Responses*, ed. Yung Suk Kim and Chin-ho Kim (Eugene, OR: Pickwick, 2013), 215–16.

PERILS OF BETRAYING A DEITY: PARALLELS BETWEEN EZEKIEL 16 AND THE SUMERIAN MYTH "UNFAITHFULNESS"

Sehee Kim

Ezekiel 16 contains a lengthy description of Jerusalem as an unfaithful wife who is harshly condemned for her infidelity to God. This text is dominated by the vivid metaphor of Jerusalem as the adulterous wife of YHWH. She was originally an abandoned child but was later rescued by God, only to be married to God. However, Jerusalem betrayed YHWH by sacrificing her children to idols and offering sexual favors to strangers: the Egyptians, Assyrians, and Babylonians.

The concept of marriage between a deity and a human is not unique to biblical texts. In Sumerian mythology, the goddess Inanna's divine union with the human king Dumuzi is well known. Their marriage rituals are described in detail in *The Sacred Marriage of Inanna and Dumuzi*. Another Sumerian myth, "Unfaithfulness,"[1] makes it clear that the sacred marriage of Inanna and Dumuzi was not peaceful. This myth and Ezek 16 have strikingly similarities, including flow of texts, plot, and characters. In this essay, I examine the parallels in concepts between these texts.

SINS OF JERUSALEM IN EZEKIEL 16

The metaphor of Israel as the adulterous wife of YHWH is not new. Ezekiel is not the first to use this metaphor in the Hebrew Bible. Hosea, in fact, was the first prophet to employ the marriage metaphor[2] to emphasize Israel's intimate relationship with God; and to describe the fearful punishment Israel endured as a result of her infidelity to God. The marriage metaphor in Hosea and further in Jeremiah, Ezekiel, and Isaiah, attracted the attention of the audiences of the texts to likely

---

[1] Thorkild Jacobsen translated this Sumerian text and entitled it "Unfaithfulness." For convenience, I use his translation and title of this text. Thorkild Jacobsen, trans. and ed., *The Harps That Once ...: Sumerian Poetry in Translation* (New Haven: Yale University Press, 1987), 24–27.

[2] Renita J. Weems demonstrates how the marriage metaphor serves to function as a poetic device, which has significant power in delivering religious words. See Renita J. Weems, "Gomer: Victim of Violence or Victim of Metaphor?," *Semeia* 47 (1989): 87–104.

bear light on the metaphorization of daily living—the punishment of wives unfaithful to their spouses.

Since Ezekiel's marriage metaphor depicts the relationship between God and Israel as husband and wife, it is important to acknowledge Israelite law codes regarding the institution of marriage and adultery (see Ahn's essay in this volume). Israel had an honor/shame value system that was aligned with its patrilineal structure. This system required honor from men and punished women by shaming them. For a man, the positive value of honor was laid upon his manliness, courage, ability to protect his family and honor, and his assertion of sexual masculinity. Meanwhile, if a woman failed to remain sexually pure, she would be rendered shameful and therefore shamed by the community. A wife's adultery was considered an extremely severe crime in the honor/shame system of ancient Israel. When a woman was unfaithful, she was viewed as defying both the husband's right of sexual intimacy with his wife and the honor of the entire family.[3]

In this sense, the sin of Jerusalem could be seen as bringing the Israelite God more than shame because she failed to preserve her virtue. She was intimate with strangers instead of her husband, like a harlot, but in ways more perverted than those of other prostitutes. She gave gifts to all her lovers rather than receiving gifts from them, whereas ordinary prostitutes were paid by their clients. This adultery metaphor obviously denotes the political alliance of Judah with Assyria, Babylonia, and Egypt, which caused the covenant that Jerusalem made with YHWH to fade away.

INFIDELITY OF DUMUZI IN "UNFAITHFULNESS"

Inanna is one of the most powerful goddesses in the Mesopotamian pantheon. She is a multifaceted goddess consisting of all possible contradictory aspects of being.[4] Her main title is "mistress of heaven," but her unique characteristics allow her to transcend all the boundaries of a female goddess. She represents the sexuality of women, but is also depicted as a warrior, which was usually regarded as a male virtue. Dumuzi, who is described as the beloved of Inanna, appears as a shepherd and is regarded as a manifestation of agriculture and natural phenomena.

---

[3] Gale A. Yee, "Hosea," in *Women's Bible Commentary*, ed. Carol A. Newsom and Sharon H. Ringe (Louisville: Westminster John Knox, 1998), 209–10.

[4] Though she has many affiliations, Inanna is best known as a daughter of the moon god Nannar and his wife Ningal. Given powers by the most superior gods, An, Enki, and Enlil, this goddess was poised to be the queen goddess, not only in heaven but also in the universe. Thorkild Jacobsen, *The Treasures of Darkness: A History of Mesopotamian Religion* (New Haven: Yale University Press, 1976), 135–43. She also seems to have had her own temple, Eduranki, which means "place of the link between heaven and earth" in Nippur. Brigitte Groneberg, "The Role and Function of Goddesses in Mesopotamia," in *The Babylonian World*, ed. Gwendolyn Leick (New York: Routledge, 2007), 323.

His Sumerian name originally meant "the good son" or "the right son,"[5] and it also appears as תמוז in Ezek 8:14, where women were wailing over his death at the north gate of the Jerusalem temple.[6]

Regarding Dumuzi's divinity, Adam Falkenstein argues that he was not originally a god but was deified later as a result of his sacred marriage to the goddess Inanna. The name of the human king Dumuzi appears twice in the Sumerian King List, once as "Dumuzi, the shepherd," king of Badtibira, and the other as Dumuzi of Kuara, king of Uruk.[7] Dumuzi's sacred marriage with Inanna is a representative example of a mortal king's marriage with a powerful goddess, and he eventually becomes a great ruler who drew on the divine power of his spouse. Along with the deification of the human king, the most significant purpose of the sacred marriage[8] was to obtain general fertility of the land. According to Samuel Noah Kramer, "It was the king's pleasant duty to marry the passionate, desirable goddess of fertility and fecundity, the alluring deity who controlled the productivity of the land and the fruitfulness of the womb of man and beast."[9] The purpose of the sacred marriage ritual for the king was to generate abundance in life and guarantee the fertility of the people, animals, and the earth as a herdsman in the human realm.

The human king Dumuzi, who is supposed to be loyal to his spouse Inanna, a goddess, betrays her in this myth by having a sexual relationship with one of the slave girls of Inanna. As in Ezekiel, the cost of betraying the deity is tremendous for both offenders, Dumuzi and the slave girl.

---

[5] Bendt Alster, *Dictionary of Deities and Demons in the Bible*, ed. Karel van der Toorn, Bob Becking, and Pieter W. van der Horst (Leiden: Eerdmans, 1999), 828.

[6] The purpose of the women's wailing is not certain at this point (possibly they were grieving the death or asking for rain from the deity), but it seems apparent that they were exposed to the Babylonian culture at certain points, which makes it no surprise that Ezekiel 16 and this myth from Mesopotamia have much in common.

[7] Alster, *Dictionary of Deities and Demons*, 829. Alster cites Adam Falkenstein, "Tammuz," Compte Rendu, Rencontre Assyriologique Internationale 3, 43–44, and Thorkild Jacobsen, "Toward the Image of Tammuz," in *Toward the Image of Tammuz and Other Essays on Mesopotamian History and Culture*, ed. William L. Moran (Cambridge: Harvard University Press, 1970), 73–103. According to Alster, Thorkild Jacobsen gives several titles of Dumuzi: (1) Ama- ushum- gal- anna: the power in storable dates, (2) Dumuzi of the Grain: the power in the grain, (3) Dumuzi the shepherd: the power in milk, and (4) Dumu: the sap that rises in trees and plants.

[8] Scholars disagree as to whether there were actual rituals of sacred marriage in Mesopotamia. See Pirjo Lapinkivi, "The Sumerian Sacred Marriage and Its Aftermath in Later Sources," in *Sacred Marriages: The Divine- Human Sexual Metaphor from Sumer to Early Christianity* (Winona Lake: Eisenbrauns, 2008), 22–28.

[9] Samuel Noah Kramer, *The Sacred Marriage Rite: Aspects of Faith, Myth, and Ritual in Ancient Sumer* (Bloomington: Indiana University Press, 1969), 49.

PARALLELS IN THE TWO TEXTS: EZEKIEL 16 AND "UNFAITHFULNESS"

In describing these two horrifying situations, the stories in the Hebrew Bible and the Mesopotamian myth have similar patterns and many elements in common. First, the mortal spouse—the personified Jerusalem in Ezek 16 and Dumuzi in "Unfaithfulness"—betrays the deity. Second, the maiden who is supposed to be loyal to her deity commits adultery and is punished. Third, the deity, with tremendous anger, plans to execute the spouse who had betrayed the deity. Last, despite the spouse's fatal blunder, in the end, the deity postpones executing the spouse. The common elements in plot and characters are as follows:

	Ezekiel 16 (NRSV)	"Unfaithfulness"[10]
The Deity Describes the Woman's Sin	[15] But you trusted in your beauty, and played the whore because of your fame, and lavished your whorings on any passer-by. [22] And in all your abominations and your whorings you did not remember the days of your youth, when you were naked and bare, flailing about in your blood. [23] After all your wickedness (woe, woe to you! says the Lord GOD), [24] you built yourself a platform and made yourself a lofty place in every square;	That [girl,] that slave woman, who did the forbidden thing, that sl[ave woman,] source of the sin, who did the forbidden thing, that [source] of the sin, that one of dire fate, that one of dire fate, with face tear-blotched—
The Woman Committed Adultery and Used Valuable Items That Belong to the God	[16] You took some of your garments, and made for yourself colorful shrines, and on them played the whore; nothing like this has ever been or ever shall be. [17] You also took your beautiful jewels of my gold and my silver that I had given you, and made for yourself male images, and with them played the whore; [18] and you took your embroidered garments to cover them, and set my oil and my incense before them.	Having sat down on the sacred throne, she then lay down in the sacred bed, came to know too the male member plied there, learned too to suck the male member.
The People Gather for the Execution	[35] Therefore, O whore, hear the word of the LORD: [36] Thus says the Lord GOD, Because your lust	"Come, let us go there, Let us go there! Us, let us go there, to the city! Let us go there to the city, to the spectacle! Let us go there,

---

[10] Jacobsen, *Harps That Once*, 24–27.

	was poured out and your nakedness uncovered in your whoring with your lovers, and because of all your abominable idols, and because of the blood of your children that you gave to them, ³⁷ therefore, I will gather all your lovers, with whom you took pleasure, all those you loved and all those you hated; I will gather them against you from all around, and will uncover your nakedness to them, so that they may see all your nakedness.	to the city, to Kullab! Let us go there, to brick-built Uruk! Let us go there to brick-built Zabalam! Let us go there to Hursag-kalamma! To the city! To the city! to brick-built Babylon! At the word spoken by Inanna!"
Execution by the People	³⁸ I will judge you as women who commit adultery and shed blood are judged, and bring blood upon you in wrath and jealousy. ³⁹ I will deliver you into their hands, and they shall throw down your platform and break down your lofty places; they shall strip you of your clothes and take your beautiful objects and leave you naked and bare. ⁴⁰ They shall bring up a mob against you, and they shall stone you and cut you to pieces with their swords. ⁴¹ They shall burn your houses and execute judgments on you in the sight of many women; I will stop you from playing the whore, and you shall also make no more payments.	The girl, the source of the sin, had thrown herself down prostrate in the dust—She (Inanna) looked at her, with that look of death, the mistress cried out, it was a cry ablaze with punishment. By the forelock she seized her, threw the girl, the source of the sin, down from the plinth of the city wall:
The Anger of the Deity and Declaration to the Sinner	⁴³ Because you have not remembered the days of your youth, but have enraged me with all these things; therefore, I have returned your deeds upon your head, says the Lord GOD. Have you not committed lewdness beyond all your abominations? ⁵⁹ Yes, thus says the Lord GOD: I will deal with you as you have done, you who have despised the oath, breaking the covenant;	[She had told her] everything, amid tears and wailing. O could but the princess's heart have held back the groans! O the heart of Inanna!—Everything! What there was and wasn't, so that he showed her favor by day, so that he spent the night with her. [O could but] her heart [have held back the groans!] [O could but her] ears [...] "I am the young lady [...] [...] I am Inanna [...] I shake the heaven, [make the earth quake] [that is my fame!"]

The Deity Gets Ready to Confront the Spouse	[60] yet I will remember my covenant with you in the days of your youth, and I will establish with you an everlasting covenant. [61] Then you will remember your ways, and be ashamed when I take your sisters, both your elder and your younger, and give them to you as daughters, but not on account of my covenant with you.	When she had sho[wered] in water, [rubbed herself with soap,] [When she had showered] in the water of the bright copper ewer, [had rubbed herself] with soap of the shiny stone jar, [had anointed herself] with the stone jar's sweet oil, she clothed herself in the queenly robe, [the robe of the queen]ship [of heaven,] her turban cloth [she wound round her head] [put] kohl on her eyes [took] her bright scepter [in hand, her kohl [....] To where food is set out, where bread from clean hands is served! To the house to which a true lord has invited! [To the house] to which a sincere lord has invited! To which a god, a lord, has invited! Accept the entreaty! To the sheepfold at the shepherd's pleading! To the pure sheepfold [at Dumuzi's] pleading! To the pure sheepfold where lives [Dumuzi!]

In the Sumerian text, one of Inanna's slave girls slept with Dumuzi. Inanna founds out about this incident. As a result, the girl who had sinned was put to death. The slave girl was supposed to be loyal to her mistress, Inanna, but by sleeping with Dumuzi on the royal bed, she betrayed her goddess. With outrage and anger, Inanna gathered the people to execute the girl. She punished the slave girl by killing her. Some time after the execution, she prepared to deal with Dumuzi. In his case, it was more complicated because he was obviously in a different position than the slave girl since he was the spouse of the goddess. In getting ready to confront her spouse, all we know is that Inanna bathed and prepared to take certain actions. Then, unfortunately, the tablet gives us no clear information about Dumuzi's fate.

The passage in Ezekiel has precisely the same narrative flow as the Sumerian myth. Although God treated Israel well and clothed her with lavish gifts in royalty, she gave herself to foreign lovers. God became deeply upset and angered, and further declared that he would judge the city of Jerusalem for her sin. Against his will, however, God remembered the covenant and reconciled with Jerusalem at the end of chapter 16. Moreover, he even established an everlasting covenant with her. The marital status of God and Jerusalem is comparable to this covenantal relationship, which is spoiled by her iniquities, but nevertheless, restored by the loving kindness of God. To present the extent of Jerusalem's sins, Ezekiel uses the highest degree of humiliation that he could devise, the image of an unfaithful wife to her husband. Accordingly, this text should be read through the lens of the social context of ancient Israel.

Conclusion

Due to the parallels between the two texts, it is plausible that Ezekiel entwined certain traces of the Sumerian myth and the Israelite tradition of the marriage metaphor, which were composed earlier, to deliver his message artistically. Comparing "Unfaithfulness" to Ezek 16, some differences are noticeable. One is that in "Unfaithfulness," Inanna is a female deity with a recognaizably different status from her slave girl and her spouse. Therefore, Inanna's rage is aimed at both the girl and her spouse, whereas the Israelite God concentrates his anger on his beloved wife Jerusalem.

The other difference is, unlike the Sumerian story, God has a distinctive "covenant" relationship with Judah. After God's harsh condemnation of Jerusalem, a dramatic reversal takes place—God makes an everlasting covenant with her once again, because he remembered the covenant that he made with her in her youth (v. 60). Although Jerusalem was not faithful as a wife, God did not reciprocate by being unfaithful to her. This is the main difference between Jerusalem's God and the betrayed goddess Inanna. In "Unfaithfulness," Inanna's angry kills the slave girl. Moreover, although the ending is not clear, the fate of Dumuzi extends into another well-known myth, *Inanna's Descent to the Netherworld*. In that story, when Inanna is suspended in the underworld and is urged to provide a substitute for herself, she sacrifices her husband Dumuzi, who had acted disgracefully against her. Whereas the goddess Inanna abandoned her spouse, the God of Israel remembered the covenant with Jerusalem and forgave her. The covenant remembered in Ezekiel's God changed the fate of Jerusalem.

CROSSING BOUNDARIES: DANIEL'S THREE FRIENDS MEET REV. KI-CHOL CHU OF COLONIZED KOREA

Hyun Chul Paul Kim

The dramatic account of the heroic courage and miraculous deliverance of Daniel's three friends from the fiery furnace has been an inspiring story for many Bible readers. Whether factual or fictional, this incredible story of resistance against an imperial ruler has significantly impacted the lives of Judeo-Christians. As an ethnic Korean, I cannot help but notice the eerie similarities between this story of the three young men refusing to bow before the Babylonian golden statue and the refusal of some Koreans to bow down before the Japanese Shinto shrine during the Japanese occupation period (1910–1945 CE). The goal of this essay is to read the story of Daniel's three friends in a sociological and hermeneutical comparison with the history of colonized Korea.

In any comparative study, there are gaps between historical accounts, particularly in terms of chronology, geography, and culture. Nevertheless, in light of postmodern and postcolonial hermeneutics, it is legitimate to compare these two distant yet, related social constructions of realities. My proposed reading crosses hermeneutical boundaries. In this study, I review some key issues of modern Korean history during the Japanese occupation. Next, I explore the dynamics between the colonizer and the colonized, exegeting and highlighting select literary and thematic topics in Dan 3. I further expound and enumerate on hermeneutical implications of "crossing boundaries" initially evident in the episodes of Daniel's three friends with Shinto shrine obeisance in Korea. I hope to arrive at an interpretive dialogue and better understanding of both the ancient and contemporary in textual and historical settings.[1]

This essay was originally presented at the 2016 International Meeting of the Society of Biblical Literature in Seoul, Korea. I am deeply grateful to The Korean Society of Old Testament Studies for inviting me as one of the keynote speakers, and also to Professor Gale Yee for her insightful feedback as a respondent. My gratitude also to Professors John Kampen and Deok-Joo Rhie for sharing invaluable input during my research processes.

[1] This study is not intended as any personal or collective attack on the country and people of Japan (I have some close Japanese friends, in addition to my obsession for Japanese food and appreciation of many beautiful aspects of Japanese culture). Rather, it is an interpretive study of a segment of history that is essential to me as a biblical reader and hopefully to

Shinto Shrine Obeisance in Colonized Korea

There is a striking similarity between the images of Daniel's three friends (along with their colonized counterparts) being compelled to bow down to the (ancient) Babylonian golden statue and colonized Koreans being forced to bow down to the (modern) Shinto shrine during the Japanese occupation.[2] The Shinto shrine became important during the early Meiji era (1868–1890), especially in the 1880s, associated with the effort to increase the national awareness and centralization of the Meiji emperor's sovereignty, to distinguish it from the feudal systems of the Tokugawa shogun era (1600–1868). In order to appeal to its own unique cultural identity, distinctive from Western imperialism, Japan resorted to the promulgation of a new ideology, namely, "national Shintoism," rooted in the Japanese people's moral values.[3] This ethical ideology of "national Shintoism" underscored the emperor as the figurative center of Japan. Actions initiated by the emperor, such as war or decrees were deemed sacred and legitimate. Full participation even unto death was marked as an honorable duty. This ideology became the thread for foundational policies implemented during the Imperial Japanese era (1890–1945).[4]

---

many others for a fuller understanding of the wrongful acts of humanity, as well as potential for mutual respect and reconciliation.

[2] Three methodological presumptions and caveats are in order: (1) first, the social location of Dan 3 is in Babylon. However, the likely compositional setting of Dan 3 points to the incidents of Antiochus IV Epiphanes with the presumable location of the land of Judah. Also, as the possible setting of Dan 3 was more likely that of the Hellenistic Ptolemaic and Seleucid empires (although some scholars argue for the Persian empire), our reading of Dan 3 against the Babylonian king Nebuchadnezzar does not presume a historical portrayal per se, but rather its literary symbolism, social cues, and cultural implications; (2) second, it is possible that Babylon and Persia are, in fact, coded ciphers for Greece, especially in the minds of the author(s) and readers. As an analogy, during the Soviet Union's censorship of revolutionary artists and musicians, Dmitri Shostakovich's fifth symphony demonstrated a kind of resistance. Though the music was acceptable to the Soviet government, the insertion of subtle folk melodies signified subversive cultures and ideals of freedom among the common people (I am indebted to a student at MTSO, Andrew Burns, in my Introduction to the Hebrew Bible class for this insight); and (3) third, it is hoped that, because our knowledge of Jewish life during the Babylonian and Persian empires remains murky, our study of Korea during the Japanese occupation may *ipso facto* shed new light on the life of colonized Judeans in Judah/Yehud during the Babylonian (and Persian and Hellenistic) occupation.

[3] Baek-yung Kim, "Colonial Assimilationism and Urban Space: Joseon Shrine in Colonial Seoul, 1920–30s," *Incheon International Studies* 11 (2009): 59–82.

[4] Osamu Kobe, "Edification Policy and 'National Shintoism,'" in *Gender Perspective on Modern and Contemporary History of Korea and Japan*, ed. Joint-Committee of Korean and Japanese Female Historians (Paju: Hanul, 2005), 110–13. Note also that in the 1900s, in most rural villages a campaign was launched to replace many independent hamlet shrines

Our study focuses on the following three topics: (1) How did this ideology of "national Shintoism" develop in occupied Korea, especially in the strategic construction of shrines—both the central shrine in the 1920s and local shrines in the late 1930s? (2) What roles did Shinto shrines play in the colonial strategies with regard to Imperial Japan's ideological, cultural, and political domination? (3) In what ways did this ideology have an impact upon colonized Koreans?

Construction of the Central and Local Shinto Shrines in Korea

Concerning the infiltration and construction of the national Shinto shrine in Korea, historians note two major incidents: the establishment of the central Joseon (state) shrine in the 1920s and the numerous local shrines of the late 1930s. The initial project of the 1920s began during Japan's annexation of Korea in 1910, during the rule of the Japanese governor-general in occupied Korea. Japan planned the construction of the central shrine replicating the state shrine in Japan, as the center of ideological domination. With the budget set up as early as 1912, the building of the central Shinto shrine (called the "Joseon Shinto" shrine) was completed at Mount Namsan in Seoul on October 15, 1925.[5] This Joseon Shinto shrine in Korea represented an extension of the state Shinto shrine in Japan.[6] Both shrines thus formed a symbolic and ideological connection, promoting the unity of the two countries under the sole sovereignty of the Japanese emperor. While local Shinto shrines prior to 1925 served primarily as religious space for Japanese residents in Korea, the Joseon Shinto shrine represented the political and ideological symbolic space for all Koreans.[7]

Historians demarcate Japan's colonial practices and policies in Korea in three phases: (1) "police takeover" in the 1910s, (2) "cultural assimilation" in the 1920s, and (3) "one empire" (or "united Japan–Korea ideal" or "Japanization of Koreans") in the 1930s–1940s. After the outbreak of the Japanese war against China in 1937, numerous local Shinto shrines were constructed as an expansion of the central Shinto shrine in Seoul. When Korea was liberated in 1945, there were as many as

---

with one central shrine per village, which then functioned to represent, "by means of ceremonial and administrative linkages with national shrines in the emerging system of state Shinto, the ideal relationship between local communities and the state." Ann Waswo, "The Transformation of Rural Society, 1900–1950," in *The Twentieth Century*, vol. 6 of *The Cambridge History of Japan*, ed. Peter Duus (Cambridge: Cambridge University Press, 1988), 572.

[5] Chul-Soo Kim, "Criticism on Religious Policies of the Japan Government-General of Choseon," *Journal for the Institute of Humanities at Soonchunhyang University* 27 (2010): 186.

[6] The name "Joseon" (or "Chosun/Choseon") represents the Joseon dynasty of Korea (1392–1910 CE). Prior to that era, the "Goryeo" (or "Corea") dynasty reigned in Korea (918–1392 CE).

[7] Baek-yung Kim, "Colonial Assimilationism," 77–78.

1,000 local Shinto shrines erected throughout the Korean peninsula.[8] Both the central and local Shinto shrines were constructed to justify and intensify Japanese colonial strategy and rule.

Ideological, Cultural, and Political Functions of Shinto Shrines

What roles did Shinto shrines play and what purposes did they serve in the colonial policies and goals of Imperial Japan? It is evident that both the central and local shrines were not merely cultural nor religious, but also ideological and political. These shrines symbolically represented the controlling power with which the colonizer wielded its will on the Korean peoples—either persuasively or by force. The shrine functioned to play "a role of reorganization and rearrangement of Korean people under Japanese government and drag them down to inferior people as the subjects of Japanese empire."[9]

The placement of the central Shinto shrine in Seoul was strategic for seminal indoctrination. Korean historians consider two constructions as significant symbols of colonial control. First, the department of the Japanese governor-general of Korea was built directly in front of the king's palace. This functioned to denote that Japan's governor had replaced Korea's king. Second, with the central Shinto shrine on Mt. Namsan, located in the heart of Seoul, national Shintoism now took precedence over other religious traditions or cultural values of Korea.[10] This is equivalent and analogous to constructing the Hellenistic shrine to replace the temple of Mt. Zion during the governance of Antiochus IV Epiphanes (175–164 BCE;

---

[8] Seonja Yoon, "The Establishment of Japanese Shrines and the Recognition of Koreans about Shrines," *Chonnam Historical Review* 42 (2011): 108–9.

[9] Yoon, "Establishment of Japanese Shrines," 137. See also Marius B. Jansen, "Japanese Imperialism: Late Meiji Perspectives," in *The Japanese Colonial Empire, 1895–1945*, ed. R. H. Myers and M. R. Peattie (Princeton: Princeton University Press, 1984), 77: "The particularity of Shintō nationalism gave the lie to assertions of brotherhood with Korea, where Japan came to combine a bland insistence on full assimilation with the virtual extinction of Korean nationality."

[10] Baek-yung Kim, "Colonial Assimilationism and Urban Space," 82: "With the completion of two monumental buildings, the new headquarter of the Colonial government and Joseon Shrine, and the vigorous promotion of a masterplan to build a colonial administration city, 1920s culminated in the spatial division of the administrative function and economic function and completion of the symbolic landscape of the colonial capital to surpass the traditional royal symbolic space."

cf. Jdt 3:8).[11] Whereas most Japanese Shinto shrines were hidden in the deep forest for the sake of sacredness, many Shinto shrines in Korea were built at readily visible spots to display the emperor's authority.[12]

Moreover, Shinto shrines functioned instrumentally to disseminate the colonizing ideology of "one empire" ("Integration of Japan and Korea"). Whereas the first decade of the Japanese occupation of Korea in the 1910s marked the "police takeover" stage, following the nonviolent independence demonstration on March 1, 1919 (which was inspired by US president Woodrow Wilson's "principle of national self-determination" promulgated in 1918), Imperial Japan changed the colonial policy to "cultural assimilation" in the 1920s. The central Shinto shrine became a crucial symbol for this policy during this decade. Similarly, together with the local shrines, it played a pivotal role in promoting the policies of one unified people, whether Korean or Japanese, in the 1930s. When Japan began to intensify its colonial domination over Korea following the war against China in 1937, the ideology of one (Japanese) empire became more overt. The proclamation of the seventh governor-general Jiro Minami best describes this "one empire" ideology as follows: "Only when Koreans ... had become Japanese both in name and in reality, in body and in soul. Under the slogans of 'Japan and Korea as one body' (*Nai-Sen ittai*) and 'harmony between Japan and Korea' (*Nissen yūwa*)."[13] Accordingly, the governor-general redefined Shinto shrine obeisance not only as a ritual of paying homage to the ancestors but also as important cultural and collective mechanisms to become citizens of Imperial Japan by paying due respect to the emperor.

Theoretically, this ideology meant equality between Koreans and Japanese, as well as the opportunity for Koreans to attain Japanese citizenship. To achieve this status and advancement, colonized Koreans were mandated to participate in programs, such as (1) Shinto shrine obeisance, (2) name change (into Japanese language), and (3) military service. In each of these programs, what seemed to be voluntary and harmless on the surface had substantial effects on the peoples of Korea. The ideas of unity, equality, and advancement were all designed to benefit Japan, not Korea.

---

[11] Leo G. Perdue and Warren Carter, *Israel and Empire: A Postcolonial History of Israel and Early Judaism* (London: T&T Clark, 2015), 189: "In 2 Maccabees 6:1 ... Antiochus sends Geron, an Athenian senator, with orders to dismantle Jewish religion. He forbids observance of the law, renames the temple the temple of Olympian Zeus, and introduces prostitutes and 'things unfit for sacrifice' into the temple." See also Seth Schwartz, *The Ancient Jews from Alexander to Muhammad* (Cambridge: Cambridge University Press, 2014), 42–43.

[12] Kyung-Soo Park, "A Strategy of Japanese Colonial Rule and Shinto Shrine: Especially from a Geographical Point of View," *Korean Journal of Japanese Language and Literature* 72 (2016): 510, 519.

[13] Carter J. Eckert et al., *Korea Old and New: A History* (Cambridge: Harvard University Press, 1990), 315–16.

Just like Shinto shrine obeisance, undergoing a name change and using the Japanese language instead of Korean was a prerequisite for survival or advancement. For example, Koreans who did not change their names were excluded from most socioeconomic benefits reserved for the citizens of Imperial Japan. Korean teachers who let the uneducated parents of students speak in Korean, when caught, were expelled and they lost their teaching license.[14] A famous Korean poet Dongju Yun wrote a poem entitled "Confessions" (January 24, 1942) describing his shame and agony upon adopting a Japanese name, Tochu Hiranuma, in order to attend university in Japan.[15]

Likewise, the slogan of the united people of Japan-Korea paved an ideological way for Koreans to "honorably" participate in Japanese wars. Again, the colonial policy of granting Japanese citizenship to Koreans was a devious plot on the part of Imperial Japan, which rationalized to conscript Koreans into military service. The ultimate goal of granting Japanese citizenship was to mobilize and turn them into readily trained combat soldiers, factory laborers (e.g., Mitsubishi), and sex slaves (aka "comfort women") for Japan's wars. Such extreme propaganda made the highest honor for (inferior) Koreans was to die in battle in the name of the emperor, comparable to (superior) Japanese. However, there was nothing comparable as Koreans were almost always deemed an inferior race. Providing these false and illusory opportunities for "equality" were nothing short of systemic discrimination and colonization. To coax or coerce them to seek death and to escape inferiority were indeed tactics to herd the colonized people to walk along the paths of self-destruction with no way out.[16]

To achieve the goal of "one empire," the "Japanization" of Koreans was a necessary evil with deep and permanent alterations to cultural, religious, social, and political dimensions in Korean way of living. Within this boundary, Koreans were coerced to embrace the prerequisites of Shinto shrine obeisance, adoption of Japanese names and language, and military service. Nevertheless, how did the Koreans react to this predicament or seduction?

---

[14] Ki Hong Kim, "A Study on the Education of 'Recreating the Imperial Subject' during the Period of the General Mobilization System in Wartime (1938–45) under the Japanese Imperialistic Rule: Centering on the Educational Activities of School Education" (Master's Thesis, Yonsei University, Seoul, Korea, 2000), 56–57: "The education of 'recreating the imperial subject' abolished some subjects like Chosun language, Chosun history, and Chosun geography in the curriculum of school education.... In addition to that, the education disciplined Chosun students to perform worship ceremonies, to read 'the Imperial Rescript about education' reverently and to recite 'the pledge as an imperial subject' in routine school events through the variety of extra-curricular activities."

[15] See Hyun Chul Paul Kim, "Dietrich Bonhoeffer, Dongju Yun, and the Legacies of Jeremiah and Suffering Servant," in *Second Wave Intertextuality and the Hebrew Bible*, ed. Marianne Grohmann and Hyun Chul Paul Kim (Atlanta: SBL Press, 2019).

[16] Ki Hong Kim, "A Study on the Education of 'Recreating the Imperial Subject,'" 46.

The Impact of Shinto Shrines on Colonized Koreans

In general, Japan's colonial policies worked effectively toward the "Japanization" of Koreans. At the risk of oversimplification, there are two historical responses from the colonized Koreans: (1) cooperate or even welcome Japan's colonial policies or (2) resist, implicitly or publicly.

Ironically, the majority of Koreans silently acquiesced, lest any of them become the target of additional oppression and persecution. One of the tactics of this process, particularly in the "cultural assimilation" policy of the 1920s, was to persuade key anti-Japanese leaders to become pro-Japanese provocateurs. Some of the most well-known anti-Japanese writers, such as Kwang-su Lee, became pro-Japanese poets and columnists, praising Imperial Japan as the harbingers of industrialization and economic advancement on primitive Korea. Through written words, these patriots-turned-puppets instigated their fellow colonized Koreans to happily embrace the programs of Imperial Japan. We should note that novelist Kwang-su Lee, a highly celebrated intellectual, was as popular as any modern celebrity. It is not hard to imagine how influential his pro-Japanese words must have been to the populace, as many Koreans were demoralized. Similarly, many Korean landowners and leaders willingly adopted Japanese names, even before Imperial Japan decreed mandatory name changes on November 1939. Likewise, many of them also actively participated not only in Shinto shrine obeisance, but also in the construction of shrines for political gains. According to the central Shinto shrine fundraising record of June 18, 1915, most Japanese persons living in Korea donated as little as 200 won per person, in contrast to some Koreans who donated 500 to 1,000 won per person exceeding the total funds for the original estimate of the construction project.[17]

Why did these colonized Koreans actively contribute to Imperial Japan's policy? What happened to these pro-Japanese supporters? Although not all of them had been identified, these pro-Japanese puppets enjoyed strong protection from Japan and received substantial economic and political privileges. While Shinto shrine obeisance was optional in the 1920s, the ritual became obligatory in the mid-1930s and Christian schools who did not participate were quickly closed.[18] In 1938, under the threat of active persecution, most leaders of Catholic, Methodist, and Presbyterian churches proclaimed that Shinto shrine obeisance was no more than a cultural and patriotic ceremony. Key Christian university leaders, alongside Buddhist and Confucian heads, endorsed and encouraged people to participate not only in Shinto shrine obeisance, but also enticed people to join forced labor overseas and recruited young persons for the empire's war. During this time,

---

[17] Yoon, "Establishment of Japanese Shrines," 124–25.

[18] A majority of Korean people "didn't recognize that such shrines had been built for a foundation to govern all the Korean people in 1910s and 1920s, until forced to visit the shrines in 1930s" (Yoon, "Establishment of Japanese Shrines," 138).

high-profile Korean church leaders took advantage of opportunities to climb within the ranks of lucrative organizations by publicly preaching that Shinto shrine obeisance was the commendable duty of all patriotic believers.[19] Interestingly, after World War II, partly due to the shift of Korea's ideological sentiment against communism during and after the Korean War of 1950–1953, many of these pro-Japanese leaders were mysteriously exonerated and continued to hold high-ranking leadership positions; some of whom enjoy their amassed wealth to this day.

What then happened to those who refused to bow to Shinto shrines? At least 2,000 Korean commoners, particularly those who were lay members of churches, were incarcerated and severely tortured.[20] At least fifty male and female Christian church leaders refused to take refuge overseas, switch their stance, but resisted Shinto obeisance to the point of death. Among them, many Korean Christians remember two heroic martyrs, Rev. Ki-chol Chu and Dame Kwan-soon Yoo. We briefly highlight the case of Ki-chol Chu.

Ki-chol Chu (1897–1944) grew up in a Christian family and received his education from some of the great thinkers and leaders of the time. Having graduated from Pyeongyang Presbyterian Seminary (currently "Presbyterian University and Theological Seminary" in Seoul) in 1925, he became the senior pastor of Sanjunghyun Church (founded in 1906) in Pyeongyang in 1936. Sanjunghyun Church was one of the key churches in Pyeongyang, known as the "Jerusalem" of Asia. With more than 1,200 members in 1929, this church became the symbol of Christian growth and social movement, since many key nationalistic leaders were members of this church.[21] When Shinto shrine obeisance became mandatory, Ki-chol Chu was one of the church leaders who vehemently defied this policy. On May 1, 1938, during a symposium gathered by key church leaders of Korea and Japan, Chu countered the proposal made by its chair Rev. Tomita asserting that

---

[19] Chung-Shin Park, *Protestantism and Politics in Korea* (Seattle: University of Washington Press, 2003), 156: "Some were forced to collaborate with the colonial government after their imprisonment and severe torture; others collaborated so that they could continue to operate their churches and schools; and still others to protect their wealth and position."

[20] Eckert et al., *Korea Old and New: A History*, 315: "The forced attendance policy split the Korean Christian church.... Some foreign missionaries were expelled and several thousand ministers arrested between 1935–38 as a large portion of the Korean Christian community continued to resist."

[21] One of Ki-chol Chu's initial achievements was helping unify the disintegrated members of this church build a new sanctuary. According to Deok-joo Rhie, Chu's leadership helped them build "the most beautiful and magnificent church in Pyeongyang." Deok-joo Rhie, *Martyrs for Love: A Study of Life and Theological Thought of the Rev. Choo Ki-Chul* (Icheon: The Korean Church History Museum, 2003), 182. In today's analogy, Chu was a "mega-church" minister and we can get a glimpse of how a mega-church minister lived out her/his authentic life back then.

enforcing Shinto shrine obeisance was a denial of religious freedom. Rev. Chu was willing to fight this proposal even if it led to death.[22]

When Ki-chol Chu was temporarily released from prison in 1939, many witnesses testified that "he stood as a tall statue and a solid rock, ready to continue his ministry and not willing to bow to any coercion or threat. Even those Christians who succumbed to Shinto shrine obeisance looked up to him."[23] When Ki-chol Chu was imprisoned for a third time on October 1939, more and more church members began to resist Shinto shrine obeisance. As the missionary C. F. Bernheisel (the former senior pastor of Sanjunghyun church) took the role of interim pastor, Bernheisel and the session leaders continued to decry the Shinto shrine obeisance policy. Yet, on December 1939, the presbytery decided to revoke Ki-chol Chu's ministry license. Soon after, on March 1940, when the presbytery delegates and Japanese police came to shut down the Sanjunghyun church, Bernheisel and 800 church members continued their Sunday worship, singing loudly, "A Mighty Fortress is our God" (cf. Jdt 4:8–12). Despite the colonizer's strategy to "divide and conquer," many leaders and members of this church became more united in their support of Ki-chol Chu and birthed the outward, resistance movement.[24] Later in the same year, the imperial police, in front of their family and others, alternately tortured Ki-chol Chu and his wife.[25] After repeated torture, Rev. Chu was martyred in 1944.

Like Ki-chol Chu, most of those who resisted Shinto shrine obeisance were incarcerated, tortured, and even killed. Those who managed to survive lost their homes, possessions, and privileges. Nonetheless, the severe colonial oppression of Shinto shrine obeisance ended up sparking an internal spirit of resistance.[26] Koo Kim, a great independence movement leader, was imprisoned where social activists and hardened criminals were housed and he recorded his experience in his diary. Before each meal, the guards made sure the prisoners bowed as an expression of gratitude to the emperor who mercifully supplied their meals. Whenever these prisoners would bow, they would mumble certain words. Curious whether they might be saying words of thanks to the emperor, Kim asked a few inmates. Their answer was uniform: "Haven't you read the imperial constitution? When the emperor or empress passes away, thousands of prisoners will be granted absolution. So, before each meal, they prayed to the deity, 'Please make them pass away soon.'"[27]

During the Japanese occupation, most Koreans had to hide their spirit of resistance. But after the demise of Imperial Japan, anti-Japanese sentiments, hidden

---

[22] Rhie, *Martyrs for Love*, 200–205.
[23] Rhie, *Martyrs for Love*, 236.
[24] Rhie, *Martyrs for Love*, 253–62.
[25] Rhie, *Martyrs for Love*, 304–5.
[26] Baek-yung Kim, "Colonial Assimilationism and Urban Space," 77–78.
[27] Jin Soon Do, ed., *Baik Beom Il Ji: An Autobiography* (Seoul: Dolbegae, 2002), 248.

deep within the psyche of the colonized people, came out to the fore. Immediately after World War II, a total of 136 local Shinto shrines in Korea were destroyed. This far exceeds the number of colonial administrative buildings that the newly freed Koreans demolished. This act demonstrates how colonized Koreans perceived these Shinto shrines as a direct symbol of Japanese imperial hegemony (cf. 2 Macc 4:35, 39).[28]

DANIEL'S THREE FRIENDS AGAINST THE IMPERIAL STATUE

With this background, we turn to the story of Daniel's three friends who were forced to bow before the golden statue in Dan 3.

First, within the larger plot, this golden statue episode is sandwiched between the two dream accounts of Dan 2 and 4. Whether or not Dan 3 was an independent account inserted at a later time is difficult to fully assess. It is noteworthy that the text is situated between dream texts. Daniel Smith-Christopher's explanation is helpful: "The dreams of Nebuchadnezzar are in reality the dreams that the Jewish author of Daniel placed in the mind of the king. The dreams therefore provide a window into the inner hopes of Diaspora Jews for the overthrow of the powers that ruled over them."[29] Likewise, although scholars consider our text to be a legend, bookended by the narratives of *dreams* (chs. 2 and 4), it is as though we have a narrative of *reality* (ch. 3). In other words, these narratives invite readers to cross boundaries and to wrestle with the tensions between a dream state and reality, between facts and interpretations.[30] Sadly, no such tension exists in the history of colonized Korea. The imposed imperial shrine obeisance, along with the startling reality of terrifying threats and painful memories, is not fictional.

Ironically, in the text, there is a punctuated change in the attitude of King Nebuchadnezzar when he "fell down" and "did obeisance" to Daniel in acknowledgment of Daniel's God after the magical dream interpretation (2:46). In the following story, the king orders all his subjects to "fall down" and "do obeisance"

---

[28] Baek-yung Kim, "Colonial Assimilationism and Urban Space," 78.

[29] Quoted from Barry A. Jones, "Resisting the Power of Empire: The Theme of Resistance in the Book of Daniel," *Review and Expositor* 109 (2012): 545; see Daniel L. Smith-Christopher, "The Book of Daniel," *NIB* 7:57–58. Consider also David M. Valeta, "Crossing Boundaries: Feminist Perspectives on the Stories of Daniel and Susanna," in *Feminist Interpretation of the Hebrew Bible in Retrospect: I. Biblical Books*, ed. S. Scholz (Sheffield: Sheffield Phoenix, 2013), 296: "Several interpretations of Dan 7–12 assert that dreams and visions are important in the narrative and apocalyptic sections of Daniel as they imagine social and political changes."

[30] Concerning the interactive tensions between "metaphor" and "reality," as well as between "memory" and "truth," see Hyun Chul Paul Kim, "Metaphor, Memory, and Reality of the 'Exile' in Deutero-Isaiah," in *Images of Exile in the Prophetic Literature: Copenhagen Conference Proceedings 7–10 May 2017*, ed. J. Høgenhaven, F. Poulsen, and C. Power (Tübingen: Mohr Siebeck, 2019), 45-61.

to the golden statue (3:6–7). Sequential readers can sense a chilling description of the "capriciousness and volatility" of a menacing emperor.[31] The emperor is utterly uncontrollable and unpredictable (cf. 2:12). Indeed, we may wonder whether Nebuchadnezzar's recognition (and even repentance) toward Daniel's God was genuine or gestural. C. L. Seow aptly observes, "Despite his obsequious response to Daniel's interpretation of the dream (2:46–49), he seems to have heard only what he had wanted to hear."[32] Nebuchadnezzar heard of the interpretation of his dream of a golden statue (2:31–32, 38) and, in response, built the golden statue for himself (or his god).

Second, the magnificent height and stature of the golden statue, accompanied with the ritualistic obeisance, makes a powerful public spectacle for the ideology of the "one empire" with its symbolic location and cultural-political domination (v. 1). In verses 1–18, the verb to "set up" (literally, "to cause to stand up") occurs nine times, as though signifying the towering magnificence of the empire.[33] The golden statue obeisance thus serves the purpose of absolutizing the imperial grip through imperial assimilation policy (e.g., Babylonization or Hellenization). Albeit a ritual, this decree has far greater cultural, religious, and political ramifications (v. 4). Notably, the act of falling down and doing obeisance (vv. 5–7) resembles similar kinds of oppression and persecution imposed by Antiochus IV Epiphanes during the Hellenistic era.[34] Inasmuch as the visible statue symbolizes power, its rhetorical force and functional impact make the statue intimidating.[35] The king is powerful enough to construct such a magnificent monument. The king is fearsome enough to control and punish all his subjects.

Thus, Nebuchadnezzar calls and assembles the satraps, prefects, governors, counselors, treasurers, judges, magistrates, and all the officials of the provinces (v. 2). In fact, the decree affects all "peoples, nations, and languages" (v. 4). The king's control over the entire political and socioeconomic sphere is a comparable

---

[31] Roy L. Heller, "'But If Not …' *What*? The Speech of the Youths in Daniel 3 and a (Theo)Logical Problem," in *Thus Says the Lord: Essays on the Former and Latter Prophets in Honor of Robert R. Wilson*, ed. J. J. Ahn and S. L. Cook (London: T&T Clark, 2009), 253.

[32] C. L. Seow, *Daniel*, Westminster Bible Companion (Louisville: Westminster John Knox, 2003), 53.

[33] Seow, *Daniel*, 52.

[34] See Eric M. Meyers and Mark A. Chancey, *Alexander to Constantine: Archaeology of the Land of the Bible*, vol. 3 (New Haven: Yale University Press, 2012), 16–17. Concerning the mechanism behind Antiochus, note Anathea E. Portier-Young's remark: "Antiochus's reprisals against Jerusalem followed the logic of reconquest and even state terror." Anathea E. Portier-Young, *Apocalypse against Empire: Theologies of Resistance in Early Judaism* (Grand Rapids: Eerdmans, 2011), 136.

[35] Smith-Christopher, "Book of Daniel," 62: "Whether Nebuchadnezzar ever erected such a statue is totally beside the point. The point was that he could—he could amass that much gold; he could assemble the leaders; he could demand obedience and threaten horrible punishment."

exhibition of the purpose of this decree.[36] The wide reach of this imperial ideology aims at creating absolute control, which no other force would dare to challenge. Carol A. Newsom observes a striking pattern of the "command and execution" sequence in the text. The king commands and all subjects obey in an instant. Both the royal command and the compliance of subjects portray the ritual of obeisance to the golden statue as an extension of the king's power that is perceived as transcendental, even divinized.[37] Put another way, participating in statue obeisance (cf. Isa 44:17) translated to adopting and venerating the value and authority of the ruler, is somewhat like "selling one's soul." As Sharon Pace elucidates: "The worshiping of idols ... was never the mere worshiping of wood and stone, but rather the acceptance of values that were symbolized and justified by the religious, economic, and governmental ideals connected with it."[38]

Third, we should note that Nebuchadnezzar gathers key leaders in a public ceremonial event. The imperial regime needs to exercise control over notable leaders who, in turn, wield influence within their own communities. In order to put these elites under imperial control, the regime makes them bow down to the imperial statue in full view of the public. Their visible abandonment of the cherished values of their subjects, as well as their acquiescence to imperial sovereignty, would have had a tremendous influence (almost like brainwashing) over the rest of the population. It is first and foremost a public ritual, accompanied by the sounds of an abundance of musical instruments (vv. 5, 7). Not unlike Shinto shrine obeisance, this is a carefully orchestrated process of the leaders marching to music and doing obeisance to the statue.[39] Not unlike the masses raising their arms to salute "Heil Hitler" in the Third Reich, the collected masses would "all bow down at once as if that bowing down were just a thoughtless reflex."[40] We should further note that the names of these Jewish delegates were changed to Babylonian ones—Shadrach, Meshach, Abednego, just like Belteshazzar (1:6–7).[41]

---

[36] Quoted from Carol A. Newsom, Pierre Briant remarks that this ideology was a way "to depict every country and every people of the Empire united in harmonious cooperation organized by and surrounding the king." Carol A. Newsom, *Daniel*, OTL (Louisville: Westminster John Knox, 2014), 105.

[37] Newsom, *Daniel*, 104: "To engage one's own body in an activity coordinated with masses of others' bodies is to experience a sense of participation in something transcendent and powerful, something to which it seems natural to give one's allegiance."

[38] Sharon Pace, *Daniel*, SHBC (Macon, GA: Smyth & Helwys, 2008), 110.

[39] During Shinto shrine ritual, participants are required to purify their bodies. Following the sound of the bell ringing, they would bow two times, clap their hands loudly two times, and then end with a bow.

[40] Seow, *Daniel*, 54.

[41] Jones, "Resisting the Power of Empire," 544: "Their Hebrew names are replaced with Babylonian names as a symbol of their new identity and their new overlord." In a way the tension between the two ethnic names is a religio-political tension between El (Dani-El), Israel's God, and Bel (Bel-te-shazzar), Babylon's deity Marduk (cf. Isa 46:1).

Thus, the regime targeted a majority of elite leaders, who succumbed to imperial pressure.

Furthermore, Daniel's three friends, whom their Chaldean oppressors tried to subjugate, were appointed as "the administrators around the province of Babylon" (v. 12). It was the policy of the suzerain to immediately place the "top dogs" of their underdog vassals firmly under control, and no matter what status these "top dogs" held, they were never considered as any more than "dogs" (or domesticated "pets") in the minds of their suzerain masters! Ironically, the more the king tried to break the backs of the colonized subjects, the more resistant some of the Jews became. To the imperial power, these three youths' disobedience threatened the king's sovereignty, igniting the first sparks of insurrection or treason. Whenever the golden statue obeisance was challenged, the king's authority was at stake. Just as Vashti's defiance was taken as a threat to the Persian king (Esth 1:12, 16–20; cf. 3:8), we can consider the civil disobedience of these youths as an outright protest against the Babylonian king.

Fourth, under imperial domination, subjugated people can easily falter and be scattered. One of the primary tactics of subjugation would thus be to disorient and cause strife—"horizontal violence"—within the subjugated community.[42] We should note that these three youths held certain administrative positions in the empire's colonial districts. Whether pro-Babylonian or not, holding positions of power as colonized subjects ironically made them more susceptible to colonial prejudice and inequality. Scholars consider that the calculated denouncement by certain Chaldeans against these three Jewish leaders (v. 8) was not so much due to their social status, but rather an example of ethnic bigotry.[43] No matter how high the official title of these youths may have been, being of an ethnic minority group made them susceptible to being stripped of their power anywhere, anytime. Similarly, Jin Hee Han insightfully delineates Daniel as a foreign exile: "Repeatedly, the exiled sage's wisdom is summoned to resolve a crisis (e.g., 2:25; 5:13), but the status of an exile can ever make him an easy suspect of lack of genuine

---

[42] Perdue and Carter, *Israel and Empire*, 186–87. Against the backdrop of the Seleucid domination of the Jews, consider the dispute and dissension over the high priesthood between Onias III and Jason, together with Jason's "Hellenistic reform" and Menelaus's alleged murder of Onias. Lester L. Grabbe, "The Seleucid and Hasmonean Periods and the Apocalyptic Worldview—An Introduction," in *The Seleucid and Hasmonean Periods and the Apocalyptic Worldview: The First Enoch Seminar Nangeroni Meeting*, ed. L. L. Grabbe and G. Boccaccini (London: T&T Clark, 2016), 21–24.

[43] Seow, *Daniel*, 54: "Certainly, the Chaldeans are provoked not by professional jealousy alone but by the fact that the foreigners are receiving promotions in their own domain." Note also Jon L. Berquist, *Judaism in Persia's Shadow: A Social and Historical Approach* (Minneapolis: Fortress, 1995), 227: "How does one maintain religious identity? How does one survive the persecutions directed toward religious minority? How does one climb the social hierarchies in ways effective for one's career? Daniel provides answers to such questions."

loyalty (cf. 6:14 [Eng. 6:13]. Here is one of the classic cases of brain drain with an overhang of xenophobic suspicion."[44]

Accordingly, dissension among the colonized people can cause major damage creating internal distrust and suspicion within the community. We may thus ask, what if one or two of Daniel's friends abandoned loyalty to YHWH and switched to follow Nebuchadnezzar's decree? What if, instead of certain Chaldeans, certain fellow Jewish subjects squealed about the disobedience of these youths?[45] Admittedly, these questions are not answerable. Yet, we can suppose that obeisance by any one of Daniel's friends would have meant an abject betrayal not only to their God but also to their comrades and community. Inasmuch as the golden statue functions as a symbol for the emperor's power, these youths' docile compliance also becomes a symbol of the collapse of courage to the colonized community.

Fifth, the youths' acts of nonviolent resistance or civil disobedience could lead to either severe persecution (the king's rage) or sweet benevolence (the king's endorsement). On the one hand, we should take note of Nebuchadnezzar's anger toward any rebellious subjects and his subsequent command to make the furnace seven times hotter (vv. 13, 19). To the colonized, the empire can be enormously benevolent, as long as they know their place and not challenge the authority of the empire. Conversely, the moment any subject dares to thwart imperial authority, benevolence can turn to brutality at a moment's notice. Once appointed as administrators of the empire's provinces, these three youths were now on the verge of being thrown into the fiery furnace, just as Daniel was thrown into the lion's den (6:17 [Eng. 6:16]).

On the other hand, the colonized subjects could comply with the empire's policy, which would provide the opportunity to ascend the sociopolitical ladder and enjoy economic prosperity. Whether for assimilation or for a greater cause, heroines and heroes like Joseph and Esther received the empire's benevolence while Moses and Mordecai were more resistant to assimilation.[46] In the central portion of Dan 3 (vv. 16–18), concerning the text-critical ambivalence of the youths' speeches, Roy Heller proposes a new translation as follows:

---

[44] Jin Hee Han, *Daniel's Spiel: Apocalyptic Literacy in the Book of Daniel* (Lanham, MD: University Press of America, 2008), 34.

[45] These "what if" questions are inspired by Danna Nolan Fewell, "Space for Moral Agency in the Book of Ruth," *JSOT* 40 (2015): 95: "At every critical juncture, alternate plots 'sideshadow' the narrative action, indicating how things might have happened differently."

[46] Hyun Chul Paul Kim, "Reading the Joseph Story (Genesis 37–50) as a Diaspora Narrative," *CBQ* 75 (2013): 219–38. Concerning the boundary crossings of identity, note Shaye J. D. Cohen, *The Beginnings of Jewishness: Boundaries, Varieties, Uncertainties* (Berkeley: University of California Press, 1999), 110: "In the second century B.C.E., the metaphoric boundary separating Judaeans from non-Judaeans became more and more permeable. Outsiders could become insiders."

O Nebuchadnezzar, who do not need to return (an answer to) you about this decree.

If it is so (i.e. if the decree is carried out), [then] our God whom we revere is able to rescue us from the burning, fiery furnace and from your hand, O king, he will rescue.

But if not (i.e. if the decree is not carried out; if you allow us to live), [then] let it be known to you, O king, that to your gods we will not give reverence, and to the image of gold that you erected we will not bow down.[47]

In this rendering, the second conditional sentence points to King Nebuchadnezzar's benevolent policy: the king can withhold the execution and let them live—and, consequently thrive with new rewards (v. 15; cf. Jdt 11:1–4; 3 Macc 2:30–31). It is often the lure of appeasement and reward, rather than threat of torture or punishment that leads the oppressed to capitulate to their oppressor: "Even more dangerous than the threat of death is the threat of a sense of duty to obey because of special treatment and clemency that might be granted by the state. In the face of death, the youths testify to their trust in God. More importantly, however, even in the face of mercy, the youths witness that devotion to God is absolutely essential."[48]

Sixth, regardless of the resistance or surrender of the subjects, there remains a theological tension between divine presence (story) and divine absence (reality) in many aspects of world history. Concerning divine presence, our *story* provides a miraculous deliverance of the three youths despite their resistance to imperial authority (vv. 25, 27). More impressively, the emperor not only blessed the God of these youths but also praised the fact that they "resisted" (literally, "changed" or "frustrated") his own royal command (v. 28). The story concludes in a somewhat happy ending, with the divine presence clearly demonstrated when an angel is sent to rescue these courageous youths (v. 28). In a story of "bold theological grounding," the righteous and the devout will be delivered and vindicated.[49]

Concerning divine absence, such an ideal plot of courageous defiance and dramatic rescue seems far too rare in *reality*. During the Persian and Hellenistic periods, many who offered resistance did not escape torture and martyrdom. It is often the case that the resistance of the powerless results in extreme torture and suffering (cf. Tob 1:18–20; 1 Macc 1:60–61; 2:29–38; 2 Macc 5:11–14; 6:1–11; 7:1–42). Despite noble ideals, the consequence of challenging the powerful so often leads to unbearable hardship. Fire in the Hebrew Bible can denote divine presence, for example, in the burning bush (Exod 3:2–4; cf. Ps 97:3). Yet, it can also connote the hard-pressed exile (Isa 43:2). Even in modern history, who can forget the horrible tragedy of the Holocaust, eerily analogous to the way Shadrach, Meshach, and Abednego were bound and thrown into the fiery furnace? The

---

[47] Heller, "'But If Not …' What?," 252.
[48] Heller, "'But If Not …' What?," 254–55.
[49] Walter Brueggemann, *Out of Babylon* (Nashville: Abingdon, 2010), 141.

memory of Shoah is so heavy to recall that a scholar expressed, "Some of us Jews cannot theologize this tragedy yet. It is too soon to do so. We are still grieving."[50] Amid the reality of seeming divine absence, the ruler of the empire looks virtually invincible and his pompous claims seem quite accurate. Indeed, Nebuchadnezzar is "arrogant enough to believe that no divine power can deliver the Jews from his power" (v. 15; cf. Isa 14:13–14; 36:18–20; 37:10–13).[51]

Nevertheless, even amid the cruel reality of a perceived divine absence, the story and testimony of these youths continue to instill powerful inspiration. Despite the indisputable reality of the colonizer's victory, the disempowered colonized have the capacity to resist and the ability to inspire others. In their courage, the boundary between happy ending and tragic ending gets blurry. In their defiance, the power differential between the mighty emperor and the helpless subjects—which seems like an immense chasm—becomes nearly equalized. Within the center of this literary plot, the king's speech ("if ... if ...") in verses 14–15 meets its daring counterpart in the youths' speech ("if ... if ...") in verses 16–18. In reality, there is no human being who is powerful like Nebuchadnezzar; yet, in this story, even Nebuchadnezzar has limits, if not weaknesses. As Carol Newsom expounds, "Nebuchadnezzar literally has no power to enforce his command, to make the Jews behave like all the rest of his officials. He can kill the three Jews; but he cannot make them worship his god. *Even if they should not be saved, in this matter they have more power than the mighty king of Babylon.*"[52] To some, the youth's defiance may appear to be a foolhardy choice, yet this is exactly the kind of story that inspires so many people.[53] Such a story holds true power—the power to say "no" to that which is wrong and abusive.[54]

---

[50] Frederick Greenspahn's comment (not verbatim) during the book review session of Marvin Sweeney, *Reading the Hebrew Bible after the Shoah: Engaging Holocaust Theology* at the Annual Meeting of the Society of Biblical Literature, New Orleans, 2009. Consider Daniel Smith-Christopher's description on the sublime courage of open defiance: "The most infuriating aspect of radical faith is its adamant refusal to be impressed *with the obvious*—namely, the subordinated status and powerlessness of the Jews before the mighty emperor—and their steadfast adherence to an alternative reality: God reigns" ("Book of Daniel," 64 [emphasis added]). Undoubtedly, it is "the obvious" that so many colonized subjects have encountered and in turn succumbed.

[51] Seow, *Daniel*, 55.

[52] Newsom, *Daniel*, 110 (emphasis original).

[53] Newsom, *Daniel*, 102: "The storyteller has a kind of sovereign power ... a means of exercising power by encouraging readers to perceive reality differently." See also Jones, "Resisting the Power of Empire," 546.

[54] Pace, *Daniel*, 112: "In saying 'no' to the idol and to Nebuchadnezzar, the three attested to the king's injustice and expressed their faith that God's justice will necessarily come, in God's own time. By not cowering, they witnessed to possibilities of a community of justice." Consider also Portier-Young, *Apocalypse against Empire*, 260: "Like the three young

When the emperor bound and executed the three resistant youths, they were clothed with shirts, trousers, hats, and garments (vv. 20–21). In one sense, the king clothed them "with every flammable item of clothing"; in another sense, readers can detect a small shred of dignity afforded to them as they were executed "in the formal attire."[55] Considering the ancient custom that prisoners were stripped before execution, readers can learn of the youths' indomitable spirit.[56] They were weak yet had nobler courage and greater honor than those who bowed down. Hoping against hope, the spirit of these courageous heroes can inspire the colonized and powerless to survive and work toward justice.

CROSSING (HERMENEUTICAL) BOUNDARIES BETWEEN THE (MODERN) FAR EAST AND THE (ANCIENT) NEAR EAST

This study has tried to cross boundaries—boundaries between ancient history and contemporary history, between Judah and Babylon, and Korea and Japan. On the one hand, there are clear distinctions between the worlds, particularly regarding the impenetrable boundaries between the histories of ancient Israel and modern Korea. Yet, these examples exhibit enough analogous aspects to make crossing boundaries worthwhile, as Paul Tillich stated, "The boundary is the best place for acquiring knowledge."[57]

Admittedly, "boundary" is a slippery concept: it functions to make distinctions on the one hand yet it is a quite arbitrary and invisible marker on the other. For example, temporal (minutes, hours, days), geographic (houses, cities, countries), or even racial boundaries can be rigid but at times quite fluid. As J. Hillis Miller posits, in the dynamics of this side versus the other side, when you cross the line, "you are now within another domain. The land you have just left is now other, strange, distant, even if it is your own homeland.... This breakdown exposes our situation to be always and at all times living in a borderland, where inside and outside overlap or are superimposed."[58] Accordingly, just as boundaries are simultaneously solid and fluid—somewhat analogous to the absence of

---

men, [the faithful] are to seek no guarantee, ask nothing of God, but give their lives for their faith simply because it is right."

[55] Seow, *Daniel*, 58.

[56] Newsom, *Daniel*, 111.

[57] Paul Tillich, *On the Boundary: An Autobiographical Sketch* (New York: Charles Scribner's Sons, 1966), 13.

[58] J. Harris Miller, "Boundaries in Beloved," *Symplokē* 15 (2007): 24, 28. Consider Homi K. Bhabha's description of "excess or slippage" in the ambivalent area between mimicry and mockery played by the colonized as "almost the same, but not quite/white." Homi K. Bhabha, "Of Mimicry and Man: The Ambivalence of Colonial Discourse," *October* 28 (1984): 125–33; also Bhabha, *The Location of Culture* (London: Routledge, 1994), 173: ["The postcolonial perspective] forces a recognition of the more complex cultural and political boundaries that exist on the cusp of these often opposed political spheres."

the "center" presented by Jacques Derrida,[59] our reading of the two (hi)stories can also traverse both dimensions. The literary position of Dan 3, sandwiched between two dreams, heightens the surreal juxtaposition between dream and reality—between ideal story and factual history. The ambivalent historical settings (i.e., Babylonian, Persian, and Hellenistic eras) likewise make the colonized world both specific and universal, inviting readers to traverse among the past, present, and future.[60]

From the observations and analyses made above, I explore the following three hermeneutical aspects that are noteworthy both in this comparative study and, hopefully, in this rapidly changing world: (1) (not) crossing *ideological* boundaries (keeping identity), (2) crossing *imperial* boundaries (keeping integrity/dignity), and (3) *hesed* (keeping justice, especially for the powerless).

First, both Dan 3 and colonized Korea exhibit the challenges and struggles associated with *ideological* boundaries. In both cases, boundary crossing is an intricate part of the ideology of imperial unity. The empire tries to compel the three young men to cross their boundaries of tradition and identity. By crossing those boundaries, these subjects would participate in accepting the legitimacy of the colonial claims. In terms of the issue of assimilation versus separation, these heroes opted to keep their identity. In doing so, they resisted the ideological values of the empire. They resisted the opportunity to cross social and ethnic boundaries from the "inferior" colonized ethnic group to the "superior" citizenship of the empire.

The majority of colonized subjects bowed to the statue switching their loyalty to the empire and thus, betraying their solidarity with one another. Only a few among the elite leaders, such as the three youths and Ki-chol Chu, kept their fidelity to God and to one another. Ki-chol Chu, a pastor of one of the "megachurches" at that time, still speaks powerfully to our time as well. It is remarkable that we do not read the stories of those who bowed. The stories of courageous resistance in the three youths' and Chu's loyalty and solidarity continue to inspire many across the generations.

Second, in their resistance to crossing ideological boundaries, they ended up crossing *imperial* boundaries. Especially in public spaces, as key leaders of their communities, their refusal to bow down was a challenge and even threat to the imperial powers. Simply put, when everyone said "yes" to the colonizers, they said "no." When every person of color had to stay in their assigned seats, "within their boundaries," heroines and heroes like Rosa Parks crossed those boundaries

---

[59] Jacques Derrida, "Structure, Sign and Play in the Discourse of the Human Sciences," in *Writing and Difference*, trans. A. Bass (Chicago: University of Chicago Press, 1967), 278–95.

[60] For a collection of insightful interpretations on the issues of boundary crossing in the Bible, see Jione Havea et al., eds., *Bible, Borders, Belonging(s): Engaging Readings from Oceania* (Atlanta: SBL Press, 2014).

set by the empire in refusing to comply. The boundaries erected by the colonizers can achieve a "win-win" situation for the empire. If the subjects, especially their leaders, bow down, their obedience benefits the imperial regime. If the subjects refuse, their disobedience provides an excuse for the empire to strengthen its abusive control through excessive violent measures.[61]

However, in a potential "lose-lose" plight for the colonized, the public defiance of a few leaders could have a significant impact. As elites, though mere youths, the act of resistance by Daniel's three friends challenged the empire. As a mega-church pastor, Ki-chol Chu's refusal to bow inspired his community. No matter how insignificant and outnumbered they may have been, their resistance stood tall against the empires. Though threatened, these few heroes contributed greatly to stymieing the imperial forces. Though terrified, their actions stirred up hope and inspired unity among the colonized. Perhaps, all was not lost. Even if their physical bodies were destroyed, their honor, dignity, and power would never be lost. As Brooke Hayes, an African American student in my Introduction class, once expressed, "To be human is to resist and to acknowledge and fight for my God-given right to be free."

Last, but not least, the three youths and Ki-chol Chu exemplify the ideals of *hesed*, for the sake of justice amid the powerless. We have noted the fluidity of boundaries, which makes it difficult to tell which action is right or wrong. Even within the book of Daniel, the youths' *not bowing* (to the golden statue) put them in danger of execution; whereas Daniel's *bowing* (to another deity, i.e., YHWH) put him in the same danger (Dan 6:8, 11 [Eng. 6:7, 10]). Qoheleth has put together such a dilemma in the well-known poem, which we may paraphrase: "a time to keep [boundary] and a time to discard [boundary]; a time to tear down [boundary] and a time to mend [boundary]" (Eccl 3:6–7). The scriptural answer to finding the right time for boundary keeping or boundary crossing often hinges on the concept of *hesed* for the disenfranchised.

In the biblical tradition, *hesed* has multiple meanings. From a comparable Korean concept, we can define it in two distinct yet interrelated meanings: (1) loyalty (*euri*) and (2) mercy (*jeong*).[62] In the same ways that boundaries are both

---

[61] Consider Portier-Young, *Apocalypse against Empire*, 138: "Revolt, then, provided an opportunity for reconquest that enabled the re-creation of empire."

[62] Consider Uriah Y. Kim's pioneering analogy of Korean concepts for the Hebrew word *ḥesed*: "The two sides of *ḥesed* are: loyalty [I propose *euri* as its Korean equivalent] and *jeong* (a rough translation of 'affection-and-kindness' in Korean).... These two aspects are not mutually exclusive; it may be better to think of *ḥesed* along a spectrum, with loyalty on one end and *jeong* on the other end." Uriah Y. Kim, "Where Is the Home for the Man of Luz?," *Int* 65 (2011): 256. See also Hyun Chul Paul Kim and M. Fulgence Nyengele, "Pursing Happiness across Cultures: Positive Psychology, Ecclesiastes, African *Ubuntu*, and Korean *Jeong* in Creative Dialogues," in *Bridging the Divide between the Bible and Pastoral Theology*, ed. D. D. Hopkins and M. Koppel (Newcastle, UK: Cambridge Scholars, 2018), 29–43.

solid and fluid, *hesed*'s meaning overlaps between loyalty and mercy. Loyalty (*euri*), with the connotations of faithfulness and fidelity, is related to obedience to God: to obey God implies the steadfast pursuit of justice and righteousness. Mercy (*jeong*), with the connotations of compassion and steadfast love, encompasses solidarity with the weak and marginalized.

In trying times when the wicked tended to outnumber and prosper over the righteous (though it is often difficult to distinguish the righteous from the wicked), these heroes represented the righteous who remained faithful to justice, and ultimately to God, in solidarity with the disempowered. We should note that, in terms of their identity, these youths are placed in the "in-between" hybrid positions of clashing cultures, languages, ethnicities, nations, and ideologies.[63] Their boundary-crossing and liminal status entails that, as Gale A. Yee describes, "the religious and political elites governing Yehud themselves were hybrids. They were ethnically Jewish but also Persian agents."[64] Rather than being intimidated, they risked their beliefs and lives, ultimately rising from their liminal place to a moral and honorable high ground, higher than that of the empire's golden statue. In their resistance, they found their true inner strength and shalom. The (heroic) faithfulness and defiance of a few outweighed the compliance and cowardice of many. Concerning the complex dynamics of boundaries in the sense of territory or power, these heroes would pale before these domineering empires. Nevertheless, these heroes preserved their own cherished boundaries (of identity, dignity, and belief) and also infiltrated—if not shattered—the empires' boundaries (of denial, subjugation, and oppression). Such is the story of a fight for justice. Such is the history of courage in the face of oppression. Such is the dream, which envisions a better world amidst the present despair.[65]

---

[63] Andrew Davison et al., "Europe and Its Boundaries: Toward a Global Hermeneutic Political Theory," in *Europe and Its Boundaries: Words and Worlds, Within and Beyond*, ed. A. Davison and H. Muppidi (Lanham, MD: Rowman & Littlefield, 2009), 92: "[Hans-Georg Gadamer] describes 'hermeneutic work' as the kind of work that happens in what he calls the 'in-between' between the 'familiarity' and 'strangeness' of a text."

[64] Gale A. Yee, "Postcolonial Biblical Criticism," in *Methods for Exodus*, ed. T. B. Dozeman (Cambridge: Cambridge University Press, 2010), 213. See also David Palumbo-Liu, *Asian/American: Historical Crossings of a Racial Frontier* (Stanford: Stanford University Press, 1999), 1: "As in the construction 'and/or,' where the solidus at once instantiates a choice between two terms, their simultaneous and equal status, and an element of indecidability, that is, as it at once implies *both* exclusion and inclusion, 'Asian/American' marks both the distinction installed between 'Asian' and 'American' *and* a dynamic, unsettled, and inclusive movement."

[65] Han, *Daniel's Spiel*, 112–13: "The book of Daniel offers such a language in apocalyptic literacy, which makes it manifest that a believing community under duress does not have to accept the powers' perversion of reality at its face value.... The paradigm of apocalyptic literacy underscores that believing communities have enormous resources to embrace hope through words that can blow away the debilitating note of despair."

The ideals and dreams inspired by these stories can spur comparable visions in today's world. We continue to envision a time of sincere apology, reconciliation, and friendship as good neighbors between Japan and Korea. We dream for lasting and reliable peace in the Middle East. We pray for a future when we can cross the DMZ boundary as safe travelers rather than spies or escapees between the two Koreas. These are bold dreams, dreams that envision good overcoming and even transforming evil, not unlike the dreams of the author(s) and readers of the book Daniel. In the meantime, stark reality of the hardships suffered by the three youths and Ki-chol Chu vividly reminds us how easy it is to forget our history, submit to the wrong ideology, or give up altogether. We ought not to erase the tragic histories of many leaders who bowed to the Shinto shrine. We ought not to deny the records of those who embraced the roles of imperial puppet leaders, amassing wealth that they possess to this day, without authentic remorse and recompense. We ought to name the trauma and painful acts inflicted by fellow human beings during this chapter of Korean history. We ought to tell and continue to retell—as the biblical writers and readers have done—the stories of the few courageous heroines and heroes who stood strong against injustice and in solidarity with the disempowered, lest the truth be distorted or concealed. It is our solemn duty to recover and preserve truth so that justice prevails and so that the *han* (the excruciating hurt and abject powerlessness caused by the act(s) of overpowering injustice) of the "comfort women" might be healed with dignity and honor. Such are the much-needed values of loyalty and solidarity. A poem by a respected Buddhist poet and independence movement leader during Korea's colonial time, Yong-woon Han, expresses the vision and action of such unwavering obedience:

"Obedience"
Others say they love freedom, but I love
obedience. Though I know freedom, I only
want to obey you. Willing obedience is
sweeter than just freedom. That is my bliss.

But if you tell me to obey some other person,
that I can never do.
For if I obey another person, I cannot obey you.[66]

---

[66] Yong-woon Han, "Obedience," in *Best Loved Poems of Korea*, trans. Chang-soo Ko (Seoul: Hollym, 1984), 48.

OF GREAT WALLS, DMZS, AND OTHER LINES IN THE SAND: THE TRUTH (OF THE GOSPEL) ABOUT BORDERS AND BARRIERS—AND CROSSING THEM IN GALATIANS

Kang-Yup Na

This essay is a hermeneutical attempt at cross-cultural comparison as a proposal for cross-fertilization between two cultures through a multidimensional reading of Galatians on the theme of borders and barriers. I intend neither a historical-critical description of Galatians nor a corrective prescription for reading it today. The aim is rather to point out what one might see in Galatians from the context of differing worldviews, particularly those native to Korea and the so-called Far East. I offer my reading in the spirit of free exchange of ideas and mutual critique. When we read with a little imagination, we can appreciate the common humanity from and into which Paul writes his letter to the Galatians, which in turn can challenge us to imagine our world and experiences in a more enriched way—toward a more humane and peaceful coexistence.

At the outset of my presentation in Korea, I provided a brief primer on some fundamental understandings of the *dao* (or *tao*) using the Korean flag as a vehicle to help orient those who may be unfamiliar. The Korean flag (태극기, *teh-geuk-ghee* in Korean[1]), unlike most flags, resists both vertical and horizontal linearity. There is not one vertical or horizontal line or framework, except the necessary boundary of the physical flag itself:

Instead of the dualistic implications of linearity, what is prominent is the harmonious, dynamic movement implied by the circular yin-yang (음양, *eum-yahng* in Korean) at the center with the emanating black symbols or trigrams for the fundamental elements of the universe: heaven, fire, water, and earth. I mention only these brief remarks to enable and enrich a better understanding of my reading of Galatians.

---

[1] 태극 (teh-geuk, 太極 in Chinese) is *tai chi* (from *I Ching*) meaning "the highest pole" and representing the "great absolute" or "supreme ultimate" as the source and beginning of the world.

BORDERS AND BOUNDARIES EVERYWHERE

Our world is full of borders and boundaries. Some are visible and palpable, even daunting, for example, the Israeli West Bank barrier. Others are more subtle, innocuous and mundane such that we are unaware of them, even when crossing over them, for example, the threshold of doors that we use every day. Borders are called various names and serve multiple functions. Among the many names are: barrier, boundary, fence, limit, margin, perimeter, and wall. Borders function chiefly to mark, contain, control, divide, exclude, isolate, protect, secure, separate, and warn. How *we* name and experience borders depends often on our experiences and *Weltanschuung* (worldview or perspective). *We* draw lines in the sand, modify them, and give them names.[2] For example, the "Israeli West Bank barrier" built by the Israeli government along the "1949 Armistice Line" can be called a "security fence" in Hebrew (גדר הביטחון, *geder ha-bitakhon*) while in Arabic it is called the "wall of apartheid."[3] Likewise, a fence around a playground may evoke unpleasant memories for a former prisoner but it is reassuring to parents whose children are at play. Although borders may seem like firm "lines in the sand," our experiences of them are always contextual.

About 30 to 40 kilometers north of Seoul is the world's most heavily fortified border dividing the Korean Peninsula. Ironically called the Demilitarized Zone (DMZ; 한반도 비무장지대), the 250-kilometer-long, 4-kilometer-wide buffer zone includes at its center the Military Demarcation Line (MDL), the "actual border" between North and South Korea "fixed" in 1953 (by mostly non-Korean parties). South of the DMZ is the Civilian Controlled Line (CCL) marking a further buffer zone covering the area of 5 to 20 kilometers from the southern boundary of the DMZ. As a border, the DMZ serves many functions, including military security and national boundary, and is one of the most palpable, sober reminders of a tragic division of one people into two nations with almost no possibility of border crossings—perhaps the most dangerous lines in the sand in our

---

[2] Cf. the critique of language and reality offered in the *Dao De Jing* as well as in continental philosophy.

[3] Other descriptions in Hebrew include "separation fence" and "separation wall." The BBC's style guide uses the term "barrier" (sometimes "separation barrier" or "West Bank barrier"), as does *The Economist*, PBS, and the *New York Times*. The Israeli Ministry of Foreign Affairs uses the phrase "security fence" in English. The International Court of Justice has used the term "wall" explaining, "the other expressions sometimes employed are no more accurate if understood in the physical sense." It is also referred to as the "Apartheid Wall" or "Apartheid Fence" in a derogatory manner. "BBC Reports on the Apartheid Wall," see http://www.palestineremembered.com/GeoPoints/Apartheid_Wall_5364/Article_2832.html., accessed Jun 26, 2016.

world. At the same time, because the DMZ has basically been an isolated forbidden zone, wildlife has been thriving there since 1953.[4] The place that is so deadly for people is life-giving, being one of the most well-preserved areas of temperate habitat in the world. Endangered animals and plants live in its biodiversity in and around a heavily fortified fence, landmines, and military posts.[5] The forbidden DMZ is also a tourist attraction. The world's fascination with borders can be seen also in Great Britain's Hadrian's Wall: begun in 122 BCE by the Romans, it is the most popular tourist attraction in Northern England.[6] Although its purpose is still debated, Hadrian's Wall seems to have been a *limes*, that is, a border defense or delimiting system that was used to mark the boundaries and provinces of the Roman Empire.[7] Still further back in history and better known to tourists around the world is the Great Wall of China, a series of fortifications built as early as the seventh century BCE to protect against various northern invaders from the Eurasian Steppe. The wall served as a border to control the Silk Road for commerce and immigration, military defense, and transportation.

Walls, especially those surrounding human settlements, have long been of interest to archaeologists, who have dug for the famed walls of Jericho, believed to be one of the oldest inhabited cities in the world (ca. 9,000 BCE) with a protective wall. As recently as 2015, archaeologists discovered a 7,000-year-old defensive wall of a prehistoric settlement mound near Hotnitsa in Central North Bulgaria that dates back to the fifth millennium BCE (Copper or Calcolithic Age). This discovery is significant because the Copper-Stone Age was associated with peaceful existence, but the arrows found by the wall indicate that there was some kind of conflict.[8] For archaeologists, anthropologists, historians, and other scholars, walls of separation, whether negative or positive, are integral to our understanding of ourselves and our world.

---

[4] Cf. the holistic insights of perfect harmony (e.g., of opposites) in the *Dao*, e.g., *Dao De Jing* 1–2.
[5] James I. Matray, Crisis in a Divided Korea: A Chronology and Reference Guide (Santa Barbara: ABC-CLIO, 2016), ix. Ecologists have identified some 2,900 plant species, 70 types of mammals, and 320 kinds of birds within the DMZ. As a place where human civilization is basically forbidden while animals and plants thrive, it can provide insight for an ecological understanding of the Garden of Eden that was guarded by cherubim and the flame of a revolving sword (Gen 3:24).
[6] Thomas J. Faulkenbury, ed., *Out of the Mist: Celtic Christianity* (Mainz: Pedia Press, 2011), 34.
[7] "Hadrian's Wall": The *limes* had a number of meanings including a path or balk delimiting fields, a boundary line or marker, any road or path, any channel, such as a stream channel, or any distinction or difference. *Limes* denotes a marked or fortified frontier and gives us the English word *limit*.
[8] Ivan Dikov, "Archaeologists Discover 7,000-Year-Old Fortress Wall in Prehistoric Settlement near Bulgaria's Hotnitsa," *Archaeology in Bulgaria* (2016),

Walls and borders often indicate conflict, which brings us to the primordial border set by the LORD God in Gen 3:22–27 to prevent the first human beings from eating from the tree of life to attain immortality, which God feared would obliterate the line separating the human from divine.[9] The human-divine boundary is symbolized by the tree of the knowledge of good and evil and by the tree of life that are simply planted in the Garden of Eden as a matter of fact (Gen 3:9), as an intended part of God's garden. The trees are an organic part of God's creation.[10] In fact, the first revelations about creation reveal that creation and order consist principally of setting borders and boundaries in the world (e.g., Gen 1:4)—what subsequent Mosaic laws articulate and maintain.

Order and border, although etymologically distant,[11] are nearly synonymous in the biblical creation narratives as well as in anthropological studies of human cultures, the most notable among which may still be Mary Douglas's *Purity and Danger: An Analysis of Concepts of Pollution and Taboo* (1966), to which I will refer later. For now, we begin with the argument that borders and boundary-setting are at the origin and heart of the Jewish tradition, the very tradition that led Paul to persecute the church of God (Gal 1:13) and the same tradition within which he argued for the unity in Christ of both Jewish and Gentilen believers (e.g., Gal 3:28). Later, I entertain Paul's argument in Galatians regarding the truth of the gospel and the Jewish practice of circumcision. Understanding Paul's argument in Galatians within the context of the larger biblical horizon and also the still larger anthropological horizon regarding borders and boundaries, I offer some ancient insights from the *dao* in East-Asian philosophies that can enrich our (mis)perceptions and (mis)conceptions about borders—that is, definitions, delineations or differences—and what it means to cross them, including the borders between the Hebrew Bible and the New Testament, biblical and anthropological studies, and Western and Eastern philosophies.

---

http://archaeologyinbulgaria.com/2016/01/21/archaeologists-discover-7000-year-old-fortress-wall-in-prehistoric-settlement-near-bulgarias-hotnitsa.

[9] Cf. the Torah observance indicating the Jew-gentile distinction, i.e., the fundamental differentiation between the sacred and the profane that mirrors the divine-human one.

[10] Here the *dao* perspective would smile-frown on the languaged prohibition that is counter to the ineffable, trans-historico-linguistic harmony of the universe within which the wise just know and go with the flow of the *dao*. There is nothing "forbidden" for the sage who perceives the *dao*. Also relevant with some resonance with the *dao* is Nietzsche's argument that there is no ultimate good and evil, e.g., *Jenseits von Gut und Böse: Vorspiel einer Philosophie der Zukunft* (*Beyond Good and Evil: Prelude to a Philosophy of the Future*).

[11] *Order* comes from the Latin word *ordo* meaning *row, series, rank. Border* derives from the Old English word *bord*, of Germanic origin, related to Dutch *boord* and German *Bort*, reinforced in Middle English by the Old French *bort*, meaning *edge* and *ship's side*, and Old Norse *borth* meaning *board, table*.

Borders and Boundaries in Paul's Jewish Weltanschaung

Without pursuing a comprehensive, historical reconstruction of Paul's beliefs and practices, we can outline some basic ideas and forces that his letters intimate regarding his understanding of what separated Jews from gentiles. Worth noting are Paul's (mission) arguments regarding Abraham, the father of Jews and the first to receive circumcision as a sign of the covenant (Gen 17:11, 24). In Gal 3:6–18, as a part of his argument against the Galatians' favorable view of circumcision and the Jewish law in general, Paul points out that Abraham was declared righteous (justified) on the basis of his trust in God's promises 430 years *before* the Mosaic law. Likewise, Paul argues in Rom 3:21–4:25 that Abraham was justified on the basis of his faith *before* he was circumcised. The simplest way to restate Paul's argument against Torah observance as a requirement for justification before God, that is, having a right relationship with God, is to say that the God of the Jews declared Abraham, the father of the Jewish covenant, to be righteous *while he was a gentile*, that is, not circumcised and before any Sinaitic law!

In both Romans and Galatians, Paul claims that God justifies Jews the same way he declares gentiles equally righteous, that is, on the basis of faith (trust) in God and not because of meritorious observance of the works of the law. What Paul insists regarding the common justification of Jews and gentiles, especially as he marshalled his exegetical points about Abraham, must have been shocking, even offensive, to most of his contemporaries, Jews and gentile proselytes alike. In demonstrating to believers in Galatia as well as in Rome that through baptism into Christ "there is no longer Jew or Greek, there is no longer slave or free, there is no longer male and female" (Gal 3:28), Paul uses the language of his world indicating ethno-religious, socioeconomic, and sexual boundaries to eliminate their significance in the new faith community that is the "church of God." As a Jew for whom the Jew-gentile distinction used to be of ultimate significance, Paul denies the boundary between Jews and gentiles as having any meaning in the light of baptismal unity in Christ: "all of you are one in Christ Jesus" (Gal 3:28).

Paul's christocentric anthropology is a long way from what he formerly embraced as a Pharisee, at least according to his own words in Phil 3:4–6 and Gal 1:13–14. His insistence on the nonsignificance of the Jew-gentile distinction in Christ would have been unintelligible in the context of his former Pharisaic, Torah-centric *Weltanschauung*. Indeed, the apostle Paul would have scandalized Paul the Pharisee (e.g., σκάνδαλον in 1 Cor 1:23; Gal 5:11).

What is so scandalous for many Jews and gentile sympathizers to contemplate is not so much that God reckoned Abraham's faith as righteousness—and thereby also the believers' faith as efficacious for justification and salvation, especially in Romans and Galatians. What is most upsetting is that Paul's scriptural observations and arguments about the fundamental and unifying significance of trust in God obliterates the very line that separated Jews from gentiles, that is, the significance of what was thought to be Jewish election and the privilege of divine covenant. Paul's christological rereading of the Jewish scriptures, his reinterpreting of Jewish traditions, and more importantly his experience of Christ led to understand the fundamental Jewish apprehension of the division among humanity not as a permanent wall but a temporary line "in the sand," that is, not set in stone (Gal 3:24). Paul's christocentric *Weltanschauung* not merely left behind his Pharisaic convictions about Jew-gentile *distinction* but through the revelation of Christ (e.g., Gal 1:13–16a) embraced the unity of Jews *and* gentiles, even though distinct, in the Abrahamic covenant with the one God of Israel (Rom 3:30; Gal 3:20) offering the same justification based on faith, that is, one gospel with twofold mission, one to Jews and the other to gentiles. The ultimate consequence of Paul's experience of Christ is that he understands the former differentiation of Jews from gentiles to be empty of any meaning: there is *no longer* Jew or Greek (Gal 3:28).[12]

The truth of the gospel as articulated in Gal 3:28 springs certainly from Paul's experience of Christ and his mission experiences, especially those involving conflict between Jews and gentiles. His experiences as an apostle, however, rested on top of layers of tradition that resonated consciously and unconsciously with his work as an apostle. Among the layers were certainly the sacred texts of Judaism, for example the Abrahamic narratives, which he uses explicitly in his arguments. More subtle and perhaps more interesting for this essay's gaze toward the Far East, are the foundational texts in the beginning of Genesis that launch the canonical imagination for Jews and now also for Christians.

GENESIS OF ORDER AND BORDERS

In the beginning when God created the skies and the earth, there was no (b)order: "the earth was a formless void and darkness covered the face of the deep" (NRSV).[13] The first word is בראשית, a grammatical puzzle that forms the absolute spatiotemporal boundary of all revelation to follow. As the phenomenal and physical point before which no epistemic access is possible, בראשית sets the limits of all epistemology.[14] It is an absolute border not to be crossed by human curiosity;

---

[12] Cf. Nagarjuna's *Mulamadhyamakakarika* in the Buddhist tradition in which we find the radical obliteration of the traditional distinction between *nirvana* and *samsara*, i.e., between ultimate salvation-freedom and the enslavement to repeated rebirth: "There is nothing whatever which differentiates the *samsara* (existence-in-flux) from *nirvana*; And there is nothing whatever which differentiates *nirvana* from *samsara*" (ch. 25). Whether in the Indian context of Nagarjuna or in the Jewish context of Paul, the offence would amount to something like declaring in Roman Catholicism that there is no difference between heaven and hell.

[13] For translations of biblical texts, I generally use the NRSV unless matters of translation are themselves at issue.

[14] Also indicating human limitations, the Torah begins with ב rather than א; a part of the divine revelation is that human beings cannot begin at *the very beginning*, that human knowledge is at most penultimate. Cf. Eccl 3:11: האדם את המעשה אשר עשה לא ימצא

it is the absolute terminus a quo of space and time.[15] The first noun in the Bible is אלהים, the absolute terminus a quo of all things that exist. Whether as the subject of a main clause or not, its grammatical, plural form is bound unmodified with the singular verb ברא in the first three words of the Bible—which I will compare to the *dao* in East-Asian thought—as if to indicate the simple elegance of creation's mystery as well as the inappropriateness and the non-sense of any epistemic attempts to uncover what lies before or behind God and creation. All epistemological approaches to the creation are greeted with poetic resistance by the first three words of a text revealing that creation is beyond the border of human perception and conception; the only truth and reality in the beginning of all beginnings are God and God's creative activity that initiates *and* delimits all space and time.

The uncreated creator of the Jewish and Christian scriptures is the axiomatic being that originates and generates all phenomenal reality that we call the universe,[16] the totality of which the Bible simply calls *skies* and *earth* (השמים והארץ).[17] These two words completing the first thoughts of the Bible also set the first phenomenal borders of intelligibility to human existence and experience: the skies, even though visible, are the realm beyond the reach of human access and always drawing the human gaze into its impenetrable, seemingly unbounded vastness; the earth is the domain of human space and time, the stage on which human history and all interpretations or stories of it unfold. Plural in form and singular in meaning, אלהים provides for us the seemingly paradoxical truth that includes simultaneously the undifferentiated one-ness and the differentiated many-ness of reality. God, whom Jews and Christians worship, can be understood in cautious comparison with the unmoved mover of Aristotelian philosophy, or the general philosophical problem of the one and the many.

In the brief foregoing remarks, those who are familiar with ancient Greek philosophy can discern my allusions to and play with Greek ideas that may yield fruitful analysis of very Jewish and subsequent Christian ideas that are articulated through conceptual formulations resembling or resonating with Greek worldviews (e.g., ἀφθαρσία and ἀθανασία in 1 Cor 15:50–57). At the same time, those who are

---

האלהים מראש ועד סוף (human beings cannot find out what God has done from the beginning to the end; cf. Sir 39:20); Rev 21:6 (ἐγώ [εἰμι] τὸ ἄλφα καὶ τὸ ὦ, ἡ ἀρχὴ καὶ τὸ τέλος), Rev 22:13 (ἐγὼ τὸ ἄλφα καὶ τὸ ὦ, ὁ πρῶτος καὶ ὁ ἔσχατος, ἡ ἀρχὴ καὶ τὸ τέλος). Furthermore, the letter ב is closed on three sides, as if to indicate human inaccessibility spatially to the skies and the waters (and the underworld) as well as temporally to "before" creation and orienting us to the open future of human history. (Elaboration and development of observations on בראשית found at http://eteacherbiblical.com).

[15] Cf. the question in Augustine's *Confessions* about what God was doing before creation.
[16] Cf. Aristotle's ὃ οὐ κινούμενος κινεῖ (Aristotle, *Metaph.* 12.1072a).
[17] Also representing the totality of the entire universe are basically the same words in East-Asian expressions, e.g., 천지 (*chuhn-jee*) in Korean and 天地 in Chinese meaning *sky-earth* in differentiated harmony.

familiar with East-Asian philosophical traditions may have noticed my playful bows to the *dao*; the Bible contains many expressions of lived-experience that resonate surprisingly with Daoistic and even Zen insights about truth, knowledge, and ethics (e.g., Ps 19:1–6). Notwithstanding similarities, biblical imagination differs significantly in various places from both ancient Greek and East-Asian thought, even though our comparing and delineating of the differences may prove to be quite a formidable challenge. In the context of our East-Asian location, that is, Korea, I draw our attention to how the one-many problem can be understood or articulated in terms of the *dao*, the absolute reality "underlying" all phenomena and experience.

HARMONY AND DIFFERENTIATION IN THE DAO

Originating in ancient Chinese thought and articulated eventually through the classic text *Dao De Jing* by Laozi (sixth century BCE), the *dao* is somewhat like *logos* in ancient Greek thought, at least in the oldest philosophical use of it in Heraclitus (ca. 535–475 BCE), for whom it was the intelligible (rational) principle in and for the world and human thought.[18] Transcending yet permeating all of reality—that is, phenomenal, humanly experienced reality—the *dao* both defies and encompasses all definition and differentiated realities.[19] As the *Dao De Jing*

---

[18] *Dao De Jing* can be roughly translated as *way-virtue-canon*, i.e., the great book or classic of *dao* and integrity. Because the *dao* is always dynamic, vital, holistic in the natural order of the universe and its being alive, it differs significantly from traditional Western ontology and metaphysics that tends to be static and atomistic. In this regard, the *logos* in Heraclitus seems to be the most comparable to the *dao*. E.g.:

> This *logos* holds always but humans always prove unable to understand it, both before hearing it and when they have first heard it. For though all things come to be in accordance with this *logos*, humans are like the inexperienced when they experience such words and deeds as I set out, distinguishing each in accordance with its nature and saying how it is. But other people fail to notice what they do when awake, just as they forget what they do while asleep. (Diels-Kranz 22B1)

> For this reason it is necessary to follow what is common. But although the *logos* is common, most people live as if they had their own private understanding. (Diels-Kranz 22B2)

> Listening not to me but to the *logos* it is wise to agree that all things are one. (Diels-Kranz 22B50[20]).

[19] The understanding of truth in terms of the *dao* may be as challenging as translating the words and ideas of *Dao De Jing*. See the following translations: Stephen Mitchell, *Tao Te Ching*, trans. Stephen Mitchell (New York: HarperCollins Publishers, 1988); James Legge

expounds, *dao* is neither a thing nor a name for a thing but the underlying natural order of the universe; it transcends and permeates all things by its being nonconceptual while evident in ubiquitous, dynamic presence.[20] In an intriguing way, the *logos* in Greek philosophies and the *dao* in East-Asian philosophies share some transcendent-permeating qualities of "the force" in the *Star Wars* movies.

The *dao* precedes all perceptible things and language, that is, the naming of things. Accordingly, Laozi uses the *dao* as a critique of language that can provide a playful counterpart to the spirit of the Buddhist philosopher Nagarjuna (ca. 150–250) in his *Mulamadhyamakakarika* that deconstructs Buddhist language and doctrine. The *dao* can also resonate playfully with the critique of language and reality found in Nietzsche, Heidegger, Gadamer, and Derrida. The *dao* is presented critically against the illusory certainty of language—somewhat like Derrida's deconstruction; it is "eternally nameless" (*Dao*, 32) and cannot be equated with or contained by the countless named things, that is, phenomenal reality and experiences, which are the manifestations of the *dao* that is the reality of all life before any namings or comprehension of life.

With regard to this critique of language in the *Dao De Jing*, we find a curious contrast in the Genesis accounts of creation. Just as God is a given in the beginning of Genesis, so is language. God's first act of creation is the utterance of words: "Let there be light"; and there was light (Gen 1:3). In Gen 1:1–2:4a we witness repeatedly the divine power of language. In the subsequent acts of creation God assigns words, that is, names (= nouns), to fundamental temporal and spatial realities: day and night (1:5), skies, earth and waters (1:8, 10).[21] But what is more surprising appears in the creation story that follows in 2:4b–24. There the LORD God invites the first human being, the earthling taken from the earth (Gen 2:7: האדם עפר מן האדמה), to participate in what had been solely a divine privilege during creation in 1:1–2:4a. God waits until the earthling names the animals and merely sanctions the names without the slightest reservation (2:19).[22]

---

et al., 道德經 - *Dao De Jing* (http://ctext.org/dao-de-jing); Derek Lin, *Tao Te Ching: Tao and Virtue Classic* (http://www.taoism.net/ttc/complete.htm).

[20] E.g., *Dao De Jing* 1, 2, 32. Here is an excerpt from chapter 32 that provides a glimpse of the *dao*: "The Dao, considered as unchanging, has no name.... As soon as it proceeds to action, it has a name. When it once has that name, (men) can know to rest in it. When they know to rest in it, they can be free from all risk of failure and error. The relation of the Dao to all the world is like that of the great rivers and seas to the streams from the valleys." (Translation by James Legge et al., http://ctext.org/dao-de-jing).

[21] Cf. *Dao De Jing* 2. E.g., "When the world knows beauty as beauty, ugliness arises. When it knows good as good, evil arises. Thus being and non-being produce each other. Difficult and easy bring about each other. Long and short reveal each other. High and low support each other. Music and voice harmonize each other. Front and back follow each other." (Translation by Derek Lin, http://www.taoism.net/ttc/complete.htm).

[22] In case this biblical endorsement of the mastery of human beings over other animals is not clear, Gen 1:26–28 stands as an explicit reminder that human beings share more in

The biblical narratives of how all phenomenal reality comes to be, that is, comes into languaged reality, feature a logocentric view of how objects of human experience are identified and ordered by name. Creation is about naming and establishing borders between day and night, between waters above and below the skies, between the waters and dry land, et cetera. Any breach of these fundamental separations means disintegration into chaos (Gen 1:2), as the story of Noah demonstrates when the waters below and above cross their created, ordered borders (7:11–12). According to this biblical tradition, knowing the universe and its order means knowing it in its division and separation (cf. *logos* in Greek philosophies, especially as reflected in Aristotelian analysis of the world). This the Bible shares in significant measure with Greek philosophical traditions at the basis of "Western thought," to which we now turn briefly.

Homo Sapiens as Homo Dividens

According to an old joke, there are two kinds of people in the world: those who divide the world into two kinds of people, and those who do not.[23] Jews are of the former kind that divide the world into two kinds of people. Both humorous and profound, this observation is a prerequisite to understanding both the Jewish and Christian canons; it is a must for understanding Paul and his letters. To the interpretation and application of Paul's letters, and in particular Gal 2:11–14 and 2:25–29 as a significant instance, I will turn later. But on the way, it is worth reflecting on the universal, human phenomenon of differentiating or categorizing and our ideas about categories, boundaries, and borders, particularly in the Western traditions.

Human beings are categorizing beings. We differentiate, that is, we compare two or more things or people and identify similarities and differences. Perhaps *the* quintessential way that we understand ourselves and our world is by categorizing, that is, by classifying objects we encounter in our experience of the world according to their distinctive characteristics. We find ourselves categorizing not because it is our conscious decision or duty but because it is a defining feature of what it means to be human. That is to say, the activity of categorizing is simply the way, perhaps the most significant way, we know how to understand ourselves and our world. Human beings categorize. It is what we do.

Although all people organize their experiences of the world through categorization, there are various ways in which the process takes place and thereby impacts theory and practice. One exemplary approach in the so-called Western tradition is the logical analysis of Aristotle, the first systematizing biologist. Aristotle provides the proto-systematic or meta-systematic analysis for subsequent

---

common with the creator than with the created, even though as earthlings they find themselves inextricably *within* the created order.

[23] Shaye J. D. Cohen, *The Beginnings of Jewishness* (Berkeley: University of California, 1999), 1.

development through a theory of definition in his logical works, according to which definition or identity is created in terms of a proximate group in which a type of thing exists, that is, a species that contains individual things sharing some common attributes and called by a common name. For example, we belong to the species (εἶδος, that which is seen, i.e., form, shape, figure)[24] called *human beings* and our proximate group is *animal*, which is the name for the larger group or *genus* (γένος, kind or family), of which the human species is a subset. The uniqueness of any species of things is circumscribed by the essential defining trait, the *differentia* (διαφορά, difference or distinction),[25] which in the case of human beings is rationality.[26] We all belong to the species of "human" within the genus of "animal," and our differentia, that is, our unique defining trait, is "rationality."

Aristotle's logical analysis of defining things[27] exhibits the fundamental approach of subsequent epistemological traditions we call Western philosophy and all manner of sciences. One example is the well-known biological taxonomy that classifies all living organisms: kingdom, phylum, class, order, family, genus, species. As powerful as Aristotelian logical analysis is, we should assess critically its epistemic approach. In fact, the word *analysis* (ἀνάλυσις) is from the verb ἀναλύειν meaning to *loose, unloose, loosen, undo, dissolve,* and thereby also *depart from life;* the divisive character of analysis typifies epistemic approaches associated with "Western" thinking that is marked by de-structive, reductionistic epistemology. Aristotle's method of division (διαίρεσις; from διαιρέω, to separate) basically follows Plato's procedure of definition and classification,[28] which is probably from Greek thought going back to at least Homer (ca. eighth century BCE). This way of thinking is fundamental to and complements the development of the atomic theory by Leucippus (ca. fifth century BCE) and his pupil Democritus (ca. 460–370 BCE), according to whose materialist view of natural phenomena everything is ultimately composed of atoms, which are physically indivisible, ἄτομος, from the verb *not able to be cut or divided.* When we want to know something, we loosen and divide until we can no longer do so. Division and separation typify all "Western" epistemic methods and explanative approaches to understanding the

---

[24] For example, εαἶδος is one of Plato's words for *form.*

[25] Διαφορά also means *disagreement,* from the verb g, meaning to *carry through* as well as to *differ,* which provides a fruitful comparison to μεταφέρω meaning to *carry over, transfer,* or *translate*—Latin-derived words *translation* and *transfer* are the same in meaning as the Greek-derived word *metaphor.*

[26] The story-telling characteristic of human beings that distinguishes us from all other animals leads us to a discussion of *logos,* which is both rationality and narrative, such that *homo sapiens* (wise/knowing human) is also *homo narrans* (story-telling human), but that discussion will have to wait for another occasion for exploration.

[27] E.g., Aristotle, *An. Pr.* 2.13.

[28] E.g., Plato, *The Sophist* 216a–236d.

world.[29] While that divisive approach is very Greek and very Western, it is also very pervasive in all parts of the world.

People everywhere have expressed the tendency, if not the practical necessity, to know things in their differentiation and contrast, for example, day and night, good and bad, and most significantly for the purposes of this essay, we and they.[30] Accordingly, categorizing, as a way of knowing, consists more of describing what a thing *is not* than prescribing what a thing is. Accordingly, categories often tend to be dualistic.

OF BORDERS AND CROSSINGS, AND *PURITY AND DANGER*

Keeping in mind the philosophical and metaphysical musings about undifferentiated reality and harmony of differences while also keeping before us the interpretation of Paul, let us consider briefly, broadly, and practically the theme of crossing borders. To enter Seoul, I arrived at Incheon Airport and had to pass through customs. Although within the geographical borders of South Korea, I would not be permitted further into the country without having my identity checked and all my things cleared.[31] It did not matter that I was born in Korea, speak Korean, eat Korean food, and have parents and most of my relatives in Korea; all that mattered was what passport I held. I stood, as I have done many times, in the customs line *for foreigners*; I am an alien, *the other*, in the land of my birth and childhood. When I travel to and from the United States with my parents or other relatives from Korea, we have to stand in different lines in both countries, although we share a genetic and familial bond (cf. Ezra 10). Customs and border control are like the Great Wall and the DMZ, a kind of border that human beings have drawn in the sand that has to be guarded, making sure that certain things and people are not permitted in or out.

A border is "the edge or boundary of something, or the part near it" (*New Oxford American Dictionary*). As neutral as that definition is, borders and boundaries in human experience come with much ideological and emotional content and history. There are many, different kinds of borders, barriers, differentiations, and divisions: among physical boundaries there are natural and artificial ones, some of which are fixed and others flexible or permeable; among artificial boundaries there are some that are harder to cross than others. There are natural boundaries

---

[29] In contradistinction is the Far-Eastern philosophical approach of the *dao*, discussed above, which is much more appreciative of holistic harmony, even at the cost of using paradoxical language.

[30] E.g., for the ancient Greeks, the world consisted of Greeks and barbarians, just as for Jews the world consisted of Jews and gentiles. Cf. "the East" and "the West" in English, which roughly approximates 동양 (*dohng-yahng* in Korean; 東洋 in Chinese, literally, east-ocean) and 서양 (*suh-yahng* in Korean; 西洋 in Chinese, literally west-ocean).

[31] This is a kind of purity-and-danger moment in the sense of Mary Douglas's anthropological insights, about which I will say more below.

that are fixed or firm according to the unbreakable "laws of physics," for example, space-time itself, molecular structures, the sound barrier, which we now can "break"[32] but nevertheless remains as a physical constant.[33] Among natural borders are those that are permeable such as the skin, which is waterproof while permitting perspiration; similarly, valves in the heart permit only one-way circulation of blood.[34] Also among natural boundaries are things like oceans, mountains, rivers, and sea shores that are fairly fixed but that change through time or human intervention. Furthermore, there are fuzzy boundaries like the shoreline that is definite-indefinite, certainly identifiably there but is in constant flux.

If borders and barriers are found in nature, human beings have done their share of constructing artificial ones. Artificial boundaries that human beings have drawn in the sand, like socioeconomic class or the Indian caste system, are not determined in the natural order, even though some coincide with natural boundaries (e.g., oceans, rivers, and mountains that mark national borders)[35] and even though some people have claimed nature as justification for segregation (e.g., the inferiority of sub-Saharan Africans or the inferiority of Jews). Although all artificial boundaries are theoretically penetrable, some, like the Korean DMZ, the Israeli West Bank barrier, and the former Berlin Wall, can cost human life when crossings are attempted. Attempted crossings of other artificial, physical boundary markers can be traumatic as well, even if short of death, for example, circumcision for gentiles, removal of circumcision for Jews (e.g., 1 Macc 1:15), and refusal by Rosa Parks to sit in the back of the bus during the civil rights movement. We can argue likewise that other nonphysical, sociocultural barriers have cost human life (e.g., segregation in the United States), even though in most cases the cost is experiences of injustice and suffering other than murder.

There are many boundaries and borders, as well as border crossings, associated with religions and rituals. Some well-known examples include dietary laws,

---

[32] Cf. other barriers we can figuratively *break* through such as "the color barrier" or "the glass ceiling."

[33] We *imagine theoretically of breaking* the time barrier with time travel, but we must wait to see its realization.

[34] Cf. the atmosphere, which rockets and astronauts have passed through. Also cf. the Karman line 100 kilometers above Earth's sea level that is considered the boundary between the Earth's atmosphere and outer space.

[35] Consider simultaneously Turkey's efforts to join the European Union and the recent Brexit vote, which many say legitimates Scotland's vote for independence from the UK and Ireland's vote for unification of the island. Consider also the cultural phenomenon called the Korean wave (*hahl-lyoo*, 한류) that crosses the peninsular borders of Korea, to "export" Korean music, K-pop, K-drama, Korean language, Korean technology (e.g., cars, electronics), Korean food, Korean games, Korean animation and webtoons all over the world. In the light of such phenomena today, reconsider the case of Paul as a West-Asian Jew evangelizing among the Celts in Galatia (= Asia) in Greek about a Jewish messiah.

circumcision, and bar mitzvah in Judaism, baptism, confirmation, and the Eucharistic "words of institution" in Christian traditions, and the washing of hands and feet as well as the removing of shoes before entering a mosque for prayer in Islam, or the burka worn by many Muslim women, which can be compared to the habit worn by Catholic nuns. Social anthropologists have noted that such boundary markers symbolize holiness and purity, often in anxious awareness of dirt and defilement.[36] While anthropologists have gained much insight from fieldwork and ethnography, texts too have been a goldmine for studying societies, religious communities, and their symbolic expressions of the sacred and the profane. An anthropological lens can bring fresh interpretations to well-known texts like Exod 3:5: "Then [the Lord] said, 'Come no closer! Remove the sandals from your feet, for the place on which you are standing is holy ground.'" Likewise, anthropological theory can illuminate the symbolic expressions of holiness in artwork, for example, the various barriers separating the angel Gabriel from Mary in paintings of the Annunciation.

The anthropologist and cultural theorist Mary Douglas argued in her seminal work, *Purity and Danger: An Analysis of Concepts of Pollution and Taboo* (1966), that what is considered impure essentially depends on context and social history. The boundaries between the pure and the impure among any people at any given time are not determined by nature or necessity but are symbolic lines drawn in the sand and continually reinforced to maintain the sacred and the profane, to preserve purity and guard against pollution. Accordingly, Douglas originally theorized that Jewish dietary laws were about symbolic boundary-maintenance.[37] Subsequently, in the preface of the 2002 edition of *Purity and Danger*, she expounded three mistakes of her earlier theory, the worst of which was that she had thought certain land animals were forbidden in the Bible for human consumption because they were abominable:

---

[36] Some notable social anthropologists are: E. B. Tylor (1832–1917), James George Frazer (1854–1941), Bronisław Malinowski (1884–1942), E. E. Evans-Pritchard (1902–73), Claude Lévi-Strauss (1908–2009), Victor Turner (1920–1983), Mary Douglas (1921–2007), Clifford Geertz (1926–2006).

Note Mary Douglas's introductory remarks on dirt and defilement that are insightful for interpreting ordinary experiences as well as biblical texts (*Purity and Danger: An Analysis of Concepts of Pollution and Taboo* [London: Routledge Classics, 2002], 2): "As we know it, dirt is essentially disorder. There is no such thing as absolute dirt: it exists in the eye of the beholder. If we shun dirt, it is not because of craven fear, still less dread of holy terror. Nor do our ideas about disease account for the range of our behaviour in cleaning or avoiding dirt. Dirt offends against order. Eliminating it is not a negative movement, but a positive effort to organise the environment."

[37] Accordingly, we can understand texts like Acts 10:9–48, 15:1–29, and Gal 2:11–14 in terms of symbolic boundary-maintenance between Jews and gentiles.

Like the Mishnah and the rabbis, I took it for granted that their abominability was the issue, which made it a case for pollution theory. I now question that they are abominable at all, and suggest rather that it is abominable to harm them ... the prohibitions on unclean animals are not based on abhorrence but are part of an elaborate intellectual structure of rules that mirror God's covenant with his people. The people's relation to their flocks and herds is implicitly parallel to God's covenanted relation to them. The land animals belong to God; He cherishes them and forbids their blood to be shed unless they are consecrated for sacrifice (Lev. xvii, 4). Of land animals, the people of Israel may only eat those which are also allowed to be sacrificed on the altar, which restricts them to eating only the species of the land animals which depend on the herdsmen entirely for safety and sustenance. What may be burned on the altar may be burned in the kitchen; what may be consumed by the altar may be consumed by the body. The dietary laws intricately model the body and the altar upon one another.[38]

Douglas makes a strong case that the biblical tradition and subsequent interpreters misunderstood the symbolic significance of the dietary prohibitions, as she had. In any case, whether misunderstood by the Jews themselves or not, the dietary prohibitions organized the Jewish world and maintained Jewish identity and purity.

With due caution, we can apply the insights from Douglas's comprehensive, humanistic perspective of anthropology to the tasks of biblical interpretation before us in Galatians. Douglas's theorizing as well as her self-correction should inform us in biblical studies where theories, especially dominant or popular ones, direct *what* we interpret and *how*. Saving that methodological-critical discussion for another time, we now direct our tortuous route back to understanding Paul, particularly through his expressions in Gal 2:11–14 and 3:25–29, the interpretation of which I will sketch in the light of insights from the *dao* and anthropology. In nuce, I propose to read Gal 3:25–29 as a quasi-*dao* expression of the harmony and unity Paul argues for Jews and gentiles, especially as articulated in verse 28

---

[38] Mary Douglas, *Purity and Danger: An Analysis of Concepts of Pollution and Taboo* (London: Routledge Classics, 2002), xv–xvi. The other two mistakes Douglas notes are as follows: "One was the temptation to circularity, such as supposing that a species must be anomalous because it was forbidden, and then setting up a search for its anomalous features. Anomaly is like similarity: anything may have anomalous features, just as any two things may have similar features. More important was the absence of any positive implications for the social system of the biblical Hebrews for whom the rules were made. The taboos did not seem to be punishing any kind of misbehaviour. Though the implications for social structure were an integral part of the theory of taboo, there are none to be found by scouring through the dietary rules. I ignored this, confident that subsequent historical research on the culture of ancient Israel would uncover the missing parts of the puzzle. But that has never happened. The dietary laws do not warn malefactors of deeds that will bring punishments down on themselves. Breaking the food rules is the sin: the rules are hard to connect indirectly to other sins against God, or other sins against people" (xiv–xv).

(οὐκ ἔνι Ἰουδαῖος οὐδὲ Ἕλλην), claiming that through Christ both Jews and gentiles are revealed to be one offspring of Abraham (εἰ δὲ ὑμεῖς Χριστοῦ, ἄρα τοῦ Ἀβραὰμ σπέρμα ἐστέ, κατ' ἐπαγγελίαν κληρονόμοι). For both Gal 3:25–29 and 2:11–14, I propose that they be understood properly with reference to their socioanthropological coordinates of an ancient intra-*Jewish* debate about what it means to be Jewish; only *thereafter* should we weigh how Paul's insights and arguments might be relevant for our use in our multifarious contexts today.

DIFFERENTIATION AND BORDERS IN PAUL

For Jews of the first century, like Paul, there were only two kinds of people: Jews and non-Jews, that is, gentiles. As would be expected of a Pharisee, Paul's way of perceiving the world was informed, on the one hand, by how Jews were an elect, privileged people of God, distinct from other people by virtue of their superior beliefs and practices, and on the other hand, in contradistinction, by how gentiles lacked true beliefs and righteous practices that had been revealed to the Jews alone.[39] So fundamental was this dualistic distinction between the pure and the impure, that even after Paul became an apostle of Jesus Christ to the gentiles, his understanding of human beings primarily through the categories of Jew and gentile persisted. For example, even as Paul argues in Galatians for the meaninglessness of those ethno-religious categories in Christ, declaring that in Christ "there is no longer Jew or Greek" (Gal 3:28), he reveals, almost in the same breath, his bias against gentiles calling them simply sinners, ἁμαρτωλοί (Gal 2:15). That is to say, while arguing *against* the separation between Jews and gentiles, he relies on precisely these categories to make his point.

What is not contested in our understanding of Jewish self-understanding in the first century is that there was this general sense of differentiation between Jews and non-Jews. What is far from clear is what constituted Jewishness.[40] Rabbinic literature, as well as other Jewish sources, like Paul's letters, corroborated by gentile sources, indicate a complex spectrum of Jewish self-understandings of what constituted a Jew and what it meant to be Jewish.[41] In the light of the literary and epigraphic evidence available to us indicating the variety of Jewish perspectives, we should recast our understanding and use of passages like Gal 2:11–14 in a way that does more justice to Paul's own ethno-religious context.

---

[39] The best work I know on this topic of Jews and gentiles in Paul's letters regarding the justification of the gentiles and Paul's critique of Jewish privilege is Hendrikus Boers's "We Who Are by Inheritance Jews; Not from the Gentiles, Sinners," *JBL* (1992): 273–81.

[40] See Shaye J. D. Cohen, *The Beginnings of Jewishness* (Berkeley: University of California, 1999) for a survey of scholarly works as well as ancient sources that deal with Jewish identity.

[41] E.g., the interesting story in Josephus, *Ant.* 20.2.1–5, of a young king of Adiabene named Izates and his queen mother Helena (d. 50 CE), in which the proselyte king is advised two different Jews about whether he must be circumcised or not. Eusebius also makes mention of this queen in his *Church History* 2.12.1, 3.

There are Pauline passages that have been understandably invoked in contemporary Christian conversations for the just cause of remedying a painful history of Christian misunderstanding and mistreatment of Jews as well as for dealing with the issue of how Christians today ought to consider the Jews. At least in the case of Paul's letters, however, it would appear appropriate to articulate more clearly that when he argues for the inclusion of gentiles in God's covenant promise *without* the generally presupposed requisite of circumcision, Paul's argument is essentially a Jewish argument—not a Christian one—against *other* Jewish perspectives, for example, the "circumcision faction" (οἱ ἐκ περιτομῆς) mentioned in Gal 2:12.[42] That is to say, what is at issue in the early church, as depicted in Galatians, Romans, and also Luke-Acts, is not Christian-Jewish relationship, although that important theme is often anachronistically projected onto Paul's letters and presupposed in our interpretations. Rather, what we have in Gal 2:11–14 is an *intra*-Jewish debate about what good Jews should think and do about gentiles, especially concerning their inclusion in the Jewish covenant and their Torah-observances (cf. Acts 8:26–39; 10:9–48; 15:1–29).

Since for Paul there is not yet a Christianity over against Judaism, but only Judaism in its ultimate revelatory stage of gentile inclusion, we must pay close attention to such historical aspects that are significant for every stage of our reading and interpretation of Paul's letters—and also significant for the ways readers appropriate Paul's writings in today's Christian-Jewish dialogues. With that in mind, we may view Gal 2:11–14 as a testing ground for understanding all of Paul's letters within their historical, Jewish—and Greco-Roman—environment. Hermeneutically speaking, I do not suggest naively that we can separate this historical understanding from our contemporary presuppositions or interests. I am a subscriber of Gadamer's keen notion that every interpretation is simultaneously an application; there is no historical understanding that can be isolated from the interpreting person.[43] That hermeneutical proviso notwithstanding, the misdirection of applying Paul too quickly in our world of needed Christian-Jewish dialogue and understanding can and should be avoided. On the positive side, understanding Paul's arguments as essentially intra-Jewish ones may permit clarity of the structure of his thought, such that, once properly configured and understood, his letters may be liberated to be *more* applicable across *more* ethno-religious contexts than the letters intended. In going beyond Paul's Jewish matrix of concerns, we can cautiously use insights from the *dao* and anthropology to

---

[42] This point would be true even if the οἱ ἐκ περιτομῆς refer to or include not just Jews but also gentiles who adopted this position on the necessity of circumcision.

[43] See part two of Hans-Georg Gadamer's book *Wahrheit und Methode* (Tübingen: Mohr Siebeck, 1960; *Truth and Method* [New York: Crossroad, 1989]) under 2.2, "The recovery of the fundamental hermeneutic problem," in which he writes about the relationship between interpretation and application.

address the scores of boundaries in our world to understand what these borders mean and what it means to (try to) cross them.

GALATIANS AND THE MEANING OF CHRIST: *CROSS*ING BORDERS

In the beginning, there was no Jew or Greek, no slave or free, no male and female. Although not quite the formulation we find in Paul, this *dao*-inspired reformulation is worth considering against the background of what creation-order means and what the new creation signaled by baptism for Christians. The warrant for my *dao* and creation orientation comes from Paul's own expressions articulating his understanding of the apocalypse of Christ (Gal 1:16: ἀποκαλύψαι τὸν υἱὸν αὐτοῦ ἐν ἐμοί), primarily in terms of Christ's crucifixion[44] and resurrection.

Creation language seems a coherent part of Paul's experience of Christ and expressions of what Christ means for him and the cosmos. For example, anyone in Christ is a new creation or perceives and participates in it (2 Cor 5:17); and new creation renders both circumcision and uncircumcision meaningless (Gal 6:15).[45] The best warrant may be the most subtle one found in Gal 3:28 itself, where in articulating the new creation or new world order in Christ, Paul enumerates three pairs of contrasting categories of human identities: the ethnoreligious (Ἰουδαῖος οὐδὲ Ἕλλην), socioeconomic (δοῦλος οὐδὲ ἐλεύθερος), and sexual identities (ἄρσεν καὶ θῆλυ).

Among the three pairs of categories, the last one does not follow the parallel structure of the first two statements: οὐκ ἔνι ... οὐδὲ. The reason that Paul writes οὐκ ἔνι ἄρσεν *καὶ* θῆλυ rather than οὐκ ἔνι ἄρσεν *οὐδὲ* θῆλυ probably has to do with the force of tradition embedded in his consciousness of the formulaic idiom from Gen 1:27: ἄρσεν καὶ θῆλυ ἐποίησεν αὐτούς.[46] Much can be made of the fact that the two adjectives are in the neuter,[47] but both the social and biological dimensions

---

[44] 1 Cor 1:13: Has Christ been divided? Was Paul crucified for you? Or were you baptized in the name of Paul? See 1 Cor 1:23; 1 Cor 2:2; Gal 2:19; Gal 3:1.

[45] Cf. Rom 8:19–23; for other *dao*-relatable reference to creation and original harmony, cf. also Rom 1:20, 25. Rom 1:18–32 would be a wonderful text for applying Mary Douglas's insights about symbolic boundary-maintenance and social order along with *dao*-understandings of *dao*'s pervasive dynamic in creation and the harmony in creation. Cf. also Col 1:15; Heb 9:11; 2 Pet 3:4.

[46] MT: זכר ונקבה ברא אתם. Cf. also the other verbatim occurrences in LXX and the New Testament: Gen 5:2, 6:19, 7:2–16; Matt 19:4; Mark 10:6. It is also reasonable to assume the force of pre-Pauline tradition in that sexual identity does not play a role in his other arguments in Galatians, whereas the Jew-gentile and slave-free categories are significant parts of his arguments in the letter.

[47] Hans Dieter Betz's commentary presents the most comprehensive *religionsgeschichtliche* discussion of possible and probable Jewish (particularly Philo), Greek, early Christian, and Gnostic sources that may illuminate the third statement in v. 28.

of human society and interrelationship are simultaneously transformed into a reality in baptism that reconciles everyone as the children of the one God (Gal 3:26).

The formulation of ἄρσεν καὶ θῆλυ in Gen 1:27 has engendered many speculations, particularly because the Hebrew text uses both the singular and plural for the creation of human beings:

ויברא אלהים את האדם בצלמו	So God created the human being in <u>his image</u>; καὶ ἐποίησεν ὁ θεὸς τὸν ἄνθρωπον, [omission of בצלמו]
בצלם אלהים ברא אתו	in the <u>image</u> of God he created <u>him</u> [human being]; κατ᾽ <u>εἰκόνα</u> θεοῦ ἐποίησεν <u>αὐτόν</u>,
זכר ונקבה ברא אתם	male and female he created <u>them</u>. ἄρσεν καὶ θῆλυ ἐποίησεν <u>αὐτούς</u>.

God is assumed to be one, but the grammatical plurality of אלהים accommodates both the singular (אתו) and plural (אתם) creation of האדם in the singular image (צלם) of God. From a *dao* perspective on language and reality, the textual problems in the Hebrew are playful, even helpful, ways to criticize human categorical language and epistemology toward the harmony of the *dao*, in which the *yin* (陰, meaning *shade, negative, feminine, the moon*) and *yang* (陽, meaning *sun, positive, male genitals*) are harmonious and complementary principles that are very different from the dualism in Greek or Western thought. A *dao* reading would be quite friendly to the notion that the one transcendent God is a *dao*-like dual-harmony of male-femaleness whose divine image becomes manifest in the sexually differentiated human beings, who though different and differentiated, are actually primordially one in creation (the singular האדם representing the archetypal human being as well as the collective of the human race as a whole).

The second creation narrative in Gen 2:4b–25, offers a variation on the male-femaleness but it still expresses the primordial unity and differentiated reality of the sexes. In Gen 2:7 the same word האדם in the singular names the first human being that became a "living being" (ויהי האדם לנפש חיה; καὶ ἐγένετο ὁ ἄνθρωπος εἰς ψυχὴν ζῶσαν) as dust fashioned from the earth (עפר מן־האדמה) and animated by the divine breath of life (נשמת חיים).[48] The first human being is revealed to be a male-female being—possibly androgynous—when later in the narrative the Lord God removes a rib from inside האדם, the sexually undifferentiated earthling,[49] to make אשה, the sexually female human being (2:21–22) as a

---

[48] ויצר יהוה אלהים את האדם עפר מן האדמה ויפח באפיו נשמת חיים ויהי האדם לנפש חיה ("Then the LORD God formed man from the dust of the ground, and breathed into his nostrils the breath of life; and the man became a living being").

[49] In Old English the suffix *-ling* on nouns indicate a person or thing belonging to or concerned with what is denoted by the primary noun (*Oxford English Dictionary*). Thus האדם

differentiated complement to the male איש—a kind of biblical yin-yang.

So in Gen 2:22 the אשה (feminine) is taken מן־האדם (masculine) paralleling the way האדם (masculine) was fashioned מן־האדמה (feminine) in 2:7.[50] Sepatated from האדם, the אשה becomes the etymological, biological counterpart (עזר, *helper*) to what remains of האדם, the formerly male-female earthling, which is now also called or given the new name איש (2:23). Notwithstanding the linear procession in the narrative from feminine אדמה to masculine אדם to feminine אשה, a *dao* twist can be found at the end of the narrative, according to which every איש must leave his parents to unite with an אשה to form בשר אחד, one family and literally one flesh in the form of an offspring, which would be either an איש or an אשה, while at the same time being a male-female being, another אדם (i.e., from a father and a mother). Consequently, human biology, although genetically linear, symbolically repeats a continual cycle of creation-procreation-recreation (from primordial unity to sexual differentiation to sexual reunion; from a male-female earthling to male and female human beings to male or female offspring). God's creation can only thrive as long as the linear pro-creation by differentiated sexes repeats the union-differentiation (i.e., creation-procreation) of the original human beings by uniting and separating repeatedly.

The ontologically axiomatic oneness of God and the differentiated human manifestation of the divine male-female image in Gen 1:27—the plural אלהים—together with the pattern of pro-creation as repeated union-differentiation in Gen 2:21–25 compare well with the primordial *dao* and its mysterious and pervasive harmony of manifest "opposites," for example, yin and yang. Additionally, the phrase עצם מעצמי ובשר מבשרי (bone of my bones and flesh of my flesh) in Gen 2:23 expresses the profound creation insight that women and men are of the same substance.[51] Or put in terms of the *dao*, male and female have no priority or privilege in the harmony that is the *dao*—a point worth remembering for Gal 3:28; they mutually, interdependently define and complement each other. Thus, biblical creation, which consists fundamentally of separating, differentiating, and (b)ordering—that is, border-formation—includes as its divine crowning expression the primordial union and unity of the divine image of male-and-female (ἄρσην καὶ θῆλυς; זכר ונקבה) in the human and in human procreation. Relexicalized into *dao* terms, yin—the cosmic-universal principle that is passive, female, sustaining, and associated with earth, cold, and dark—is inextricably coconstitutional and co-original in the universe with yang—the harmoniously opposing principle that is

---

from האדמה can be understood as an *earthling*. Translating האדם as *earthling* also avoids the potential English problem of understanding *man* as exclusively masculine.

[50] Cf. the language of interdependent genesis of male and female in 1 Cor 11:8–12, one of the best places for a *dao* reading (e.g., recognition of difference and harmonious interdependence, although linearly expressed in 1 Corinthians).

[51] Cf. the ancient Greek philosophical problem of the one and the many.

active, male, creative, and associated with sky, heat, and light. As two complementary cosmic forces and energy, their fusion and their differentiation in(to) physical matter accounts for the entire phenomenal world.

When understood in the light of the biblical creation narratives through the lens of *dao*, Paul's baptismal formulation in Gal 3:28 of the new creation in Christ entreats the Galatians, as well as all Jews and gentiles, to recognize the primordial (baptismal) oneness of each of the differentiated categories in human society.[52] Paul shares the Jewish and Stoic view that the unity of human beings corresponds to the oneness of God.[53] At the least, Paul argues in Galatians, as also in Romans, that Jews have temporal-covenantal priority but not ultimate privilege.[54] The cosmic reconciliation that Christ effects constitutes a new creation that unifies the very distinctions and order that creation set in place, especially the distinction between the chosen people of Israel and the rest of the world—for Paul, still distinct but ultimately not to be separated.[55]

In Gal 2:11–14 the boundary of dietary and ritual purity in the Mosaic tradition asserts the dominant Jewish understanding of how the world ought to be ordered, that is, with Jews and gentiles separated. Even as Cephas, Barnabas, and other Jews seem to have had no problems in Antioch with commensality with gentiles, the crossing of ritual borders in the table fellowship of Christ was intolerable to those who saw the dangers of chaos breaking into a Jewish world order. For some believers—Jews sent by James or Galatian gentiles—dietary laws and circumcision were sacred lines of separation drawn by God indicating covenantal election, with no expiration date. Admittedly, what Paul calls hypocrisy (2:13) was basically Jewish obedience to the Torah. Yet Paul's understanding of the gospel would insist that Mosaic borders must be crossed in Christ to reach new creation, the baptismal oneness in Christ (3:27–28).

Unlike in Antioch and Galatia, Jewish views on commensality and circumcision no longer constitute the issues of contention for today's gentile-dominated churches. Yet the analogical application of Paul's convictions and theological hermeneutics may prove to be ever relevant and fruitful for all who read Paul's letters as authoritative for Christian faith and life. Paul's report of the Antioch incident

---

[52] Although with judicious caution, we may invoke the insights of Mircea Eliade (1907–1986) in his *Myth of the Eternal Return: Cosmos and History* (1954) to discern on some levels a Pauline "eternal return" to creation and Eden, e.g., Paul's creation language and his references to Adam in expressing the meaning of Christ (Rom 5:14; 1 Cor 15:22, 45).

[53] Hans Dieter Betz, *Galatians*, Hermeneia (Philadelphia: Fortress, 1979), 192.

[54] Cf. Gal 3:24a: ὥστε ὁ νόμος παιδαγωγὸς ἡμῶν γέγονεν εἰς Χριστόν (So the law was our teacher until Christ came). See Boers for the best explication of the misunderstanding of both circumcision and baptism as privilege.

[55] Gal 3:28, 5:6, 6:15; Rom 3:22, 29, 10:12; 1 Cor 7:19, 12:13; 2 Cor 5:17–20. Also cf. Col 3:9–11; Eph 2:15, 4:24. Cf. the Isaian vision of the wolf and the lamb, the leopard and the kid, the calf and the lion (Isa 11:6; 65:25; cf. Sir 47:3; also cf. Sir 13:17; Luke 10:3).

prompts us to ask how Christians today should handle ecclesiological (comm)union among them with regard to differences in beliefs and practices. For example, if we see the analogical features of circumcision and baptism as rites of initiation into the covenant community, we may be justified in applying some of Paul's arguments in today's Christian disputes surrounding the meaning and practice of baptism, for example, differences of opinion about the significance and validity of baptizing infants.[56] Likewise, although dietary purity may no longer apply to Christians, ritual eating of the Eucharist, as well as ordinary eating, could provide a comparable forum for discussing Christian identity and communal life in the light of Paul's strong convictions in Galatians. If this kind of analogical application is reasonable, then although many Christian traditions have not and do not permit table fellowship at the eucharistic table, they must take seriously the injunction that reaches us from Paul two millennia ago, namely, the unity in Christ that transcends those differences of beliefs and practices.

In these and other instances, Paul's uncompromising insistence on ecclesiastical unity in Gal 3:28 may be recontextualized analogically among diverse Christian traditions or among opposing factions within one particular tradition, that is, as an intra-Christian debate. The question of covenantal unity and identity in Christ remains as fundamental to current Christian contexts as it was to Paul's Jewish context; if baptism is the new circumcision, then Paul's old arguments against circumcision can levy the most serious critique of Christian-covenantal privilege.[57] To be faithful to the spirit of Paul while being mindful of his historical context, perhaps we may reformulate his conviction in Gal 3:28 in order to ponder that in Christ there is no Orthodox or Roman Catholic, no Catholic or Protestant, no Presbyterian or Baptist. Such a reformulation should not be suggested lightly, especially if we recognize the complexities of theological developments in the history of Christianity and seek to respect the integrity of differing Christian traditions. Nevertheless, even if a bit bold, this hermeneutical application of Galatians—with its new, Christian coordinates for Paul's intra-Jewish argument—may be the most appropriate one for contemporary theology—and for questions regarding non-baptized people, including Abraham.

Concluding Thoughts

People say that rules are meant to be broken. They mean that rules stifle creativity and progress, so it is important to break the occasional rule to create and progress; it does not mean that all rules should be wantonly abandoned for the sake of fun.

---

[56] This analogical-hermeneutical approach is precisely what John Calvin used in his *Institutes of the Christian Religion* (4.16) to articulate and defend his understanding of infant baptism.

[57] See Hendrikus Boers, "We Who Are by Inheritance Jews; Not from the Gentiles, Sinners," *JBL* 111 (1992): 273–81. This is perhaps the best interpretation of the apparent contradiction in Rom 2:13 and 3:20 regarding the justification by faith without works of the law.

If rules are meant to be broken, borders are meant to be crossed and transgressed, at least some. For Paul, the crucifixion and resurrection of Christ breaks through the barrier that is sin and death (1 Cor 15:20–28); Christ crosses the borders of alienation between God and enslaved, sinful humanity (Phil 2:6–8) reconciling God and humanity (2 Cor 5:18). One primary way of understanding the meaning of Christ in Paul is to see that Christ is the border-crossing agent of God who unites what has been separated—a kind of a *dao* critique or remedy for a Jewish and Greek problem of separation and division.

In 1 Cor 15:53 Paul says that the mystery of resurrection-transformation consists of putting on imperishability and immortality, a formulation contrary to Platonic philosophy. If Platonic dualism and Greek philosophies in general speak of separation (e.g., soul from body), in which the immaterial soul must be liberated from material corruptibility, Paul speaks of reconciliation and new creation, that is, the restored harmony, in which corruptibility takes on incorruptibility and mortality immortality (1 Cor 15:50–57). In Paul's play with Greek language and concepts, his is an articulation or vision closer to that of the *dao* that only knows of eternal harmony of manifestly opposite reality. If Plato et alii represent "the European" or "the Western" traditions,[58] then Paul of Tarsus (in Asia Minor), writing to the Galatians in Asia Minor, is more of a "little Asian" in his experience of Christ, more resonant with *dao*-like intuition.

The meaning of Christ that Paul articulates in his argument against the Galatian believers' desire for circumcision takes on a focused expression in Gal 3:28. What a *dao*-oriented reading might suggest is to recognize the harmonious oneness in-of differentiated reality. What Paul negates is not the reality of distinctions—he was neither blind nor ignorant—but their significance in and for the community of faith. Paul's understanding of the meaning of Christ includes a renewing of the mind (ἡ ἀνακαίνωσις τοῦ νοός, Rom 12:2) that must reconfigure the ordinary, mundane, and even sacred categories of human society.[59] The newness (καινός) is transformative of the traditional Jewish understanding of not only

---

[58] Alfred North Whitehead (1861–1947), who himself crossed over from being a British mathematician to become an American philosopher, said famously, "The safest general characterization of the European philosophical tradition is that it consists of a series of footnotes to Plato" (*Process and Reality: An Essay in Cosmology* [1929], 1.2.2). Consider also: "The term many presupposes the term one, and the term one presupposes the term many" (*Process and Reality*, 1.2.2).

[59] Although Paul's authorship of Colossians and Ephesians is contested, Col 3:9–11, Eph 2:15, and Eph 4:24 express Paul's ideas through familiar formulations. Particularly relevant for this paper is the fact that the language of these passage interconnects the ideas I connect, namely, language of new identity (humanity), renewal, image of God, creation, non-significance of differentiating categories and ritual holiness ("Greek and Jew, circumcised and uncircumcised, barbarian, Scythian, slave and free" in Col 3:11), and the harmony of everything in Christ.

justification but also creation—compare 2 Cor 5:17: καινὴ κτίσις.⁶⁰ Whether the ἀνά in ἡ ἀνακαίνωσις τοῦ νοός of Rom 12:2 is taken in the spatial sense of *up* or the temporal sense of *back*, both are significant for expressing the radical nature of baptismal identity that requires nothing short of death of the self (along with its ideas; Rom 6:2–4) for the transformation into new (resurrection) life.⁶¹

Paul's letters contain language bearing a predictable perspective or bias within the spectrum of ancient Jewish beliefs and practices, for example, Jew-gentile division. Yet, because of the gospel of Jesus Christ, Paul came to declare and insist on the unity of believers in Christ *without requiring uniformity* in their ethno-religious, socioeconomic, and gender identities: "There is no longer Jew or Greek, there is no longer slave or free, there is no longer male and female; for all of you are one in Christ Jesus" (Gal 3:28). What is of interest for understanding Paul's experience of Christ through the lens of the *dao* is the *dao*'s non-negation, even affirmation, of differentiation (i.e., the reality of practical human experience) and the fundamental harmony-unity of all differentiation (i.e., negation of differentiation, e.g., Jews basically look like gentiles, too similar to require clear boundaries)—we can speak of a harmony in and of differentiation or harmonious differentiation. For the *dao* there is neither purity nor danger; borders and boundaries in a world of differences are places of harmonious insight, not of erroneous segregation.

Of special interest in Paul's letters is his articulation of baptismal identity or unity in Christ (e.g., Rom 6:1–11), particularly regarding the ultimate meaning (lessness) of being a Jew or gentile in Christ. Paul never denies the differences between Jews and gentiles, even when emphasizing that both Jews and gentiles are justified before God in the same way, that is, διὰ or ἐκ πίστεως Χριστοῦ. While he chastises the Galatians not to become circumcised, he never insists the same for Jews. Yet in Christ, that is, from the viewpoint of the new identity in baptism, the Jew-gentile difference becomes meaningless (cf. 2 Cor 5:16–17: εἴ τις ἐν Χριστῷ, καινὴ κτίσις). Seen through a *dao* lens, Paul's use of κτίσις and his allusions to creation signal the ultimate border-crossing, from this age into the apocalyptic age to come, from separation and alienation to the primordial dynamics of undifferentiated reality—in a sense, a crossing of borders that never were (primordially) and are not (ultimately). Perhaps Paul would not approve of *dao*-hearings of his words; but surely, his vision of humanity and the world would find a home in the harmony of the *dao*.

---

⁶⁰ E.g., Galatians and Romans.

⁶¹ The aorist tense of παρέρχομαι in 2 Cor 5:17 indicates that the "old things" were indeed real, not illusions; the point is that they are no longer significant in the light of Christ: εἴ τις ἐν Χριστῷ, καινὴ κτίσις· τὰ ἀρχαῖα **παρῆλθεν**, ἰδοὺ γέγονεν καινά.

EVE AND NOREA RETOLD: THE POWER OF STORYTELLING IN NATURE OF THE RULERS

Eunyung Lim

The Genesis story of creation (chs. 1–6) played a crucial role in the formation of early Christianity. This account of God and the origins of the world and humanity functioned as a reference point whereby early Christians not only constructed and developed soteriology and theological anthropology, but also rhetorically promoted and defended their sociocultural and political stances in the church and society. Since the creation story was crucial to understanding how the world *should* be, many contested interpretations of Genesis arose in the first few centuries of Christianity. Among them is the Nature (or Reality) of the Rulers in the Nag Hammadi library (NHC II 4), which is also known as the Hypostasis of the Archons.[1] This text does not merely provide a commentary on the creation story in the Hebrew Bible, but its narrative takes the form of a fresh, and even de-familiarizing, retelling of Gen 1–6, in which innovative and shocking gender and sex images are deployed. For example, unlike what we see in Gen 1–3, the carnal part of Eve is raped by the archons and later her daughter, Norea, is presented as a savior figure. The problem is that our unfamiliarity with this kind of retelling often leads to the labeling of the Nature of the Rulers as heretical or gnostic. It is considered a deviant or abnormal interpretation of Genesis in which its understanding of God, the human world, and salvation is seen as entirely invalid or misleading.[2] Obviously, this approach—not much different from that of some early Christians, especially the heresiologists,[3] who won the history of normative

---

[1] For English translation and numbering system of the Coptic text, I use Bentley Layton, ed., *Nag Hammadi Codex II, 2-7: Together with XIII*, 2, Brit. Lib. Or. 4926(1), and P. OXY. 1, 654, 655*, vol. 1 (NHS 20; Leiden: Brill, 1989), 234–59.

[2] This happens when people interpret Genesis within the framework of origins discourse or the "doctrinal-canonical" paradigm, insisting that there is only one true meaning in Genesis and their literal reading of it is the only legitimate way to approach Genesis's factual truth. Elisabeth Schüssler Fiorenza, *Rhetoric and Ethic: The Politics of Biblical Studies* (Minneapolis: Fortress, 1999), 39–41.

[3] Scholars have assumed that the Nature of the Rulers was originally written no later than the late third century CE. Yet, it appears that the only surviving copy included in the Nag Hammadi Codices was buried around the late fourth or fifth century in Egypt. As King

Christianity—cannot do justice to the Nature of the Rulers, but only precludes the possibility of evaluating the meaningfulness of this text.

Emerging from such a concern, this essay explores a preliminary yet viable way in which to duly appreciate the Nature of the Rulers, focusing on its startling sex and gender imagery. A careful literary analysis of the accounts of Eve and Norea will be provided with special emphasis on this text's retelling per se. As these female characters' stories pinnacle the text's creative and "critical appropriation of tradition,"[4] they enable us to explore the ways in which the Nature of the Rulers tries to fill in the fissures of the Genesis account. For this purpose, the present research draws upon Michael D. Jackson's existential-phenomenological insight into storytelling. Jackson argues that "storytelling is a modality of working with others to transform what is given, or what simply befalls us, into forms of life, experience, and meaning that are collectively viable."[5] If we consider the Nature of the Rulers' retelling to be a "collectively-shared narrative" between the storyteller and her listeners, our attention to the transformative effects of storytelling will help unpack the text's unfamiliar elaborations of Genesis from a fresh perspective.[6] We will then take the opportunity to understand how this ancient text creates "a world of meaning,"[7] asking this set of questions: How do the shocking gender and sex images of Eve and Norea function in this storytelling? To what kind of "transgression" and "social critique" does the Nature of the Rulers invite its readers?[8] Does its retelling of Genesis carry any transformative power in itself?[9] Our attention to these questions will allow us to reflect on this text's

---

notes, it is the time when "the content of the buried manuscripts was considered to be heretical by the standards of emerging orthodoxy." Karen L. King, *The Secret Revelation of John* (Cambridge: Harvard University, Press, 2006), 20; see also, King, "The Book of Norea, Daughter of Eve," in *A Feminist Commentary*, vol. 2 of *Searching the Scriptures*, ed. Elisabeth Schüssler Fiorenza (New York: Crossroads, 1994), 80–82.

[4] King, "Book of Norea, Daughter of Eve," 66.

[5] Michael D. Jackson, *The Politics of Storytelling: Violence, Transgression, and Intersubjectivity* (Copenhagen: Museum Tusculanum Press, 2002), 25.

[6] Cf. Jackson, *Politics of Storytelling*, 9. In this paper I will refer to the author's gender as "her" for the sake of convenience.

[7] Cf. Anne McGuire, "Virginity and Subversion: Norea against the Powers in the *Hypostasis of the Archons*," in *Images of the Feminine in Gnosticism*, ed. Karen L. King (Philadelphia: Fortress, 1988), 241.

[8] Jackson, *Politics of Storytelling*, 14–15, 25–30, 251–66; These two notions are to be discussed in the following section.

[9] Jackson argues that "storytelling is a modality of working with others to transform what is given, or what simply befalls us, into forms of life, experience, and meaning that are collectively viable" (*Politics of Storytelling*, 252).

theological significance, as well as to speculate about the storyteller and her listeners' plausible existential conditions, under which this text's storytelling functions as "a critical and creative force."[10]

STORYTELLING: BOUNDARIES, TRANSGRESSION, AND SOCIAL CRITIQUE

The stories of Eve and Norea constitute the main plot of the Nature of the Rulers. When compared with Gen 1–6, they present a strikingly different image of the female gender. For example, the hierarchical relationship between Adam and Eve in Genesis (esp. 3:16) is reversed in the Nature of the Rulers (Nat. Rulers). The spirit-endowed Eve (Nat. Rulers 89.11) awakens Adam from his deep sleep. She appears to have the higher nature (i.e., spirit) than Adam, and she is even portrayed as a "savior figure" who gives Adam life (89.13–17).[11] In addition, this text introduces a new female character, Norea, who not only stands up against the wicked rulers in her world but also receives the true knowledge of her spiritual roots in the last half of the narrative (92.32–97.20).[12] In contrast to Eve in Genesis, Nature of the Rulers emphasizes that neither Eve nor Norea are completely overwhelmed by the male authorities of the world. The provocative images of the female gender cause us to wonder how and why the author(s) of the Nature of the Rulers had to retell the creation story in such a way, overturning the conventional notions of Eve in Genesis.

The stories of Eve and Norea, however, cannot be considered at face value to reflect the social construction of reality of real women at that time, given that such ancient texts as Nature of the Rulers were formed in a largely patriarchal society.[13] Besides, the scarcity of historical information about this text would make it challenging to reconstruct the real communities behind the text and their evaluation of women. The question of what such portrayals of Eve and Norea may have meant for the ancient audience, therefore, can be discussed within the literary realm of the Nature of the Rulers. This is where Jackson's theory of storytelling

---

[10] Jackson, *Politics of Storytelling*, 9.

[11] King, "Book of Norea," 68; see also, Elaine H. Pagels, "Adam and Eve and the Serpent in Genesis 1–3," in *Images of the Feminine in Gnosticism*, 414.

[12] Norea is absent from the creation account in Genesis, but Pearson convincingly argues that "Norea has been developed out of the Jewish material featuring the biblical Naamah" (cf. Gen 4:22). Birger A. Pearson, "Revisiting Norea," in *Images of the Feminine in Gnosticism*, 265–66.

[13] Many scholars have discussed this issue. See, for example, Karen L. King, "Editor's Forward," in *Images of the Feminine in Gnosticism*, xvii; King, "Ridicule and Rape, Rule and Rebellion: *Hypostasis of the Archon*," in *Gnosticism and the Early Christian World*, ed. James Goehring et al. (Sonoma: Polebridge, 1990), 4; Elaine H. Pagels, "Adam and Eve and the Serpent in Genesis 1–3," 415; Elisabeth Schüssler Fiorenza, *In Memory of Her: A Feminist Theological Reconstruction of Christian Origins* (New York: Crossroad, 1983), 274.

can serve as a useful ground on which to assess the text's female imagery. Nature of the Rulers is set within a storytelling scene in which the narrator secretly tells her audience a story about "the reality of the authorities" (89.20–27).[14] As the narrator retells–and even twists up–the all too familiar story of Genesis, the audience is asked to participate in an unpredictable situation that this retelling creates.[15] Such nature of storytelling makes it possible to examine the effects of Eve and Norea's story in light of "the dual potentiality of stories to either reinforce or degrade [the] boundaries" in society.[16] As Jackson puts it:

> Whether considered in the light of their function, form, or performance, stories create indeterminate and ambiguous situations that involve contending parties, contrasted locations, opposing categories of thought, and antithetical domains of experience. In traversing the borderlands, stories have the potential to take us in two very different directions. On the one hand, they … validat[e] the illusions and prejudices [the status quo] customarily deploys in maintaining its hold on truth. On the other hand, stories may confound or call into question our ordinarily taken for granted notions of identity and difference, and so push back and pluralise our horizons of knowledge. In the first case, storytelling seals off the possibility of critique; in the second, critique becomes pivotal.[17]

While the Genesis narrative's Eve is often interpreted as more congruent with a traditional wife/mother image in the patriarchal household,[18] the retelling in the Nature of the Rulers presents provocative gender images of Eve and Norea that divert from the subordinate female stereotype.[19] As this observation exemplifies,

---

[14] Bullard regards this text as "an esoteric work, written for a self-conscious community which probably felt pressure from a Christian community that defined itself as orthodox and others as heretical." Roger A. Bullard and Bentley Layton, "The Hypostasis of the Archons (II, 4)," in James Robinson, ed., *The Nag Hammadi Library in English*, 3rd ed. (San Francisco: HarperSanFrancisco, 1990), 161.

[15] At the beginning of the text, the narrator refers to "us" as those to whom the great apostle told the message of Eph 6:12; then, she introduces the following narrative as the message that "I" sent to "you" (Nat. Rulers 86.20–27). Also, in Norea's dialogue with Eleleth, it is observed that the narrator's voice is synchronized with Norea's voice (93.13ff). We can presuppose an original storytelling setting from these scenes, in which the audience listened to the storyteller.

[16] Jackson, *Politics of Storytelling*, 25.

[17] Jackson, *Politics of Storytelling*, 25.

[18] As King points out, according to the ideal gender construction in the ancient Mediterranean world, "women (being weaker and more timid [than men]) are charged with the duties of nurture and service.… They are to be concerned for shame, to be shy, submissive to authority, and deferential, passive and restrained." See, "Ridicule and Rape, Rule and Rebellion: *Hypostasis of the Archon*," 3–7.

[19] However, it should be questioned whether these two figures are entirely at odds with patriarchal social gender roles. I will discuss this issue later.

it is possible to assume that the Nature of the Rulers's storyteller may have witnessed that the extant narrative in Genesis, having obtained authority of canon in both Jewish and burgeoning Christian communities, is read to "validate" the existing social order.[20] However, by retelling this traditional narrative "in a highly creative and critical mode,"[21] Nature of the Rulers calls into question the "ordinarily taken for granted notions of identity and difference." Thus, Nature of the Rulers, through the stories of Eve and Norea, suggests to what extant boundaries may be crossed ("transgression"), and challenge the status quo.[22]

EVE AND NOREA RETOLD

What does the storyteller see as the status quo and how does transgression take place in Nature of the Rulers? The rape of Eve and the attempted rape of Norea respond to these questions in detail. In both scenes, first of all, we observe that Nature of the Rulers traverses the extant conventional boundaries between God and humanity and between male and female. Nevertheless, it should first be pointed out that Nature of the Rulers, prior to Eve's rape, introduces the creator God in Genesis as the chief ruler (also called Samael, Yaldabaoth, or Sakla) and his archontic powers (also called authorities of darkness, wicked rulers, or forces), which lack "the spirit" (ΠΝΑ or ΠΝΕΥΜΑΤΙΚΟC) in their nature and only involve the creation of this inferior, material world (86.27–88.16; cf. 96.16–18).[23] On the contrary, the God of mercy, in the Hebrew Bible, is located in the invisible world above (96.20).[24] In so doing, the storyteller sets out a new relationship between the Creator(s) and humanity and this is more fully developed in Eve's rape (89.18–31).

While the creation of Eve ensues from the chief ruler and his archons' clumsy action to put Adam into a deep sleep of "Ignorance" (ΤΜΝΤΑΤCΟΟΥΝ, 89.7), this spirit-endowed woman is not only superior to Adam, but also outwits all the spirit-less authorities in their rape of her. These wicked rulers, enamored of Eve, sexually pursue her. Yet, Nature of the Rulers tells that what is defiled is only her carnal form (ΤΕCϨΑΪΒΕC, "shadowy reflection") that they modeled with their

---

[20] In reality, many "orthodox" writings of early Christianity available to us stand in this line of exegesis; to name only a few here, 1 Cor 11:2–16, Tim 2:8–15, Tertullian, *On the Apparel of Women* 1.1. Meanwhile, Jackson also remarks that "the stories that are approved or made canonical in any society tend to reinforce extant boundaries," yet "storytelling also questions, blurs, transgresses, and even abolishes these boundaries" (*Politics of Storytelling*, 25).

[21] King, "Book of Norea," 81.

[22] Jackson, *Politics of Storytelling*, 25–26. Jackson's "notion of transgression" is based on Michel de Certeau's insight; see, Michel de Certeau, *The Practice of Everyday Life*, trans. Steven Rendall (Berkeley: University of California Press, 1984), 129.

[23] These worldly rulers obviously stem from the Nature of Rulers' interpretation of the plural of Gen 1:26–27. King, "Book of Norea," 82 n9.

[24] King, "Book of Norea," 81.

own fleshly image,[25] which results in their self-condemnation (89.26–30). Therefore, at the moment when the "female spiritual principle" (†ⲠⲚⲈⲨⲘⲀⲦⲒⲔⲎ) leaves her carnal form behind and laughs at the rulers' foolishness (89.24), their vices—such as ignorance, blindness, arrogance, lustfulness, and emotional agitation (cf. 86.27–88.10)—culminate more aggravatingly than ever before.[26] In effectively employing the rape theme in its interpretation of Genesis, Nature of the Rulers "transgresses" the social convention of male domination and female submission, so that it discloses and ridicules the wicked rulers' authoritarian and unrighteous control over the human world.

A similar thematic move to this is also found in the rulers' attempt to rape Norea (Nat. Rulers 92.18–93.2). Their failure in defiling her reveals their powerlessness as well as their vices one more time. However, the dissimilarities between Eve's and Norea's stories should be considered together with their similarities. For, not modeled by the wicked rulers but born to Adam and Eve, Norea eventually represents a new possibility for humanity.

Even before the attempted rape, the text underscores Norea's virginity (ⲦⲠⲀⲢⲐⲈⲚⲞⲤ), which "the forces did not defile" (92.2–3). Her assertive and rebellious actions, shown in her encounters with Noah (cf. 6:5–22) and the wicked rulers, contradict the typical weak and submissive female gender role. When the rulers strive to control her on the pretext of the carnal Eve's "service" to them (Nat. Rulers 92.20–21, 30–31),[27] Norea overtly resists this deceptive attempt by debunking their evil identity and proclaiming her spiritual origin (92.22–26). Again, Norea's story transgresses the hierarchical male-over-female convention, yet, similar to Eve's rape, it points to the text's strong critique of the "unrighteous" and illegitimate authorities in the world (93.1–2).

While the stories of Eve and Norea "work to deconstruct [the] divisions between the powerful and the powerless" in reality, Norea's story, more clearly than Eve's, displays the new "antithetical domains of experience" that Nature of the Rulers creates.[28] As the split of Eve's spiritual principle from her corporeal form implies (89.26), the story rejects the idea that "the carnal body is to be experienced as one's true self."[29] This dissociation between the spirit and the soul/body, intertwined with the sharp division between the invisible and the visible worlds, respectively, reaches a climax in Norea's ruthless refusal of the carnal Eve as her

---

[25] This text's interpretation of Gen 1:27 and 2:21–22 is noticeable here. Those worldly creators (alluding to the God of Genesis) formed Eve "according to their image," but their spirit-less condition results in their impotence to seize Eve's true self (the spiritual principle).

[26] These attributes of the archons contradict the male virtues in the ancient Mediterranean, such as "male perfection" and "self-control" in sexual desires, thereby revealing that they are more powerless and weaker than the woman. See, King, "Ridicule and Rape, Rule and Rebellion," 6–10.

[27] See n. 16 above.

[28] Cf. Jackson, *Politics of Storytelling*, 25, 28.

[29] King, "Ridicule and Rape, Rule and Rebellion," 14.

mother: "You [i.e., the wicked rulers] did not know my mother; instead it was your female counterpart (ⲧⲉⲧⲛ̄ϣⲃⲣⲉⲓⲛⲉ) that you knew!" (92.23–25). Even though Norea seems to be born of Adam and Eve's bodily procreation (91.30–34), Nature of the Rulers claims that her real origin is in the invisible world above. This logic is well couched in the symbolic combination between voice and virginity. From Eve's 'wake-up' call to Adam before her rape scene, to Norea's speech and dialogue (92.23–97.20), to the Incorruptibility and Zoe's exclamations ("You're mistaken, Samael/Sakla!"; 87.1–3; 94.24–26; 95.6–8), the story connects the voices of the female characters to "the divine faculty of speech."[30] At the same time, it also associates the mouth with the vagina "as orifices of penetration."[31] The defilement of the stamp of Eve's voice (89.29) signifies the carnal Eve's sexual impurity,[32] and conversely, Norea's spiritual power is highlighted in her virginity. In sync with this idea, the story further reveals that the virgin Norea plays "an assistance [role] for mankind," and she and her offspring will be saved because of the spirit of truth present within them (92.1–4; 96.19–25). In turn, the portrait of Norea makes a stark contrast with the carnal Eve, whose destiny is unknown after her giving birth to Norea (91.35).

Accordingly, we can argue that the retelling of Genesis, while confounding and contradicting the extant boundaries between the authorities in this world and the humans and between male and female, opens up a new horizon of existence and association[33] in which virginity and spirituality prevail over sexuality and materiality.[34] In this respect, whether Nature of the Rulers entirely overturns the conventional patriarchal system should be put into question. For when Nature of the Rulers denounces the male-over-female hierarchy in the rape scenes, it only aims to critique the unrighteous authorities' vices and highlight the spiritual element in humanity. This analysis also turns our attention to the fact that the text's storyteller often refers to "the father" (ⲡⲉⲓⲱⲧ), the absolute power in the spiritual world.[35] Furthermore, Norea, on her own, cannot escape the dangerous confrontation with the rulers of unrighteousness and has to request a rescue from the male angel Eleleth, who eventually foreshadows the coming of "the true man" (ⲡⲣⲱⲙⲉ ⲛ̄ⲁⲗⲏⲑⲓⲛⲟⲥ, 96.33-34), the ultimate savior of all. Therefore, it is important to note that the patriarchal social order itself may not be the status quo that Nature of the Rulers denies. As the text's main argument underlines, the status quo that this storytelling actually critiques and challenges is the injustice, violence, and

---

[30] McGuire, "Virginity and Subversion," 256.

[31] King, "Book of Norea," 71.

[32] King, "Book of Norea," 71.

[33] Jackson, *Politics of Storytelling*, 31.

[34] Cf. Elaine H. Pagels, "Pursuing the Spiritual Eve: Imagery and Hermeneutics in the *Hypostasis of the Archons* and the *Gospel of Philip*," in *Images of the Feminine in Gnosticism*, 191.

[35] Note such expressions as "the father of truth," "(by the will of) the father," "the father of the entirety," and "the primeval father" in 86.21, 87.22, 88.11, 88.35, 96.12, 96.20, 97.18, etc.

oppression of the worldly authorities that humans have to suffer under their material condition.[36]

SURVIVAL AND TRANSFORMATION IN NATURE OF THE RULERS

The sophisticated retelling of Genesis in Nature of the Rulers conveys a social critique of power relations in the world,[37] and the sex and gender images in Eve and Norea are operative in supporting this. As the text's transgression of the existing boundaries has shown (e.g., the powerlessness of the creator and rulers, gender subversion, and denial of the body), this storytelling does not represent or conserve "what *is* the case" in social realities, but imagines and "speaks otherwise."[38] In the process of its twisting and retelling of Gen 1–6, the audience is invited to see the authorities in the world through the pluralized and demeaned creator God of Genesis. By doing so, Nature of the Rulers critiques "illegitimate power,"[39] alluding to those unrighteous rulers of reality who pretend to be the absolute God over all of humanity. This aspect becomes clear when Nature of the Rulers, using an inter-textual strategy, mocks the chief ruler, who claims, "It is I who am [the] God [of the entirety]; there is none apart from me" (Nat. Rulers 86.30–31; 94.21–22; 95.5; cf. Exod 3:14; Isa 45:5). As the accounts of Eve and Norea have explicitly asserted, such an arrogant self-identification only "reveals the frailty of authority"[40] and unmasks the unrighteous power's reality.[41] From this point, the transformative exegesis in Nature of the Rulers proceeds to yield an important theological reflection: the wicked rulers' control over humanity is limited to only one's material existence, so they cannot defile his or her true spiritual self (96.15–26). In Nature of the Rulers, therefore, Eve and Norea are the ontological locus where the human condition is exposed and the salvation of humanity is anticipated.

This so-called "fictional reworking" or "counter-factuality" in such retelling of Genesis leads us to a strong critique of illegitimate power and at the same time encourages us to consider Nature of the Rulers not as mere "make-believe," but as existential imperative for "survival."[42] Even though it is impossible to have

---

[36] Concerning the Nature of the Rulers' critique of imperial power, see Celene Lillie, *The Rape of Eve: The Transformation of Roman Ideology in Three Early Christian Retellings of Genesis* (Minneapolis: Fortress, 2017).
[37] Jackson, *Politics of Storytelling*, 253. Cf. King, *Secret Revelation of John*, 158, 340.
[38] Jackson, *Politics of Storytelling*, 26.
[39] King, "Ridicule and Rape," 15; King, "Book of Norea," 76.
[40] Cf. Jackson, *Politics of Storytelling*, 27.
[41] Note that the text's title is also translated as "the Reality of the Rulers" (86.20, 27; 97.21–22).
[42] In Jackson's terms, the counter-factual power of Nature of the Rulers' storytelling, namely, the story's ability to contradict or deny reality, can be understood in line with those

access to the storyteller and her community's sociohistorical context or exact life situation, through this retelling we hear their plausible theological and existential questions: How can our world be full of evil if God is good? How can we face violence and oppression that we so vividly suffer in our bodies? Ultimately, their struggle for "being" directs our attention to those whose existence and life cannot be recognized or "livable" in this world unless a normative or conventional reading of Genesis is entirely challenged.[43] If this understanding can be articulated in light of an existential-phenomenological thought, we can argue that the retold stories of Eve and Norea function as the storyteller and her listeners' "vital human strategy," which empowers them to overcome their sense of powerlessness "in the face of disempowering circumstances"[44] and to recover their existential footing as "the children of the light" (Nat. Rulers 97.14). In Jackson's words, what this retelling would have meant for them is their experience of transformation from a "*what*"—an object for others—to a "*who*"—a subject for themselves.[45]

This transformative nature allows us to ponder the power of the Nature of the Rulers' storytelling. As already implied, this mythical story carries an open possibility to be used for deconstruction of the status quo or for "anti-social ends."[46] Yet we should note that Nature of the Rulers, in engaging Gen 1–6, does not take the form of polemic—"which cultivates a disinterested, objective, abstract, and

---

"narratives whose 'truth effects' are more blatantly tied to the struggles and tensions of personal existence" (see, *Politics of Storytelling*, 26–27).

[43] Cf. Judith Butler, *Undoing Gender* (New York: Routledge, 2004), 205, 213; My argument here is also influenced by Jackson. As he states, "what is possible for a person is always preconditioned by the world into which he or she is born and raised, but a person's life does more than conserve and perpetuate these pre-existing circumstances; it interprets them, negotiates and nuances them, re-imagines them, protests against them, and endures them in such complex and subtle ways that, in the end, human freedom appears as 'the small movement which makes of a totally conditioned social being someone who does not render back completely what his conditioning has given him.'" Michael Jackson, *Things as They Are: New Directions in Phenomenological Anthropology* (Bloomington: Indiana University Press, 1996), 30. See also, Jean-Paul Sartre, "A Sketch of a Phenomenological Theory," in *The Emotions: Outline of a Theory*, trans. Bernard Frechtman (New York: The Wisdom Library, 1948), 90–91; Jackson, *Minima Ethnographica: Intersubjectivity and the Anthropological Project* (Chicago: University of Chicago Press, 1998), 20.

[44] Jackson, *Politics of Storytelling*, 15. Jackson's understanding of storytelling's existential aspect is influenced by what Sartre calls "emotive" or "magical" action, which also stands with Jackson's another important concept, "ritualization." See, Sartre, "A Sketch of a Phenomenological Theory," 58–64; Jackson, *Things as They Are*, 6.

[45] Jackson, *Minima Ethnographica*, 8. Here Jackson notes, "Each person is at once a subject for himself or herself—*a who*—and an object for others—*a what*. And though individuals speak, act, and work toward belonging to a world of others, they simultaneously strive to experience themselves as world makers." See also, Hannah Arendt, *The Human Condition* (Garden City, NY: Doubleday, 1958), 181–88.

[46] Jackson, *Politics of Storytelling*, 27.

authoritative view from afar"—but the form of story.[47] Not promoting its own dogma or point of view in a forceful way, but "destabilizing habitual thinking" by inviting imagination, the Nature of the Rulers' retelling "inspires judgment and critique—the ability to see one's immediate situation as it appears from another vantage point."[48] Therefore, if we imagine this text's initial storyteller and her listeners in this collectively-shared narrative, while telling and listening to this story, they would have not only regained their existential grip "in the face of suffering and injustice,"[49] but also been invited to live in the story, thereby seeing the world in another way.

From such conceptions, two strands of reflection invite further study. First, I envision that by approaching such stories as Nature of the Rulers in the light of storytelling and its existential-phenomenological insight, we are provided an opportunity to understand them as they are, neither merely stereotyping them into Gnosticism or heretical literature nor making any normative judgment on them. At the same time, without necessarily distancing ourselves from the ancient world, we can obliquely speculate about existential motivations behind those texts, so as to gain new insights into human existence and religious experience that may resonate with our modern life.

Second, I would like to point out that the Nature of the Rulers' retelling, with its "hermeneutic openness and probing, and [its] straying beyond the bounds of orthodox viewpoints,"[50] exemplifies a fluid and fruitful way to explore various theological meanings of Scriptures. In addition, it encourages us to critically think about and communicate our own and also others' religious, cultural, and political lives in another point of view. In this sense, to whom and for what the Nature of the Rulers' storytelling can be, and will be, is a "critical and creative force" that is open-ended. As long as the stories of Eve and Norea are told and live in an "existing web of human relationships,"[51] Nature of the Rulers never remains the sole storyteller's own story; its theological meanings will always remain open to inquiring minds.

---

[47] Jackson, *Politics of Storytelling*, 252.
[48] Jackson, *Politics of Storytelling*, 169, 264–65.
[49] King, "Book of Norea," 67.
[50] Jackson, *Politics of Storytelling*, 169.
[51] Arendt, *Human Condition*, 184.

BIBLIOGRAPHY

Aaron, David H. *Etched in Stone: The Emergence of the Decalogue*. London: T&T Clark, 2006.

Abadie, Philippe. "From the Impious Manasseh (2 Kings 21) to the Convert Manasseh (2 Chronicles 33): Theological Rewriting by the Chronicler." Pages 89–104 in *The Chronicler as Theologian: Essays in Honor of Ralph W. Klein*. Edited by Matt Patrick Graham, Steven L. McKenzie, and Gary N. Knoppers. JSOT Sup 371. London: T&T Clark, 2003.

Abasil, Alexander Izuchukwu. "Was It Rape? The David and Bathsheba Pericope Re-examined." *VT* 61.1 (2011): 1–15.

Abbott, Andrew. *Processual Sociology*. Chicago: University of Chicago Press, 2016.

Adam, A. K. M., ed. *Handbook of Postmodern Biblical Interpretation*. St. Louis: Chalice, 2000.

Ahn, John. "A Light to the Nations: The Sociological Approach in Korean American Approach." Pages 112–22 in *Ways of Being, Ways of Reading*. Edited by Mary F. Foskett and Jeffrey Kah-Jin Kuan. St. Louis: Chalice, 2006.

———. *Exile as Forced Migration*. BZAW 417. Berlin: de Gruyter, 2011.

———. "Ezekiel 15: A מָשָׁל." Pages 101–19 in *The Prophets Speak on Forced Migrations*. Edited by Mark J. Boda, Frank Ritchel Ames, John Ahn, and Mark Leuchter. AIL 21. Atlanta: SBL Press, 2015.

———. "Rising from Generation to Generation: Lament, Hope, Consciousness, Home, and Dream." Pages 459–74 in *The Oxford Handbook of the Psalms*. Edited by William P. Brown. New York: Oxford University Press, 2014.

———. "Story and Memory." Pages 332–43 in *The Oxford Encyclopedia of the Bible and Theology*. Edited by Samuel E. Balentine. New York: Oxford University Press, 2014.

Ahn, Young-Sung. "For a Better Future in Korean Biblical Studies: Dialoguing within Myself in a Different Context." Pages 67–79 in *The Future of a Biblical Past: Envisioning Biblical studies on a Global Key*. Edited by Roland Boer and Fernando R. Segovia. Atlanta: Society of Biblical Literature, 2012.

Albeck, Shalom. "The Ten Commandments and the Essence of Religious Faith." Pages 261–90 in *Ten Commandments in History and Tradition*. Edited by Ben-Tsiyon Segal and Gershon Levi. Magnes Press, the Hebrew University of Jerusalem, 1990.

Alter, Robert. *The Art of Biblical Narrative*. New York: Basic Books, 1981.

Amaru, Betsy Halpern. "The Killing of the Prophets: Unraveling a Midrash." *HUCA* (1983): 153–80.
Anderson, A. A. *2 Samuel*. WBC. Dallas: Word Books, 1989.
Andrews, Edward E. "Christian Missions and Colonial Empires Reconsidered: A Black Evangelist in West Africa, 1766–1816." *JCS* 51.4 (2009): 663–91.
Arendt, Hannah. *The Human Condition*. New York: Doubleday, 1958.
Arnold, Bill. "The Use of Aramaic in the Hebrew Bible: Another Look at the Bilingualism in Ezra and Daniel." *JNSL* 22 (1996): 1–16.
Assmann, Jan. *Religion and Cultural Memory*. Translated by Rodney Livingstone. Stanford: Stanford University Press, 2006.
———. *Religion und kulturelles Gedächtnis*. München: Beck, 2000.
Avigad, Nahman. *Corpus of West Semitic Stamp Seals*. Revised and Completed by Benjamin Sass. Jerusalem: Israel Academy of Arts and Sciences/Israel Exploration Society/Institute of Archaeology, Hebrew University, 1997.
Avioz, Michael. "The Motif of Beauty in the Books of Samuel and Kings." *VT* 59 (2009): 341–59.
Bailey, Randall C., Tat-siong Benny Liew, and Fernando F. Segovia, eds. *They Were All Together in One Place? Toward Minority Biblical Criticism*. Atlanta: Society of Biblical Literature, 2009.
Bakhtin, Mikhail M. "Discourse in the Novel." Pages 3–32 in *The Dialogic Imagination: Four Essays by M. M. Bakhtin*. Edited by Michael Holquist. Translated by Caryl Emerson and Michael Holquist. Austin: University of Texas Press, 1981.
———. "Dostoevsky's Polyphonic Novel and Its Treatment in Critical Literature." Pages 14–17 in *Problems of Dostoevsky's Poetics*. Edited and translated by Caryl Emerson. Minneapolis: University of Minnesota Press, 1984.
Bhabha, Homi. "Of Mimicry and Man: The Ambivalence of Colonial Discourse." *October* 28 (1984): 125–33.
Baltzer, Klaus. *The Covenant Formulary: In Old Testament, Jewish and Early Christian Writings*. Translated by David E. Green. Philadelphia: Fortress, 1971.
Bar-Efrat, Shimon. "The Narrative of Amnon and Tamar." Page 239–82 in *Narrative Art in the Bible*. Sheffield: Almond, 1989.
Barton, John. *The Nature of Biblical Criticism*. Louisville: Westminster John Knox, 2007.
Becking, Bob, Meindert Dijkstra, Marjo Korpel, and Karel Vriezen. *Only One God? Monotheism in Ancient Israel and the Veneration of the Goddess Asherah*. Sheffield: Sheffield Academic, 2001.
Belazi, Hedi M., Edward J. Rubin, and Almeida Jacqueline Toribi. "Code Switching and X-Bar Theory: The Functional Head Constraint." *Linguistic Inquiry* 25 (1994): 221–37.

Berger, Peter, and Hansfried Kellner. "Marriage and the Construction of Reality: An Exercise in the Microsociology of Knowledge." *Diogenes* 46 (1964): 1–23.

Berger, Peter, and Thomas Luckmann. *The Social Construction of Reality*. New York: Anchor Books, 1966. Berkeley: University of California Press, 1984.

Berman, Joshua. "The Narratological Purpose of Aramaic prose in Ezra 4:8–6:18." *Aramaic Studies* 5 (2007): 165–92.

———. "The Narratorial Voice of the Scribes of Samaria: Ezra iv 8–vi 18 Reconsidered." *VT* 56 (2006): 313–26.

Berquist, Jon L. *Judaism in Persia's Shadow: A Social and Historical Approach*. Minneapolis: Fortress, 1995.

Betz, Hans Dieter. *Galatians*. Hermeneia. Philadelphia: Fortress, 1979.

Bhabha, Homi K. *The Location of Culture*. London: Routledge, 1994.

Bhatia, Tej K., and William C. Ritchie, eds. *The Handbook of Bilingualism and Multilingualism*. Oxford: Wiley Blackwell 2012.

Blenkinsopp, Joseph. *David Remembered: Kingship and National Identity in Ancient Israel*. Grand Rapids: Eerdmans, 2013.

———. *Ezra-Nehemiah*. Louisville: Westminster John Knox, 1988.

———. *Isaiah 1–39: A New Translation with Introduction and Commentary*. New York: Doubleday, 2000.

Blount, Brian, ed. *True to Our Native Land: An African American New Testament Commentary*. Minneapolis: Fortress, 2007.

Boase, Elizabeth, and Christopher G. Frechette, eds. *Bible through the Lenses of Trauma*. Atlanta: SBL Press, 2016.

Boda, Mark, Frank Ritchel Ames, John Ahn, and Mark Leuchter, eds. *The Prophets Speak on Forced Migration*. AIL 21. Atlanta: SBL Press, 2015.

Boers, Hendrikus. "We Who Are by Inheritance Jews; Not from the Gentiles, Sinners." *JBL* (1992): 273–81.

Bolin, Thomas. *Ezra-Nehemiah*. Collegeville: Liturgical, 2012.

Boose, Donald W., Jr. "Portentous Sideshow: The Korean Occupation Decision." *Parameters: USAWCQ* 25.4 (1995–1996): 112–29.

Booth, Wayne. *The Rhetoric of Fiction*. Chicago: University of Chicago Press, 1961.

Bosman, Henrik. "Adultery, Prophetic Tradition, and the Decalogue." Pages 21–30 in *Wünschet Jerusalem Frieden: Collected Communications to the XIIth Congress of the International Organization for the Study of the Old Testament, Jerusaelm 1986*. Edited by Marrhias Augustin and Klaus-Dietrick Schunk. Frankfurt am Main: Lang, 1988.

Bosworth, David. "Faith and Resilience: King David's Reaction to the Death of Bathsheba's Firstborn." *CBQ* 73.4 (2011): 691–707.

Breed, Brennan. "A Divided Tongue: The Moral Taste Buds of the Book of Daniel." *JSOT* 40 (2015): 113–30.

Brenner, Athalya. "Job the Pious? The Characterization of Job in the Framework of the Book." *JSOT* 43 (1989): 37–52.

———. "The Integrity of Job 1 and 42:11–17." *CBQ* 76 (2014): 230–51.
Brichto, Herbert Chanan. "Case of the the *Śōṭā*," *HUCA* 46 (1975): 55–70.
Broshi, Magen. "Expansion of Jerusalem in the Reigns of Hezekiah and Manasseh." *IEJ* 24 (1974): 21–26.
Brown, William P., ed. *The Oxford Handbook of the Psalms*. New York: Oxford University Press, 2014.
Brueggeman, Walter. "Introduction." Page vii in *A Whirlpool of Torment: Israelite Traditions of God as an Oppressive Presence*. Edited by James L. Crenshaw. Philadelphia: Fortress, 1984.
———. "Faith in the Empire." Pages 25–40 in *In the Shadow of Empire: Reclaiming the Bible as a History of Faithful Resistance*. Edited by Richard A. Horsley. Louisville: Westminster John Knox, 2008.
———. *Out of Babylon*. Nashville: Abingdon, 2010.
Bullard, Roger A. "The Hypostasis of the Archons (II, 4)." Page 161–69 in *The Nag Hammadi Library in English*. Edited by James Robinson. New York: Brill, 1996.
Butler, Judith. *Undoing Gender*. New York: Routledge, 2004.
Byron, Gay, and Vanessa Lovelace, eds. *Womanist Interpretations of the Bible: Expanding the Discourse*. Atlanta: Society of Biblical Literature, 2016.
Camp, Claudia V. "The Wise Women of 2 Samuel: A Role Model for Women in Early Israel?" *CBQ* 43 (1981): 14–29.
Carmichael, Calcum M. *The Origins of Biblical Law: The Decalogues and the Book of the Covenant*. Ithaca: Cornell University, 1992.
Ch'oe, Young-Ho, ed. *From the Land of Hibiscus: Koreans in Hawai'i 1903–1950*. Honolulu: University of Hawai'i Press, 2006.
Cha, Marn J. *Koreans in Central California (1903–1957): A Study of Settlement and Transnational Politics*. Lanham, MD: University Press of America, 2010.
Chan, Sucheng, ed. *The Vietnamese American 1.5 Generation: Stories of War, Revolution, Flight and New Beginnings*. Philadelphia, PA: Temple University Press, 2006.
Charlesworth, J. H. "Manasseh, Prayer of." *ABD* 4:499–500.
Childs, Brevard S. *Exodus*. OTL. Louisville: Westminster, 1974.
Chin, Gabriel J., and Rose Cuison Villazor, eds. *The Immigration and Nationality Act of 1965: Legislating a New America*. New York: Cambridge University Press, 2015.
Cho, Eunsik. "The Great Revival of 1907 in Korea: Its Cause and Effect." *Missiology* 26.3 (1998): 289–300.
Cho, Haejoang. "Male Dominance and Mother Power." Pages 187–207 in *Confucianism and the Family*. Edited by Walter H. Slote and George A. De Vos. SUNY Series in Chinese Philosophy and Culture. Albany, NY: State University of New York Press, 1998.

Cho, K-K. "Job 2 and 42:7–10 as Narrative Bridge and Theological Pivot." *JBL* 136 (2017): 857–77.

———. "'I Have Become a Brother of Jackals': Evolutionary Psychology and Suicide in the Book of Job." *BibInt* (forthcoming).

———. "The Integrity of Job 1 and 42:11–17." *CBQ* 76 (2014): 230–51.

Choi, Jin Young. "Asian/Asian American Interpretation." Pages 1–9 in *The Oxford Encyclopedia of the Bible and Gender Studies*. Edited by Julia M. O'Brien. Oxford: Oxford University Press, 2014.

Chong, Joong-Ho. "A Study on Manasseh's Religious Policy." *Studies in Religion* 17 (1999): 213–33.

Clark, Francis E. "Do Foreign Missions Pay?" *NAR* (1898): 268–80.

Cleath, Lisa. "Reading Ceremonies in the Hebrew Bible: Ideologies of Textual Authority in Joshua 8, 2 Kings 23, Nehemiah 8." UCLA, PhD Dissertation, 2016.

Clines, D. A. *Ezra, Nehemiah, Esther*. Grand Rapids: Eerdmans, 1984.

Clines, David J. *Job 38–42*. WBC 18B. Nashville: Thomas Nelson, 2011.

Cogan, Mordechai and Hayim Tadmor. *II Kings: A New Translation*. Garden City: Doubleday, 1988.

Cohen, Shaye J. D. *The Beginnings of Jewishness: Boundaries, Varieties, Uncertainties*. Berkeley: University of California Press, 1999.

Collins, John J. *Daniel*. Hermeneia. Minneapolis: Fortress, 1993.

———. *The Bible after Babel: Historical Criticism in a Postmodern Age*. Grand Rapids. Eerdmans, 2005.

Coltrane, Scott, and Randall Collins. *Sociology of Marriage and the Family: Gender, Love, and Property*. 5th ed. Wadsworth, 2000.

Confucius. *Confucius Analects: With Selection from Traditional Commentaries*. Translated by Edward Gilman Slingerland. Indianapolis: Hackett, 2003.

Conroy-Krutz, Emily. *Christian Imperialism: Converting the World in the Early American Republic*. New York: Cornell University Press, 2015.

Coogan, Michael. *The Ten Commandments: A Short History of an Ancient Text*. New Haven: Yale University Press, 2014.

Coser, Lewis A., ed. *Maurice Halbwachs On Collective Memory*. Chicago: University of Chicago Press, 1992.

Crenshaw, James L. "Popular Questioning of the Justice of God in Ancient Israel." *ZAW* 82 (1970): 380–95.

———. *Defending God: Biblical Responses to the Problem of Evil*. Oxford: Oxford University Press, 2005.

———. *Theodicy in the Old Testament*. Philadelphia: Fortress, 1983.

Crompton, Samuel Willard. *Cyrus the Great*. New York: Chelsea House, 2008.

Cross, Frank Moore. *Canaanite Myth and Hebrew Epic: Essays in the History of the Religion of Israel*. Cambridge: Harvard University Press, 1973.

Cumings, Bruce. *The Origins of the Korean War*. 2 vols. Princeton: Princeton University Press, 1981–1992.

———. "American Policy towards Korean Liberation." Pages 39–93 in *Without Parallel: The American-Korean Relationship since 1945*. Edited by Frank Baldwin. New York: Pantheon, 1974.

Curtis, John Briggs. "On Job's Response to Yahweh." *JBL* 89 (1979): 497–511.

Dailey, Thomas F. "And Yet He Repents—On Job 42,6." *ZAW* 105 (1993): 205–9.

Danico, Mary Yu. *The 1.5 Generation: Becoming Korean American in Hawaii*. Honolulu: University of Hawaii Press, 2004.

"Dao De Jing 1, 2, 32." Translated by James Legge et al. http://ctext.org/dao-de-jing.

"Dao De Jing 2." Translated by Derek Lin. http://www.taoism.net/ttc/complete.htm.

Darr, Katheryn P. "Ezekiel." Pages 192–200 in *Women's Bible Commentary*. Edited by Carol Newsom and Sharon H. Ringe. Louisville: Westminster John Knox Press, 1998.

Davison, Andrew et al. "Europe and Its Boundaries: Toward a Global Hermeneutic Political Theory." Pages 83–111 in *Europe and Its Boundaries: Words and Worlds, Within and Beyond*. Edited by A. Davison and H. Muppidi. Lanham, MD: Rowman & Littlefield, 2009.

de Boer, P. A. H. "Does Job Retract? (Job xlii 6)." Pages 179–95 in *Selected Studies in Old Testament Exegesis*. Edited by C. van Duin. OTS 27. Leiden: Brill, 1991.

de Certeau, Michel. *The Practice of Everyday Life*. Translated by Steven Rendall. Berkeley: University of California Press, 1984.

der Lugt, Pietervan. "Who Changes His Mind about Dust and Ashes? The Rhetorical Structure of Job 42:2–6." *VT* 64 (2014): 623–39.

DeMaris, Alfred. "Burning the Candle at Both Ends: Extramatrial Sex as a Precursor of Martial Disruption." *Journal of Family Issues* 34.11 (2013): 1474–1499.

Derrida, Jacques. *Writing and Difference*. Translated by A. Bass. Chicago: University of Chicago Press, 1967.

Deuchler, Martina. *The Confucian Transformation of Korea: A Study of Society and Ideology*. Harvard-Yenching Institute Monograph Series 36. Cambridge: Council on East Asian Studies, Harvard University Press, 1992.

———. Propagating Female Virtues in Choson Korea." In *Women and Confucian Cultures in Premodern China, Korea, and Japan*. Edited by Dorothy Ko, JaHyun Kim Haboush, and Joan R. Piggott. Berkeley: University of California Press, 2003.

Dhorme, Édouard. *A Commentary on the Book of Job*. Translated by Harold Knight. Nashville: Nelson Publishers, 1984.

Dikov, Ivan. "Archaeologists Discover 7,000-Year-Old Fortress Wall in Prehistoric Settlement near Bulgaria's Hotnitsa." *Archaeology in Bulgaria* (2016).

Dillard, Raymond B. *An Introduction to the Old Testament*. Grand Rapids: Zondervan, 1994.

Douglas, Mary. *Purity and Danger: An Analysis of Concepts of Pollution and Taboo*. London: Routledge Classics, 2002.

Driver, Samuel Rolles, and George Buchanan Gray. *A Critical and Exegetical Commentary on the Book of Job, Together with a New Translation*. Edinburgh: T&T Clark, 1977.

Duncan, John. "The Korean Adoption of Neo-Confucianism: The Social Context." In *Confucianism and the Family*. Edited by Walter H. Slote and George A. De Vos. SUNY Series in Chinese Philosophy and Culture. Albany, NY: State University of New York Press, 1998.

Dunn, James. *The New Perspective on Paul*. Grand Rapids: Eerdmans, 2008.

Durham, John I. *Exodus*. WBC. Waco, TX: Word Books, 1987.

Eckert, Carter J., et al. *Korea Old and New: A History*. Cambridge: Harvard University Press, 1990.

Eden, Anthony. *The Reckoning: The Memoirs of Anthony Eden, Earl of Avon*. Boston: Houghton Mifflin, 1965

Ecklund, Elaine Howard. *Korean American Evangelicals: New Models for Civic Life*. New York: Oxford University Press, 2008.

Elliott, John. "Envy, Jealousy, and Zeal in The Bible: Sorting out the Social Differences and Theological Implications—No Envy for YHWH." Pages 344–64 in *To Break Every Yoke: Essays in Honor of Marvin L. Chaney*. Edited by Robert Coote and Norman Gottwald. Sheffield: Sheffield Phoenix, 2007.

———. "God-Zealous or Jealous but Never Envious: The Theological Consequences of Linguistic and Social Distinctions." In *Social Sciences and Biblical Translation*. Edited by Dietmar Neufeld. Atlanta: Society of Biblical Literature, 2008.

Erbil, Yiğit, and Alice Mouton. "Water in Ancient Anatolian Religions: An Archaeoloigcal and Philological Inquiry on the Hittite Evidence." *JNES* 71 (2012): 53–74.

Eril, Astrid, and Ansgar Nünning, eds. *A Companion to Cultural Memory Studies*. Berlin: de Grutyer, 2010.

Feinstein, Eve L. "The 'Bitter Waters' of Numbers 5:11–31." *VT* 62 (2012): 300–306.

Feinstein, J. Sasson. "Numbers 5 and the 'Waters of Judgment.'" *BZ* 16 (1972): 249–51.

Felder, Cain Hope, ed. *Stony the Road We Trod: African American Biblical Interpretation*. Minneapolis: Fortress, 1991.

Fewell, Danna Nolan. "Judges." Pages 73–83 in *Women's Bible Commentary*. Expanded Edition. Edited by Carol A. Newsom and Sharon H. Ringe. Louisville: Westminster John Knox, 1998.

———. "Space for Moral Agency in the Book of Ruth." *JSOT* 40 (2015):79–96.

Finkelstein, Israel. "Saul, Benjamin and the Emergence of 'Biblical Israel': An Alternative View." *ZAW* 123 (2011): 348–67.

———. "The Settlement History of Jerusalem in the Eighth and Seventh Century BC." *RB* 115 (2008): 499–515.
Fiorenza, Elisabeth Schüssler. *In Memory of Her: A Feminist Theological Reconstruction of Christian Origins*. New York: Crossroad, 1983.
———. *Rhetoric and Ethic: The Politics of Biblical Studies*. Minneapolis: Fortress, 1999.
Fishbane, Michael. "Jeremiah IV 23–26 and Job III 3–13: A Rediscovered Use of the Creation Pattern." *VT* 21 (1971): 151–67.
Fohrer, Georg. "The Righteous Man in Job 31." Pages 3–22 in *Essays in Old Testament Ethics. J. Philip Hyatt, In Memoriam*. Edited by James L. Crenshaw and John T. Willis. New York: Ktav, 1974.
———. *Das Buch Hiob*. KAT 16. Gütersloh: Gütersloher Verlagshaus G. Mohn 1963.
Foley, John Miles. "Plenitude and Diversity: Interactions between Orality and Writing." Pages 116–17 in *The Interface of Orality and Writing: Speaking, Seeing, Writing in the Shaping of New Genres*. Edited by Annette Weissenrieder and Robert B. Coote. WUNT 260. Tübingen: Mohr Siebeck, 2010.
Foskett, Mary, and Jeffrey Kuan, eds. *Ways of Being, Ways of Reading: Asian American Biblical Interpretation*. St. Louis: Chalice, 2006.
Foucault, Michel. *The History of Sexuality*. Vintage Books ed. New York: Vintage Books, 1990.
———. *Discipline and Punish: The Birth of the Prison*. Translated by Alan Sheridan. 2nd ed. New York: Vintage Books, 1995.
Fox, Michael V. "God's Answer and Job's Response." *Biblica* 94 (2013): 1–23.
———. "Job the Pious." *ZAW* 117 (2005): 351–66.
———. "Reading the Tale of Job." Pages 145–62 in *A Critical Engagement: Essays on the Hebrew Bible in Honour of J. Cheryl Exum*. Edited by David J. A. Clines and Ellen van Wolde. HBM 38. Sheffield: Sheffield Phoenix, 2011.
Fox, Michael V. *Proverbs 10–31: A New Translation with Introduction and Commentary*. AB 18B. New Haven: Yale University Press, 2009.
Fram, Edward. "Two Cases of Adultery and the Halakhic Decision Making Process." *AJS Review* 26.2 (2002): 277–300.
Fretheim, Terence. *Exodus*. IBC. Louisville: John Knox.
Freud, Sigmund. "On Narcissism: An Introduction." In *The Freud Reader*. Edited by Peter Gay. New York: Norton, 1995.
———. "A Special Type of Choice of Object Made by Men (Contributions to the Psychology of Love I)." In *The Freud Reader*. Edited by Peter Gay. New York: Norton, 1995.
Fried, Lisbeth S. *Ezra: A Commentary*. Sheffield: Sheffield Phoenix, 2015.
Frymer-Kensky, Tikva. "Strange Case of the Suspected Sotah (Numbers V:11–31." *VT* 34 (1984): 11–26.
Fullerton, Kember. "The Original Conclusion to the Book of Job." *ZAW* 42 (1924): 116–36.

Gadamer, Hans-Georg. *Wahrheit und Methode*. Tübingen: Mohr Siebeck, 1960.

———. *Truth and Method*. New York: Crossroad, 1989.

Galambush, Julie. *Jerusalem in the Book of Ezekiel: The City as Yahweh's wife*. Atlanta: Scholars Press, 1992.

Gardner-Chloros, Penelope. *Code-Switching*. Cambridge: Cambridge University Press, 2009.

Garsiel, Moshe. "The Story of David and Bathsheba: A Different Approach." *CBQ* 55.2 (1993): 244–62.

Giddens, Anthony. *Modernity and Self-Identity*. Stanford: Stanford University Press, 1991.

Girard, René. *The Scapegoat*. London: Athlone, 1986.

Goetze, Albrecht, trans. "Instructions for Temple Officials." *ANET* (1955): 207–11.

Goffman, Erving. *The Presentation of the Self in Everyday Life*. Garden City, NY: Doubleday, 1959.

Good, Edwin M. *In Turns of Tempest: A Reading of Job, with a translation*. Stanford: Stanford University Press, 1990.

Gordis, R. *The Book of God and Man: A Study of Job*. Chicago: University of Chicago Press, 1965.

Grabbe, Lester L. "The Seleucid and Hasmonean Periods and the Apocalyptic Worldview—An Introduction." Pages 11–31 in *The Seleucid and Hasmonean Periods and the Apocalyptic Worldview: The First Enoch Seminar Nangeroni Meeting*. Edited by L. L. Grabbe and G. Boccaccini. London: T&T Clark, 2016.

Grabbe, Lester L., ed. *Good Kings and Bad Kings*. LHBOTS 393. London: T&T Clark, 2005.

———. *Ezra-Nehemiah*. New York: Routledge, 1998.

Granados, Jos, Carolos Granados, and Luis Snchez-Navarro, eds. *Opening Up the Scriptures: Joseph Ratzinger and the Foundations of Biblical Interpretations*. Grand Rapids: Eerdmans, 2008.

Grätz, Sebastian. *Das Edikt des Artaxerxes: Eine Untersuchen zum religionspolitischen und historischen Umfeld von Esra*. Berlin: de Gruyter, 2004.

Greenberg, Moshe. "The Decalogue Tradition Critically Examined." Pages 83–119 in *The Ten Commandments in History and Tradition*. Magnes Press, Hebrew University of Jerusalem, 1990.

———. *Ezekiel 1–20: A New Translation with Introduction and Commentary*. NY: Doubleday, 1993.

Greenstein, Edward L. "In Job's Face/Facing Job." Pages 301–17 in *The Labour of Reading: Desire, Alienation, and Biblical Interpretation*. Edited by Fiona C. Black, Roland Boer, and Erin Runions. Atlanta: Society of Biblical Literature, 1999.

Gruen, Erich S. *Heritage and Hellenism: The Reinvention of Jewish Tradition*. Berkeley: University of California Press, 1998.

Guillaume, Philippe. "Jerusalem 720–705 BCE: No Flood of Israelite Refugees." *SJOT* 22 (2008): 195–211.

Gumperz, John J., and Jan-Petter Blom. "Social Meaning in Linguistic Structures: Code Switching in Northern Norway." Pages 407–34 in *Sociolinguistics: Current Trends and Prospects*. Edited by R. Shuy. Georgetown: Georgetown University Press, 1972.

Gunn, David M. "Narrative Criticism." Pages 201–29 in *To Each Its Own Meaning: An Introduction to Biblical Criticisms and Their Application*. Edited by Steven L. McKenzie and Stephen R. Haynes. Louisville: Westminster John Knox.

Gunn, David M., and Danna Nolan Fewell. *Narrative in the Hebrew Bible*. New York: Oxford University Press, 1993.

Gunnerweg, Antonius. *Esra*. Gütersloh: Gütersloh Verlagshaus Mohn, 1985.

Habel, Norman C. "The Verdict on/of God at the End of Job." Pages 27–38 in *Job's God*. Edited by Ellen van Wolde. London: SCM, 2004.

———. *The Book of Job: A Commentary*. Philadelphia: Westminster, 1985.

Hadjiev, Tchavdar. "Adultery, Shame, and Sexual Pollution in Ancient Israel and in Hosea: A Response to Joshua Moon." *JSOT* 41.2 (2016): 221–36.

Han, Jin Hee. *Daniel's Spiel: Apocalyptic Literacy in the Book of Daniel*. Lanham, MD: University Press of America, 2008.

Han, Ju Hui Judy. "Contemporary Korean/American Evangelical Missions: Politics of Space, Gender, and Difference." PhD diss., University of California, Berkeley, 2009.

Han, Sharon K. "Cross-Discipline Trafficking: What's Justice Got to Do with It?" Pages 76–103 in *Orientations: Mapping Studies in the Asian Diaspora*. Edited by K. Chuh and K. Shimakawa. Durham: Duke University Press, 2001.

Harrelson, Walter J. *Ten Commandments and Human Rights*. Macon, GA: Mercer University Press, 1997.

Havea, Jione, and Peter H. W. Lau, eds. *Reading Ruth in Asia*. Atlanta: SBL Press, 2015.

Havea, Jione, Margaret Aymer, and Steed Vernyl Davidson, eds. *Island, Islanders, and the Bible*. Atlanta: SBL Press, 2015.

Havea, Jione, David J. Neville, and Elaine M. Wainwright, eds. *Bible, Borders, Belonging(s): Engaging Readings from Oceania*. Atlanta: SBL Press, 2014.

Heller, Roy L. "'But If Not …' What?: The Speech of the Youths in Daniel 3 and a (Theo)Logical Problem." Pages 244–55 in *Thus Says the Lord: Essays on the Former and Latter Prophets in Honor of Robert R. Wilson*. Edited by John J. Ahn and Stephen L. Cook. LHBOTS 502. New York: T&T Clark, 2009.

Henderson, Gregory. *Korea, the Politics of the Vortex*. Cambridge: Harvard University Press, 1968.

Hobbs, T. R. *2 Kings*. Waco, TX: Word Books, 1985.

Hoffner, Harry A., Jr., and H. Craig Melchert. *A Grammar of the Hittite Language*: *Part 1 Reference Grammar*. Winona Lake: Eisenbrauns, 2008.
Hogue, Timothy. "Return from Exile: Diglossia and Literary Code-Switching in Ezra 1–7." *ZAW* (forthcoming).
Holter, Knut. "Geographical and Institutional Aspects of Global Old Testament Studies." Pages 3–14 in *Global Hermeneutics: Reflections and Consequences*. Edited by Knut Holter and Louis C. Jonker. Atlanta: Society of Biblical Literature, 2010.
Horovitz, Haim S., ed. *Siphre d'be Rab: Siphre ad Numeros adjector Siphre zutta*. Jerusalem: Wahrmann, 1917. Repr., Leipzig, 1966.
Howard, Cameron. "Writing Yehud: Textuality and Power under Persian Rule." PhD Diss., Emory University, 2010.
Hwang, Yong-Yeon. "The Person Attacked by the Robbers Is Christ: An Exploration of Subjectivity from the Perspective of Minjung Theology." Pages 215–31 in *Reading Minjung Theology in the Twenty-First Century: Selected Writings by Ahn Byung-Mu and Modern Critical Responses*. Edited by Yung Suk Kim and Chin-ho Kim. Eugene, OR: Pickwick, 2013.
Hunermann, Heinrich Denzinger-Peter. *Enchiridion Symbolorum*: *A Compendium of Creeds, Definitions and Declarations of the Catholic Church*. San Francisco: Ignatius Press, 2012.
Hurvitz, Avi. "Hebrew and Aramaic in the Biblical Period: The Problem of 'Aramaisms' in the Linguistic Research of the Hebrew Bible." Pages 24–37 in *Biblical Hebrew: Studies in Typology and Chronology*. Editor Ian Young. Sheffield: Sheffield Academic Press, 2003.
Hyung muk, Choi, and Cho Ha mu. "한국 그리스도교 민중공동체의 성서해석" ["Methods of Biblical Interpretation in Korean Minjung Christian Communities"]. *Theological Thought* 63 (1988): 811–45.
Jacbos, Sandra, ed. *The Dynamics of Early Judean Law: Studies in the Diversity of Ancient Social and Communal Legislation*. BZAW. Berlin: de Gruyter, forthcoming.
Jackson, Bernard. "The 'Institution' of Marriage and Divorce in the Hebrew Bible." *JSS* 56.2 (2011): 221–51.
Jackson, Michael D. *Minima Ethnographica: Intersubjectivity and the Anthropological Project*. Chicago: University of Chicago Press, 1998.
———. *The Politics of Storytelling: Violence, Transgression, and Intersubjectivity*. Copenhagen: Museum Tusculanum, 2002.
———. *Things as They Are: New Directions in Phenomenological Anthropology*. Bloomington, Indiana: Indiana University Press, 1996.
Jacobsen, Thorkild. *The Harps that Once …: Sumerian Poetry in Translation*. New Haven: Yale University Press, 1987.
Jakobson, Roman. "Closing Statement: Linguistics and Poetics." Pages 360–77 in *Style in Language*. Edite by Thomas A. Sebeok. New York: The Technology Press of the Massachusetts Institute of Technology, 1960.

———. "Part II: Two Aspects of Language and Two Types of Aphasic Disturbance." Pages 67–96 in *Fundamentals of Language*. Edited by Roman Jakobson and Moris Halle. Rev. and repr., Berlin: de Gruyter, 1975.

Jang, Se-Hoon. *Particularism and Universalism in the Book of Isaiah: Isaiah's Implications for a Pluralistic World from a Korean Perspective*. Bern: Lang, 2005.

Jansen, Marius B. "Japanese Imperialism: Late Meiji Perspectives." Pages 61–79 in *The Japanese Colonial Empire, 1895–1945*. Edited by R. H. Myers and M. R. Peattie. Princeton: Princeton University Press, 1984.

Janzen, J. Gerald. *Job*. Atlanta: John Knox, 1985.

Jones, Barry A. "Resisting the Power of Empire: The Theme of Resistance in the Book of Daniel." *Review and Expositor* 109 (2012): 541–56.

Jones, Stanton L. "My Genes Made Me Do It: Evolutionary Psychology May Explain Why We Commit Adultery–But Not Why We Don't." *Christianity Today* 39.5 (1995): 14–18.

Jonker, Louis C. "Living in Different Worlds Simultaneously. Or: A Pleas for Contextual Integrity." Pages 107–19 in *African and European Readers of the Bible in Dialogue: In Quest of a Shared Meaning*. Edited by J. H. de Wit and G. O. West. Leiden: Brill, 2008.

———. "The Global Context and Its Consequences for Old Testament Interpretation." Pages 47–56 in *Global Hermeneutics: Reflections and Consequences*. Edited by Knut Holter and Louis C. Jonker. Atlanta: Society of Biblical Literature, 2010.

Joselit, Jenna Weissman. *Set in Stone: America's Embrace of the Ten Commandments*. Oxford: Oxford University Press, 2017.

Jung, Seokgyu. "Dual Functions of Manasseh's Sin (2 Kings 21: 1–18) in the Deuteronomistic History." *Korean Journal of Old Testament Studies* 16.2 (2010): 30–52.

Kaminsky, Joel S. "The Sins of the Fathers: A Theological Investigation of the Biblical Tension between Corporate and Individualized Retribution." *Judaism* 46 (1997): 319–32.

Kang, In-ch'ŏl. 한국기독교회와 국가, 시민사회 [*Church, State, and Civil Society in Korea: 1945–1960*]. Seoul: The Institute of Korean Christian History, 2003.

Kang, Nam-Soon. *Diasporic Feminist Theology: Asia and Theopolitical Imagination*. Minneapolis: Fortress, 2014.

Kang, Sa-Moon. *Divine War in the Old Testament and in the Ancient Near East*. BZAW 177. Berlin: de Gruyter, 1989.

Kautzsch, E. *Die Aramaismem im Alten Testament. I: Lexicalischer Teil* (Halle), 1902.

Kelly, Brian E. "Retribution Revisited: Covenant, Grace, and Restoration." Pages 206–27 in *The Chronicler as Theologian: Essays in Honor of Ralph W. Klein*.

Edited by M. Patrick Graham, Steven L. McKenzie, and Gary N. Knoppers. JSOTSup 371. London: T&T Clark, 2003.

Kim, Baek-yung. "Colonial Assimilationism and Urban Space: Joseon Shrine in Colonial Seoul, 1920–30s" [Korean]. *Incheon International Studies* 11 (2009): 59–82.

Kim, Chan-Hie. "Reading the Bible as Asian Americans." *NIB* 1:161–66.

Kim, Chul-Soo. "Criticism on Religious Policies of the Japan Government-General of Choseon" [Korean]. *Journal for the Institute of Humanities at Soonchunhyang University* 27 (2010): 155–91.

Kim, Dong-choon. *Why, South Korea* [Korean]. Seoul: Sakyejul, 2015.

Kim, Hakseo. "A Re-evaluation on King Manasseh and the Theological Implications: 2 Kings 21:1–18 and 2 Chronicles 33:1–20." Th.M. Thesis. Yonsei University, 2013.

Kim, Hyun Chul Paul, and M. Fulgence Nyengele. "Pursing Happiness across Cultures: Positive Psychology, Ecclesiastes, African *Ubuntu*, and Korean *Jeong* in Creative Dialogues." Pages 29–43 in *Bridging the Divide between the Bible and Pastoral Theology*. Edited by D. D. Hopkins and M. Koppel. Newcastle, UK: Cambridge Scholars, 2018.

Kim, Hyun Chul Paul. "Currents in Korean-American Biblical Interpretation" *Journal of Korean American Ministries and Theology* (2012): 7–19.

———. "Dietrich Bonhoeffer, Dongju Yun, and the Legacies of Jeremiah and Suffering Servant." In *Intertextuality and the Hebrew Bible: Whence and Whither?* Edited by M. Grohmann and H. C. P. Kim. Atlanta: SBL Press, forthcoming.

———. "Metaphor, Memory, and Reality of the 'Exile' in Deutero-Isaiah." In *Images of Exile in the Prophetic Literature: Copenhagen Conference Proceedings 7–10 May 2017*. Edited by J. Høgenhaven, F. Poulsen, and C. Power. Tübingen: Mohr Siebeck, forthcoming.

———. "Reading the Joseph Story (Genesis 37–50) as a Diaspora Narrative." *CBQ* 75 (2013): 219–38.

Kim, Ki Hong. "A Study on the Education of 'Recreating the Imperial Subject' during the Period of the General Mobilization System in Wartime (1938–45) under the Japanese Imperialistic Rule: Centering on the Educational Activities of School Education" [Korean]. Master's Thesis, Yonsei University, Seoul, Korea, 2000.

Kim, Sebastian C. H., and Kirsteen Kim. *A History of Korean Christianity*. New York: Oxford University Press, 2015.

Kim, Seong Hee. *Mark, Women and Empire: A Korean Postcolonial Perspective*. Bibles in the Modern World. Sheffield: Sheffield Phoenix, 2010.

Kim, Sŭng-t'ae, and Hye-jin Pak, eds. 내한선교사 총람 [*A Comprehensive Survey of Missionaries in Korea*]. Seoul: The Institute of Korean Christian History, 1994.

Kim, Uriah Y. "Where Is the Home for the Man of Luz?" *Int* 65 (2011): 250–62.

King, Karen L. "The Book of Norea, Daughter of Eve." Pages 80–82 in *A Feminist Commentary*, vol. 2 of *Searching the Scriptures*. Edited by Elisabeth Schüssler Fiorenza. New York: Crossroads, 1994.

———. Editor's Forward to *Images of the Feminine in Gnosticism*. Edited by Karen L. King. Philadelphia: Fortress, 1988.

———. "Ridicule and Rape, Rule and Rebellion: *Hypostasis of the Archon*." Page 4 in *Gnosticism and the Early Christian World*. Edited by James Goehring et al. Sonoma: Polebridge, 1990.

———. *The Secret Revelation of John*. Cambridge: Harvard University Press, 2006.

Kirk, Alan, and Tom Thatcher, eds. *Memory, Tradition, and Text: Uses of the Past in Early Christianity*. SemeiaSt 52. Atlanta: Society of Biblical Literature, 2005.

Klein, Melanie. "Envy and Gratitude (1957)." In *Envy and Gratitude and Other Works 1946–1963: The Writings of Melanie Klein Volume III*. New York: The Free Press, 1975.

Knauf, Ernst Axel. "The Glorious Days of Manasseh." Pages 164–88 in *Good Kings and Bad Kings*. Edited by Lester L. Grabbe. LHBOTS 393. London: T&T Clark, 2005.

Knoppers, Gary. *Jews and Samaritans: The Origins and Histories of Their Early Relations*. Oxford: Oxford University Press, 2013.

Ko, Haboush, Ko Piggott, Haboush Dorothy, JaHyun Kim, and Joan R. Piggott. *Women and Confucian Cultures in Premodern China, Korea, and Japan*. Berkeley: University of California Press, 2003.

Kobe, Osamu. "Edification Policy and 'National Shintoism'" [Korean]. Pages 110–13 in *Gender Perspective on Modern and Contemporary History of Korea and Japan*. Edited by Joint-Committee of Korean and Japanese Female Historians. Paju: Hanul, 2005.

Koch, Klaus. "Is There a Doctrine of Retribution in the Old Testament?" In *Theodicy in the Old Testament*. Edited by James L. Crenshaw. Philadelphia: Fortress, 1983.

Kohut, Heinz. "On Courage (Early 1970s)." *Self Psychology and the Humanities: Reflection on a New Psychoanalytic Approach*. Edited by Charles Strozier. New York: Norton, 1985.

———. "On Leadership (1969–70)." *Self Psychology and the Humanities: Reflection on a New Psychoanalytic Approach*. Edited by Charles Strozier. New York: Norton, 1985.

———. "Thoughts on Narcissism and Narcissistic Rage (1972)." *Self Psychology and the Humanities: Reflection on a New Psychoanalytic Approach*. Edited by Charles Strozier. New York: Norton, 1985.

———. "On the Continuity of the Self and Cultural Selfobjects (February 26, 1981)." *Self Psychology and the Humanities: Reflection on a New Psychoanalytic Approach*. Edited by Charles Strozier. New York: Norton, 1985.

Kratz, Reinhard. *The Composition of the Narrative Books of the Old Testament*. Translated by John Bowden. London: T&T Clark, 2005.
Kreitzer, Larry J. and Deborah W. Rooke, ed. *Ciphers in the Sand: Interpretations of the Woman Taken in Adultery* (John 7:53–8:11). Biblical Seminar 74. Sheffield: Sheffield Academic, 2000.
Kuyper, Lester J. "The Repentance of Job." *VT* 9 (1959): 91–94.
Kwon, Ho-Young, and Kwang Chung Kim. *Korean Americans and Their Religions: Pilgrims from a Different Shore*. University Park: Penn State University Press, 2001.
Kynes, Will, ed. *An Obituary for "Wisdom Literature": The Birth, Death, and Intertextual Reintegration of a Biblical Corpus*. Oxford: Oxford University Press, forthcoming.
Lambert, David A. "Job 2 and 42:7–10 as Narrative Bridge and Theological Pivot." *JBL* 136 (2017): 857–77.
———. *How Repentance Became Biblical: Judaism, Christianity, and the Interpretation of Scripture*. Oxford: Oxford University Press, 2016.
Lasine, Stuart. "Manasseh as Villain and Scapegoat." Pages 163–83 in *The New Literary Criticism and the Hebrew Bible*. Edited by J. Cheryl Exum and David J. A. Clines. JSOT Sup 143. Sheffield: JSOT Press, 1993.
Lee, Jung Young. *Marginality: The Key to Multicultural Theology*. Minneapolis: Fortress, 1995.
Lee, Kyung Sook, and Kyung Mi Park, eds. *Korean Feminists in Conversation with the Bible, Church, and Society*. Sheffield Phoenix, 2011.
Lee, Kyung-Ha. "A Woman Intellectual in Fifteenth Century, Insu-Daebi." *Research of Korean Classical Women's Literature* 12 (2006): 149–77.
Lee, Kyung-Sook. "Neo-Confucian Ideology in the Interpretation of the Book of Ruth: Toward a Cross-checking Hermeneutics." Pages 1–13 in *Korean Feminists in Conversation with the Bible, Church and Society*. Edited by Kyung Sook Lee and Kyung Mi Park. Sheffield: Sheffield Phoenix, 2011.
Lee, Poong-In. "The Sewol Ferry Disaster and the Scapegoat Mechanism." *Presbyterian Theological Quarterly* 319 (2014): 87–112.
Lee, Sang Hyun. *From a Liminal Place: An Asian American Theology*. Minneapolis: Fortress, 2010.
Lee, Soon Gu. "The Exemplar Wife: The Life of Lady Chang of Andong in Historical Context." In *Women and Confucianism in Choson Korea: New Perspectives*. Edited by Youngmin Kim and Michael J. Pettid. Albany: State University of New York Press, 2011.
Lee, Yoon Kyoung. "Postexilic Jewish Experience and Korean Multiculturalism." Pages 3–18 in *Migration and Diaspora: Exegetical Voices from Northeast Asian Women*. Edited by Hisako Kinukawa. Atlanta: Society of Biblical Literature, 2014.
Legge, James et al., "道德經 - Dao De Jing." http://ctext.org/dao-de-jing.

Létourneau, Anne. "Beauty, Bath, and Beyond: Framing Bathsheba as a Royal Fantasy in 2 Sam 11, 1–5." *SJOT* 32 (2018): 72–91.
Leuchter, Mark. "The Aramaic Transition and the Redaction of the Pentateuch." *JBL* 136 (2017): 249–68.
Levenson, Jon D. *Creation and the Persistence of Evil: The Jewish Drama of Divine Omnipotence.* San Francisco: Harper & Row, 1988.
Levine, Baruch. *Numbers 21–36.* New York: Doubleday, 2000.
Lévêque, Jean. *Job et son Dieu: Essai d'exégèse et de théologie biblique.* 2 vols. Paris: Librairie Lecoffre, 1970.
Li, Chichang. "Doing Theology in Chinese Context: the David-Bathsheba Story and the Parable of Nathan." *East Asia Journal of Theology* 3.2 (1985): 243–57.
Liew, Tat-siong Benny, ed. *The Bible in Asian America.* Atlanta: Society of Biblical Literature, 2002.
———. *What Is Asian American Biblical Hermeneutics: Reading the New Testament.* Honolulu: University of Hawaii Press, 2008.
Lillie, Celene. *The Rape of Eve: The Transformation of Roman Ideology in Three Early Christian Retellings of Genesis.* Minneapolis: Fortress, 2017.
Lin, Derek. "Tao Te Ching: Tao and Virtue Classic." Online: http://www.taoism.net/ttc/complete.htm.
Lind, Millard. *Monotheism, Power, Justice: Collected Old Testament Essays.* TRS. Elkhart, IN: Institute of Mennonite Studies, 1990.
———. *Yahweh Is a Warrior: The Theology of Warfare in Ancient Israel.* Scottdale, PA: Herald Press, 1980.
Lochhead, David. "Monotheistic Violence." *Buddhist-Christian Studies* 21 (2001): 3–12.
Luhmann, Niklas. "Society, Meaning, Religion–Based on Self Reference." *Sociological Analysis* 46.1 (1985): 5–20.
———. *A Systems Theory of Religion.* Translated by David A. Brenner with Adrian Hermann. Stanford: Stanford University Press, 2013.
———. *Die Funktion der Religion.* Frankfurt: Suhrkamp, 1977.
———. *Die Gesellschaft der Gesellschaft.* Frankfurt am Main: Suhrkamp, 1997.
———. *The Differentiation of Society.* New York: Columbia University Press, 1982.
Lummis, C. Douglas. *Gandhi's "Dangerous" Peace-law* [Korean]. Translated by Jongchul Kim. Seoul: Greenreview, 2014.
Lyke, Larry L. *King David with the Wise Woman of Tekoa: The Resonance of Tradition in Parabolic Narrative.* LHBOTS 255. Sheffield: Sheffield Academic, 1997.
MacSwan, Jeff. "Code Switching and Linguistic Theory." Pages 221–37 in *Handbook of Bilingualism and Multilingualism.* Edited by T. K. Bhatia and W. Ritchie. Oxford: Blackwell, 2013.

Mandolfo, Carleen. *Daughter Zion Talks Back to the Prophets: A Dialogic Theology of the Book of Lamentations*. Atlanta: Society of Biblical Literature, 2007.

Mannheim, Karl. "The Problem of Generations." Pages 276–322 in *Karl Mannheim: Essays*. Edited by Paul Kecskemeti. New York: Routledge, 1952.

Markl, Domink. *The Decalogue and Its Cultural Influence*. Sheffield: Sheffield Phoenix, 2013.

Masoga, Alpheus, Norman K. Gottwald, Tinyiko S. Maluleke, Justin S. Ukpong, Gerald O. West, Jeremy Punt, Vincent L. Wimbush, and Musa W. Dube. *Reading the Bible in the Global Village: Cape Town*. GPBS 8. Leiden: Brill, 2002.

Matsutani, Motokazu. "Church over Nation: Christian Missionaries and Korean Christians in Colonial Korea." PhD diss., Harvard University, 2012.

McCarthy, Dennis J. *Treaty and Covenant: A Study in Form in the Ancient Oriental Documents and in the Old Testament*. 2nd ed. Analecta Biblica: Investigationes Scientificae in Biblicas. Rome: Biblical Institute Press, 1978.

McCourt, David M. "The 'Problem of Generations' Revisited: Karl Mannheim and the Sociology of Knowledge in International Relations." Pages 47–70 in *The Theory and Application of the "Generation" in International Relations and Politics*. Edited by Brent J. Steele and Jonathan M. Acuff. New York: Palgrave Macmillan, 2012.

McGuire, Anne. "Virginity and Subversion: Norea against the Powers in the Hypostasis of the Archons." Pages 239–58 in *Images of the Feminine in Gnosticism*. Edited by Karen L. King. Philadelphia: Fortress, 1988.

McKeating, H. "Sanctions against Adultery in Ancient Israelite Society, With Some Reflections on Methodology in the Study of Old Testament Ethics." *JSOT* 11 (1979): 57–72.

McKenzie, Steven L. *Covenant*. UBT. St. Louis: Chalice, 2000.

———. *How to Read the Bible: History, Prophecy, Literature—Why Modern Readers Need to Know the Difference, and What It Means for Faith Today*. New York: Oxford University Press, 2005.

———. *The Chronicler's Use of the Deuteronomistic History*. HSM 33. Atlanta: Scholars Press, 1985.

McKinlay, Judith E. *Troubling Women and Land Reading Biblical Texts in Aotearoa New Zealand*. Sheffield Phoenix, 2014.

McMahon, Gregory. "Instructions to Priests and Temple Officials (1.83)." IPages 217–21 in vol. 1 of *The Context of Scripture: Canonical Compositions from the Biblical World*. Edited by William W. Hallo and K. Lawson Younger Jr. Leiden: Brill, 1997.

Melammed, Ezra Zion. "'Observance' and 'Remember' Spoken in One Utterances." Pages 191–218 in *The Ten Commandments in History and Tradition*. Magnes Press, the Hebrew University of Jerusalem, 1990.

Mendels, Doron. *The Rise and Fall of Jewish Nationalism*. New York: Doubleday, 1992.
Meshorer, Ya'akov. *Ancient Jewish Coinage: Volume 1 Persian Period through Hasmoneans*. New York: Amphora Books, 1982.
Meyer, Esias E. "The Reinterpretation of the Decalogue in Leviticus 19 and the Centrality of the Cult." *SJOT* 30.2 (2016): 198–214.
Meyers, Eric M., and Mark A. Chancey. *Alexander to Constantine: Archaeology of the Land of the Bible*. Vol. 3. New Haven: Yale University Press, 2012.
Milgrom, Jacob. *Cult and Conscience: The Asham and the Priestly Doctrine of Repentance*. SJLA 18. Leiden: Brill, 1976.
———. *Leviticus 1–16: A New Translation with Introduction and Commentary*. AB 3. New York: Doubleday, 1991.
———. *The JPS Torah Commentary: Numbers*. Philadelphia: The Jewish Publication Society, 1990.
Miller, J. Hillis. "Boundaries in *Beloved*." *Symplokē* 15 (2007): 24–39.
Miller, Jared L. *Royal Hittite Instructions and Related Administrative Texts*. Edited by Mauro Giorgieri. WAW 31. Atlanta: Society of Biblical Literature, 2013.
Miller, Patrick D. *The Divine Warrior in Early Israel*. Atlanta: Society of Biblical Literature, 2006.
Miller, Stephen R. *Daniel*. Nashville: Broadman & Holman, 1994.
Mitchell, Stephen. *Tao Te Ching*. Translated by Stephen Mitchell. New York: HarperCollins Publishers, 1988.
Moffet, Samuel. *History of Christianity in Asia*. Vol 2. Maryknoll, NY: Orbis Books, 2005.
Moon, Cyris Heesuk. *A Korean Minjung Theology: An Old Testament Perspective*. Maryknoll: Orbis Books, 1995.
Moon, Seungsook. "Begetting the Nation: The Androcentric Discourse of National History and Tradition in South Korea." Pages 33–66 in *Dangerous Women: Gender and Korean Nationalism*. Edited by Elaine H. Kim and Chungmoo Choi. New York: Routledge, 1998.
———. *Militarized Modernity and Gendered Citizenship in South Korea*. Durham: Duke University Press, 2005.
Moore, Stephen. *Literary Criticism and the Gospels: The Theoretical Challenge*. New Haven: Yale University Press, 1989.
Morgan, Robert. *Biblical Interpretation*. Oxford: Oxford University Press, 1988.
Morrow, William. "Consolation, Rejection, and Repentance in Job 42:6." *JBL* 105 (1986): 211–25.
Muenchow, Charles. "Dust and Dirt in Job 42:6." *JBL* 108 (1989): 597–611.
Musharbash, Yasmine. "Marriage, Love Magic, and Adultery: Warlpiri Relationships as Seen by Three Generations of Anthropologists." *Oceania* 80 (2010): 272–88.

Na, Zhang, William L. Parish, Yingying Huang, and Suiming Pan. "Sexual Infidelity in China: Prevalence and Gender-Specific Correlates." *Arch Sex Behav* 41 (2012): 861–73.

Na'aman, Nadav. "The Growth and Development of Judah and Jerusalem in the Eighth Century BCE: A Rejoinder." *RB* 116 (2009): 321–35.

Nam, Roger S. "Unsettled Homecomings: A Repatriate Reading of Ezra-Nehemiah." In *Reading in These Times*. Edited by Benny Tat-siong Liew and Fernando Segovia. Atlanta: SBL Press, forthcoming.

———. *The Theology of the Books of Ezra and Nehemiah*. Cambridge: Cambridge University Press, forthcoming.

Na'aman, Nadav. "When and How Did Jerusalem Become a Great City? The Rise of Jerusalem as Judah's Premier City in the Eighth-Seventh Centuries B.C.E." *BASOR* 347 (2007): 21–56.

NCCK Sewol Disaster Task Force, ed. *Theology of the Remnants: The Memory, Fury, and Thereafter*. Seoul: Dongyeon, 2015.

Nelson, Richard D. *The Double Redaction of the Deuteronomistic History*. JSOTSup 18. Sheffield: University of Sheffield, 1981.

Neusner, Jacob. "The Ten Commandments." Pages 157–58 in *Common Ground: A Priest and a Rabbi Read Scripture Together*. Edited by Andrew M. Greeley and Jacob Neusner. Cleveland: Pilgrim, 1996.

Newell, Lynne. "Job Repentant or Rebellious?" *WTJ* 46 (1984): 298–316.

Newsom, Carol A. "The Book of Job." *NIB* 4:317–637.

———. *Daniel*. OTL. Louisville: Westminster John Knox, 2014.

Oh, Taek Hyun. "Manasseh in the Deuteronomistic History." *Theology and Ministry* 31 (2009): 63–76.

Olson, Dennis. *The Death of the Old and the Birth of the New: The Framework of the Book of Numbers and the Pentateuch*. Chico, CA: Scholars Press, 1985.

———. "Negotiating Boundaries: The Old and New Generations and the Theology of Numbers." *Interpretation: A Journal of Bible and Theology* 51.3 (1997): 229–40.

Ortlund, Dane C. *Zeal without Knowledge: The Concept of Zeal in Romans 10, Galatians 1, and Philippians 3*. LNTS 472. London: T&T Clark, 2012.

Oswalt, John N. *The Book of Isaiah: Chapters 40–66*. NICOT 16. Grand Rapids: Eerdmans, 1998.

Pace, Sharon. *Daniel*. SHBC. Macon, GA: Smyth & Helwys, 2008.

Page, Hug R. Jr., ed. *The Africana Bible: Reading Israel's Scriptures from Africa and the African Diaspora*. Minneapolis: Fortress, 2010.

Pagels, Elaine H. *Adam and Eve and the Serpent in Genesis 1–3*. Berkley: University of California, 2009.

———. "Pursuing the Spiritual Eve: Imagery and Hermeneutics in the *Hypostasis of the Archons* and the *Gospel of Philip*." Pages 187–210 in *Images of the Feminine in Gnosticism*. Edited by Karen L. King. Harrisburg: Trinity Press International, 1988.

Palumbo-Liu, David. *Asian/American: Historical Crossings of a Racial Frontier.* Stanford: Stanford University Press, 1999.

Park, Chung-Shin. *Protestantism and Politics in Korea.* Seattle: University of Washington Press, 2003.

Park, Kyeyoung. *The Korean American Dream: Immigrants and Small Business in New York City.* Ithaca, NY: Cornell University Press, 1997.

Park, Kyung-Soo. "A Strategy of Japanese Colonial Rule and Shinto Shrine: Especially from a Geographical Point of View" [Korean]. *Korean Journal of Japanese Language and Literature* 72 (2016): 501–22.

Park, Yungsik. *Where Was God on That Day? Sewol and the Task of Christian Faith.* Seoul: Holy Wave Plus, 2015.

Patrick, Dale Patrick. "Job's Address of God." *ZAW* 91 (1979): 268–82.

Patterson, Wayne. *The Ilse: First-Generation Korean Immigrants in Hawaii 1903–1973.* Honolulu: University of Hawaii Press, 2000.

Pearson, Birger A. "Revisiting Norea." Pages 265–66 in *Images of the Feminine in Gnosticism.* Edited by Karen L. King. Harrisburg: Trinity Press International, 1988.

Perdue, Leo G., and Warren Carter. *Israel and Empire: A Postcolonial History of Israel and Early Judaism.* London: T&T Clark, 2015.

Philips, Anthony. "Another Look at Adultery." *JSOT* 20 (1981): 3–25.

———. *Ancient Israel's Criminal Law: A New Approach to the Decalogue.* New York: Schocken, 1970.

Polak, Frank H. "Sociolinguistics and the Judean Speech Community in the Achaemenid Empire." Pages 589–628 in *Judah and Judeans in the Persian Period.* Edited by O. Lipschitz and M. Oeming. Winona Lake: Eisenbrauns, 2006.

Pole, Marvin H. *Job.* AB 15. Garden City, New York: Doubleday, 1965.

Polzin, Robert. *Moses and the Deuteronomist: A Literary Study of the Deuteronomic History: Deuteronomy, Joshua, Judges.* Bloomington: Indiana University Press, 1980.

———. *Samuel and the Deuteronomist: A Literary Study of the Deuteronomic History: 1 Samuel.* San Francisco: Harper & Row, 1989.

Poplack, Shana. "Sometimes I'll Start a Sentence in Spanish Y TERMINO EN ESPAÑOL: Toward a Typology of Code-Switching." *Linguistics* 18 (1980): 581–618.

Portier-Young, Anathea. "Languages of Identity and Obligation: Daniel as Bilingual Book." *VT* 60 (2010): 98–115.

———. *Apocalypse against Empire: Theologies of Resistance in Early Judaism.* Grand Rapids: Eerdmans, 2011.

Pritchard, James B. *Ancient Near Eastern Texts Relating to the Old Testament.* 2nd ed. Princeton: Princeton University Press, 1955.

Prior, Michael. *The Bible and Colonialism: A Moral Critique.* Sheffield: Sheffield Academic, 1997.

Pui-Lan, Kwok. *Postcolonial Imagination and Feminist Theology*. Louisville: Westminster John Knox, 2005.

Purdue, Leo G. *Wisdom Literature: A Theological History*. Louisville: Westminster John Knox, 2007.

Quddus, Abul Hasnat Golam. "Behind the Myth of Puritan Bangladesh: Pre-and Extra Marital Sexual Reality Among Lower-Class Urban Men." *Journal of Comparative Family Studies* 46.4 (2015): 451–66.

Queen Sohye. *Naehun*. Edited by Kyung Ha Lee. Seoul: Hangil-Sa, 2011.

Raisanen, Heikki, Elisabeth Schüssler Fiorenza, R. S. Sugirtharajah, Krister Stendahl, and James Barr. *Reading the Bible in the Global Village: Helsinki*. Atlanta: Society of Biblical Literature, 2000.

Rendsburg, Gary. "Linguistic Variation and the 'Foreign' Factor in the Bible." Pages 1–16 in *Language and Culture in the Near East*. Edited by Shlomo Iz'real and Rina Drory. Leiden: Brill, 1995.

Reuven, Firestone. "Holy War Idea in the Hebrew Bible." Center for Muslim-Jewish Engagement, University of Southern California. http://www.usc.edu/org/cmje/articles/holy-war-bible.php.

Reventlow, Henning Graf and Yair Hoffman Yair, eds. *The Decalogue in Jewish and Christian Tradition*. LHBOTS 509. London: T&T Clark, 2011.

Rhie, Deok-Joo. *Martyr for Love: A Study of Life and Theological Thought of the Rev. Choo Ki-Chul* [Korean]. Icheon: The Korean Church History Museum. 2003..

Rhode, Deborah L. *Adultery: Infidelity and the Law*. Cambridge: Harvard University Press, 2016.

Robertson, David. "The Book of Job: A Literary Study." *Soundings* 56 (1973): 446–69.

———. "The Comedy of Job: A Response." *Semeia* 7 (1977): 41–44.

Robinson, James M., ed. *The Nag Hammadi Library in English*. 3rd ed. San Francisco: Harper San Francisco, 1990.

Roth, Martha T. *Law Collections from Mesopotamia and Asia Minor*. 2nd ed. WAW 6. Atlanta: Scholars Press, 1997.

Rowley, H. H. *Job*. Melbourne: Nelson, 1970.

Ruiz, Jean-Pierre. "The Bible and Latino/a Theology." Pages 111–28 in *The Wiley Blackwell Companion to Latino/a Theology*. Edited by Orlando O. Espin and Chichester West Sussex. UK: Wiley & Sons, 2015.

Ryu, Dae Young. "Understanding Early American Missionaries in Korea (1884–1910): Capitalist Middle-Class Values and the Weber Thesis." *ASSR* 46 (2001): 93–117.

Sáenz-Badillos, Angel. *A History of the Hebrew Language*. Translated by John Elwolde. Cambridge: Cambridge University Press, 1988.

Sakenfeld, Katharine. *Journeying with God: A Commentary on the Book of Numbers*. Grand Rapids: Eerdmans, 1995.

Sanders, Seth L. *The Invention of Hebrew*. Urbana: Illinois University Press, 2009.
Sankoff, David, and Poplack, Shana. "A Formal Grammar for Code Switching." *Research on Language and Social Interaction* 1 (1981): 3–45.
Sarna, Nahum M. *Exodus*. JPS Torah Commentary. Philadelphia: JPS, 1991.
Sarte, Jean-Paul. "A Sketch of a Phenomenological Theory." Pages 90–91 in *The Emotions: Outline of a Theory*. Translated by Bernard Frechtman. New York: The Wisdom Library, 1948.
Schipper, Jeremy. "'Why Do You Still Speak of Your Affairs?': Polyphony in Mephibosheth's Exchanges with David in 2 Samuel." *VT* 54 (2004): 350.
Schmidt, Brian B. *Israel's Beneficent Dead: Ancestor Cult and Necromancy in Ancient Israelite Religion and Tradition*. Winona Lake: Eisenbrauns, 1996.
Schneidewind, William M. *A Social History of Hebrew: Its Origins through the Rabbinic Period*. New Haven: Yale University Press, 2013.
———. "The Source Citations of Manasseh: King Manasseh in History and Homily." *VT* 41 (1991): 451–55.
Schottroff, Louise and Wacker, Marie-Theres, eds. *Kompendium Feministische Bibelauslegung*. Gütersloh: Chr. Kaiser Gütersloher Verlagshuas, 1999.
———. *Feminist Biblical Interpretation: A Compendium of Critical Commentary on the Books of the Bible and Related Literature*. Grand Rapids: Eerdmans, 2012.
Schüssler Fiorenza, Elisabeth. "Introduction: Feminist Liberation Theology as Critical Sophialogy." Pages viii–xxxix in *The Power of Naming: A Concilium Reader in Feminist Liberation Theology*. Edited by Elisabeth Schüssler Fiorenza. Maryknoll, NY: Orbis Books, 1996.
———. *Rhetoric and Ethic: The Politics of Biblical Studies*. Minneapolis: Fortress, 1999.
Schwartz, Seth. *The Ancient Jews from Alexander to Muhammad*. Cambridge: Cambridge University Press, 2014.
Seow, C. L. *Daniel*. Westminster Bible Companion. Louisville: Westminster John Knox, 2003.
Sérandour, Arnaud. "Hébreu et Araméen dans la Bible." *Revues des Études juives* 159 (2000): 345–55.
———. "Remarques sur le Bilinguisme dans le Livre d'Esdras." Pages 131–44 in *Mosaïque de Langues, Mosaïque Culturelle: Le bilinguisme dans le Proche-Orient Ancien*. Edited by F. Briquel-Chatonnet. Paris: Librairie d'Amérique et d'Orient, 1996.
Shils, Edward Albert. *Center and Periphery: Essay in Macrosociology*. Chicago: University of Chicago, 1975.
Shimoff, Sandra. "David and Bathsheba: The Political Function of Rabbinic Aggada." *JSJ* 24 (1993): 246–56.

Slote, Walter H. Slote and George A. De Vos., eds. *Confucianism and the Family*. SUNY Series in Chinese Philosophy and Culture. Albany: State University of New York Press, 1998.

Smelik, K. A. D. "The Portrayal of King Manasseh: A Literary Analysis of II Kings Xxi and II Chronicles Xxxiii." in *Converting the Past: Studies in Ancient Israelite and Moabite Historiography*. Leiden; New York: Brill, 1992.

Smith-Christopher, Daniel L. "The Book of Daniel." *NIB* 7:17–152.

———. *A Biblical Theology of Exile*. Minneapolis: Fortress, 2002.

Smith, Daniel Jordan. "Promiscuous Girls, Good Wives, and Cheating Husbands: Gender Inequality, Transitions to Marriage and Infidelity in Southeastern Nigeria." *Anthropology Quarterly* 83.1 (2010): 123–52.

Smith, Mark S. *The Early History of God: Yahweh and the Other Deities in Ancient Israel*. BRS. 2nd ed. Grand Rapids: Eerdmans, 2002.

———. *God in Translation: Deities in Cross-Cultural Discourse in the Biblical World*. Tübingen: Mohr Siebeck, 2008.

———. *The Origins of Biblical Monotheism: Israel's Polytheistic Background and the Ugaritic Texts*. New York: Oxford University Press, 2001.

Sneed, Mark, ed. *Was There a Wisdom Tradition? New Prospects in Israelite Wisdom Studies*. Atlanta: SBL Press, 2015.

Snell, Daniel. "Why Is There Aramaic in the Bible?" *JSOT* 18 (1980): 32–51.

Sŏ, Chŏng-min. 일본기독교의 한국인식 [서정민, 일본기독교의 한국인식 [*Japanese Christianity's Recognition of Korea*]. Seoul: Hanul Akademi, 2009.

———. 건국대통령 이승만 [*Syngman Rhee, the First President of South Korea*]. Seoul: Institute of Korean Church History Studies, 2013.

Sohn, Ho Hyun. "Plurality and Ambiguity: Theodicy Models in the Old Testament." *Korean Journal of Christian Studies* 82 (2012): 147–76.

Son, Jong-Hee. "'אני אמלך': 다윗 왕위 계승순위의 뒤틀림." 구약논단 22.2 (2016): 98–131.

Spencer, William David. "Cyber-Marriage, Virtual Adultery, Real Consequences, and the Need for a Techno Sexual Ethic." *Africanus Journal* 2 (2010): 14–23.

Spolsky, Bernard. *The Language of the Jews: A Sociolinguistic History*. Cambridge: Cambridge University Press, 2014.

Stager, Lawrence. "The Archaeology of the Family in Ancient Israel." *BASOR* 260 (1985): 1–35.

Stavrakopoulou, Francesca. "The Blackballing of Manasseh." Pages 248–63 in *Good Kings and Bad Kings*. Edited by Lester L. Grabbe. LHBOTS 393. London: T&T Clark, 2005.

———. *King Manasseh and Child Sacrifice: Biblical Distortions of Historical Realities*. BZAW 338. Berlin: de Gruyter, 2004.

Sternberg, Meir. *The Poetics of Biblical Narrative: Ideological Literature and the Drama of Reading*. Bloomington: Indiana University Press, 1985.

Stubbs, David. *Numbers*. Grand Rapids: Brazos Press, 2009.
Sturtevant, Edgar H., and George Bechtel. *A Hittite Chrestomathy*. Baltimore, Massachusetts: Waverly, 1935.
Süel, Aygül. "Hitit Kaynaklarinda Tapinak Görevlileri ile ilgili bir Direcktif Metni." Ph.D. diss. AÜDTCFY 350. Ankara Üniversitesi, 1985.
Sugirtharajah, R. S. *Asian Biblical Hermeneutics and Postcolonialism: Contesting the Interpretations*. Maryknoll, NY: Orbis Books, 1998.
―――. *Exploring Postcolonial Biblical Criticism: History, Method, Practice*. Chichester, West Sussex: Wiley-Blackwell, 2011.
―――. *The Bible and Asia: From the Pre-Christian Era to the Postcolonial Age*. Cambridge: Harvard University Press, 2013.
―――. *The Bible and Empire: Postcolonial Explorations*. Cambridge: Cambridge University Press, 2005.
―――. *Still at the Margins: Biblical Scholarship Fifteen Years after Voices from the Margin*. New York: T &T Clark, 2008.
Sunoo, Harold Hakwon. *Korea: A Political History in Modern Times*. Columbia, MO: Korean-American Cultural Foundation, 1970.
Sweeney, Marvin A. "King Manasseh of Judah and the Problem of Theodicy in the Deuteronomistic History." Pages 264–78 in *Good Kings and Bad Kings*. Edited by Lester L. Grabbe. LHBOTS 393. London: T&T Clark, 2005.
―――. *King Josiah of Judah: The Lost Messiah of Israel*. Oxford: Oxford University Press, 2001.
―――. *Reading the Hebrew Bible after the Shoah: Engaging Holocaust Theology*. Minneapolis: Fortress, 2008.
―――. *Reading the Hebrew Bible After the Shoah: Engaging Holocaust Theology*. Minneapolis: Fortress, 2008.
Taggar-Cohen, Ada. *Hittite Priesthood*. Heidelberg: Universitätsverlag, 2006.
Thatcher, Tom, ed. *Memory and Identity in Ancient Judaism and Early Christianity: A Conversation with Barry Schwartz*. SemeiaSt 78. Atlanta: Society of Biblical Literature, 2014.
The Society of Korean Cultural Theology, ed. *Theology after Sewol: Weep with Those Who Weep*. Seoul: Mosinunsaramdeul, 2015.
Tamez, Elsa. "The Bible and the Five Hundred Years of Conquest." Pages 13–26 in *Voices from the Margin: Interpreting the Bible in the Third World*. Edited by R. S. Sugirtharajah. Maryknoll, NY: Orbis Books, 2006.
Tillich, Paul. *On the Boundary: An Autobiographical Sketch*. New York: Scribner's Sons, 1966.
Timmer, Daniel. "God's Speeches, Job's Responses, and the Problem of Coherence in the Book of Job: Sapiential Pedagogy Revisited." *CBQ* 71 (2009): 286–305.
Torrey, C. C. *The Composition and Historical Value of Ezra-Nehemiah*. Giessen: J. Ricker'sche Buchhandlung, 1896.
Tsevat, Matitiahu. "The Meaning of the Book of Job." *HUCA* 37 (1966): 73–106.

Tu, Wei-Ming. *Confucian Thought: Selfhood as Creative Transformation*. SUNY Series in Philosophy. Albany: State University of New York Press, 1985.

Tur-Sinai, N. H. *The Book of Job: A New Commentary*. Jerusalem: Kiryath Sepher, 1967.

Tuttle, Joshua D. and Shannon N. Davis. Religion, Infidelity, and Divorce: Reexamining the Effect of Religious Behavior on Divorce Among Long-Married Couples." *Journal of Divorce and Remarriage* 56 (2015): 475–89.

Ullendorf, E. "C'est de l'hébreu pour moi!" *JSS* 13 (1968): 125–35.

United Methodist Church. "Korea: Peace, Justice, and Reunification." Pages 650–57 in *The Book of Resolutions of the United Methodist Church 2016*. Nashville: United Methodist Publishing House, 2016.

Vaka'uta, Nasil. *Reading Ezra 9–10 Tu'a-Wise: Rethinking Biblical Interpretation in Oceania*. Atlanta: Society of Biblical Literature, 2011.

Valeta, David M. "Crossing Boundaries: Feminist Perspectives on the Stories of Daniel and Susanna." Pages 290–307 in *Feminist Interpretation of the Hebrew Bible in Retrospect: I. Biblical Books*. Edited by Susanne Scholz. Sheffield: Sheffield Phoenix, 2013.

van Keulen, P. S. F. *Manasseh through the Eyes of the Deuteronomists: The Manasseh Account (2 Kings 21:1–18) and the Final Chapters of the Deuteronomistic History*. New York: Brill, 1996.

van Wolde, Ellen. "Job 42,1–6: The Reversal of Job." Pages 223–50 in *The Book of Job*. Edited by W. A. M. Beuken. Leuven: Leuven University Press, 1994.

Wallerstein, Immanuel. *Essential Wallerstein*. New York: The New Press, 2000.

———. *The Modern World System II: Mercantilism and the Consolidation of the European World Economy 1600–1750*. New York: Academic Press, 1980.

———. *The Modern World System III: The Second Era of Great Expansion of the Capitalist World-Economy, 1730–1840*. New York: Academic Press, 1989.

———. *The Modern World System: Capitalist Agriculture and the Origins of the European World-Economy in the Sixteenth Century*. New York: Academic Press, 1974.

Wang, Tai Il. "Performing the Scripture: Understanding the Bible from Korean Biblical Hermeneutics." Pages 37–52 in *Mapping and Engaging the Bible in Asian Cultures: Congress of the Society of Asian Biblical Studies 2008 Seoul Conference*. Edited by Yeong Mee Lee and Yoon Jong Yoo. Seoul: Christian Literature Society of Korea, 2009.

Waswo, Ann. "The Transformation of Rural Society, 1900–1950." Pages 541–605 in The Twentieth Century. Vol. 6 of *The Cambridge History of Japan*. Edited by Peter Duus. Cambridge: Cambridge University Press, 1988.

WcWhorter, John. *The Power of Babel: The Natural History of Languages*. New York: Harper, 2001.

Weber, Max. *Protestant Ethic and the Spirit of Capitalism*. Translated by Talcott Parsons. Introduction by Anthony Giddens. London: Routledge, 2001.

Weinfeld, Moshe. "The Uniqueness of the Decalogue." Page 1–44 in *Ten Commandments in History and Tradition*. Edited by Ben-Zion Segal and Gershon Levi. Jerusalem: The Magnes Press, The Hebrew University of Jerusalem, 1990.

Wellhausen, Julius. *Prolegomena to the History of Ancient Israel: With a Reprint of the Article Israel from the Encyclopedia Britannica*. New York: Meridian Books, 1957.

Wells, Bruce. "The Cultic Versus the Forensic: Judahite and Mesopotamian Judicial Procedures in the First Millennium B.C.E." *JAOS* 128 (2008): 205–32.

West, Gerald. "Reading Shembe 'Re-Membering' the Bible." *Neotestamenica* 40.1 (2006): 157–84.

Westbrook, Raymond. "Adultery in Ancient Near Eastern Law." *RB* 97 (1990): 542–80.

———. *Property and the Family in Biblical Law*. Sheffield: JSOT Press, 1991.

Williams, William Appleman. *The Tragedy of American Diplomacy*. 2nd rev. and enl. ed. New York: Dell, 1972.

Williamson, Hugh. "The Aramaic Documents in Ezra Revisited." *JTS* 59 (2008): 41–62.

———. *Ezra, Nehemiah*. Waco, TX: Nelson, 1985.

Wilson, Robert R. *Prophecy and Society in Ancient Israel*. Philadelphia: Fortress, 1984.

Wolters, Al. "'A Child of Dust and Ashes' (Job 42, 6b)." *ZAW* 102 (1990): 116–19.

World Council of Churches. "Statement on Peace and Reunification of the Korean Peninsula." Statement filed under the World Council of Churches 10th Assembly. Busan, Republic of Korea, 08 November 2013.

Yee, Gale A. "Postcolonial Biblical Criticism." Pages 193–233 in *Methods for Exodus*. Edited by T. B. Dozeman. Cambridge: Cambridge University Press, 2010.

Yoder, Christine Elizabeth. *Wisdom as a Woman of Substance: A Socioeconomic Reading of Proverbs 1–9 and 31:10–31*. BZAW 304. Berlin: de Gruyter, 2001.

Yoo, David K. *Contentious Spirits: Religion in Korean American History 1903–1945*. Stanford: Stanford University Press, 2010.

Yoo, Yani. "Women's Leadership Fragmented: Examples in The Bible and The Korean Church." In *Korean Feminists in Conversation with the Bible, Church and Society*. Edited by Kyung Sook Lee and Kyung Mi Park. Bible in the Modern World 24. Sheffield: Sheffield Phoenix, 2011.

Yoon, Seonja. "The Establishment of Japanese Shrines and the Recognition of Koreans about Shrines" [Korean]. *Chonnam Historical Review* 42 (2011): 107–40.

Contributors

John Ahn, PhD (Yale University)
Associate Professor of Hebrew Bible
Howard University School of Divinity
Washington, DC, USA

Hannah S. An, PhD (Princeton Theological Seminary)
Assistant Professor of Old Testament Studies
Torch Trinity Graduate University
Seoul, Republic of Korea

Paul K.-K. Cho, PhD (Harvard University)
Associate Professor of Hebrew Bible
Wesley Theological Seminary
Washington, DC, USA

SungAe Ha, PhD (Graduate Theological Union)
Visiting Scholar Claremont School of Theology
Claremont, CA, USA

Koog-Pyoung Hong, PhD (Claremont Graduate University)
Associate Professor of Old Testament
Yonsei University
Seoul, Republic of Korea

Sun-Ah Kang, PhD Candidate (Garrett-Evangelical Theological Seminary)
Garrett-Evangelical Theological Seminary
Evanston, IL, USA

Hyun Chul Paul Kim, PhD (Claremont Graduate University)
Harold B. Williams Professor of Hebrew Bible
Methodist Theological School in Ohio
Delaware, OH, USA

Sehee Kim, PhD Candidate (Boston University)
Boston University
Boston, MA, USA

Eunyung Lim, ThD (Harvard Divinity School)
Assistant Professor of New Testament
Lutheran School of Theology at Chicago
Chicago, IL, USA

Kang-Yup Na, PhD (Emory University)
Associate Professor of Religion
Westminster College
New Wilmington, PA, USA

Roger S. Nam, PhD (UCLA)
Dean of the Seminary/Professor of Biblical Studies
Portland Seminary/George Fox University
Portland, OR, USA

Hee-Kyu Heidi Park, PhD (Claremont School of Theology)
Assistant Professor of Practical Theology
Ewha Womans University
Seoul, Republic of Korea

Kyungmi Park, DLitt (Ewha Womans University)
Professor of New Testament
Ewha Womans University
Seoul, Republic of Korea

SuJung Shin, PhD (Drew University)
Adjunct Professor of Biblical Studies
New Brunswick Theological Seminary
New Brunswick, NJ, USA

INDEX OF PRIMARY SOURCES

HEBREW BIBLE /OLD TESTAMENT

Genesis
1	171
1–3	243
1–6	18, 241, 243, 248
1:1–2:4a	225
1:2	226
1:3	171, 225
1:4	220
1:5	225
1:8	225
1:10	225
1:26–27	245
1:26–28	225
1:27	235, 246
2	82
2–3	171
2:4b–24	225
2:4b–25	235
2:7	225, 236
2:19	225
2:21–22	246
2:21–25	236
2:22	236
2:23	236
3:7–8	172
3:9	220
3:16	243
3:17–19	172
3:22–27	220
3:24	177, 219
4:22	243
5:2	234
6:5–22	246
6:6	153
6:7	153
6:19	234
7	177
7:2–16	234
7:11–12	226
12:10	80
17:11	221
17:24	221
18:27	173, 174
20:1	80
22	54
31:47	122
37–50	7
38	75
46:26	32
49	177

Exodus
1:5	32
3:2–4	209
3:5	230
3:14	248
13:17	153
14:14	177
14:21	177
15:3	177
20:5	38
20:13–15	73
20:13–17	74
20:14	93
23:13	91
32	38
32:12, 14	153
34:7	7
34:14	38

Leviticus
4–5	28
5:1	23, 35
20:10	87, 92

-279-

Numbers

4:15	28
4:20	28
5	30
5:11–15	88
5:11–31	16, 19, 20, 23, 30, 31, 32, 35, 78
5:12–14	30
5:12–28	32, 33, 34
5:13	30, 31
5:14	32, 41
5:15	32
5:18	32
5:19	32
5:22	31
5:23	32
5:24	32
5:27	32, 33
5:28	32, 33, 34
5:29	33
5:29–31	32, 33, 34
5:30	33, 35
5:31	16, 23, 31, 33, 34, 35
5:31a	31
5:31b	31
10:35	178
13–14	38
22:31	177
25	16, 37, 38, 39, 43, 47
25:4	39
25:11	41
25:11–13	39

Deuteronomy

4:24	38
5:9	38
5:17	91
5:17–19	73
5:18	93
6:14–15	38
11:14	170
22:22	78, 87
22:23–27	78
23:3	127
24:16	7
28–30	175
32:8–9	176

Joshua

5:13	177

Judges

2:18	153
5	54, 177
5:31	178
8:30	32
11	16
11:1–40	54
11:3	54
11:24	176
11:29–31	54
11:40	54
19	16, 54, 88

1 Samuel

2:25	40
4:4	178
5:5–6	127
6:19	28
8	177
9:2	67
15:11	153
15:29(2)	153
15:35	153
16	66
16:6–7	67
16:12	67
16:13–14	69
16:14	66
18:9	66
18:12–13	66
18:29	66
19:17	66
21:12–14	66
26:10	66
26:19	176
29:9	68
31:9–13	69

2 Samuel

1	66
2–4	66
2:4	66
2:8–11	66
2:23	66

3:1	66	15:30	69
3:27	66	15:37	70
4:7	66	16:16	70
4:12	66	16:17	70
5:1–3	66	16:21–22	69
6:6	28	18	70
11	75, 87, 88	18:9	70
11–12	16, 73, 80, 94, 95	19	70
11:1–5	87	19:1	71
11:3–4	88	19:22	70
11:6	94	19:27–28	70
11:11	178	19:28	68
11:15	94	19:43–44	71
11:27	88	20:1–2	71
12:7–12	89	20:6	71
12:10–11	69	20:3	71
12:13	89	22	177
12:13–14	70	23:1–7	177
12:22	95	24:16	153
13:19	154	24:16–17	177
13:23	69		
13:32	67	1 Kings	
14:1–24	67	1	95
14:6–7	68	1:6	67
14:11	68, 69	2	95
14:13	68	17	104, 170
14:14	68	17:2–9	105
14:17	68	17:8	105
14:17, 20	68	17:9	105
14:20	68	17:10	105
14:21	69	17:10–15	105
14:24	69	17:11	105
14:25	67	17:15	105
14:26	70	17:12	105
14:28	69	17:13	105
14:32	69	17:13–15	105
14:33	69	17:15	105
15	66	17:16	105
15:1ff	69	17:17	105
15:6	66, 69	21:1–21	105
15:13	69	21:2	105
15:14	69	21:3	105
15:16	95	21:4	105
15:23	69	21:5	105
15:25	70	21:6	105
15:26	70	21:7	105
15:28	70	21:8	105

21:9	105	33:18–19	106
21:11	105	33:18–20	106
21:26	105	33:20	106

2 Kings / Ezra

14:5–6	7	1:1	124, 125, 126
16:10–16	104	1–4	121
17:12	105	1–7	123
17:16	105	4–7	119, 122, 126
21	103, 104	4:2–3	125
21:1	104	4:7	120
21:1–18	103, 104	4:8–11	120
21:2	104	4:8–6:18	119, 121, 125
21:2–9	104	4:12	125
21:2–16	104	4:13	125
21:3	104, 105	4:15	125
21:4	104, 105	4:19	125
21:5	104, 105	4:24	120
21:6	104, 105	5:1	121
21:7	104, 105	5:1–2	120
21:10–15	104	5:1–4	121
21:16	111	5:2	121
21:17–18	104	5:3	121
23	106, 124	5:4	121
23:25–27	106	5:8	125
23:29–30	106	5:14	126
		5:16	126

1 Chronicles

		6:19–21	128
21:15	153	7	121
21:27–40	177	7:12–26	119
		10	228

2 Chronicles / Nehemiah

26:6	127	2:19	125
33	106	6:6	125
33:1	106	8	124
33:1–20	104	13	127
33:2–9	106	13:24	127
33:2–17	106		
33:3	106	Esther	
33:5	106	1:12	207
33:6	106	1:16–20	207
33:10–11	106	3:8	207
33:12–13	106, 107		
33:14	107	Job	
33:14–17	106	1	17, 146, 148, 161, 162
33:15	107	1–2	161
33:16	107		

1:1	168
1:8	166, 168
1:10	147
2	147, 161, 162
2:3	166, 168
2:8	153, 154
2:12	153
3	171
3–27	161
3–28	163, 173
3–31	148
3–42:6	161, 162
3:1	151
3:4	171
3:8	171
4–5	164
4:7	114
7:16	151
9:21	151
21–37	169
22	164
27:2	185
28	161, 162
29	161, 164, 166, 167, 168, 169, 170, 172
29–31	17, 147, 148, 151, 152, 153, 164, 166, 168, 172, 174
29:2	166
29:3–6	167
29:7–10	167
29:8–10	169
29:11–13	169
29:11–17	169
29:14	169
29:15–16	169
29:17	169
29:23	170
29:24	170
29:25ab	170
30	167, 170
30:1–2	170
30:1–8	170
30:15	170
30:16–19	170
30:19	153, 173
30:20	171
30:21	171
30:23	171
30:24	171
30:25	171
30:29	171
30:31	167
31	161, 164, 167, 168, 171, 172
31:2–4	167
31:5	167
31:5–6	165
31:7–8	167
31:9–10	167
31:13	167
31:13–15	168
31:14–15	167
31:16–17	167
31:29	167
31:33	168, 172
31:35	167
31:36	172
31:37	172
31:40	172
32–37	161, 162
34:33	151
38–39	165
38–41	151
38:1–42	147
38:1–42:6	17, 148, 159, 161
38:2	164, 173
38:3	166
39:1–42:6	164
40:4-5	159, 165
40:2b	165
40:6–41:26	166
40:7	166
40:12–14	166
40:15	166, 173
41:4–5	166
41:26	173
42:1–6	147, 163
42:2–6	145, 146, 156, 159
42:3	151
42:6	17, 145, 146, 147, 148, 150, 151, 154, 158, 159, 160, 161, 162, 163, 164, 166, 167, 168, 173, 174
42:7b	163
42:7–8	163, 164, 166
42:7–10	148, 161, 162, 163, 164

42:7–17	161	31:27	136, 139
42:8–9	164	31:27–29	139
42:10	164	31:28	139, 140
42:11–17	17, 146, 148, 161, 162	31:28–31	139
42:25	166	31:29	136, 139, 140
		31:30	139, 140
Psalms		31:31	136, 140
18	177		
19:1–6	224	Ecclesiastes	
29	177	3:6–7	213
50:18	93	3:11	222
68	178		
68:1	178	Isaiah	
72	170	1:24	153
72:6	170	10:1–7	175
89:39	151	11:6	237
90:13	153	11:6–9	179
97:3	209	14:13–14	210
104:26	170	36:18–20	210
106:45	153	37:10–13	210
106:30	40	40–55	176
110:4	153	40:2	178
132:9	169	43:2	209
		44:17	206
Proverbs		44:28–45:13	17, 175, 176
1–9	137	45:1–13	175
8	169	45:5	248
17:14	68	46:1	206
31:10–31	17, 133, 135, 136, 138, 139, 140, 141, 142, 143	50:1	178
		51:17–23	178
31:10–11	140	57:3	93
31:13	139	57:6	153
31:13	136	58:5	154
31:14	136, 139	59:17	169
31:15	136, 139	61:10	169
31:16	136	65:25	237
31:17	136, 139		
31:18	136, 139	Jeremiah	
31:19	136, 137, 139	3:3	170
31:20	139	3:8–9	81, 93
31:21	136, 139	4:28	153
31:22	136, 139	5:24	170
31:23	139, 140	5:7	81
31:24	136, 139	5:7–8	93
31:24–25	139	6:26	154
31:25	136, 137	7:9	81, 93
31:26	139	8:6	153

9:1	93	2:31–32	205
9:2	93	2:38	205
15:6	153	2:46	204
15:14	107	2:46–49	205
18:8, 10	153	3	195, 196, 204, 205, 207, 208, 212
20:16	153	3:1–18	205
23:10	93	3:2	205
23:14	93	3:4	205
25	178	3:5	206
25:1–11	175	3:5–7	205
25:20	127	3:6–7	205
26:3	153	3:7	206
26:13	153	3:8	207
26:19	153	3:12	207
27:1–15	17, 175	3:13	208
27:6–7	175	3:14–15	210
27:8	176	3:15	209, 210
27:11–12	178	3:16–18	208, 210
29:23	81, 93	3:19	208
31:29–30	7	3:20–21	211
42:10	153	3:25	209
		3:27	209
Ezekiel		3:28	209
8:14	189	4	204
16	17, 187, 190, 193	5:13	207
16:32	93	6:7	213
16:38	39, 93	6:8	213
16:42	39	6:10	213
18	114	6:14	208
18:1–4	7	6:15	210
23	178	6:16	208
23:25	39	6:17	208
23:37	93	6:16–18	208
23:43	93	7–12	204
23:45	93	8–12	123
24:14	153		
27:30	153, 154	Hosea	
36:6	39	1–2	75, 87
39:21–24	178	3	75, 87
		3:1	93
Daniel		4:2	93
1	123	4:13	93
1:6–7	206	4:14	93
2	204	6:3	170
2–7	123		
2:12	205		
2:25	207		

Joel		Acts	
2:13	153	8:26–39	233
2:14	153	10:9–48	233
2:18	39	15:1–29	233

Amos		Romans	
3:9	127	1:18–32	234
7:3	153	1:20	234
7:6	153	1:25	234
		2:13	238
Jonah		3:20	238
3:9	153	3:21–4:25	221
3:10	153	3:22	237
4:2	153	3:29	237
		3:30	222
Nahum		5:14	237
1:2	39	6:1–11	240
		6:2–4	240
Zephaniah		7	82
1:18	39	7:4	82
3:8	39	8:19–23	234
		10:12	237
Zechariah		12:2	240
1:14	39		
8:2	39	1 Corinthians	
8:14	153	1:13	234
9:6	127	1:23	234
		2:2	234
NEW TESTAMENT		7:19	237
		7:39	82
Matthew		11:2–16	245
1:1–15	56	11:8–12	236
1:16	55	12:13	237
19:4	234	15:20–28	239
		15:22	237
Mark		15:45	237
10:6	234	15:50–57	223, 239
		15:53	239
Luke			
10:3	237	2 Corinthians	
		5:16–17	240
John		5:17	240
7:53–8:11	75	5:17–20	237
8:3–4	81	5:18	239
9	113, 114, 115, 116		
9:2	114	Galatians	
9:3	114	1:13	220

1:13–14	221	Judith	
1:13–16a	222	11:1–4:3	209
1:16	234		
2:11–14	226, 230, 231, 232, 233, 237	1 Maccabees	
2:12	233	1:60–61	209
2:13	237		
2:15	232	2 Maccabees	
2:19	234	5:11–14	209
2:25–29	226	6:1–11	209
3:1	234	7:1–42	209
3:6-18	221		
3:20	222	3 Maccabees	
3:24	222, 237	2:30–31	209
3:25–29	231		
3:26	235	Ecclesiasticus (Sirach)	
3:27–28	237	10:9	173
3:28	220, 234, 236, 238, 239, 240		
5:6	237	DEAD SEA SCROLLS	
5:11	221		
6:15	234, 237	1QH	
		18.5	173
Ephesians			
2:15	237, 239	4Q266 [4QD^a]	173
4:24	237, 239		
6:12	244	4Q277 [4QpsJub^c]	173

Philippians
2   47
2:6–8   239
3:4–6   221

Colossians
1:15   234
3:9–11   237, 239
3:11   239

Hebrews
9:11   234

2 Peter
3:4   234

DEUTEROCANONCIAL BOOKS

Tobit
1:18–20   209

ANCIENT NEAR EASTERN TEXTS

CTH 264
1–9   24
2–8   24
3 i 38   28
5.59   24
6–8   26
7 ii 29   28
8.58   24
9–19   28
10   23, 24
10–11   24, 25, 29
10.20   24
10 iii 3–6   24
10 iii 4–5   25
10 iii 5–6   25
10 iii 9–14   24
10 iii 15–16   23
11   24
11 iii 26–34   25

11 iii 30	25	NAG HAMMADI	
11 iii 30–31	25		
11 iii 30–34	23	Nature of the Rulers	
11 iii 34	25	86.21	247
13 iii 54	28	86.27–88.10	246
14	23, 24, 26, 27	86.27–88.16	245
14 iii 68–83	20	86.30–31	248
14 iii 7–83	26	87.1–3	247
14 iii 57	28	87.22	247
14 iii 71–77	23	88.11	247
14 iii 82–83	29	88.35	247
15–19	20	89.7	245
15.10	23	89.11	243
15 iv 7–8	23	89.26	246
16	20	89.13–17	243
16.23	23	89.18–31	245
16 iv 12–22	23	89.20–27	243
16 iv 12–23	20	89.24	246
17–18	34	89.26–30	246
17.31	23	89.29	247
17 iv 25–30	23	91.30–34	247
17 iv 31	20, 29	91.35	247
18 iv 40	21	92.1–4	247
18 iv 32–33	21	92.2–3	246
18 iv 43–46	23	92.18–93.2	246
18 iv 46–47	20	92.20–21	246
18 iv 47	21	92.22–26	246
18 iv 32–33	21	92.23–25	247
18 iv 45–46	21	92.30–31	246
18 iv 46–47	29	92.32–97.20	243
18 iv 49–52	21	93.1–2	246
18 iv 52–53	21	94.21–22	248
19 iv 68	20	94.24–26	247
19 iv 69	21	95.5	248
19 iv 47	21	95.6–8	247
19 iv 61–66	23	96.12	247
19 iv 68–69	21	96.15–26	248
19 iv 32	21	96.16–18	245
		96.19–25	247
		96.20	247
		96.33–34	247
		97.14	249
		97.18	247

INDEX OF MODERN AUTHORS

Aaron, David H.	74	Betz, Hans Dieter	234, 237
Abadie, Philippe	103	Beuken, W. A. M.	147
Abasil, Alexander I.	87	Bhabha, Homi K.	211
Abbott, Andrew	1, 11	Bhatia, Tej K.	123, 130
Acuff, Jonathan M.	6	Black, Fiona C.	153
Adam, A.K.M.	5	Blenkinsopp, Joseph	120, 125
Agosto, Efrain	2	Blom, Jan-Petter	122
Ahn, John	vii, ix, 1, 2, 13, 16, 18, 56, 73, 81, 89, 188, 205, 277	Blount, Brian K.	14
		Boase, Elizabeth	5
Ahn, Young-Sung	2	Boccaccini, G.	207
Albeck, Shalom	90, 91	Boda, Mark	5, 89
Alster, Bendt	189	Boer, Roland	2, 153
Alter, Robert	61	Boers, Hendrikus	232, 237, 238
Amaru, Betsy Halpern	111	Bolin, Thomas	119
An, Hannah S.	vii, 16, 18, 19, 277	Bonhoeffer, Dietrich	200
Anderson, Arnold A.	88	Boose, Donald W., Jr.	179
Andrews, Edward E.	175	Booth, Wayne	60, 61
Arendt, Hannah	249, 250	Bosman, Henrik	80, 92
Arnold, Bill	120, 121	Bosworth, David	87
Assmann, Jan	13	Brenner, Athalya	146
Augustin, Marrhias	80	Briant, Pierre	206
Avigad, Nahman	125	Brichto, Herbert Chanan	32
Avioz, Michael	15, 67	Briquel-Chatonnet, F.	121
Aymer, Margaret	13	Broshi, Magen	109
Bailey, Randall C.	10, 14	Brown, William P.	2
Bakhtin, Mikhail M.	16, 59, 60, 62, 63, 64, 65, 66, 70, 71, 72	Brueggemann, Walter	183, 209
		Buber, Martin	91
Baldwin, Frank	181	Bullard, Roger A.	244
Baltzer, Klaus	74	Butler, Judith	249
Bar-Efrat, Shimon	67	Byron, Gay L.	14
Barton, John	5	Camp, Claudia V.	5, 68
Bechtel, George	19, 27	Carmichael, Calcum M.	74
Becking, Bob	176, 189	Carter, Warren	199, 207
Belazi, Hedi M.	122	Castelli, Elizabeth A.	61
Bentham, Jeremy	141, 143	Ch'oe, Young-Ho	13
Berger, Peter	6, 8, 92	Cha, Marn J.	12
Berman, Joshua	121	Chan, Sucheng	6
Berquist, Jon L.	207	Chancey, Mark A.	205

Charlesworth, J. H.	111	Dikov, Ivan	219
Childs, Brevard S.	5, 10, 91	Dillard, Raymond B.	113
Chin, Gabriel	13	Do, Jin Soon	203
Cho, Eunsik	12	Douglas, Mary	220, 228, 230, 231, 234
Cho, Haejoang	137, 138, 140	Dozeman, Thomas B.	214
Cho, Paul K.-K.	viii, 17, 18, 145, 162, 165, 277	Drivers, Samuel Rolles	155
Choi, Chungmoo	181	Drory, Rina	120
Choi, Jin Young	130	Duncan, John	133
Chong, Joong-Ho	104	Dunn, James	40
Chuh, K.	129	Durham, John I.	92
Clark, Francis E.	179	Durkheim, Emile	92
Cleath, Lisa	124	Duus, Peter	197
Clines, David J. A.	5, 103, 120, 145, 146, 150, 151, 152, 153, 154, 155, 160, 169, 173	Dyne, Linn Van	3
		Eckert, Carter J.	199. 202
		Ecklund, Elaine Howard	2
Cohen, Shaye J. D.	208, 226, 232	Eden, Anthony	180
Collins, John J.	15	Elliot, John	40, 41
Collins, Patricia Hill	7, 15	Emerson, Caryl	59, 60
Collins, Randall	92	Eril, Astrid	13
Coltrane, Scott	92	Espin, Orlando O.	2
Conroy-Krutz, Emily	179	Evans-Pritchard, E. E.	230
Coogan, Michael	86	Exum, J. Cheryl	103, 160
Cook, Stephen L.	205	Falkenstein, Adam	189
Coote, Robert B.	40, 112	Feinstein, Eve L.	32
Coser, Lewis	13	Felder, Cain Hope	14
Crenshaw, James	99, 105, 114, 168	Fetalsana-Apura, Lily	15
Crompton, Samuel W.	176	Fewell, Danna Nolan	54, 55, 61, 64, 208
Cross, Frank Moore	103, 106		
Cumings, Bruce	180, 181, 182	Finkelstein, Israel	109
Curtis, John Briggs	146, 147, 152, 153, 155, 160, 161, 174	Fishbane, Michael	5, 171
		Fohrer, Georg	155, 168, 171
Dailey, Thomas F.	152, 155	Foley, John Miles	112
Davidson, Steed Venyl	13	Foran, John	7
Danico, Mary Yu	6	Foskett, Mary F.	2, 14, 130
Davies, Philip	5	Foucault, Michel	17, 133, 141, 142, 143
Davis, Shannon N.	86		
Davison, Andrew	214	Fox, Michael V.	146, 152, 155, 159, 160, 161, 162
de Boer, P. A. H.	153, 155		
de Certeau, Michel	245	Fram, Edward	75
De Wit, J. H.	1	Frazer, James George	230
DeMaris, Alfred	86	Frechette, Christopher G.	5
der Lugt, Pietervan,	156	Frei, Hans	113
Derrida, Jacques	212, 225	Fretheim, Terrance	92
Deuchler, Martina	132, 134, 135, 137	Freud, Sigmund	41, 42, 43, 44, 45
DeVos, George A.	133, 137	Fried, Lisbeth S.	125, 128
Dhorme, Édouard	155	Frymer-Kensky, Tikva	32

Fullerton, Kember	160, 163
Gadamer, Hans-Georg	214, 225, 233
Gafney, Wil	15
Gamaliel, Hananiah b.	75
Gardner-Chloros, Penelope	122
Garsiel, Moshe	87
Geertz, Clifford	8, 230
Giddens, Anthony	16, 73, 94, 95, 96
Giorgieri, Mauro	19
Girard, Rene	100
Goehring, James	243
Goetze, Albrecht	19
Good, Edwin	155, 165, 167, 168, 169, 170, 171
Gordis, Robert	146, 155
Gottwald, Norman	40
Grabbe, Lester L.	101, 103, 105, 107, 120, 207
Graham, Matt Patrick	103
Granados, Carlos	4
Granados, Jose	4
Grätz, Sebastian	120
Gray, George Buchanan	155
Greeley, Andrew M.	75
Greenberg, Moshe	90, 91
Greenspahn, Frederick	210
Greenstein, Edward L.	153, 163
Grohmann, Marianne	200
Groneberg, Brigitte	188
Guillaume, Philippe	109
Gumperz, John	122
Gunn, David M	61, 64
Gunnerweg, Antonius	125
Ha, SungAe	viii, 17, 18, 175, 277
Habel, Norman C.	145, 152, 156, 168, 169, 171
Habermas, Jürgen	8, 10
Hadjiev, Tchavdar	87
Halle, Moris	148
Hallo, William W.	21
Han, Jin Hee	207, 208
Han, Ju Hui Judy	182
Han, Sharon K.	129
Harrelson, Walter J.	92
Hartley, John E.	156
Havea, Jione	13, 15, 212
Heller, Roy L.	205, 208, 209
Henderson, Gregory	182
Hidalgo, Jacqueline M.	2
Hiles, Dave	42
Hobbs, T. R.	111
Hoffman, Yair	74
Hoffner, Harry A.	24
Hogue, Timothy	123
Holquist, Michael	60
Holter, Knut	1, 15
Hong, Koog-Pyoung	vii, ix, 16, 18, 99, 277
Hooks, Bell	7, 15
Hopkins, D. D.	213
Horovitz, Haim S.	34
Horsley, Richard A.	183
Howard, Cameron	124
Huang, Yingying	84
Hunermann, Denzinger-Peter	4
Hurvitz, Avi	126
Hwang, Yong-Yeon	185
Iz'real, Shlomo	120
Jacobs, Sandra	7
Jackson, Bernard	75
Jackson, Michael D.	18, 242, 243, 244, 245, 246, 247, 248, 249, 250
Jacobsen, Thorkild	187, 188, 189, 190
Jaegerstaetter, Frank	41, 46
Jakobson, Roman	17, 147, 148, 149, 151, 154, 158, 160
Jang, Se-Hoon	2
Jansen, Marius B.	198
Janzen, J. Gerald	156
Jones, Barry A.	204, 210
Jones, Stanton L.	76
Jonker, Louis C.	1, 15
Joselit, Jenna Weissman	86
Jung, Seokgyu	104
Kaminsky, Joel S.	105
Kampen, John	195
Kang, Nam-Soon	136, 140
Kang, Sa-Moon	177
Kang, Sun-Ah	17, 133, 277
Kautzsch, E.	128
Kecskemeti, Paul	6
Kellner, Hansfried	92
Kim, Baek-yung	196, 197, 198, 203, 204

Kim, Chan-Hie 3
Kim, Chin-ho 185
Kim, Chul-Soo 197
Kim, Dong-choon 50
Kim, Elaine H. 181
Kim, Hakseo 104
Kim, Hyun Chul Paul viii, 4, 7, 17, 129, 145, 195, 200, 204, 208, 213, 277
Kim, Ki Hong 200
Kim, Kirsteen 12
Kim, Sebastian C. H. 12
Kim, Sehee viii, 17, 187, 277
Kim, Seong Hee 2
Kim, Kwang Chung 2
Kim, Uriah 15
Kim, Yung Suk 185
King, Karen L. 242, 243, 245, 246, 247, 248, 250
Kinukawa, Hisako 2, 15
Kirk, Alan 103
Klein, Melanie 42, 43, 44
Knauf, Ernst Axel 101, 108, 109
Knoppers, Gary N. 103, 121
Kobe, Osamu 196
Koch, Klaus 105
Kohut, Heinz 16, 37, 41, 43, 44, 45, 46, 47
Koppel, M. 213
Kramer, Samuel Noah 189
Kratz, Reinhard 119
Kreitzer, Larry J. 75
Kuan, Jeffrey Kah-Jin 2, 14, 130
Kuyper, Lester J. 151, 156
Kwon, Ho-Young 2
Kynes, Will 80
Lambert, David A. 147, 152, 153
Lapinkivi, Pirjo 189
Lapsley, Jacqueline 15
Lasine, Stuart 103, 104, 105, 108
Lau, Peter H. W. 13, 15
Lawson, George 7
Layton, Bentley 241, 244
Lee, Jung Young 6
Lee, Kwang-su 201
Lee, Kyung Sook 2, 12, 138
Lee, Kyung-Ha 141

Lee, Poong-In 100
Lee, Sang Hyun 6
Lee, Yeong Mee 2
Lee, Yoon Kyoung 2
Legge, James 225, 244
Leick, Gwendolyn 188
Lessem, Peter A. 43
Létourneau, Anne 87
Levenson, Jon D. 102
Lévêque, Jean 154
Lévi-Strauss, Claude 230
Levi, Gershon 76
Li, Chichang 87
Liew, Tat-siong Benny 3, 10, 14, 129
Lillie, Celene 248
Lim, Eunyung vii, 18, 241, 278
Lin, Derek 225
Lind, Millard 177
Lipschitz, O. 123
Livingstone, Rodney 13
Lochhead, David 47
Lovelace, Vanessa 14
Lombaard, Christo 15
Lozada, Francisco 15
Luckman, Thomas 6, 8
Luhmann, Niklas 6, 8, 9, 10, 11, 96
Lummis, C. Douglas 52, 53
Lyke, Larry L. 88
MacSwan, Jeff 123
Maimonides, Moses 40
Malinowski, Bronishaw 230
Mandolfo, Carleen 102
Mannheim, Karl 6
Markl, Domink 7, 74
Masoga, Alpheus 11
Matsutani, Motokazu 182
McCarthy, Dennis 74
McCourt, David M. 6
McGuire, Anne 242, 247
McKeating, H. 81
McKenzie, Steven L. 61, 103, 109, 178
McKinlay, Judith E. 13
McMahon, Gregory 21, 24, 25, 26
Melammed, Ezra Zion 91
Melchert, H. Craig 24
Meshorer, Ya'akov 125
Meyer, Esias E. 74

Index of Modern Authors

Meyers, Eric M. 205
Milgrom, Jacob 19, 24, 26, 28, 40
Miller, J. Hillis 211
Miller, Jared L. 19, 21
Miller, Patrick D. 177
Mitchell, Stephen 224
Moffet, Samuel 12
Moon, Cyris Heesuk 2
Moon, Seungsook 181
Moore, Stephen 60, 61
Moran, William L. 189
Morgan, Robert 5
Morrow, William 146, 147, 150, 151, 154, 156
Mouton, Alice 25
Muenchow, Charles 147, 167
Muppidi, H. 214
Musharbash, Yasmine 85
Myers, R. H. 198
Na, Kang-Yup 4, 17, 18, 217, 278
Na'aman, Nadav 109
Nam, Roger S. 17, 18, 119, 129, 278
Nelson, Richard D. 105
Neufeld, Dietmar 41
Neusner, Jacob 75
Newell, Lynne 156
Newsom, Carol A. 54, 146, 147, 157, 163, 185, 188, 206, 210, 211
Nofoaiga, Vaitusi 15
Nünning, Ansgar 13
Nyengele, M. Fulgence 213
O'Brien, Julia M. 130
Oeming, M. 123
Oh, Taek Hyun 104
Olson, Dennis 37, 43
Ortlund, Dane C. 40
Oswalt, John N. 176
Pace, Sharon 206
Page, Hugh R. Jr. 14
Pagels, Elaine H. 243, 247
Palumbo-Liu, David 214
Pan, Suiming 84
Parish, William L. 84
Park, Chung-Shin 202
Park, Hee-Kyu Heidi vii, 16, 37, 278
Park, Kyeyoung 2
Park, Kyungmi vii, 2, 12, 16, 18, 49, 138, 278
Park, Kyung-Soo 199
Park, Yungsik 99
Patrick, Dale 152, 157
Patterson, Wayne 2
Pearson Birger A. 243
Peattie, M. R. 198
Perdue, Leo G. 199, 207
Philips, Anthony 80, 81
Phillips, Gary A. 61
Polak, Frank H. 123
Polzin, Robert 61, 62, 63, 64
Pope, Marvin H. 157
Poplack, Shana 122
Portier-Young, Anathea 123, 124, 205, 210, 213
Poulsen, F. 204
Power, C. 204
Prior, Michael 175
Pritchard, James B. 73
Pui-Lan, Kwok 129
Purdue, Leo G. 156
Quddus, Abul Hasnat Golam 83, 84
Rabin, Chaim 40
Raisanen, Heikki 11
Rendsburg, Gary 120, 121
Reventlow, Henning Graf 74
Rhie, Deok-Joo 195, 202, 203
Rhode, Deborah L. 76
Ringe, Sharon H. 54, 188
Ritchie, William C. 123, 130
Robertson, David 146
Robinson, James 244
Rooke, Deborah W. 75
Roth, Martha T. 20
Rowley, H. H. 157
Rubin, Edward J. 122
Ruiz, Jean-Pierre 1, 2
Runions, Erin 153
Ryu, Dae Young 182
Saenz-Badillos, Angel 128
Sakenfeld, Katharine 38, 40
Sanchez-Navarro, Luis 4
Sanders, James 5
Sanders, Seth L. 127
Sankoff, David 122

Sarna, Nahum M.	91	Sternberg, Meir	61, 62, 88
Sartre, Jean-Paul	249	Stole, Walter H.	133, 137
Sass, Benjamin	125	Strozier, Charles	43, 44, 45
Sasson, Jack M.	32	Sturtevant, Edgar H.	19, 24, 27
Schipper, Jeremy	68	Süel, Aygül	19
Schmidt, Brian B.	111	Sugirtharajah, R. S.	5, 9, 175
Schniedewind, William M.	110, 125, 128, 129	Sunoo, Harold Hakwon	182
Scholz, S.	204	Sweeney, Marvin	10, 101, 102, 103, 105, 210
Schottroff, Louise	5	Taggar-Cohen, Ada	19, 21
Schunk, Klaus-Dietrick	80	Tamez, Elsa	175, 183
Schüssler Fiorenza, Elisabeth	140, 183, 241, 242, 243	Thatcher, Tom	103
		Tillich, Paul	211
Schwartz, Regina M.	61	Timmer, Daniel	152
Schwartz, Seth	199	Tolbert, Mary Ann	15
Sebeok, Thomas A.	148	Toribi, Almeida Jacqueline	122
Segal, Ben-Zion	76	Torrey, C. C.	120
Segovia, Fernando F.	1, 2, 10, 15, 129	Trible, Phyllis	15
Seow, C. L.	205, 206, 207, 210, 211	Tsevat, Matitiahu	159
		Tu, Wei-Ming	133
Sérandour, Arnaud	120, 121	Tur-Sinai, N. H.	157
Sherwood, Stephen	39	Turner, Victor	230
Shils, Edward Albert	3	Tuttle, Joshua D.	86
Shimakawa, K.	129	Tylor, E. B.	230
Shimoff, Sandra	87	Ukpong, Justin S.	11
Shin, Kwang-Yeong	180	Ullendorff, Edward	127
Shin, SuJung	16, 18, 59, 278	Uspensky, Boris	120
Shuy, R.	122	Vaka'uta, Nasili	13, 15
Slote, Walter H.	133, 137	Valeta, David M.	204
Smelik, K. A. D.	105	van der Horst, Pieter W.	189
Smith-Christopher, Daniel	128, 204, 205, 210	van der Lugt, Pieter	156
		van der Toorn, Karel	189
Smith, Daniel Jordan	82, 83	van Duin, C.	153
Smith, Mark S.	178, 179	van Keulen, P. S. F.	103
Smith, Mitzi	15	van Wolde, Ellen	145, 147, 153, 160
Sneed, Mark	80	Villazor, Rose Cuison	13
Snell, Daniel	120, 121	Wacker, Marie-Theres	5
Son, Jong-Hee	87	Wallerstein, Immanuel	3
Soon, Ang	3	Wang, Tai Il	ix, 2
Spencer, William David	75	Waswo, Ann	197
Spillers, Hortense	15	WcWhorter, John	130
Spolsky, Bernard	127	Weber, Max	12
Stager, Lawrence	77	Weems, Renita J.	187
Stavrakopoulou, Francesca	103, 105, 107, 108, 110, 111	Weinfeld, Moshe	76, 91
		Weissenrieder, Annette	112
Steele, Brent J.	6	Wellhausen, Julius	109, 119
Steffan, Melissa	184	Wells, Bruce	30

West, Gerald	1, 82
Westbrook, Raymond	75, 92
Whitehead, Alfred North	239
Williams, William Appleman	179
Williamson, Hugh	120
Willis, John T.	168
Wilson, Robert	5, 10, 93, 205
Wolters, Al	153, 157
Yang, Seung Yi	15
Yee, Gale A.	188, 195, 214
Yoder, Christine R.	139
Yoo, David K.	12
Yoo, Yani	138
Yoo, Yoon Jong	2
Yoon, Seonja	198
Young, Ian	126
Younger, K. Lawson Jr.	21
Yun, Dongju	202
Zhang, Na	84

www.ingramcontent.com/pod-product-compliance
Lightning Source LLC
Chambersburg PA
CBHW021651230426
43668CB00008B/591